THE TRANSITIONAL HUMAN BEING

Purdue Studies in Romance Literatures

Editorial Board

Íñigo Sánchez-Llama, Series Editor
Elena Coda
Paul B. Dixon

Beth Gale
Laura Demaría

Howard Mancing, Consulting Editor
Floyd Merrell, Consulting Editor
R. Tyler Gabbard-Rocha, Production Editor

Associate Editors

French
Jeanette Beer
Paul Benhamou
Willard Bohn
Thomas Broden
Mary Ann Caws
Allan H. Pasco
Gerald Prince
Roseann Runte
Ursula Tidd

Italian
Fiora A. Bassanese
Peter Carravetta
Benjamin Lawton
Franco Masciandaro
Anthony Julian Tamburri

Luso-Brazilian
Marta Peixoto
Ricardo da Silveira Lobo Sternberg

Spanish and Spanish American
Catherine Connor
Ivy A. Corfis
Frederick A. de Armas
Edward Friedman
Charles Ganelin
David T. Gies
Roberto González Echevarría
David K. Herzberger
Emily Hicks
Djelal Kadir
Amy Kaminsky
Lucille Kerr
Howard Mancing
Floyd Merrell
Alberto Moreiras
Randolph D. Pope
Elżbieta Skłodowska
Marcia Stephenson

PSRL volume 95

THE TRANSITIONAL HUMAN BEING

Literary, Journalistic, and Cinematographic Representations of the Twentieth- and the Twenty-First-Centuries Italy

Ron Kubati

Purdue University Press
West Lafayette, Indiana

Copyright ©2025 by Purdue University. All rights reserved.

Cataloging-in-Publication Data on file at the Library of Congress.

Cover image: Industrial coal mine, abstract sendimentation tank of mine in Poland. Industrial lake Aerial drone photo view: Mariusz Pietranek/iStock via Getty Images Plus

978-1-62671-153-2 (hardcover)
978-1-62671-157-0 (paperback)
978-1-62671-158-7 (epub)
978-1-62671-159-4 (epdf)

Content

1 Introduction

15 Part One
The "New Man"

15 Chapter One
The "New Man" and the Universal Man

21 Chapter Two
Fascism, Nazism and Bolshevism in Alvaro

27 Chapter Three
Soldiers and Mothers of the Race
   28 Gentile and Marinetti
   35 Soldiers, mothers of the race and heroes

45 Chapter Four
The Stripped Man
   55 De-individualization and the interruption of tradition

55 Chapter Five
The Interruption of Tradition
   60 Material conditions and social matters

65 Chapter Six
From Berlin to Rome
   65 *Germania anno zero:* A thesis film
   69 Return to Rome

73 Conclusion to Part One

79 Part Two
The Urban Explorer

83 Chapter Seven
Excluded and Transformed

97 Chapter Eight
Different Readings of Pasolini
   97 Pasolini's assassination and the interpretation of his late work
   100 The subject as the new political battlefield

111 Chapter Nine
Literature as Re-Representation: Calvino and the Encyclopedic Novel
114 The incomplete human being in the city
118 *If on a Winter's Night:* The network novel
121 Different readings of Calvino
125 The network subject

129 Chapter Ten
Fellini's Invisible Cities
129 The symbols of *La dolce vita*
130 Marcello as "the self-confessed sinner" male in Celati's reading
133 Homo eligens
137 The open form
141 The incomplete human being is young
146 New representations, new geographies

153 Conclusion to Part Two

165 Part Three
The Geographic Human Being

171 Chapter Eleven
The Italo-Albanian Cinematographic Confrontation on Fascism and Immigration
171 *Lamerica* and the controversy on its release
174 A novel, two sets of propaganda, three films
179 Migrants, nightmares, and dreams
187 The outlook on modernity and the Italian imaginary of Africa: Pasolini, Di Carlo, and Celati

187 Chapter Twelve
Lampesuda: The New Border
187 The outlook on modernity and the Italian imaginary of Africa: Pasolini, Di Carlo, and Celati
193 Toward Italy
199 The mobile border and European citizenship

203 Chapter Thirteen
The Modesty of Representation
203 Media and migration projects
207 On this side of the sea
214 The representation of sea crossings and the role of the documentary
220 Like a documentary: *Terra di mezzo* (1997), and *La mia classe* (2014)

227 Chapter Fourteen
On Communities
228 Closed communities: *Io sono Li, La Giusta distanza* and *Cose dell'altro mondo*
241 Lakhous' closed rooms
244 The community of the communities

249 Chapter Fifteen
The Multi-Belonger
249 Multibelonging in literature
255 Cultural capital
258 Impossible returns and organized returns

263 Conclusion to Part Three

277 A Final Note

281 Notes

305 Works Cited

321 Filmography

325 Index

337 About the book

338 About the author

Introduction

> [...] l'uomo nuovo sarebbe un essere spoglio d'ogni interesse personale e privato, d'ogni influenza di vita occidentale dopo averla assorbita tutta, che abbia di sé il concetto d'un uomo transitorio e sacrificato al sogno di benessere di domani, e di quelli che verranno, pronto a mandare avanti ogni forza tecnica e intellettuale, dedicato alla collettività e solidale con essa.
>
> The new man seems like a being stripped of all personal and private interests, of any Western influence after having absorbed it all. He is someone who thinks of himself as a transitional man that has been sacrificed to the dream of tomorrow's well-being, and to those who will come, he is ready to keep every technical and intellectual force moving forward, dedicated and loyal to the community, (Alvaro, *I maestri del diluvio: Viaggio in Russia* 69).[1]

There are some images from films and literature, as well as from reportages by writers, journalists, and philosophers that profoundly affect our consciousness. Edmund Kohler, an eleven- or twelve-year-old boy, climbs up the skeleton of a recently bombed Berlin and kills himself by jumping to his death. The film is Rossellini's *Germania anno zero* (*Germany Year Zero*), and the landscape of ruins in a destroyed Berlin is not simply a background. Temporally and spatially adjacent to Edmund's tragedy there is the incredible category of "Muslims" walking towards the gas chambers of Auschwitz. Significantly, Primo Levi's book is entitled *Se questo è un uomo* (*If This Is a Man*). Then there are

Introduction

other men, "new men" from the East, the vast majority of whom come from tribal and medieval environments of whom we read in the pages of *I maestri del diluvio: Viaggio in Russia* (*Travel in Russia*) by Corrado Alvaro. Through purges and totalitarian organization these "new men" are quickly remodeled and urbanized according to an avant-garde profile designed by the Soviet elite and creatively inspired by both philosophies and social analyses born from the contradictions of Western modernity. Other, additional more recent pictures: migrants, already "new men," crammed onto a small fleet of rusty ships, fleeing failed metropolitan projects, apparently called by the lights of far more successful metropolises. They can be found in the television chronicles of the 1990s, and in the film *Lamerica* by Gianni Amelio. Finally, there are those who describe cities from within as laboratories devoted to literally going beyond the human being. Calvino does just that in several important novels.

Going beyond human for the benefit of whom or what? This is a question without a clear answer. And what is the very definition of a human being? Do we have answers that are valid for all eras? No, we do not. On the contrary, the mutations of possible answers left a profound mark on the last century and the destinies of millions of people. Nazism and Bolshevism, in particular, put the idea of the "new man" at the center of their political actions.

In post WWII Eastern Europe, the project of the new man was declined very clearly in all of its stages: from the decision made at the Congress of the Communist Party to the breakdown of the strategy that reached classrooms, televisions, radios, newspapers, music festivals, writers' associations, and thence became lyrics, songs, novels, movies, and reportages. Disobedient poets were hung in public squares, writers were exiled, and musicians influenced by Western culture were imprisoned. They called it socialist realism; its duty to forge the new man being experienced in a wider area and geography. Its theory and practice were elaborated first in Moscow and then spread to other countries in the Communist camp where, once the social engineering methods were mastered, the new man's profile was modified and modeled according to local needs. Even the bodies, looks, dresses, and the schedules of "new men" were carefully forged (as can be seen in Corrado Alvaro's reportage). Gender equality was energetically pursued fighting against a long-lasting patriarchal tradition. According to Corrado Alvaro, the massive industrialization of the Soviet Union would not have been possible without women's contributions. It was easy to notice all the proclaimed traits of "new men" showing in lyrics, melodies, pictures, frames, genres and composing the fil rouge of the cultural discourse that needed to stay uncontaminated by other (Western) cultural discourses. The latter forged a different human dubbed as "bourgeois," "corrupted" and "consumerist."

In the twentieth century all the contexts, Eastern and Western, had their cultural discourses with their own articulated ideas as to what it meant to be a human being. Keeping the collective imaginary uncontaminated by other ideologies was crucial. This cultural "war of the worlds" ran through movies, TV shows, and big border antennas that faced neighbors. Italy built its own antennas facing its eastern border and relentlessly projected its own cultural discourse. After 1991—when massive waves of immigrants reached the Italian coast—many considered it a call which tens or even hundreds of thousands of migrants had answered. Some Italian Studies scholars (who will be quoted in the third part of this book), consider the Italian media influence in Albania during the second half of the twentieth century as a colonizing weapon. Both systems engaged cinema, literature, music, newspapers, TV shows, and universities in an attempt to forge the profile of citizens. Included in this book are the analyzes proffered by many works of different genres. The post WWII "bourgeois," "corrupted" and "consumerist" Italian-Western profile was "new" in its own right. It had to start from the erasing of the previous Fascist draft. When Bolshevism outlined its profile of its "new man," Fascism and Nazism had their own ideas. "Dobbiamo rifare l'uomo" (We must remake the man) wrote Giovanni Gentile in 1921 (*Preliminari allo studio del fanciullo*,137). The Fascist elaboration of the profile of human beings opened to the racist theories wanted by Hitler and, consequently, to the discrimination of many starting with Jewish people and continuing with black Africans without forgetting to relegate Italian women to the role of the mothers of the race. The demographic concerns of a colonial expansive regime that needed to rely on a large army and a strong industry had a big impact on the regime's gender policies. Fascist manhood was represented by solders and aviators who were considered in the pre-neorealistic Rossellini's *Il pilota ritorna* (*The*

Introduction

Pilot Returns), "knights of modern times." This volume considers a variety of representations that Italian culture has made out of these issues and the resulting impact that the same has had on Italian culture's current discourses, in particular, and western ones more generally. The works of Alvaro, Levi and Rossellini are the primary texts examined in the first part of this work. Within this section, particular attention is paid to the figure of the stateless person in the vicinity between and during the two world wars, with frequent references being made to the work of Arendt, Levi and Agamben. The works of Alvaro, Levi, and Rossellini are read in contrast to the regime's cultural discourse which was clearly expressed by some of its political and cultural protagonists such as Gentile and Marinetti (while the focus is on human beings, in Marinetti there is an explicit masculine component), and by the Italian Colonial Cinema (one of its most important propaganda tools, considered almost an extension of the Fascist army.)

The urban and modern character of Europe's main cities (Moscow, Berlin, Rome), within which traditional spatial and cultural geographies have been constantly challenged, makes them central laboratories for this discourse. Eric Hobsbawm, in his well-known work *The Age of Extremes: The Short Twentieth Century 1914–1991*, stressed the absolute centrality of capitals and major cities in the history of the twentieth century. It is clear, he observed, that every major change and every revolution, had to first pass through the capitals and major cities of individual nations. Jacques Attali, too, in *A Brief History of The Future* (*Une brève histoire de l'avenir*), traced the history of the development of our societies in the last millennium through the history of some of the most important cities in the world, which he called "hearts": Bruges, Venice, Antwerp, Genoa, Amsterdam, London, Boston, New York City and Los Angeles. It is clear that the so-called Italian contribution is not limited to Venice and Genoa; there is no need to recall here the historical centrality of imperial Rome. Evoking the latter, Mussolini imagined a modern and totalitarian empire capable of making radical changes that also focused on Man's profile. The term "totalitarianism" was invented in Italy in the 1920s but many believe that it was Mussolini himself who coined the word in an attempt to create an auto-interpretation of his regime. In a study devoted to totalitarianism, Simona Forti (*Il totalitarismo* [*The totalitarianism*]) believes, on the contrary, that the word began to circulate among opponents of the Fascist regime in the early 1920s. She identifies Giovanni Amendola as the first person to use the adjective "totalitarian." Amendola used it in a series of articles published in *Il Mondo* on 12 May and 28 June 1923, in which he denounced the local elections scandal. Mussolini's government was totalitarian, according to Amendola, because it sought absolute domination of political and administrative life. Fascism was not, however, to become the emblem of totalitarianism. The latter showed its sharpest and most significant features in Berlin and Moscow. It is no coincidence that Rossellini himself explored the issue in *Germania anno zero*. Rossellini and Alvaro made this choice out of their need to broaden the perspectives of their work and as a means by which to look for explanations of local events that occurred where the epicenter the twentieth-century earthquake appeared to be. It is evident that Corrado Alvaro, born in Calabria, traveled to Russia with the problems of Southern Italy in mind and was interested in investigating Bolshevik solutions.

The undeniable importance of Levi's work does not require further comment. In this context the reading that Agamben makes of Levi and his concept of the non-human is important. A Foucauldian idea reinterpreted by Agamben (*Quel che resta di Auschwitz [Remnants of Auschwitz]*)—specifically the idea of the use of a racial caesura as well as other kinds of caesura (national, one might add), becomes very helpful in understanding the new biopolitical techniques that were used in Nazism and Soviet Communism. The isolation of an individual or a group of individuals made possible a control that was powerful enough to strip individual human beings of their humanity. What is meant by humanity is a problem but, in this context, it refers to a set of cultural, political, emotional, linguistic, social and professional constructs, up to one of human beings' basic characteristics: their will. The extreme control dedicated to transforming individuals into a mere group of conditioned reactions produced what Levi (*Se questo è un uomo*) called the non-human, interpreted by Agamben (*Quel che resta di Auschwitz*) as the subhuman. Connections between Agamben's and Arendt's work are also highlighted. Agamben's term "simply man" recalls Arendt's conceptual and political analysis of the errors of the French Revolution that became apparent with the experiences of stateless persons during

Introduction

the early twentieth century. Their being "simply men" who were not legally protected by a political affiliation to a state opened the way to making human beings superfluous. Non-belonging in a world now organized according to the national model opened the abyss of non-humans.

Totalitarian regimes can, in any case, as Simona Forti states, be regarded as a tragic response to the problems posed by modernity. Its variants, or at least some elements, some needs, and some questions have, then, certainly spread to countries that were not totalitarian. Their coexistence was not only possible but can be seen to have evolved and subsequently penetrated cultural contexts characterized by postmodernity. As can be seen from the work of Rossellini, Levi, and Alvaro, Italian culture has thought deeply about totalitarianism and has also reflected on aspects close to what is called postmodernity (as focused upon in the second part of this work).

The Post WWII era brought deep political, economic, and cultural changes to Italy and western countries. Italy needed to overcome the destruction, trauma, internal conflicts and divisions, and poverty to build a new unified country from the point of view of the economy, the infrastructure, the language and the cultural, social, and political beliefs. There was a need to establish a strong discontinuity from its recent past. Even its political geography became somehow different. The country came to look towards the United States, and it was from America that it received many of its economic and cultural impulses. If the Fascist idea of the human being was at some point influenced by Hitler's Germany, a very different idea on the society and its members was inspired by the western economies and democracies. The Fascist legacy, including the conception of woman as the mother of race, needed to be dismantled. The Italian economic boom made these change very evident so much so that Pasolini called it an anthropological shift, while Fellini's *La dolce vita* showed new cultural and social patterns to a country that was not yet aware of the deep currents of change that were affecting it. According to Pasolini, the "new" Italian was a consequence of the anthropological shift caused by consumerism and a different mode of production, the impact of which was, in his eyes, much deeper than that of Fascism. For Pasolini there was no distinction between the (new) Italian—who spoke the official national language (Italian)—and bourgeois (using almost the same terminology as Eastern Europe used when referring to the West) as opposed to, for example, the Neapolitan who spoke Neapolitan dialect. Pasolini's focus on those who were excluded from the new dynamics offers only a negative picture of this transformation. Calvino, on the other hand, without hiding his criticism, looked with unconcealed hope to modernity, embraced the change, and tried to channel it. In Calvino's early work interrogation of the new man is also present. Critics such as Alberto Asor Rosa see in the first part of Calvino's writings characters—mostly workers—that they consider "uomini nuovi" (new men) almost in Bolshevik terms. The "new man" however soon becomes the 'incomplete human being' who looks a lot like the 'new post war Italian', and needs to be completed (with the new Italian national culture, one might think) but never will be. The updates are temporary, and they change dynamically with the contextual needs. His idea of the 'incomplete human being' is a re-elaboration of Marx's alienated individual and the Freudian repressed one. In his reportage in Russia, Corrado Alvaro called the new (Bolshevik) man "transitional." The incomplete human being of Calvino who is never complete—but is always completed according to the needs of context—has a similar meaning. The main prototype is Marcovaldo, a newcomer in the city (seen almost as a laboratory that tries to complete human beings), who Calvino literally calls "an immigrant." The condition of the immigrant is the condition of new urban inhabitants; alienated and amazed, naïve, and brilliant, who explores the city with disappointment and enthusiasm. They evolve over time into explorers like Marco Polo and Ludmilla (middle class, like the new profile of the post economic Italian boom). They deal now with a new geography, with an enlarged environment, both in spatial and knowledge terms. They fight fragmentation and succeed in managing plurality; giving life to a kind of network human able to live a new global geography almost preparing and anticipating the post 1990's world. To this dynamic completion he dedicated many reflections on language, culture, environment, and geography, going from local to international. The geography of the works of these authors was important in my choice to focus on their work. The Italy of the economic boom needs to be understood within the Western block from which a multitude of aspects from consumerism to the fight for civil rights arrived. These aspects, which also

Introduction

included gay and women's rights, directly inspired local efforts. The sharp debate around Pasolini's work and figure—which are commented upon in the second part of this book—is also helpful for registering the 1970's debate of the Italian gay movement. I extend briefly these analyzes to Mario Mieli's *Elementi di critica omosessuale* (1977; Elements of homosexual criticism).

According to Gianni Celati "Fellini's cinema is a kind of anthropological telescope" ("Fellini on the Italian male" 223) in which the cultural constructs of the Italian male's profile are also examined. Celati, who stated that, without an invitation from The University of California, San Diego, he would not have analyzed Fellini's observations on the Italian male spanning the entire output of Fellini's films (223), outlined the profile of the Italian mail against the backdrop of "a sick eros that currently bombards our societies" and the influence of the Catholic Church as "being the [body] most responsible for this type of Italian stuck in a chronic infantilism" (231). Fellini's anthropological telescope is, however, very wide.

The new economic, cultural, and civil rights geography offers the context for Fellini's *La dolce vita*. Within this, the closeness of Rome to the United States is highlighted, while Calvino's internationalism and direct interest in Paris and New York inspire a global cultural map that almost senses the transportation revolution, as well as the era of the internet. Many other aspects of our time show on Marcello and Ludmilla. The improved conditions of life and the extension of youth postpone many of the traditional aspects of a human being's existence. Marcello is told by an American poet to choose to not chose, almost like Zygmund Bauman "homo eligens" (in Bauman's analysis there is a direct reference to Calvino's *Le città invisibili [Invisible Cities]*) who is always asked to choose without ever making a definitive choice.

Other authors could, of course, have been considered, but the depth and influence of these author's works on the main cultural discourses made the choice to focus upon them both appropriate and necessary. Though possessed of different ideological agendas, Calvino and Pasolini had in mind a pedagogical mission towards Italy. According to Alfonso Berardinelli, who compares Calvino's pedagogic role to that of Collodi and De Amicis, it is hard to imagine a literary destiny more successful than that

Introduction

of Italo Calvino. Calvino in Italy is read from elementary school to university, taking "us from childhood to senility" (Berardinelli 91, see note 30). Rarely has any other author had such an impact. Fellini's *La dolce vita* turned into a huge cultural event that participated in the lively social debate that culminated with the referenda on divorce and abortion, which finally dismantled the last elements of the Fascist woman's profile as the mother of the race. Pasolini's idea of the extra modern immense peasant's world—that goes from the outskirts of Rome to the Italian south, and from the Italian south to Africa—directly influences the work of more recent protagonists of Italian culture like Amelio, Celati and Giordana and the outlook on modernity along with the representation of immigration; addressed in the third part of this volume. Outlooks upon modernity are an important topic within this book. The part of the world that adopted communism as its political ideology expected to obtain, from the modernization of their countries, the means to redeem the human condition. The East European immigrants considered the missed modernization to be a broken promise and looked towards the West, where some critics of capitalism saw those countries and others as alternative worlds and a natural reserve of diversity.

Many elements that emerge from Calvino's and Fellini's work coexist now with new aspects imposed by new geographies, new demographies, and new cultural contexts. The "middle-class" Italian (let's repeat it again: in Pasolini's analyses of the anthropological shift *Italian* and *middle-class* are synonyms) is suddenly woken up by the end of the Cold War which had frozen international mobility and, with it, a certain world order and economy. This is the reason why many aspects addressed in Part I of this book re-emerge in Part 3, entitled "The Geographic Human Being."

In the 1990s, massive migrant fluxes began a process that brought big changes to Italy's ethnic balance. Tens of thousands of Albanians, former "new men," broke into Apulia in 1991. Just two years later, Gianni Amelio tried to make an artistic synthesis of their story. Italy is now "Lamerica" recalling the beginning of last century's dream destination for Italian immigrants, and the Albanians, today's immigrants, are simply "the new poor." This thesis is supported by an entire cultural discourse of the Left, as many subsequent publications show. The consequence of this cultural discourse is evident in present legislation on migration

Introduction

(the Bossi-Fini law completed by the Decree Law Salvini of 2018 and 2025)[2] that establishes an economic threshold below which one cannot be an Italian citizen; constricting the opportunity to live within and be part of the Italian community. This is how the modern birth of the nation-state and colonial experiences have crystallized in the economic profile of the "national man." The importance of the cultural aspect—already at the core of the idea of the "new man"—seems to be taken into consideration for the very profile of the new Italian citizens born in Italy from migrant parents. Two proposed laws (*Ius culturae*—2017, and *Ius scholae*—2022) seek to replace the concept of *Ius solis*.

The end of the Cold War and the arrival of new waves of migration, along with a new European cultural, economic, political, and even territorial map, as well as new demographics, internet, new media, better transportation and the birth of a new state, the European Union, rapidly changed the old internal and external balances and caused another important shift in the cultural discourse. A new state needs a new nationalism as Sandro Mezzadra wrote in his "The New European Migratory Regime" (2002); highlighting the relationship of mobility to different levels of European citizenship. In the first part of this book, we see how the Soviet Union—and all the totalitarian systems, including Fascist Italy—used the control of mobility in their immense territories as a powerful tool. A vast territory transformed into a "bread factory" (as Alvaro calls it), on the one hand, and the Nazi's extreme experiment of the concentration camps (to say it with Agamben), on the other, are some clear examples of the control of mobility. Mobility and borders are, today, very important once more. The borders of the European Union, as Mezzadra points out, are now increasingly mobile, and project different degrees of citizenship and related rights. Within national territories, mobility rates translate into different levels of inclusiveness. With the fall of the Eastern border, and the increase of mobility, the human being's profile may have discovered the importance of geography like never before. If in Part II, thanks to improvements in transportation and media, we see the emerging of a new geography that is gradually also open to the middle classes, in part III we see the coexistence of old and new geographies along with inequalities. Immigration today has become, once again, an important factor bringing with it demographic, political, social, and cultural challenges. This is the reason why the third part of this book presents a geographic trip. It starts with the Balkans, with the analyzes of *Lamerica*, the arrival of the first massive immigrant crowds in Apulia; continues with Andrea Segre's representation of African immigration in the new millennium; then arrives in Italy, starting in the South and continuing in the small northeastern industrialized cities in need of migrant labor; and ends in the capital, in Rome.

The new media panorama is more articulated than ever before. The contrast between mainstream representations and small productions is sharp. The reading of mainstream representations of border crossings in comparison to documentaries about the same topic is very revealing. Mainstream production, whose directors such as Amelio and Giordana do not have direct experience of the realities that they are representing, are read in contrast with documentaries made with little money by authors such as Segre, Ymer, Garrone, and Rosi who spent a long time in Africa, Lampedusa, and the outskirts of Rome and included in their filmmaking processes some protagonists of these trips (Segre does so in a methodical way). Amelio and Celati—along with Pasolini never, in a certain way, leave Italy. They represent respectively, Albanian migrants (Amelio with *Lamerica*) and life in remote Senegal (Celati in *Passare la vita a Diol Khad [Spending Life in Diol Kadd]*) through a lens that has an outlook on modernity. Their ideological closeness to Pasolini's take on "extra modern people" is evident. Pasolini, who used to call the Yemenites "clowns" who wanted to behave and look like the people of the modern West, seems to have inspired Amelio's and Celati's perspectives when dealing with very distant and different realities such as Albania and Senegal. They implicitly deny the right of immigrants coming from this "extra modern" geography to live within the standards and comfort of modern life. This 'extra modern' geography is matched with an 'extra modern' time that refers to Italy's history of emigration. The immigrants are like Italian grandfathers of the past (Amelio literally refers to his grandfather in an interview, whilst Celati uses similar comparisons many times in his reportage) who emigrated to the United States: poor, analphabets but with a great heart.

The "middle class" aspirations of the new Italian generation who, even when they come from worker's families, aspire to a

Introduction

certain category of jobs along with relatively good health after retirement has created a demographic, social and economic condition into which 'extra modern' immigrants—who are expected to be employed in non-qualified jobs that Italians do not want anymore—fit perfectly. Many of the aspects considered in Part II are still true but happen somehow in parallel, protected, and isolated social bubbles or closed communities that characterize our current urban realities (I refer to Bauman analyzes (2001) of the phenomenon he calls "desire for community" and his analyzes on "gated communities"). In this part of the book, I examine Italian "closed communities" in the films *Io sono Li* (Segre, 2012; *Shun Li and the Poet*), *La giusta distanza* (Mazzacurati, 2007; *The Right Distance*) and *Cose dell'altro mondo* (Patierno, 2011; *Things of Another World*). These directors do an excellent job in representing urban realities that they know well and offer a very lucid reading. The same reality of closed communities, now seen through migrant eyes, is offered by Amara Lakhous's novel *Scontro di Civiltà per un Ascensore a Piazza Vittorio* (2006; *Clash of Civilizations over an Elevator in Piazza Vittorio*). Set in Rome, these closures do not characterize only the different approaches of locals and newcomers but also forms a sort of archipelago of closures even among the newcomers. The choice of these authors was necessary—and simple—given the topics and the quality of their representations.

The quality of mainstream representations improves a lot from the point of view of insights and knowledge of territory, when the movies are set in Italian cities that the directors know well. Mazzacurati's and Segre's movies converge in representing closed communities in the industrialized Italian northeast, as does Amara Lakhous' novel which is set in Rome. Many aspects however, seen in Part II when analyzing Calvino and Fellini, do not disappear but coexist with new elements poised by the complexity of the present. The consequences of economic growth and the extension of youth have triggered social, economic, and demographic challenges that have become complementary to the need for migrant labor. The crisis of the family—as the main social model—has now become the background for relationships between emancipated female characters (like, for example, Mazzacurati's Mara) who are willing to experience the many possibilities of the world (without ever making final choices), and male migrants who instead want a family and a traditional life having been forged by other cultural discourses. What makes the difference in Mazzacurati's and Segre's movies is their direct knowledge of their cities. Knowledge, imaginary and global media now play a crucial role in the formation of subjectivities that are no longer informed and influenced only by controlled local media. As Gabriele del Grande puts it in his book reportage *Mamadou va a Morire: La Strage dei Clandestini nel Mediterraneo* (2009), skype chat between two cousins in Tunisia and Turin is much more real than the song of a muezzin from a nearby mosque. Its changed demography has brought challenges to Italy that could not have been imagined only a few decades ago. Economic inequalities, fear, phobia, and closure reveal both a missing multicultural model and the need for one. Giving cohesion to plurality and diversity via a new culture which is able to forge a new Italian, an Italian-European-Mediterranean multibelonging one, seems to be the new challenge.

There are several writers "in Italian," as some critics call them, who write in more than one language. The last section of the book starts with an analysis of two literary works, *Lasciami andare, madre* (2001; Mother, Let Me Go) by Helga Schneider, and the volume of poetry *Corpo Presente* (1999; Present Body) by Gëzim Hajdari. Schneider writes in Italian to deny the German part of herself that connects the writer to her ex-SS mother but, unable and not wanting to entirely remove bonds with her mother and her mother tongue, she moves from one language to another, from one belonging to another, according to need. Another poet and writer, Hajdari, is an Albanian migrant. Already a "new man," he calls the motherland Medea without idealizing the Italy that confines him to the margins. Hajdari, horrified by the abyss of non-belonging, always writes in two languages, entrusting the construction of his condition of non-belonging precisely to this bilingual writing. The metaphor of the bad mother is very present in both works. The stepmother, however, is not nature, as in Leopardi, but the motherland; thereby emphasizing the shift from the "Natural Man" to the "National Man" first, and to the post-national, multibelonging thereafter. It is no coincidence that the possession of two passports speaks of Italian-Americans, French-Germans and so on. Stateless persons, illegal immigrants, uprooted or non-belongers bring back to mind the category of non-humans, as they emerge from Arendt's, Agamben's and Primo Levi's work. That legal hyphen is the thread of multibelonging that is also a very important cultural issue. That hyphen is a temporary condition without which one risks falling into the abyss of the non-human. Also taken into consideration is Alvaro's analysis of how the USSR sought to address the issue of multi-ethnicity through the forced acceptance of a package of knowledge and a vision of the world that was generically defined as culture. It is this kind of culture—revisited, as if it were Calvino's open encyclopedia, according to the needs and parameters of our time—that is needed as the roof where pluralities are housed. In order to house diversities and plurality within the same context, some universals are needed. Today, a group of educated migrants use an international cultural capital (I refer to Bourdieu's 1980 analysis) to create a multibelonging status. This trend also seems to prevail among younger Western generations who are willing to interact globally. New technologies and a world with improved transportation can make this a successful trend.

Today, Italian cinema and literature highlight, (as does Giordana, for example, in his *Quando sei nato non puoi più nasconderti* (2005; *Once You're Born You Can No Longer Hide*), among other aspects, the need for the formation of a "post-Italian" or, rather, an Italian European and Mediterranean Italian. This new profile would be an auspiciously multibelonging Italian which is open to multiethnic and multicultural cohabitations, and interacts with a much vaster and plural territory. A clear shift in discourses about Rome is also noticeable. If Fellini's *La Dolce Vita* stressed the modernity and closeness between Rome and New York, Ferrente's *L'Orchestra di Piazza Vittorio* (2006; *The Orchestra of Piazza Vittorio*), inspired by Fellini's *Prove d'orchestra* (1978; *Orchestra Rehearsals*) and sponsored by the Rome-Europa festival, now highlights the multiethnic and Mediterranean profile of the city.

Italy has been and remains a crossroads for diverse cultural and political currents. It is no coincidence that, for several decades, it was in Italy that the most important Western Communist Party existed. It is also no coincidence that Italy gave life in literature and cinema to neorealism and also inspired cultural products such as Fellini's *La Dolce Vita* that registered and anticipated changes in urban anthropology that could well have related to New York City instead of Rome. Italy continues to be a work in progress site that is open to Mediterranean cultural influences while remaining within a typically Western cultural context. Current so-called globalizing tendencies make Rome a very significant site today.

Part One: The "New Man"

Chapter One
The "New Man" and the Universal Man

The absence of a stable profile for human beings was accompanied by the absence of a corresponding stable design for him. It follows, that even the "new man" is subject to continuous revision. Philosophy has targeted the same issues as literature. The question "Who is a human being?" along with the many existentialist, political, and literary implications that flow from that question, has always been at the core of philosophical elaborations. There is something elusive about this supposed essence because constant change has never made an affirmative and satisfactory response possible. A profile of human beings is more traceable in their evolution, in their historicity. As Nietzsche wrote polemically in *Human, All Too Human:* "They involuntarily think of 'man' as an *aeterna veritas*, as something that remains constant in the midst of all flux, as a sure measure of things. Everything the philosopher has declared about man is, however, at bottom no more than a testimony to the man of a very limited period of time. Lack of historical sense is the family failing of all philosophers" (Nietzsche 12–13).

After him, philosophy no longer showed a "lack of historical sense." In answer to the question "Who is a human being?" Hannah Arendt (*The Human Condition*) posed the question, "Who was the human being?" It was the only question she thought could be answered. Indeed, we long ago abandoned Earth, now exposed, as Arendt states, to universal cosmic forces alien to its nature. The place of our spatiality, our gravitational geometry, our appearance, our visibility, of metaphysics, of our anti-gravitational anxiety, and of our being, has been replaced by mathematics, fluctuations, the unseen, and the concept of "process." The human being's heir would have had to undergo a kind of a biological process of mutation in which, in order to adapt to new conditions,

Chapter One

"human bodies are gradually covered with shells of steel." These look like sentences from *A Cyborg Manifesto* by Donna Haraway but are, instead, from the pages of a much earlier essay entitled *The Human Condition*, which is the theoretical background to Arendt's analysis of twentieth-century totalitarianism. In *Homo Sacer: Il potere sovrano e la nuda vita* (*Sovereign Power and Bare Life*), Giorgio Agamben points out that Arendt's book anticipated Michel Foucault's analysis on questions of biopolitics (in particular *La Volonté de savoir* and *The History of Sexuality*) by almost twenty years. Agamben claims that Foucault, strangely, did not use the central places of modernity where biopolitics was exercised: concentration camps and totalitarian states, as examples. The same may be said of Arendt who, in Agamben's view, did not include the perspective of biopolitics in her analysis of totalitarianism. More recently, Arendt's reading of both totalitarianism under the same paradigm and the known imbalance between the analysis of Nazism and Communism in *The Origins of Totalitarianism* became the main target of Roberto Esposito's critique (*Termini della politica*). Here, Esposito considered Nazism not as a "filosofia compiuta" ("fulfilled philosophy")—like, for example, Communism which, according to Esposito "fulfills," albeit in an exasperated and extreme form, a philosophical tradition of modernity—but as a "biologia compiuta" ("fulfilled biology") born from the decomposition of modernity itself. As Esposito points out, Nazism lost the war and was defeated militarily and politically, but its cultural and linguistic elements survived; providing some characteristics of today's context where the centrality of *bios* as political subject and object is, according to Esposito's *Termini della politica*, confirmed. The imbalance of analysis regarding the study of Nazism and Bolshevism does not only apply to Arendt. It is true of many scholars, not only with regards to Marx and Marxism, but also with regard to the much-longer-lived and, to them, less-familiar reality of eastern European totalitarianism. It seems that they prefer to move in a territory that they know better. Agamben (*Quel che resta di Auschwitz*), for example, places the study of *lagers* at the center of his reflections. He borrows and develops further a later Foucauldian idea—that of a necessary caesura—as a way to distinguish different groups inside a population in order to exercise as much biopolitical power as possible. The caesurae can be of different types; racial and spatial. As is illustrated in the first part of this volume, in the transition from the universal man of the Enlightenment to the homologated one of the ideologies and then to the national one (as Arendt's *The Origins of Totalitarianism* seems to suggest), the importance of applied caesurae becomes evident.

It is clear how the idea of the human being progressively formed in the modern West is a thread that runs through contexts and issues. It does so conserving, of course, contextual peculiarities and characteristics, and anticipates issues that are now crystallizing. It was evidently modernity which radically overhauled the idea of the "human being" and asked society to manufacture a "new man" with features tailored to the new challenges being posed. It was the heart of modern Europe which generated contrasting ideas and profound contradictions, even when they were first applied in the East, where a big problem had to be faced: the metamorphosis in a few decades (or at least, equally significantly, the nagging needs) of the "tribal" human being into a "new man" possessed of an avant-garde package of knowledge and traits. Illiteracy and the confused pagan-religious consciousness were replaced by an atheism characterized by an irresistible attraction to science (a deep source of redemption and hope), and a lifestyle marked by materialism. Not blue eyes, not blonde hair, and not selection; but education and ideologically imposed culture became the main features of the new modern "man" in the East. Biopolitical studies have paid less attention to this variant of totalitarianism, the study of which would offer much. The two main ideologies displayed substantial and not inconsequential differences. It is clear that the Germans really believed in biological selection, while the Bolsheviks believed blindly in cultural indoctrination. Both wanted to produce what the Soviets called the "new man": biologically selected by the former, culturally manufactured by the latter. However, as this chapter illustrates, before selecting or transforming them, both totalitarian regimes stripped them of their former identity. The only certainty lay in the deep dissatisfaction that existed regarding the human being as he was. What was certain was his malleability and adaptability to specific contextual needs. No one believed in the immutable universal man any longer. That man was probably dead, together with his god. Nor did the "natural man" of the Enlightenment, equally universal, survive. The twentieth-century experiences of stateless persons, as is subsequently discussed, demonstrated how vulnerable the "simply man" was when not accompanied by adjectives such as German, Italian, American or Russian; in other words, adjectives of nationality. Religion retreated, making space for nationalism, and was often used as a surrogate ideology for the benefit of the former. The body of the community received unprecedented biopolitical attention. Racism came to power in Germany with the purpose of emphasizing alleged ethnic differences as if they were different species; its goal was the manufacture of nothing less than Aryans being the new dominant species. The means to pursue this inconceivably crazy project were financial. Germany, though frustrated and battered by the crisis that brought power to Nazism, had important resources. The Soviets were chasing the same economic development. Both knew that their economies were the means and the ends to their respective imperialistic processes. The "new man" of the East was needed to relaunch on Western economies, while Germany's imperialistic economy was needed to self-preserve and produce the Aryan species. The economic development was needed to renew human beings, and the renewal of human beings was needed for economic development—so "new men" are members of a new, modern, and certainly rich society.

The horizon and the future were now drawn by ideologies. The "new man" of tomorrow had to be better. The improvement, whatever that meant, started from what was believed to be the inadequacies in the human being. For the Nazis this included: race, physical frailty, illness and, potentially, being socially weak. For the Bolsheviks it included: backwardness, ignorance, wealth, and independence; together with diversity and individuality for both. The urgent task for both was to homologate, to monitor and adapt to the changing needs of the state. Differences are frightening. This is why the migration of yesterday and today contained and contain something subversive with respect to the *status quo*. This is why the stranger is the element that disturbs this kind of order—which fights him back. Primo Levi thought it was among the main causes of the Holocaust, so much so that he highlighted it in the introduction to *Se questo è un uomo*:

> A molti individui o popoli, può accadere di ritenere, più

The "New Man" and the Universal Man

> o meno consapevolmente, che "ogni straniero è nemico." Per lo più questa convinzione giace in fondo agli animi come una infezione latente; si manifesta solo in atti saltuari e incoordinati, e non sta all'origine di un sistema di pensiero. Ma quando questo avviene, quando il dogma inespresso diventa premessa maggiore di un sillogismo, allora, al termine della catena, sta il Lager. (*Se questo è un uomo* 9)

> Many people—many nations—can find themselves believing, more or less wittingly, that 'every stranger is an enemy'. For the most part this conviction lies deep down like some latent infection; it betrays itself only in random, disconnected acts, and does not lie at the base of a system of reason. But when this does come about, where the unspoken dogma becomes the major premise in a syllogism, then, at the end of the chain, there is the *Lager*. (*If This Is a Man*, 15)

The conceptual void left by the universal man urgently needed to be filled by the homologated human being, by the citizen of a given political entity. Plurality was heterogeneous to power. The "new man" of the East, in particular, whose sphere of necessity was taken care of by the state through the exploitation of the workforce and the trapping of people in a defined role in order to dispose of all that was excessive in absolute terms, was subjected to hellish thought control in order to be conditioned and dominated. And there is no doubt that the terrorist barbarism characterized by mass and systematic physical elimination was first and foremost a specialty of the Nazis.

Chapter Two

Fascism, Nazism, and Bolshevism in Alvaro

There are some constant themes present in the work of Corrado Alvaro, the reasons for which must be sought in an exceptionally troubled historical context: two world wars, three forms of totalitarianism—Fascism, Nazism, and Stalinism—and a city–countryside dichotomy, the result of urbanization as never before accelerated; promoted by both Fascism and Bolshevism. At the center of all this is an anthropological reflection on the new profile of man. The titles of novels such as *L'uomo nel labirinto* (*The Man in the Labyrinth*) and *L'uomo è forte* (*The Man is Strong*), interspersed with reports in Russia, Agro Pontino, Berlin and the short stories *Gente in Aspromonte* (*People in Aspromonte*), are enough to realize how urbanization, the form of the government and the new profile of man compose a single intertwining at the center of the work of the Calabrian writer. This section highlights how the city–countryside dichotomy, central in the first novel, the Agro Pontino chronicles and, to a certain extent in *Gente in Aspromonte*, is connected to the fear transformed into Brechtian and Orwellian anguish which characterizes *L'uomo è forte*.

Babel, the protagonist of *L'uomo nel labirinto*, a former southern fighter, cannot fit into the labyrinthine urban context. As much fascinated by, as lost in, the relational multiplicity, he returns to his place of birth. Babel however ends up underlining the disenchantment of the return and discovering the eradication and alienation as dominant existential characteristics of his historical context. Alvaro's biography matters a lot, and the tension between the problems of the south, especially those of his native Calabria, and the exploration of new and modern urban reality, remain constant in his work. It declines both as a reflection of the dichotomy civilization–nature, and as a political reflection on the modalities and consequences of the acceleration of urbanization of its time. "È un fatto che qui manca la nozione geometrica della ruota" ("It is a fact that the geometric notion of the wheel is missing here"), Alvaro writes in *Gente in Aspromonte*, "ma per poco ancora. Come al contatto dell'aria le antiche mummie si polverizzano, si polverizzò così questa vita. È una civiltà che scompare, e su di essa non c'è da piangere, ma bisogna trarre, chi ci è nato, il maggior numero di memorie" ("but for a while yet. As when ancient mummies come in contact with air and disintegrate, this life has also been pulverized. It is a civilization that disappears, with nothing to cry about it, and those who were born here must drag out the greatest number of memories") (15). A civilization disappears, together with a landscape, an anthropological profile, a way of living, relating, working, and a mode of production. The new possible profile of the human being within an economic and political system, often presents insidious unknowns. This moment is the favorite location of the observer, Alvaro, who tries to capture the image of the sudden collapse of the world of yesterday, and the irruption of a radically different reality. But it is now the Fascists and the Soviets who drive the bulldozers that destroy the dams:

> Sono gli ultimi ad abbandonarlo, dopo le volpi, i cinghiali, gl'insetti maligni. L'umanità avanza qui con le vanghe, le zappe, le roncole, irta come un treno armato. Basta consultare la storia di questa regione.—Qui siamo nell'Agropontino, cui è dedicato questo reportage.—Il 6 novembre 1931 l'Opera Nazionale Combattenti prende possesso di questa landa. Il 7 novembre 1931 arrivano i primi 1.300 operai. Il 21 gennaio 1932 si fonda la prima casa colonica. Il 5 aprile 1932 il Duce visita la contrada.

> They are the last to abandon it, after the foxes, the boars, the evil insects. Humanity advances here with spades, hoes, billhooks, bristling like an armed train. All one must do is consult the history of this region. Here we are—in the Agropontino, to which this report is dedicated—on 6 November 1931, when the Opera Nazionale Combattenti (National Fighters Movement) took possession of this land. On 7 November 1931, the first 1,300 workers arrived. On 21 January 1932, the first farmhouse was founded. On 5 April 1932, the Dux visited the district. (Alvaro, *Terra nuova* 15–16)

The powerful impact of modernity on the world of yesterday produces a constant curiosity in Alvaro, along with an anxiety that, in the novel *L'uomo è forte*, turns into an Orwellian vision.[3] This curiosity also becomes the lens through which, beyond the Soviet experience, Alvaro reads the story of the Agro Pontino, in a report published by the National Institute of Fascist Culture in 1934. "Il sistema dell'Agro Pontino ha questo di straordinario," Alvaro writes enthusiastically, "che riproduce in un'estensione di tempo assai breve quello che l'uomo e la sua opera compiono in un lungo giro d'anni. Talvolta secoli. È l'intervento dell'uomo nella biologia..." ("This is what is extraordinary about the Agro Pontino system," Alvaro writes enthusiastically, "it reproduces what man and his work complete in many years, sometimes centuries, but within a very short period of time. It is a human intervention in biology ...") (*Terra nuova* 45–46). The profound changes are surrounded by rather dramatic social and political phenomena. The deep wounds of the First World War and the triumphalist tones that incite another, even more sanguine one, must somehow be felt in the present, and must disturb the consciences of those who, like the author from Calabria, widen their gaze to the whole country and the whole continent. Despite the celebratory occasion, Alvaro does not hold back. "Guerra ed emigrazione," he writes, "le due fasi della vita italiana, e della lotta italiana per vivere, fanno qui un solo eloquente spettacolo; per questo due esperienze: gli ottantamila ettari di terra dell'Agro Pontino sono un mondo, una storia di civiltà e di lavoro." ("War and emigration," he writes, "the two phases of Italian life, and of the Italian struggle for life, make here only one eloquent show; for this, two experiences: the 80,000 hectares of land of the Agro Pontino are a world, a history of civilization and work") (*Terra nuova* 48). The disruption of the human habitat has multiple consequences that are often extreme. The type of social and political organizations that accompanied these efforts is a question that, in the first half of the twentieth century, had tragic answers. It seems evident that Alvaro was asking himself the question of how to avoid slipping into extreme experiences, how to avoid the massification and de-individualization seen elsewhere, and how to guarantee the existence of a bourgeoisie capable of enacting a political regime different, for example, from the collectivizing of the Soviet Union. "È l'utopia dell'Italia di piccoli proprietari divenuta fatto vivo: difatti in questo lembo di terra nasce un nuovo ordine, si tenta una costituzione umana che ha più d'un punto di contatto coi sogni di tutti i pensatori che fantasticano su uno Stato ordinato, senza servi né padroni, la comunità che assorbe gli individui e tuttavia non ne fa un numero" ("It is the Italian utopia of small owners that has become a living fact: indeed in this strip of land a new order is born. It is a human constitution which attempts to extend over more than one point of contact with the dreams of all the thinkers who fantasize about an ordered state, without servants or masters, a community that absorbs individuals and yet does not make them numbers") (*Terra nuova* 49–50). Expressions like "ordered state," "without servants nor masters" signal a vision, a utopia whose nature, unfortunately, becomes evident in some cloying pages of Chapter VI, "Mussolini tra i pionieri" ("Mussolini among the pioneers"). Alvaro praises the Dux regime. The decision to write this reportage for the National Institute of Fascist Culture certainly undermines its results. Avoiding a good deal of pure and simple propaganda was evidently impossible. The banal praise then comes: "Aveva piovuto quasi tutta la mattina. Quando egli apparve sul bancone venne fuori un sole caldo in un cielo sgombro. 'È naturale', diceva un giornalista americano. 'Quando esce lui il tempo si fa buono'" ("It had rained almost the whole morning. When he appeared at the counter, a hot sun came out in a clear sky. 'It's reasonable', said an American journalist. 'When he comes out, the weather changes for the better'") (Alvaro, *Terra nuova* 73). His tormented relationship with Fascism is, however, well known and was probably the reason for his stay in Berlin between 1928 and 1929.[4] When he returned to Italy, Alvaro was too aware of the reality of things. For Walter Mauro, the publication of the reportage was "un cedimento verso il regime" ("a surrender to the regime") but one which served to "rendere più aspra e polemica la sua pagina" ("make his page more harsh and polemical") (Mauro, 47) in the many anti-totalitarian writings. The Agro Pontino chronicles should not, however, be neglected as a simple "failure" as they offer elements of contiguity with the rest of Alvaro's work that help us to better understand the wider context to which his writings refer. The search for the common elements of Fascism, Nazism, and Bolshevism present in *L'uomo è forte* does not occur suddenly. Instead, it is a constant feature of all the work of the Calabrian writer. The reportage on the Agro Pontino was supposed to exalt land remediation work that could be extended to other parts of Italy. Nor does Alvaro forget it.[5] The modernization of the country accomplished by the "ordered" state had plans to transform the face of the whole country.

Quite different are the tones of Alvaro in his Soviet reportage—the analysis is less celebrative and much sharper. Alvaro had nothing to fear. The new profile of the modern human being, already in the urban labyrinth of the post-World War I period, was here a declared political program. According to scholars such as Domenico Scarpa, Alvaro was obsessed with Mussolini—as can be seen more in the diari but it is also concealed in his fiction—and finds him in Stalin that considers a mediocre dictator who has pervaded the whole country with his invisible presence (Scarpa 113). In Alvaro's *L'uomo è forte,* the dictator cannot be seen and cannot be nominated. For Scarpa, this novel refers to Fascism when it describes the human condition in everyday life (115). The order that Alvaro talked about in the Agro Pontino chronicles is not missing here. While the Nazis, using the brute force of modernity, closed the plurality in sealed trains and then burned it in the gas chambers, the Bolsheviks tried other social engineering solutions through the forced metamorphosis of all in "new men." In both cases, the combination of propaganda with terror and fear was essential. It is exactly this atmosphere that dominates the novel *L'uomo è forte*—the original title of which was *Paura sul mondo* (Fear in the World). However, the censors did not approve (see the volume *Paura sul mondo* edited by Aldo Maria Morace, and Angelo R. Pupino, Edizioni ETS, Pisa, 2013). Alvaro had to specify that he was inspired by the Russian experience and that the novel did not concern Fascist Italy. If the latter had been the case, then the use of neutral names, the nuanced context, and the universalization of the story would remain incomprehensible. Another warning from the author explicitly pointed to the censorship of the regime after the fall of Fascism. According to the critics, there is no lack of references to Nazi-Fascist regimes[6], which is why the novel was considered suspect in Italy and banned in Nazi Germany.

Alvaro was concerned with finding the unique matrix of these regimes that dominated the entire continent. He found it in the terror, in the propaganda, in the isolation of individuals, in the atomization of society, and in the hallucinated alteration of reality. He also found it in the ongoing urban upheaval, and in the use of technological means never before available to human beings. The impression of impotence mixed with fascination, while describing the powerful and unstoppable progress of urbanization, is complementary to the state of loss, and to the ineluctable control of depersonalized power. Dale, the protagonist, sees the arrival of the tsunami and runs off, clumsily and vulnerable, waiting for the inevitable. Yet he does not stop.

Chapter Three

Soldiers and Mothers of the Race

Anna Banti wrote and published *Le donne muiono* (*Women Die*), a dystopian short story—composed between 1938 and 1950—about a distant future where one gender is destined to immortality, and the other to perpetual submission and death. This kind of catastrophic imaginary should not surprise readers considering the years of the holocaust and the racial laws. If a race, a group of people, or the believers of a particular religion could be targeted and killed, any kind of mega collective suppression was suddenly thinkable. In 2617, in the city of Valloria, which takes the place of today's Venice, men discover that they can remember past lives. This "*seconda memoria*" (second memory) opens the way for men to claim immortality through constant reincarnation, while women become procreation machines. Many women end up retreating into female communities similar to the old convents. As Carol Lazzaro-Weis, the editor of a 2001 MLA edition of Banti's collection of short stories *Le donne muoiono* points out, this volume was published two years after Simone de Beauvoir's novel *Tous les hommes sont mortels* (*All Men Are Mortal*) with which it shared many themes. "While Beauvoir's book is situated within a debate about existential philosophy, Banti's story, a parody of Fascism's attempts to revive Italy's glorious past, emphasizes how men's desire for immortality excludes women" (Lazzaro-Weis, xix). The consequence of all this, in Banti's words, was that "il genere umano, insomma, s'era spaccato in due come una mela" ("in short, mankind had been split in two like an apple") (85). The symbol of the apple is not a casual one. The defeat of many battles for emancipation are not attributable exclusively to Fascism. The communities to which women retreat in Banti's short story look like churches without confessions, places where a faith was cultivated. "Il mito arcaico di Eva colpevole e punita vi serpeggiava, a insinuare che certo la donna aveva peccato più dell'uomo, con maggior coscienza, e bisognava dunque che più dell'uomo soffrisse per meritare l'eternità del ricordo." ("The archaic myth of Eva, who is guilty and punished, slithered there, insinuating that, certainly, women had sinned more than men, with greater conscience, and therefore it was necessary that, more so than men, they suffered to deserve the eternity of the memory") (73). Banti's pessimism about the future was justified if we agree with Victoria de Grazia that it was only in the 1970s that Fascist policies about women were completely erased. The Resistance (1943–1945) offered to both women and men the ability to act freely after two decades of inaction but, when the time came to celebrate its victories, the new Republic maintained laws "that had been codified under fascist rule" (de Grazia, 278). Victoria de Grazia's book *How Fascism Ruled Women* is the most important study on this topic. Her work confirms that only in the late 1930s did Fascism adopt the same Nazi eugenicist precepts that relegated women into the home as "custodians of race, culture and sentiment" (xi). Mussolini's dictatorship is generically considered lighter when compared to the extreme mobilized totalitarian organization of Nazism. Nonetheless, concludes de Grazia, "the antifeminist zeal of the two dictatorships, their laws relegating women to the home, and their public cult of motherhood in the name of building national-state power were similar to justify speaking of a common Fascist politics toward women" (xi). In this chapter, I highlight both the elements that Fascism shared with Nazism and the specificities of Fascism. The standardized public discourse about women, as de Grazia notes, can be traced in official policies reinforced by stereotypes circulated through mass media. I analyze these stereotypes—both in the official propaganda, through selected readings by Gentile and Marinetti, and in the Fascist cinema—to determine which discourse was reinforcing and complementary to the regime's position.

Gentile and Marinetti

Giovanni Gentile, Minister of Education from 1922 to 1924 and a neo-idealist philosopher who proclaimed the alliance between culture and Fascism, promoted the notorious *Manifesto degli intellettuali del fascismo* (1925; *Manifesto of Fascist Intellectuals*).

In 1921, Gentile wrote and published *Preliminari allo studio del fanciullo* (Preliminaries to the Study of the Child), which contains a final chapter entitled "La donna e il fanciullo" ("The woman and the child"), which was published in "*Levana*" in 1922–1923, and republished as a book in 1924.

For Giovanni Gentile, feminism and its adversary, which used to live exclusively through polemics, were both dead in 1921: "La donna oggi non desidera più i diritti per cui lottava; ma la donna si è elevata dinanzi all'uomo e dinanzi a sé stessa per merito di quelle stesse polemiche, che esasperavano in lei la coscienza della sua dignità morale e inducevano l'uomo al riconoscimento dell'alta missione che alla donna spetta nella famiglia e quindi nella società." ("The woman today no longer desires the rights she fought for; but woman's prominence has been elevated before man and herself. The credit is due to those same controversies, which had exacerbated her awareness of moral dignity and these controversies also engendered men to recognize the high mission that falls upon women within the family and, therefore within society.") (*Preliminari* 82). There was no longer a need to talk about equal rights between men and women since, instead of rights, they had duties towards the (Fascist) state. Gentile's principal model of his assessment of woman was, according to Lucia Re, Hegel, "who places woman squarely within the economy of the family, and therefore of the state" ("Fascist Theories of 'Women' and the Construction of Gender" 82). Gentile lists right from the start as interrelated aspects the "healthy and well-ordered society," the growing respect for woman and for the family along with a religious feeling (*Preliminari* 85). The "well-ordered society"— evidently, in his view, legitimated by religious feeling—is a key phrase and an obsession of the totalitarian propaganda of those years, as we saw in Alvaro's *Terra Nuova. Prima cronaca dell'Agro Pontino*. In the Italian Fascist case, however, and especially from Gentile's religious perspective, it establishes its coordinates as opposite to those of the atheist Soviet Union. "La società è in crisi e in disgregazione—esempio, oggi, la Russia sovietica—strappano l'individuo alla famiglia, rallentando ogni vincolo familiare, esaltando il cosiddetto "libero amore" (che è l'amore meno libero, cioè meno umano che si possa essere), e predicando insieme l'ateismo." ("Society is in crisis and disintegration—for example, today, the Soviet Union tear the individual from the family unit while impeding every familial tie in exaltation of the so-called "free love" (which is the least free love, or that is, the least human a person can be) and, at the same time, preaching atheism.") (*Preliminari* 85). For Gentile, Atheism is materialism, and incapable of recognizing the value of the family. Materializing the woman "spegne quella luce ideale che la cinge dell'aureolo, che la difende dalle perversioni bestiali della vita sessuale." ("turns off that ideal light which girds her with the Aureolus, which defends her from the bestial perversions of the sexual life.") (*Preliminari* 87). Gentile, in an attempt to emphasize the importance of the family, distinguishes two main categories and two spheres of activity in which human life is shared: the private and the public. In his view, family is the real strength of the man who always, and continuously, goes back to the private dimension after experiencing enriching public life. Gentile does not miss the chance to condense in the family metaphor, which, in his words, is the foundation of the "well-ordered-society," an important part of the Fascist ideology which lists categories of people that the regime considered enemies: "E guai all'ebreo errante, al senza tetto, all'uomo che, tornando, trova il focolare deserto!" ("Woe to the errant Jew, to the homeless, to the man who, returning, finds the hearth empty") (*Preliminari* 91). This private dimension has an essential element. To explain how central the woman is in this articulation, Gentile explains, first, that part of this private dimension, similar to the home, is also the body, "al centro saldo di questo sé" ("the solid center of the self") (*Preliminari* 91). Man's body lives, he explains, within a limit—that is, in relation to what limits it; to the other; to the other sex, to the woman, who is, "come la terra e più della terra, il complemento dell'essere naturale dell'uomo" ("like the earth and is also more than the earth, the complement of the natural being of man") (*Preliminari* 92). At the same time, however, in this happy portrait of the private dimension man is dialectically equally essential to woman, to her alleged nature, and to her alleged fulfillment. Here is "la donna che è del marito, ed è quel che è in quanto è di lui; ecco la donna a realizzare in quello di lui la sua propria individualità" ("the woman, who belongs to the man, is who she is because she is his; here is the woman realizing in him her own individuality") (*Preliminari* 92). This complementary reciprocal completion is not enough, and beyond such dialectical interactions the woman in Gentile's description is, thanks to a sort of religious investiture, by nature not just a mother but a "virginal" one. Motherhood, seen as a virtue that transcends man, is the most important aspect of all that describes woman and her role in society; elevated even to the sacred by evoking "virginal love." "Non è lui a renderla madre; essa è tale per sua propria virtù, per quella sua originaria natura che già noi intravvediamo in lei andandole incontro, quando essa ci saluta col suo sorriso… Chi non rispetta nella donna, vedendola sia pure oscuramente, quella sua 'verginale maternità'—che è poi quell'eterno femminino che il poeta col suo acuto sguardo ha visto in lei—distrugge nella donna la donna, e spegne nel mondo l'amore." ("He is not the one who makes her a mother; she is a mother because of her own virtue; we see her inherent nature when we go towards her, when she greets us smiling… Who does not respect the woman, seeing her, albeit obscurely, her 'virginal motherhood'—which is then that eternal femininity that the poet saw in her with his sharp gaze—destroys in the woman the woman, and turns love off to the world") (*Preliminari* 97). This virginal mother is the source of (Christian) love for all of society. She shapes man's life and is a "anello prezioso della catena che stringe l'uomo a Dio" ("precious link in the chain that bonds man close to God") (*Preliminari* 99). Her almost transcendent and irreplaceable role protects "modern man," enabling him to overcome the current civilization crises by consolidating "le basi morali e religiose della vita con un concetto serio di tutti i suoi elementi" ("the moral and religious foundations of life with a serious concept of all its elements") (*Preliminari* 99). Gentile, by resorting to the Italian tradition, elaborates a rhetorical and cultural discourse that highlights the much-needed role of woman as the mother of the race in the Fascist context. The rhetoric of restoring a lost glorious past includes all the aspects of the Fascist program. "'Restaurare' è la nostra parola d'ordine" ("'Restore' is the key word") (*Preliminari* 135). The moral powers, the school, the family and the state, all need to be "restored" according to the totalitarian agenda. First of all, within this new restored family must be reinstated the man, that is the essence of the family, of the school, of the State. (*Preliminari* 136). This restored human being is the new man (and woman) of Fascism. It is the central part of Fascist ideology: "Bisogna rifare la coscienza dell'uomo, bisogna rifare l'uomo." ("We must remake man's conscious, we must remake man") (*Preliminari* 137).

Chapter Three

Gentile, who was very close to Mussolini, was considered to be the official thinker of the regime. His "essay is to a large extent a careful, thoroughly constructed, and in many ways sophisticated argument about sexual difference, rather than about the inferiority of women" (Re, "Fascist Theories" 81).

Filippo Tommaso Marinetti, best known as the author of the *Manifesto Futurista* (1909; *Futurist Manifesto*), was one of the first affiliates of the Italian Fascist Party. In 1919 he co-wrote with Alceste De Ambris "Il manifesto dei Fasci italiani di combattimento" ("The Manifesto of the Italian Fasces of Combat"); the Fascist Manifesto. Marinetti had a more independent position towards Mussolini to the point that he opposed him "in 1920 when he left the Fascist party, and in 1938 when, after years of uneasy support of the regime, he published an open letter condemning anti Semitism in the arts" (Flint 8). His position on the role of women in Italian society went far beyond Gentile's. What is most relevant in our context is not the differences in their perspectives but the constants. Gentile and Marinetti share what the Fascist ideology claims; the end point.

In *The Founding and Manifesto of Futurism*, published in Paris' *Le Figaro* on 20 February 1909, Marinetti expressed "scorn for women," and committed to fighting feminism. In 1919 he wrote a paragraph entitled "Contro il matrimonio" ("Against Marriage"), which was included in *Democrazia futurista. Dinamismo politico* (*Futurist Democracy. Political Dynamism*), where he critically articulated analysis of the current situation of Italian families and highlighted the paramount importance of women as the mother of the race. In "Contro il matrimonio," included by Flint in *Marinetti, Selected Works* as "Marriage and the Family," Marinetti exposed "anarco-libertarian ideas that are often contradictory but are clearly aimed at destroying hereditary power" (Flint 33).

Before doing so, Marinetti took sides in favor of divorce. "La famiglia come è costituita oggi dal matrimonio senza divorzio è assurda, nociva e preistorica. Quasi sempre un carcere. Spesso una tenda di beduini con la lurida mescolanza di vecchi invalidi, donne, bambini, porci, asini, cammelli, galline e sterco." ("Contro il matrimonio" 61; "The family of marriage-without-divorce is absurd, harmful and pre-historic. Almost always a prison. Often a Bedouin tent covering a lurid mixture of old invalids, women, babies, pigs, asses, camels, hens, and filth"; "Marriage and the Family" 76). The anti-family stance was meant to empower women, not by simply emancipating them but by freeing them from assisting the weak, the ill, the poor, and the old so that they might be free to select healthy pleasant men and have with them hundreds of presumably healthy babies who would be collectively raised for the benefit of the race. "La donna non appartiene a un uomo, ma bensì all'avvenire e allo sviluppo della razza. Noi vogliamo che una donna ami un uomo e gli si conceda per il tempo che vuole; poi, non vincolata da contratto, né da tribunali moralistici, metta alla luce una creatura che la società deve educare fisicamente e intellettualmente ad un'alta concezione di libertà italiana. Una sola educatrice basta a favorire e difendere senza costrizione il primo sviluppo di 100 bambini..." ("Contro il matrimonio" 63–64; "Woman does not belong to a man but rather to the future and to the race's development...We want a woman to love a man and give herself to him for as long as she likes; then, not chained by contract or by moralistic tribunals, she should bear a child whom society will educate physically and intellectually to a high conception of Italian freedom...A single woman suffices to support and defend the first growth of a hundred babies, without constriction"; "Marriage and the Family" 78). Marinetti drew parallels between ownership of land and ownership of women. The healthy and the strong are the only ones who deserve (fertile) land and woman. "Chi non sa lavorare il campo deve esserne spodestato. Chi non sa dare gioie e forza alla donna non deve imporle il suo amplesso né la sua compagnia." ("Contro il matrimonio" 63; "Whoever cannot work his land should be dispossessed. Whoever cannot give his woman strength and joy should never force his embrace or his company upon her"; "Marriage and the Family" 78).

"Underlying anxieties about masculine identity were intensified by modern warfare" (96),—wrote Cinzia Sartini Blum in her "Marvelous Masculinity: Futurist Strategies of Self-Transfiguration through Maelstrom of Modernity" (2014). Its traumatic impact also affected the perceived 'emasculation' of Western man (88). Marinetti in the "Contro il matrimonio" seems to complicate his positions about gender roles and the superhuman that he longed for. Blum states that futuristic discourses on woman and love are much more complex and contradictory than they are purported to be.

Chapter Three

Marinetti's contradictions can be understood in terms of varying but ultimately convergent strategies. On the one hand, he takes on the avant-garde role of formulating a radical blueprint for the future; on the other, he addresses practical concerns, such as the immediate challenges posed by women's emancipation. The ultimate goal—the 'utopia' of immunity to all affective needs—will be attained only when man completes his evolutionary metamorphosis into a superhuman type. (Blum 95-96)

Gender difference as a binary logic, already highlighted in Gentile's writing, remains central in Marinetti's discourse. Free and selective women will help fight the effeminizing of men in the same way that rejecting of any kind of mixture will: "Sarà finalmente abolita la mescolanza di maschi e femmine che—nella prima età—produce una dannosa effeminazione dei maschi." ("Contro il matrimonio" 64; "We will finally do away with the mixture of males and females that—during the earliest years—produces a damnable effeminizing of the males"; "Marriage and the Family" 78). 1919 was also a pivotal year for the exclusion of women from the labor market. It was the year of the promulgation of the Sacchi law on this matter (17 July 1919) that listed the professions which were forbidden to women (Guida 33). Marinetti, by enforcing the discourse of gender difference as a binary logic, reached the necessary conclusion. Along with the mixture of genders, he opposed what he saw as the subversion of roles through the absence of men from the working scene—to the advantage of working women. "La vasta partecipazione delle donne al lavoro nazionale prodotto dalla guerra, ha creato un tipico grottesco matrimoniale: Il marito possedeva del denaro o ne guadagnava, ora l'ha perduto e stenta a riguadagnarne... Rovesciamento completo di una famiglia dove il marito è diventato una donna inutile con prepotenze maschili e la moglie ha raddoppiato il suo valore umano e sociale." ("Contro il matrimonio" 65; "The wide participation in the national workforce produced by the war has created a typical matrimonial grotesque: the husband had money or was earning it, now he has lost it or can't win it back... Complete subversion of a family in which the husband has become a useless woman with masculine vanities, and his wife has doubled her social and human value"; "Marriage and the Family" 79).

In her article "Fascist Women and the Rhetoric of Virility," Barbara Spackman makes an important point by stating that "stepping out into the public sphere 'masculinizes' and 'sterilizes' women, whereas the loss of the position in the public sphere necessarily 'devirilizes' men" (101). The entry of women into the public, economic sphere was, in Spackman's view, a threat not only to the reproduction of the means of production, but also the woman's own reproductive equipment. The association of "masculine woman" with feminism was often repeated. This "Fascist topography of gender and sex" was also enforced and highlighted because it was directly related to historical context, to the perceived threat from the participation of women in the workforce during WWI, and to the decision to expel them from the labor market in 1919. Women's presence in the male sphere of action was associated with masculine attitudes to the extent that Fascist propaganda "spread the Mussolinian word that work masculinizes women and robs their husbands of their virility" (102).

The inclusion or exclusion of women from the workforce was one of the key factors in gender politics—along with demographic concerns—that becomes even more evident when the Italian Fascist context is compared to that of the Soviet Union in which every social category, including women and peasants, was forcefully proletarianized and involved in the country's industrialization. Whilst Gentile and Marinetti adopted very different perspectives, especially towards what was considered traditional in the Italian context, they reached the same conclusion about women. Their main characteristics were, according to both authors, to be mothers for the benefit of the race. The biological politics of Fascism had decided on the exclusion of women from the labor market and their relegation to the role of child-bearers.

Soldiers, mothers of the race and heroes

Italian cinema was heavily supported by funding from Fascist state; the Third Right Cinema and The Soviet Cinema were supported by their respective states. The regime also saw its great potential as a propaganda instrument for colonial purposes. The preferred genre was documentaries because it was very adaptable to quickly presenting contemporary events, including military accomplishments. Documentaries were important for propaganda purposes, too, especially with regards to delineating Fascist gender ideology. *Madri d'Italia* (*Mothers of Italy*), a silent documentary made for the Opera Nazionale Maternità e Infanzia, and OMNI (the National Institute for Mother and Child Welfare) outlined the role that the Fascist regime assigned to women, whilst *Figli d'Italia caduti in Africa* (*Sons of Italy Fallen in Africa*), did the same thing regarding Italian men, are the two most important examples (Cottino-Jones, *Women, Desire, and Power in Italian Cinema*). Italian cinema expanded representations of the gender ideology to full-length movies. In order to justify such expansive propaganda, the regime pushed for historical feature films which idealized the past—Imperial Rome and the Renaisance were the preferred topics as shown in movies such as *Scipione l'Africano* and *Ettore Fieramosca*. Both drew useful parallels with the imperial aspirations of the present that were, of course, very much in focus. According to Ruth Ben-Ghiat who, in her study *Italian Fascism's Empire Cinema*, examines empire features within the context of contemporary newsreels and documentaries, by the early 1940s "the close relationship between feature and documentary film[s] had become a hallmark of Italian empire cinema culture" (xx). In her book, instead of using the term "colonial cinema" as some scholars do, Ben-Ghiat chooses the term "empire cinema" to refer to "Italian features and documentaries made on imperial themes between 1936 and 1943" (xv), thereby privileging movies that were created by imperial conquest rather than films about remote eras, such as *Gallone's Scipione l'Africano* (1937) (xxi).

Ben-Ghiat also looks at representations of gender roles in empire cinema, and observes that military men were the protagonists in all of those films. It is the uniformed male body that "stood at the center of the particular cult of masculine appearance fostered by empire cinema," fashioning rituals of militarized masculinity (*Italian Fascism's Empire Cinema* 11). White women, on the other hand, were present only remotely, as mothers or wives, while numerous indigenous women featured as objects of desire (*Italian Fascism's Empire Cinema* 14).

After colonial films such as Mario Camerini's *Il grande appello* (*The Great Appeal*), Augusto Genina's *Lo squadrone Bianco* (*White Squadron*), and Romolo Marcellini's *Sentinelle di bronzo* (*Sentinels of Bronze*) produced at the same time as Gallone's *Scipione l'Africano* (*Scipione the African*), the Fascist films sought to represent the postwar era and Italian people's need for land and work (Ben-Ghiat, *Italian Fascism's Empire Cinema* 191). Guido

Brignone's 1938 film *Sotto la croce del sud* (*Under the Southern Cross*) is set in Abyssinia following its recent Italian occupation. Throughout the movie the settlers repeatedly state that everybody, both locals and Italians, "must work." They arrive with trucks full of Italian workers, agricultural tools and machines, and plan to build new plantations, farms, and warehouses. Marco, the old owner, and his partner, the young, handsome Paolo, there meet the fake owner Simone Aeropouluos and his accomplice, the beautiful Mailù. Throughout the entire movie, numerous indigenous people can be seen in the background; they communicate in pidgin Italian, mostly working, singing or performing rituals that invoke the rain. They display a distant otherness. During these rituals, the young indigenous women are shown half-naked; singing and dancing. Rosetta Giuliani Caponetto, whose *Fascist Hybridities* analyzes the role of racial purity in the context of Italian Fascism, observes that the representation of nude and semi-nude indigenous women in late-nineteenth-century Eritrea and Somalia was used to attract the Italian male population and encourage their participation in the colonial enterprise. In this context, the native woman is often referred to as a *concubina* or *madama* (Giuliani Caponetto 114). In the late 1930s both the need for, and the strategy of, Italian colonialism changed, as did representations of non-Italian women. Italian men were now reminded of their obligations to their original families and the Italian state. Lasting relationships with native women were discouraged, while Italian women were invited to join their husbands abroad. In *Sotto la croce del sud*, shortly after the arrival of the Italian workers, we see the arrival of their wives. The beautiful Mailù is perceived as a threat. An old Italian man tells Marco that her presence distracts the workers and, as a consequence, their commitment and productivity fade. The idleness of the indigenous lifestyle is hinted at in the film, and in its main song title "La croce del sud," (which in turn refers to the Southern Cross), "the dominant constellation of the South Pole, just as the North Star indicates the North Pole" (Giuliani Caponetto 114). The southern lands, as the film intended, symbolize the indolent lifestyles of their inhabitants as opposed to the laborious way of life of the Italian settlers. Mailù spends her days doing nothing but listening to sweet nostalgic melodies like the lyric *Sotto la croce del sud*; evoking a decadent atmosphere. "Io mi perdo volentieri a sognare." ("I willingly get lost in dreaming"), she tells Paolo. "È la mia razza" ("It's my race") concludes Mailù who, in the film, is said to be a "Levantine." The origins of both Mailù and the male coprotagonist Simone are very important in a movie whose colonial setting and year of release (1938) activated a series of very complex mechanisms that tried to address questions about then-current definitions of Italian identity. The 1938 racial laws adopted anti-Semitic discriminatory policies that "become immediately questionable in light of other groups, such as the Italian Levantines and *insabbiati* living in the Italian colonies" (Giuliani Caponetto 126). In 1936, the legislation limited permissible reasons for granting Italian citizenship and, in 1937, punished Italians living with a *madama* while, in 1940, it categorized meticcio offspring as blacks (Giuliani Caponetto 116).

Mailù's origins are never fully articulated but they play an important role in the plot. She tries to seduce Paolo in order to be allowed to remain on the plantation, while Simone secretly exploits the rich mines. At the end of *Sotto la croce del sud* Simone is punished by the quicksands of moralizing nature, while the Levantine woman decides to leave despite her growing feelings for Paolo. Mailù—played by a then famous Italian actress, Doris Duranti, who was not actually "biracial"—lives in transitory places, her existence characterized by a high degree of mobility, while her comfortable lifestyle is supported by men like Simone. Her being both "biracial" and a negative character reminds Italian women that the features of her life are not a good example and that they should be avoided. Mobility, idleness, and love affairs are characteristic of "biracial" women. Motherhood, and a steady, stable lifestyle rooted in the home describe, instead, Italian women.

According to Giuliani Caponetto, the term "Levantine" was used to refer to those Italian residents of Africa who embraced cultural intermingling with other ethnic groups. She defined Levantines as "not quite the same, not quite the other" (124). Ruth Ben-Ghiat, in her *Italian Fascism's Empire Cinema* invests both the origins of Simone and the term "Levantine" with a broader meaning. She suggests that it refers to people of the Eastern basin, including not only Jews but also Turks (193). The character of Simone Aeropouluos, whose name signals his Italian-Greek descent, is called *meticcio* (mestizo) in the film. Ben-Ghiat, referring to the legislative context of those years, suggests that Simone also had a Jewish affiliation.

Robin Pickering-Iazzi, in her article "Ways of Looking in Black and White," comments more on the meaning of the word "*meticcio*." She notes that it means mestizo which, in Italian, indicates a person of mixed white and East Indian race. According to her, the word "*meticcio*" in the 1930s denoted "individuals with one parent of an African race and the other of European origin" (209). However, these scholars do not highlight that Simone, defined by Marco as "*meticcio*," is the half-Greek villain because of the planned invasion of the Balkans.

While the "biracial" Simone and Mailù are the only negative characters in *Sotto la croce del sud*, the hard-working settlers are presented as people possessed of high morals, whilst the indigenous are presented as docile. Brignone's film clearly reinforces the discourses that were behind the racial laws, and addresses concerns pertaining to failing to comply with those laws. Despite the outlawing of marriage and cohabitation between Italians and indigenous people, Pickering-Iazzi points out that between 1936 and 1940, 10,000 biracial children were born in East Africa (206).

Ruth Ben-Ghiat in *Italian Fascism's Empire Cinema* highlights the links between Empire cinema and war. Films, she states, quoting writing of that time by a young militant called Giuseppe Lombrassa, were envisaged as "machines of war" and aids to governance (43). For this reason, after 1939, Albania, Greece and Russia replaced Ethiopia and Somalia as settings. According to Ben-Ghiat, "empire films were structured around stories of male abjection and redemption that moved them beyond the desiring body" (244) and, since the early 1930s, she reminds us, the emblem of Fascist manhood had been the aviator (245). *Il pilota ritorna*, is the second movie of Roberto Rossellini's Fascist trilogy (the other two are *La nave bianca*/The White Ship, and *Uomo della croce*/ Man of the Cross). This movie is dedicated to the fighter pilots who did not return from their missions over the Greek front during the war. Like many other films of the Fascist period that do not focus on gender issues, it nevertheless carefully reflects Fascists gender policies. There is a masculinity; more precisely, a "Fascist militarized masculinity" (*Italian Fascism's Empire Cinema* 73) that emerges clearly from this movie in which "'real' military men" also feature (*Italian Fascism's Empire Cinema* 62).

Chapter Three

In the very first scene of the movie, the mother of the protagonist, a piano teacher, shows her young student a picture of Lieutenant Gino Rossati with great pride. After offering this detail about Gino Rossati's family, the mother does not appear again in the movie. These "heroes," we are told later, sacrificed everything, leaving homes, mothers, and wives behind them. The young lieutenant joins a combat team of pilots who are supporting, through their airstrikes, the Italian army that is fighting on the Albanian–Greek border. We see and hear many loud combat planes aligned high in the sky dispatching hundreds of bombs down onto the Greek landscape. After their day of combat, the pilots attend a spectacle in the evening. However, we do not see it, because the lights go off. The female dancers join the pilots after the performance and one of them reads for everybody, viewers included, the portrait of these soldiers, depicted by a newspaper as "eroi alati che solcano i cieli portando alla vittoria" ("winged heroes that sail the skies leading to victory"), "cavalieri dei tempi moderni" ("knights of modern times") who offer all they have—"houses," "wives" and "their own destiny." These Fascist "knights of modern times" keep flying during the film, casting "the usual bombs of 50," supposedly kilograms. They do not show the slightest psychological or moral dilemma. Man and plane almost form a united cyborg being of steel which, empowered by loud engines, is destructive and senseless, cold and detached. They fly fast and so high that the pilots cannot feel empathy for other beings in flesh and blood. Far from the ground, far from other human beings: this is the Fascist "knight of modern times."

The movie is divided into two very different parts. In the first part the perspective is from above, from the planes, from the viewpoint of "the modern knights" who cast bombs down upon a distant landscape that looks just like a map. In this first part, the female presence is limited to that of the mother in the first scene and to the dancers. The soldiers are away from their "wives" and the "houses" where the women live. Since the film is dedicated to the pilots who did not come back from the Greek front, it is no surprise that, during a combat fight, Gino's plane is hit. The pilot parachutes into Greece, where he is captured and taken to a British military outpost.

From this point on, the perspective of the movie radically changes. The point of view is no longer from above, but instead shown at a human scale. The ugly face of war is depicted. The difficult conditions in the prison camps seem almost like neorealist scenes. People are scared; they feel cold, and they are hungry. Children remain as orphans, and soldiers are mutilated. Misery, pain, and long slow marches under rain and bombs fill the screen. Ben-Ghiat, in another article dedicated to this film, "The Imperial Moment in Fascist Cinema," considers this film to be a transitional movie that foreshadows a big turn in Rossellini's cinema. "Within Rossellini's career, it prepared his exit from the universe of empire cinema into that of the neorealist movement, which dismissed the Fascist temporalities of revolution and eternity in the name of everyday and small events happening on a human scale" (78). "E pensare che nel mondo c'è tanta gente che si sveglia nella propria casa, nel proprio letto" ("And just think that there are many people in the world who wake up at home, in their own bed") says Gino, introducing one of the most important themes represented by neorealism; housing and living conditions. The destructions of war caused Rossellini to instinctively address what mattered most in those years. His interlocutor is 18-year-old Anna, born in Athens, the daughter of Italian parents, who assists the wounded and the sick in the prison camps. At the Pargas concentration camp, they meet the rest of Gino's flying crew, who had been captured and sent to the same camp. They remain behind when Gino—on board a stolen British plane—flees, satisfying both the need to tell the story of the hero who makes it back to his country, and the need to represent the pilots who did not make it. The film ends with rhetorical close-ups of Gino landing a stolen plane at his military base, while the Fascist's triumph is shown in the newspapers' grotesque headlines but not on screen.

In 1944, Roberto Rossellini began shooting *Roma città aperta* (*Rome Open City*). The director had to film on location because the Cinecittà studios were still occupied by war refugees (Cottino-Jones 54) and, consequently, several neorealist techniques—such as authentic settings, a preference for non-professional actors (although in this movie several famous actors were involved), and the improvisation and rejection of elaborate plots—were often adapted out of necessity. "This film is a rare capturing of wartime experiences drawing along at a near frantic pace by a searing ethical vision. The pace reflects the urgency of every moment in wartime, and lengthy soul-searching would be out of place in such a context of barbarity and authoritarianism" (Riviello 22). The movie was released in the following year and was a major cultural and political event because neorealism was one of the most important contributions that Italian culture has given to world cinema, and because it started to elaborate the foundational values for the post-war Italian Republic. Discussion of the issue of women is, this time, central, with four female characters who are each crucial both for the plot and the film's meaning.

Rossellini's particular ideological blend of Marxism and Catholicism is very evident in *Roma città aperta*, which starts with hungry people raiding a bakery. The majority of them are women, and it is there that we first meet Pina, an iconic and articulated character who is highly inspirational and likable and was played by Anna Magnani. Pina, is generous, solid, a widow, a mother, a currently unemployed worker, an active member of the anti-Nazi resistance movement, pregnant, and engaged to Francesco who is another resistance comrade. Through her character traits, Pina represents both a continuity with tradition and a break from it, partly heroic and partly "the image of the 'good' woman and mother canonized by Italian tradition and prescribed by fascism" (Cottino-Jones 55). In contrast, her sister Lauretta is the first of three negative female characters. She is a weak woman who likes to perform in night clubs as a way of leaving behind the poverty of her roots. This denial of her belonging makes her a helpless and useless person. Lauretta's beautiful childhood friend Marina is more significant for the movie's plot. Marina takes drugs and wants to escape misery at any cost. Her lover is Giorgio Manfredi, one of the national leaders of the Italian resistance movement. Drugs, lovers, and a desire for life's comforts are characterizing negative elements that make Marina betray Manfredi and her people towards the final part of the movie. The third female negative character, Ingrid, is—a Nazi who is a manipulative and cruel woman with suggested lesbian tendencies. She corrupts Marina with drugs and beautiful dresses and is both the most negative and the least-articulated character of the three. The positive aspects of Pina's nature versus the negative traits of the other three women give us a complete idea of Rossellini's reading of the issue of women.

Pina, the positive character bears the new values that, in the director's mind, are auspicious for women; she blends her love for her children, husband, and family with active participation in the public arena as a worker, a member of the resistance and, ultimately, a heroine. Rossellini has a girl tell Pina's son: "E perché, le donne non possono fare l'eroismo!" ("And what, can't girls be heroic too?!"). This shows that the imaginary of the new generation raised during the war has moved away from the passive and submissive Fascist female stereotype. However, Pina remains first and foremost a mother who believes in marriage and is ready to sacrifice everything for her family. Rossellini pays particular attention, in building her portrait, to stylistically emphasizing her traits as a mother, a woman in love, and a heroine. In the sequences where Pina and Francesco are on the screen at the same time, Rossellini frames them together, using mostly close-up shots that "convey their personal and private situation as individuals in love" (Cottino-Jones 56). In contrast, when Francesco is captured by the Nazis, we see Pina from his tragic point of view, with the camera placed inside the truck moving away with him while the distance between Pina's body—just gunned down by the soldiers—and Francesco "multiplies with a very strong dramatic effect" (Cottino-Jones 57). Don Pietro, too, is conveniently nearby, blessing the heroine's dead body before, only a moment later, comforting Marcello, Pina's son, whose desperate reaction is also shown to the viewer.

The negative female characters are neither mothers nor workers. Marina does not have the right perceptions of the war or the value of secrecy. Her reckless phone call endangers Giorgio Manfredi right from the start and anticipates what will happen later. Pina, with her generous motherly empathy, is the only one who offers a positive and understanding portrait of Marina; thereby implicitly highlighting the dogmatic intransigence of Giorgio. In her view, Marina would change for love but Giorgio remains skeptical. Rossellini seems to adopt Giorgio's perspective when, in contrast to Pina's heroic and tragic death, he has Marina, in a later scene, listening to American jazz and drinking as though this path to a bourgeois lifestyle will lead her to the big betrayal. Marina is very caring to Giorgio and Francesco but Giorgio breaks up with her because of her dependence on drugs and, more generically, because of the fact that her comfortable lifestyle

Chapter Three

has been made possible by her lovers. For Giorgio Manfredi, who preaches to Marina, happiness (for a woman) is (should be) love, "l'amore per il proprio uomo, per i propri figli, i propri compagni" ("love for the woman's man, for her own children, for her own comrades"), depicting implicitly—as the ideal female portrait—Pina, who was all that he respected. Marriage, family, and class solidarity as a blend of catholic and Marxist values is highlighted by Rossellini in this film.

Rossellini's ideological position becomes more evident in the words of Don Pietro who is the priest who actively took part in the resistance along with Francesco, Giorgo, and Pina. The priest is the moral authority in the movie who also intimidates the enemy. His path never crosses that of the negative female characters which can be seen as an effective metaphor by which to suggest that there is no possible redemption for them; Marina, did not give up her comfortable lifestyle and Giorgio's Marxism punished her. The betrayal of her own class equals, in Marina's case, the betrayal of her country. Don Pietro's path instead crosses Pina's and Giorgio's path, contrasting the Nazi commander, Major Bergmann, who recalls his atheism. The fight for freedom is blessed by moral authority which helps the viewer to understand the director's ideological blend. "Credo che chi combatte per la giustizia e per la libertà cammini nelle vie del signore" ("I believe that whoever fights for justice and freedom walks in the lord's path"), Don Pietro says to Major Bergmann, "E le vie del signore sono infinite." ("And the lord's paths are infinite.").

Chapter Four

The Stripped Man

In an attempt to fill a gap, Giorgio Agamben uses the analytical tools of biopolitical studies and applies them to both Levi's novel *Se questo è un uomo* and the tragic Nazi experience. He then took a similar approach to Arendt and Foucault. An idea of the latter, taken up and developed here by Agamben, is very interesting: "In the biological continuum of the human species, the opposition and hierarchy of races, the qualification of certain races as good and others, by contrast, as inferior, are all ways to fragment the biological domain whose care power had undertaken; they are ways to distinguish different groups inside a population. In short, to stabilize a caesura of a biological type inside a domain that defines itself precisely as biological" (Foucault in *Remnants of Auschwitz* 84). In fact, it is the notion of caesura that seems analytically fertile. Agamben uses it to talk about the transformation of people into a population; that is, the transformation of a political body into a biological body whose fertility, mortality, health, and sickness are controlled and regulated. "Con la nascita del biopotere, ogni popolo si raddoppia in popolazione, ogni popolo democratico è, insieme, un popolo demografico." (*Quel che resta di Auschwitz* 79; "With the emergence of biopower, every people is doubled by a population; every democratic people is, at the same time, a *demographic* people"; *Remnants of Auschwitz* 84). It would be worthwhile seeing whether these caesurae have evolved today into other forms; if the city itself can be seen as a spatial caesura, if there are classist caesurae or, using a less Marxist tone, economic ones that, through access to the most sophisticated medical innovations and wider knowledge (here called culture), are capable of transforming a transnational group into a "transitional" (enhanced) group that has a much longer life expectancy and greater physical capabilities. Hitler evidently aimed to do something like this: "Nel 1937, nel corso di un convegno segreto, Hitler formula per la prima volta un concetto biopolitico estremo, sul quale occorre soffermarsi. Riferendosi all'Europa centro-orientale, egli dice di aver bisogno di un volkloser Raum, di uno spazio privo di popolo" (*Quel che resta* 79–80; "In 1937, during a secret meeting, Hitler formulates an extreme biopolitical concept for the first time, one well worth considering. Referring to Central-Western Europe, he claims to need a *volkloser Raum*, a space empty of people"; *Remnants* 85).

In Agamben's reading, the caesura is a space, a group, a race, class, something that, for the sake of experimentation, is initially limited but then extended on a larger scale. Foucault's concept of caesura becomes, for Agamben, a kind of state of exception; it is the focus of his work. That is why Auschwitz, for him, is nothing more than a laboratory, inexpressibly horrible and tragic but still a laboratory.

"Prima di essere il campo della morte, Auschwitz è il luogo di un esperimento ancora impensato, in cui, al di là della vita e della morte, l'ebreo si trasforma in musulmano, e l'uomo in non-uomo." (*Quel che resta* 47; "Before being a death camp, Auschwitz is the site of an experiment that remains unthought today, an experiment beyond life and death in which the Jew becomes *Muselmann*, and the human being turns into a non-human"; *Remnants* 52). This transformation is a process clearly shown by Primo Levi in *Se questo è un uomo*. It is a process during which the prisoner is stripped of his clothing, his name, his relationships, from belonging, from memory, from hope, from the dimension of time, from emotions, and is left naked; with only his most basic instincts left intact. He is even powerless to retaliate with a single judging glance:

> Allora per la prima volta ci siamo accorti che la nostra lingua manca di parole per esprimere questa offesa, la demolizione di un uomo. In un attimo, con intuizione quasi profetica, la realtà ci si è rivelata: siamo arrivati al fondo. *Più giù di così non si può andare: condizione umana più misera non c'è, e non è pensabile.* Nulla più e nostro: ci hanno tolto gli abiti, le scarpe, anche i capelli; se parleremo, non ci ascolteranno, e se ci ascoltassero, non ci capirebbero. Ci toglieranno anche il nome: e se vorremo conservarlo, dovremo trovare in noi la forza di farlo, di fare sì che dietro al nome, qualcosa ancora di noi, di

> noi quali eravamo, rimanga ... Si immagini ora un uomo a cui, insieme con le persone amate, vengano tolti la sua casa, le sue abitudini, i suoi abiti, tutto infine, letteralmente tutto quanto possiede: sarà un uomo vuoto, ridotto a sofferenza e bisogno. (*Se questo è un uomo* 23)

> Then, for the first time, we became aware that our language lacks words to express this offense, the demolition of a man. In a moment, with almost prophetic intuition, the reality was revealed to us: we had reached the bottom. *It is not possible to sink lower than this; no human condition is more miserable than this, nor could it be conceivably be so* [my italics]. Nothing belongs to us anymore; if we speak, they will not listen to us, and if they listen, they will not understand. They will even take away our name: and if we want to keep it, we will have to find, ourselves, the strength to do so, to manage somehow so that behind the name something of us, of us as we were, still remains ... Imagine now a man who is deprived of everyone he loves, and at the same time of his house, his habits, his clothes, in short, of everything he possesses: he will be a hollow man, reduced to suffering and needs. (*If This Is a Man* 32–33)

This contextual uprooting and subsequent decontextualization and re-contextualization that takes place in the camp produces what, for Agamben, is the biopolitical material that was the ultimate goal of the camp: a *Muselmann*, a non-human. What seems implicit in Agamben's thesis is that establishing the boundary between man and non-man (non-human) is useful for an overriding biopolitical control of society members. Extension of this extreme control by society towards the remaining impulses, the purely organic biological impulses, that strips the man from the man and removes any space for independent decision-making that makes the individual an individual. This, in turn, transforms them into nothing else than a range of conditioned responses, into nothing other than "Pavlov's pervert dog," to quote Arendt (*The Origins of Totalitarianism*), or the non-man as subhuman then, or drowned, to quote Levi (*I sommersi e i salvati*). Subhuman and not *other from human*, it is better to stress [my italics]. We should pay attention to the subhuman and not to supermen, Agamben (*Remnants of Auschwitz*) emphasizes. The interest of the Italian philosopher, author of *Homo Sacer* and *Lo stato di eccezione* (*State of Exception*),[7] is in targeting the fluid boundary that exists between legality and illegality, between rule and exception, and between social body and outcast where the latter is used to better define the former and open up new territory by which to control the former.

The framing of the individual in space and time inside the *Lager*, is essential for the realization of all this, as is the method—the modern, new technique by which everything is achieved. The unprecedented dimensions of the horror make us reflect not only on *why* but on *how*. Levi writes: "Innumerevoli sono le proibizioni: avvicinandosi a meno di due metri dal filo spinato; dormire con la giacca, o senza mutande […] , non andare alla doccia nei giorni prescritti, e andarvi nei giorni non prescritti" (*Se questo è un uomo* 29; "The prohibitions are innumerable: to not approach nearer to the barbed wire than two yards; to sleep with one's jacket on, or without one's pants […], not to go for a shower on the prescribed days, or to go there on a day not prescribed"; *If This Is a Man* 39–40). He continues in this vein for a full page and beyond. "Infiniti e insensati sono i riti da compiersi: ogni giorno al mattino bisogna fare il "letto," perfettamente piano e liscio…, alla sera, bisogna sottoporsi al contro dei pidocchi… alla domenica, sottoporsi al controllo generale della scabbia…" (*Se questo è un uomo* 29; "The rites to be carried out were infinite and senseless: every morning one had to make the 'bed' perfectly flat and smooth […], in the evening one had to undergo control for lice […], on Sunday, undergo a general control for skin diseases and control of buttons on one's jacket, which had to be five"; *If This Is a Man* 40). A few pages later he continues with the definition of time. "Una domenica ogni due è regolare giorno lavorativo; nelle domeniche cosiddette festive, invece di lavorare in Buna si lavora di solito alla manutenzione del Lager, in modo che i giorni di effettivo riposo sono estremamente rari." (*Se questo è un uomo* 31; "One Sunday in every two is a regular working day; on the so-called holiday Sundays, instead of working at Buna, one works normally on the upkeep of the *Lager*, so that days of real rest are extremely rare"; *If This Is a Man* 42). Finally we have the desired result of this organization. "Quando questa musica suona, noi sappiamo che i compagni, fuori nella nebbia, partono in marcia come automi: le loro anime sono morte e la musica li sospinge, come il vento le foglie secche, e si sostituisce alla loro volontà. Non c'è più volontà…" (*Se questo è un uomo* 45; "When this music plays we know that our comrades, out in the fog, are marching like automatons; their souls are dead and the music drives them, like the wind drives dead leaves, and takes the place of their wills"; *If This Is a Man* 57).

Let us here recall the Foucauldian intuition of caesura. It is useful to do so because controlling everything is impossible. The *Lager* is a first spatial caesura. In order to exercise extreme control, one part needs to be isolated. There are functional similarities between the two totalitarian systems that are interesting to note. If the Germans applied the caesura in *Lagers*, then the Soviets, in addition to responding with the gulag, arguably embarked on a much bigger endeavor. It was necessary to transform the masses where they were. Selection was unthinkable. The dramatic metamorphosis, quick and imposed, was the option chosen. The isolation of the individual through spatial-temporal framing, even in a vast territory, was their invention:

> E poi v'è l'adempimento dei doveri di "civismo," di propaganda, di ore straordinarie di lavoro gratuite a benefizio della collettività, il lavoro sociale delle riunioni serali in cui si parla della costruzione socialista, e i corsi speciali di scienze economiche e politiche marxiste su cui bisogna sostenere annualmente un esame: tutto questo conta molto nella conservazione dell'impiego. Nessuno può mancare a tali riunioni, le uscite sono guardate, i tentativi di evasione segnalati. A casa qualcuno aspetta, i negozi si chiudono, e bisognerebbe fare anche la fila per comperare qualcosa da far bollire sotto il fornello "Primus."

> Then there is the fulfillment of the duties of "good citizenship," propaganda, overtime work gratis for the benefit of the community, the social work during the evening gatherings where the discussion is about socialist construction, and special courses in economics and Marxist policies about which an annual examination is required: all of this matters greatly in maintaining employment. No one can miss these meetings, the exits are monitored, attempts to escape are reported. At home someone is waiting, the shops are closed, and one should also stay in line to buy something to boil on the Primus stove. (Alvaro, *Viaggio in Russia* 97)

In Eastern society, the individual has precise coordinates. Change of home or city, alongside choices of study, work, marriage, separation, and career all pass through the filter of collegial organisms that cover society completely; both vertically and horizontally. The relationships of all individuals are also determined: it is enough to know an individual's age, house, the social range where they belong, or their place of work or study for the components

Chapter Four

of their day to be guessed in detail. There is a rigidly determined daily routine for everyone: projects, desires, possibilities are born within this "fitting routine." Everyone is inserted into one of the few social groups and, depending on where they belong, most of their days are spent in the kind of work or study that the state has decided is appropriate for them. To disobey is impossible: a student must go to school, a peasant must work in a cooperative, a worker must work in a factory. The economic possibilities of every person are largely calculable. Among the various social groups, economic differences are limited. The part of the day that is not devoted to work or study is filled by meetings of a political nature, whether they be: condo meetings, neighborhood meetings, union meetings (controlled by the party), company meetings, or assemblies of any kind for students. The most important figure of every organization is the party secretary—for a residential block, a neighborhood, a district, or a township. For the last two there are party committees that control and authorize administrative power. A party secretary of a city is more important than a mayor. The party secretaries of the condominium join in meetings for their neighborhoods, the neighborhood secretaries are controlled by that for the district, and so on.

This line of control was supervised in turn by the powerful secret police, whose shadow infiltrated all relationships and came between friends, fathers and sons, and brothers and sisters. One of the biggest expenditures of the economy was the costs of the secret police who used to target any kind of harmony between people, so as to weaken individual's protective networks and render them totally powerless against the fatal force of the state. The atmosphere became one in which everyone feared everyone else and, to defend themselves, controlled the other. The stranger, most of all, was regarded as a spy: "Ma nei miei riguardi tutti hanno un certo timore della mia guida; sanno che questa a un certo momento cava fuori il suo taccuino e scrive diligentemente: 'Il signor Alvaro ha conosciuto in battello la cittadina...'" ("But everyone, at least when it comes to me, is afraid of my guide; they know that at some point he pulls out his notebook and accurately writes: 'Mr. Alvaro met the citizen on the boat...'") (*Viaggio in Russia* 120).

The values that circulate in the "fitting routine" (the individual's environment) become the individual's values because it is in this routine where problems, hopes, and possibilities are consumed. The logic that runs this routine determines the space and breadth of an individual's thoughts: human nature drives him to improve his life. A totalitarian state, through the type of organization described, is able to control an individual's opportunities. The Soviets in some sense went the farthest. Not only did they strip individuals of their traditional roles but they re-contextualized and re-dressed them in an attempt to fabricate the "new man." The achievement of a sort of ground zero was ruthlessly programmed for the successive relaunch of the "new man" in the desired direction: "Nella sua parte incivile questo paese ha fatto con la rivoluzione la conquista che fece l'Europa con la Rivoluzione Francese; nella sua parte civile s'è veduto un mondo che, spogliatosi di tutto, dove l'uomo reca con sé ogni bene, ricomincia a gustare il sapore del pane e della vita..." ("In its uncivilized part, this country, did the same that Europe did with the French Revolution, by making the revolution into conquest. In its civilized one can see a world where, stripped of everything, a man who carries every good with him starts enjoying the taste of bread and life again...") (*Viaggio in Russia* 138).

The caesura mentioned by Foucault and Agamben is the true extreme ground zero of this process. The intensity and horror of the *Lager* are unthinkable elsewhere. According to Agamben, its function was to produce degradation: "Così il non ariano transita nell'ebreo, l'ebreo nel deportato (umgesiedelt, ausgesiedelt), il deportato nell'internato (Häftling), finché, nel campo, le cesure biopolitiche raggiungono il loro limite ultimo. Questo limite è il musulmano." (*Quel che resta* 79; "Thus the non-Aryan passes into the Jew, the Jew into the deportee (*amgestedelt, ausgesiedelt*), the deportee into the prisoner (*Häftling*), until biopolitical caesurae reach their final limit in the camp. This limit is the *Muselmann*"; *Remnants* 85). The degradation process described here is one of progressively stripping the human being of what we think of as his or her humanity. So, at first, de-contextualization of the individual and uprooting from their family, their social network, their role, their personal history, their culture, and their memories is achieved through geographical uprooting. Then literally stripping them of their clothes, their habits, their name, their rights, dignity and decision-making autonomy and, finally, re-contextualizing them in the *Lager*, with the new clothes of a deported person, and their re-naming with a serial number: "L'operazione

Chapter Four

è stata lievemente dolorosa, e straordinariamente rapida: ci hanno messi tutti in fila, e ad uno ad uno, secondo l'ordine alfabetico dei nostri nomi, siamo passati davanti a un abile funzionario munito di una specie di punteruolo dall'ago cortissimo. Pare che questa sia l'iniziazione vera e propria: solo "mostrando il numero" si riceve il pane e la zuppa." (*Se questo è un uomo* 24; "The operation was slightly painful and extraordinarily rapid: they put us all in a row and, one by one, according to the alphabetical order of our names, we filed past a skillful official, armed with a sort of pointed tool with a very short needle. It seems that this is the real, true initiation: only by 'showing one's number' can one get bread and soup"; Levi, *If This Is a Man* 32–33). What remains at the end of this process is the non-human: "Anche i nazisti si servono, in riferimento alla condizione giuridica degli ebrei dopo le leggi razziali, di un termine che implica la dignità: entwürdigen. L'ebreo è l'uomo che è stato privato di ogni Würde, di ogni dignità: *semplicemente uomo*—e, appunto per questo, non-uomo." (*Quel che resta* 62; "When referring to the legal status of Jews after the racial laws, the Nazis also used a term that implied a kind of dignity: *entwürdigen*, literally to 'deprive of dignity'. The Jew is a human being deprived of all *Würde*, all dignity: he is *merely human*[8]—and, for this reason, non-human"; Agamben, *Remnants* 68).

The term "merely human," intentionally or not, reminds us of Arendt's proposed analysis. In her work she is very sensitive to the discontinuities and fractures relative to the advent of modernity. Particularly significant, according to Arendt, were the changes accomplished by the French Revolution. Rousseau's axiom of the goodness of man in a state of nature, given a critique by Arendt in her essay *On Revolution*, does nothing but pull the man backwards in history, erasing everything that has been built, and reducing him to only his biological part. Rousseau's stripped man is the man stripped of centuries of civilization and culture, the primitive man: "However, the men of the French Revolution had no conception of the persona, and no respect for the legal personality which is given and guaranteed by the body politic [...] They believed that they had emancipated nature herself, as it were, liberated the natural man in all men, and given him the Rights of Man to which each was entitled, not by virtue of the body politic to which he belonged but by virtue of being born" (*On*

Revolution 104). The consequence of this was the emptying out of the concept of person; the end result of a long tradition. In an attempt to make everyone equal, the natural man was seen as a source of rights that, dangerously, did not rely on the protecting mask of legal personality. This legal mask, mentioned by Arendt in the essay *On Revolution*, reminds us of the problem of nationality, and brings us to the stateless issue that she addresses in another book, *The Origins of Totalitarianism*, in which, among other things, she points out the reversals that followed the French Revolution. It was precisely the latter, as Arendt observes here, that combined the declaration of human rights with the proclamation of national sovereignty. Either the ultimate source of laws was human rights, or it was national sovereignty in terms of laws that privileged chosen ethnicity; the two principles excluded each other. The sad consequence of this was the transformation of human rights, generally, into national rights: a transformation which, combined later with the great migrations, also created the conditions for emptying out the concept of man and turning stateless people into superfluous millions. The real issue was related to the ambiguity of the abstract idea of man. An equally ambiguous conceptual interdependence of man/people during the nineteenth century forced the emancipation of man to pass through national emancipation. The source of law no longer became man but humanity as the family of nations. The *en masse* appearance of stateless persons made it clear that the loss of community was a loss of rights. The distinctive new aggravating factor was that the loss of a country made a person unable to find a new one. It follows that stateless persons—no longer protected by a community—were expelled from humanity because they were "*nothing but men.*" This situation was not foreseeable from the categories that had been developed during the eighteenth century. Human rights that were initially thought of as autonomous from history now had to rely on human "nature" and the belief that this would provide an obvious and strong reference in, and of, itself. Being human became a matter of status granted by a given context. Legislative coverage includes them in social biopolitics that determine their form (even more so today now that knowledge lies in the hands of power) and makes the invasiveness of the latter almost unlimited, just as Foucault was concerned that it would.

Chapter Five

The Interruption of Tradition

De-individualization and the interruption of tradition

There are different readings of the Holocaust and the works of an author such as Levi, whose literary writings and essays are at the core of these reflections, clearly do not belong to Italian literature alone. However, his Italianness is considered of great importance in critical readings relative to the issue of the Holocaust. Italianness in these readings is equivalent to the humanist tradition hybridized with the Enlightenment perspective of a chemist through education. In Levi's work, the problem of the individual and individuality is central. Recognizing in the other person the individual, his/her singularity, his/her humanity, is equivalent to having an awareness of ourselves, to recognizing ourselves as human beings. The other is co-human. Not even those who were guilty of mass murder were indifferent to the suffering of an individual, and seem to have been almost conscious of killing something that was as intangible as singularity. "Forse solo ai santi è concesso il terribile dono della pietà verso i molti; ai monatti, a quelli della Squadra Speciale, ed a noi tutti, non resta, nel migliore dei casi, che la pietà saltuaria indirizzata al singolo, al Mitmensch, al co-uomo: all'essere umano di carne e sangue che sta davanti a noi, alla portata dei nostri sensi provvidenzialmente miopi." (*I sommersi e i salvati* 42; "Perhaps the dreadful gift of pity for the many is granted only to saints; to the Monatti, to the members of Special Squad, and to all of us there remains in the best of cases only the sporadic pity addressed to the single individual, the *Mitmensch*, the co-man: the human being of flesh and blood standing before us, within reach of our providentially myopic sense"; *The Drowned and the Saved* 56).

Chapter Five

Levi then tells the story of Muhsfeld, one of the SS men attached to the death installations who, faced a 16-year-old survivor of the gas chamber, decided that she had to die, anyway, because she was a witness, young, immature and, therefore, unreliable. Yet, a man whose "razione quotidiana di strage era trapunta di episodi arbitrari e capricciosi" (*I sommersi* 42; "daily ration of slaughter was studded with arbitrary and capricious acts"; *The Drowned* 57) does not kill her with his own hands, because "neppure lui era un monolito" (*I sommersi* 42; "not even he was a monolit"; *The Drowned* 57). Muhsfeld was executed in 1947. "Se fosse vissuto in un ambiente ed in un'epoca diversi, è probabile che si sarebbe comportato come qualsiasi altro uomo comune" (*I sommersi* 42; "Had he lived in a different environment and epoch, he probably would have behaved like any other common man"; *The Drowned* 57) writes Levi, who evidently recorded a cultural shock, a sudden change, the mutation of those cultural references that anticipate and inspire organizational codes. In *The Drowned and the Saved* he appeals to a morality "comune a tutti i tempi e a tutte le civiltà... mentre Hitler ha rotto con questa morale" (*I sommersi* 84; "common to all times and all civilizations ... while Hitler broke with this morality"; *The Drowned* 107), which obviously for him was the guarantor of the idea of a universal and timeless human being. Nicholas Patruno, who sees the *Lager* Levi experienced as "a modern version of Dante's city of Dis" (13), in his *Understanding Primo Levi*, notes that Levi's use of Dante "is an example of his belief that literature can help bolster human endurance in suffering and provide uplifting moments that strengthen ones resistance" (22). Jonathan Druker, on the other hand, believes that what Levi had faith in was a form of secular humanism that was nourished as much by Dante as it was by Darwin. The Enlightenment matrix of Levi's worldview seems to be foremost behind his understanding of the final solution as having its beginnings in the sacrifice of the particular, and the different, for the universal.[9]

Reflecting on the new Soviet man, Corrado Alvaro also highlights (*Viaggio in Russia*) de-individualization (here, it would be fair to also emphasize the importance of an Italian's perspective on this case). The trend towards the de-individualization of Sovieticus man was a dominant feature of the Soviet regime, and contrasted to the importance of individuality (a consequence of christianity) in the Western tradition: "Tuttavia il cristianesimo rimane sempre l'origine della concezione dell'individualità umana quale per quasi duemila anni s'è coltivata, cioè libertà di coscienza, di arbitrio, senso di sé e della libertà individuale, tutto quello che insomma è venuto all'uomo dal cristianesimo e che forma la differenza con la civiltà pagana composta di aggregati, civiltà di massa, come diremmo oggi. Socialmente, oggi, è la fine della concezione cristiana dell'individuo; il bolscevismo fa dell'individuo un prodotto sociale, una conseguenza fisiologica e ambientale [...]" ("However, Christianity remains the origin of the conception of human individuality which Christianity has cultivated over nearly 2,000 years. That is to say, freedom of conscience, of will, of sense of self and individual freedom come from Christianity. We could say, in short, that everything that has come to man from Christianity and that it forms the difference with pagan civilization which is made up by aggregates and mass civilization. Socially, today, is the end of the Christian conception of the individual; Bolshevism makes the individual a social product, a physiological and environmental consequence ...") (*Viaggio in Russia* 192). As noted by Alvaro, apart from the fact that the fabrication of the "new man" could not have been built on anything but a cliché decided upon by leadership, another reason for de-individualization success was the absence of tradition in Russia. Ferrying the masses who lived in rural and medieval conditions directly into the most advanced modernity was one of the true purposes of the October Revolution. Alvaro, however, wrote in the 1930s. The impending war was felt strongly in Russia. Given this, how does one explain that Nazism sprang up and thrived in the same Germany that produced Communism as an ideology? This question is answered by Arendt (*The Origins of Totalitarianism*). Totalitarianism was made possible due to a break, or at least a deep fracture, in tradition that arose as a consequence of the advent of modernity. Levi understood this when he openly opposed Nietzsche who, in turn, had made his attack on Christianity one of the cornerstones of his work (*Human, All Too Human: A Book for Free Spirits*) leading to what he will call "the Superman." The difference with the Nazis was underlined by Levi himself:

> Il verbo di Nietzsche mi ripugna profondamente; stento a trovarvi un'affermazione che non coincida con il contrario di quanto mi piace pensare; mi infastidisce il suo tono oracolare; ma mi pare che non vi compaia mai il desiderio della soffer-

> enza altrui. L'indifferenza sì, quasi in ogni pagina, ma mai la Schadenfreude, la gioia per il danno del prossimo, né tanto meno la gioia del far deliberatamente soffrire. Il dolore del volgo, degli Ungestalten, degli informi, dei non-nati-nobili, è un prezzo da pagare per l'avvento del regno degli eletti; è un male minore, comunque sempre un male; non è desiderabile in sé. Ben diversi erano il verbo e la prassi hitleriani. (*I sommersi* 84–85)

> Nietzsche's message is profoundly repugnant to me; I find it difficult to discover an affirmation in it which is not contrary to what I like to think. His oracular tone irritates me, yet it seems to me that a desire for the suffering of others cannot be found in it. Indifference, yes, almost on every page, but never *Schadenfreude*, the joy in your neighbor's misfortune and, even less, joy in deliberately inflicting suffering. The pain of the *hoi polloi*, of the *Ungestalten*, the shapeless, the non-noble-born, is a price that must be paid for the advent of the reign of the elect—it is a minor evil, but an evil nonetheless; it is not in itself desirable. Hitlerian doctrine and practice were much different. (*The Drowned* 106–07)

Rossellini also addressed the problem of the interruption of tradition and the attack against Christianity. He began his film *Germania anno zero* with a written statement declaring that disconnection from Christian values was the cause of the tragedy that was about to be narrated: "Quando le ideologie si discostano dalle leggi eterne della morale e della pietà cristiana, che sono alla base della vita degli uomini, finiscono per diventare criminale follia. Persino la prudenza dell'infanzia ne viene contaminata e trascinata da un orrendo delitto ad un altro non meno grave, nel quale con la ingenuità propria dell'innocenza, crede di trovare una liberazione dalla colpa." ("When the ideologies differ from the eternal laws of morality and Christian piety, which are the basis of life of human beings, end up as criminal folly. Even the prudence of childhood is contaminated and is driven by a terrible crime to another no less serious, in which the proper naivety of innocence believes to find a release from guilt"). The background of the ruins of Berlin were transformed into the graveyard of a humanity that was not developed by Rossellini himself, but given as obvious and supported by Christianity. The invocation of Christianity is a problem within a problem given that we must be careful to separate Christianity—understood as a tradition devastated by modernity—from Christianity that, as a philosophy, supports and constructs an idea of the human being. There is, however, something profound that unites Levi's and Rossellini's approaches: neither of them saves "men." Although Levi tries to find positive elements, scattered here and there, his indignant gaze never tires of collecting humanity's darkest miseries, as highlighted by the *Lager*. For example, in *Se questo è un uomo* he narrates the story of the engineer Alfred L. to show how "sia vano il mito dell'uguaglianza originale fra gli uomini" ("pointless is the myth of the original equality among men") (84). Although Alfred was a former entrepreneur, he entered the *Lager* "nudo, solo e sconosciuto" ("naked, alone and unknown"), like everyone else in the camp. Through a thousand invisible sacrifices, he exudes an image of a strong and healthy man who has potential: he wears a crisp suit and is clean-shaven unlike his "sordidi e sciatti" ("sordid and sloppy") colleagues. He also survived. Then there is the thief, Elias Lindzin, who survives the destruction from the outside because he is physically strong and resists the annihilation from within due to his dementia. Elias survives because he is "idoneo a questo modo di vivere" ("suited to this way of life"). There is also Henri, who "muove con languida naturale eleganza" ("moves with languid natural elegance") and uses his mild image to incite pity. "Henri ha scoperto che la pietà, essendo un sentimento primario e irriflesso, alligna assai bene, se abilmente instillata, proprio negli animi primitivi dei brutti che ci comandano..." (*Se questo è un uomo* 89; "Henri has discovered that pity, being a primary and instinctive sentiment, grows quite well if ably cultivated, particularly in the minds of the brutes who command us ..."; *If This Is a Man* 105). Finally, there is old Kuhn, who thanks God for not having been chosen. "Se io fossi Dio, sputerei a terra la preghiera di Kuhn" (*Se questo è un uomo* 116; "If I was God, I would spit at Kuhn's prayer"; *If This Is a Man* 136), comments Levi who, as a free man, had no desire to see even the survivor Henri: "Distruggere l'uomo è difficile, quasi quanto *crearlo*: non è stato agevole, non è stato breve, ma ci siete riusciti, tedeschi. Eccoci docili sotto i vostri sguardi: da parte nostra nulla più avete a temere: non atti di rivolta, non parole a sfida, neppure uno *sguardo giudice*." (*Se questo è un uomo* 132; "To destroy a man is difficult, almost as difficult as to *create* one: it has not been easy, nor quick, but you Germans have succeeded. Here we

Chapter Five

are, docile under your gaze; from our side you have nothing to fear; no acts of violence, no words of defiance, not even *a look of judgment*"; *If This Is a Man* 156; my italics). The "man" is he who is able to rebel, maintain autonomy, and able to judge—this is precisely Arendt's conclusion in *Eichmann in Jerusalem: A Report on the Banality of Evil*—atrophy of the judgment faculty, the inability to judge. Here it is interesting to note that Levi's man was created, but not by God: "Ogni anno che passa ci rende più soli: non soltanto l'uomo non è il centro dell'universo, ma l'universo non è fatto per l'uomo, è ostile, violento, strano." (*La ricerca delle radici* 229; "Every year that passes leaves us more alone. Not only are we not at the center of the universe, but the universe is not made for human beings; it is hostile, violent, alien"; *The Search for Roots* 214). In the gallery of characters narrated by Levi there is also Lorenzo who, with "il suo modo così piano e facile di essere buono" (*Se questo è un uomo* 130; "his so easy and slow way of being good"; *If This Is a Man* 152) shows Levi that there was still a just world outside our own, something and someone still pure and possessed of integrity. Lorenzo is one of the few positive characters; this speaks volumes about Levi's perspective. Whilst there are some of the positive traits of "man" created by our society, they are then destroyed by the Nazis: goodness, fairness, and purity of soul. According to Levi, these traits were cultivated throughout our history. Certainly, many of the characters about whom Levi writes entered the *Lager* already corrupt. However, it was the *Lager* that chose their characteristics as winning ones to be rewarded. It follows, that it seems to have always been the duty and right of the collective to create the human being's profile in one way or another. In this reading, the Nazis had both the intent and the means to subvert a long process.

Rossellini (*Germania anno zero*), on the other hand, has a child commit suicide, a being whose postulated humanity should still be uncontaminated. For Rossellini, too, protection and salvation seem to be secured from above, through a social discourse on Christianity. It is from here that he wants to start; from the restoration and reset of the social discourse.

Material conditions and social matters

Selection is the quintessence of Nazi ideology, the first building block of the "new" and "pure" man. It is selection that is the distinguishing feature between the two totalitarian regimes: the Soviet one took human beings as they were and tried to change them through terror tactics combined with social, cultural and political engineering, whilst the cruder Nazi regime was obsessed by, amongst other issues, biology. The Germans were apparently planning on discarding the socially weaker as well. At least Rossellini's *Germania anno zero* (*Germany Year Zero*) seems to suggest it. Let us consider the case of Edmund's father. Weak, sick, useless, and cumbersome, he is eliminated by the Nazi ideology. He is eliminated by his child, a son of the just-ended war and the radical ruins of a destroyed Berlin. Against the backdrop of a landscape of death and destruction, Edmund becomes the obedient soldier of the selection algorithm. There is no social bond that holds, neither family nor blood ties, nor strong affections. Edmund, 11 or 12 years old,[10] is in a direct and solitary relationship with Nazism, without any form of mediation. The network of relationships that define and protect the individual have been destroyed. Teaching a child to select and eliminate his or her own parents means projecting him/her into the darkest recesses of isolation, thereby de-socializing him/her at the beginning of his/her life.

Edmund is the most disquieting child in the history of cinema and literature. He kills with consciousness, but a consciousness that is not his. After the non-humans of the *Lager*, stripped of individuality and judging capacity, here is the "new man," a former member of the Hitler Youth movement. His conscience is given to him by an ideology and, in this, he is not very different from the "new man" of the East, even if the substance of the ideologies are at variance. He is a soldier, a robot who, perhaps tragically, becomes an individual by committing suicide. However, suicide is too obvious a reading, a synthesis of what could be seen with the naked eye in postwar Berlin. "Io non credo che Berlino potrà essere ricostruita" ("I do not believe that Berlin will be rebuilt"), the assistant director Carlo Lizzani writes in a letter during filming to Trombadori, at the time director of the Cultural Section of the Italian Communist Party. "Dappertutto c'è odore di cadavere. Migliaia di berlinesi (e di tedeschi, perché quasi tutte le città tedesche sono ridotte così) si suicideranno il prossimo inverno soprattutto perché non si vede assolutamente una via d'uscita." ("Everywhere there is the smell of corpses. Thousands of Berliners (and Germans, because almost all German cities are in the similarly ruined) will commit suicide next winter especially because no one quite sees a way out" (Lizzani 37). The suicide of a child is, however, radical. It is the "new man's" suicide, the complete abortion of Nazism that has no future. It is what Rossellini hopes for, as he sees in this desperate act a return to consciousness. Suicide is a rebellion. As Levi also says in *I sommersi e i salvati*, animals do not commit suicide, human beings do. The younger brother of a former Nazi soldier also becomes a human being by committing suicide! Dramatically, it is the suicide that rekindles the "divine spark." It has the appearance of a painful rebirth of the individual within the ruins of Berlin which is, itself, at the heart of a horrible, failed project. It is also the dawning of a new social and urban design that begins by recognizing the horror in order to stem it. Partly for budgetary reasons and partly because of Rossellini's anxiety to return to Rome where, as Lizzani recounts, the anxious Anna Magnani was waiting for him, many of the film's interiors are Roman, interweaving Berlin and Rome within this film even more specifically. It seems appropriate, therefore, to emphasize the great attention which neorealism paid, in general to housing conditions as a central aspect of the postwar human condition. The idea of the human being as not being separated from its material conditions was beginning to find its way in Italy and the West.

The loneliness of the individual contributes to the creation of an atomized society. The socially weaker may be physically weaker or may be what the Soviets called the objective enemy; that is, a person who has not yet done anything against the regime but who would have an interest in doing so. Examples would include; the *kulaks* or affluent peasants, who were first conceived of as a category, and then as a class enemy by the designers of the grand plan, and subsequently destroyed and sacrificed *en masse* in the *gulag*). However, it could also be the poorest of the poor (after all, it is poverty and a lack of food that makes necessary, according to the Nazi teacher, the elimination of Edmund's sick father, whose sustenance had become a problem in a Berlin that has been razed to the ground). Here we find the extension of a perverted racism, in which discarding the sick intersects with selection and thus becomes a form of class war. One notes how, in these extreme circumstances, a rudimentary economic mechanism alongside theories of selection merge with racism. Or *vice versa*: here a kind of primitive Social Darwinism within classist tensions can be found.

The Interruption of Tradition

> Nella storia e nella vita pare talvolta di discernere una legge feroce, che suona "a chi ha, sarà dato; a chi non ha, a quello sarà tolto." Con gli adatti, con gli individui forti e astuti, i capi stessi mantengono volentieri contatti, talora quasi camerateschi, perché sperano di poterne trarre forse più tardi qualche utilità. Ma ai musulmani, agli uomini in dissolvimento, non vale la pena rivolgere la parola… (Levi, *Se questo è un uomo* 80)

> In history and in life one sometimes seems to glimpse a ferocious law which states: 'to he that has, will be given; from he that has not, will be taken away'. In the *Lager*, where man is alone and where the struggle for life is reduced to its primordial mechanism, this unjust law is openly in force, is recognized by all. With the adaptable, the strong and astute individuals, even the leaders willingly keep contact, because they hope later to perhaps derive some benefit. But with *muselmann*, the men in decay, it is even not worth speaking… (Levi, *If This Is a Man* 94–95)

Levi was a partisan from Turin at the time of his capture, and the Nazis took him to the camp where he would be a prisoner. In Italy, during the 1980s, Levi revisited these topics in the last work of his life, greatly expanding the perspective:

> Non c'è dubbio che il disegno fondamentale del nazionalsocialismo aveva una sua razionalità: la spinta verso Oriente (vecchio sogno tedesco), *la soffocazione del movimento operaio*, l'egemonia sull'Europa continentale, *l'annientamento del bolscevismo e del giudaismo, che Hitler semplicisticamente identificava fra loro*, la spartizione del potere mondiale con Inghilterra e Stati Uniti, l'apoteosi della razza germanica con l'eliminazione "spartana" dei malati mentali e delle bocche inutili: tutti questi elementi erano fra loro compatibili, e deducibili da alcuni pochi postulati già esposti con innegabile chiarezza nel *Mein Kampf*. (*I sommersi* 84)

> There is no doubt that the fundamental design of National Socialism had a rationale of its own: the eastward drive (an old German dream); stifling the workers' movement, hegemony over continental Europe; annihilation of Bolshevism and Judaism, which Hitler simplistically identified with one another; sharing world power with England and the United States; the apotheosis of the Germanic race with the "Spartan" elimination of the mentally ill and useless mouths. All these elements were

> mutually compatible and can be deduced from a few postulates already presented with undeniable clarity in *Mein Kampf.* (*The Drowned* 106)

This class war was ideologically central to the Bolsheviks. The Communist utopia envisaged a future in which an individual's economic condition was to be elevated, a tomorrow in which the state would not be necessary. The existence of the state seemed to be a requirement for managing the tensions of a society that was not wealthy and its task was to build a prosperous and cultured society in which fully self-aware individuals were motivated to make fair contributions to society. There are plenty of references and comparisons that Alvaro (*Viaggio in Russia*) makes with prosperous America, which was then taking its first steps. The Russians seem to have been inspired by nothing else. Arendt also approached the same problem, but via other paths. According to her (*On Revolution*), the American Revolution succeeded better than the French Revolution—a certain template of which is present in the October Revolution—because of the prosperous American context. What matters to us in this context is that one of the ideal characteristics of the Soviet "new man" is an elevated economic status, as put forward by Alvaro:

> L'ideale comunista va verso l'abolizione del commercio e del denaro, lo scambio dei prodotti, l'abolizione dello Stato; ma tutto questo, dice Stalin, in una epoca fantastica di ricchezza e di abbondanza di merci, e anche, direi, in un'epoca ideale di perfezione di lavoro e di rapporti umani che si possano dispensare dall'autorità regolatrice dello Stato. Ma si sa che se il mondo è ricco lo è per tutti, come lo fu in America ai bei tempi, quando perfino qualche mendicante aveva la sua automobile per correre meglio alle poste ...

> The communist ideal is to seek the abolition of trade and money, the exchange of products, the abolition of the State; but this, says Stalin, in an era of great wealth and abundance of goods, and also, I would say, in an ideal era of the perfection of work and human relations that can be dispensed by the regulatory authority of the State. However, it is known that if the world is wealthy it is wealthy for everyone, as it was in America in the good old days, when even a beggar had a car in order to run faster to the post office ... (*Viaggio in Russia* 83)

Chapter Six

From Berlin to Rome

Germania anno zero: A thesis film

After the great interest that Mussolini showed in cinema, in the post-war period the PCI (The Italian Communist Party) showed great attention to the sector, so much so that, at its direction in 1947, a Department of Cinema was founded. Carlo Lizzani tells how a PCI official convinced him not to travel to Sicily, where he had planned to make a documentary about the regional elections of the following year. The PCI wanted him alongside Rossellini, who was, at that time, in Paris meeting the *Germania anno zero* film producer. Visconti was asked to make the documentary set in Sicily, which became nothing less than *La terra trema* (*The Earth Trembles*). *Germania anno zero* is a kind of continuation of *Roma città aperta*[11] and, although the topics addressed in the film are international in scope and importance, its context is Italian (an Italy that about to be rebuilt) and Rossellini's readings are determined by, or at least deeply concerned with, the Italian context. That Christian-Communist sensibility, a particularly Italian amalgam, ends up influencing the various layers of the film. In Peter Bondanella's eyes (*Italian Cinema. From Neorealism to the Present* 38), the message of Christian humanism prevails in *Roma città aperta*. While from the point of view of Millicent Marcus (*Italian Film in the Light of Neorealism*), which is the one, as already said, that I also adopt in reading this film, Rossellini seeks a balance between Marxism and Christian humanism.[12] This is how Rossellini arrives in Germany. Berlin feels a bit like Rome.

Chapter Six

It took the Allies' bombing to break down the organizational architecture of the Nazis in Berlin and their inherent organization—evidently the allies did not succeed completely. Ideological skeletons held up for a short time while, from the general chaos, there also germinated a new order that was carried symbolically by the modern trams that ran surreally throughout the city that had been razed to the ground. "Bisogna insegnare ai bambini tedeschi di riamare la vita" ("We need to teach German children to love life again"), says the voiceover at the beginning of *Germania anno zero*. "Vivono nella tragedia come nel loro elemento naturale" ("They live in tragedy as in their natural element"). The narrator then concludes that what is to come will be a "serena constatazione dei fatti" ("serene statement of facts"). Rossellini, however, did not limit his film to a straightforward statement of facts. The director's sad loss of his own child shortly before the movie was shot and a representation that ends with the suicide of a child meant that that was impossible and, instead, Rossellini does the opposite. The film is constructed slowly, with a well-thought-out development, and aims for precise goals. Indeed, *Germania anno zero* can be considered a film with a thesis. Despite this, important elements of realism are not absent, nor could they have been absent. The film was shot in Berlin in the summer of 1947. It was enough to move the camera through the streets of a city razed to the ground to document the extreme conditions that three and a half million Germans were living in. The ruins are the constant background of the entire movie. The representation of the ruinous landscape in post-war cinema implicates an imperative for reconstruction. According to Noa Steimatsky (*Italian Locations: Reinhabiting the Past in Postwar Cinema*), the ruinous landscape "evolves as a late-modern trope inflecting not only the space but the consciousness and the agencies of post-war cinemas" (44). The need to clear up the space as well as the urgency of habitation were more important than the conservation of the ruins as monuments. "In a landscape of ruins neorealism was reconstruction" (45). Steimasky convincingly pointed out that "realism" should be understood as intervention rather than as a passive moment in modern culture, and that neorealist cinema was a "lively participant in the production of postwar Italy" (46). In Rossellini's films, the ruins "proclaim the imperative of shelter, of housing" (43).

The story of the characters seems to mirror the ruins, doubling their visual impact. This film was not as successful as the previous two in the *War Trilogy*. Nevertheless, according to James Quandt (*Roberto Rossellini's War Trilogy, Myth and Manipulation*), great directors such as Truffaut and Godard shot their own films inspired by this trilogy, while Bertolucci and Haneke considered it to be one of the best films in the history of cinema. The delicate issue of Germans' historical responsibility for Nazism on the one hand, and Rossellini's demonstration of their vulnerability on the other, as well as the raw ending that shows a child commit suicide, and the absence of humor and heroism, are among the likely causes of the film's unpopularity.

The film opens with men who work for a pittance opening tombs in which to bury the dead. A blonde boy named Edmund digs a grave too—and that says it all. In order to keep digging and send food home he claims to be 15 years old, but really he is 12, at most. Although always walking amongst the ruins, he is carefully and precisely dressed. The streets are grey with dust but his clothes appear flawless. His image is clean-cut, almost the icon of the exemplary German child desired by Nazism. Edmund was and, in a certain sense, continues to be a "Young man of Hitler."

The next sequence is typically neorealist. We are in someone's home. It is not that of Pina in *Roma città aperta* but its colors are those of poverty (in fact, most of the interior sequences were filmed in Rome). The living conditions inside the apartments are a central theme of the film. Ten people, forming different family units, live together in an apartment and they lack food as well as electricity. These simple elements make up the central theme of the city. Work that is not available, a person's right to housing and energy, and the conditions of urban life are what really form the thematic horizon of Rossellini's reflections.

The tram that never stops winds surreally amidst the ruins. It does not stop even after the suicide of the child. Modernity continues; unstoppable. The tram carries on regardless as if impelled by an indifferent force, a force of things that transcends the individual, whether the child to whom the city should have belonged or Umberto D, the old Roman citizen—in the film of the same name by De Sica—who, tired and contemplating suicide, sees the tram proceeding indifferently without him at all hours through the streets of Rome. The same indifferent tram makes its path through Berlin, in the background, while the child's lifeless body lies on the ground.

A Berlin in ruins opens all the sequences, like a premise that affects their development. From this point of view, the monologue by Edmund's father is programmatic: "Tutto mi è stato tolto, il danaro dall'inflazione, i figli dai nazisti." ("Everything has been taken away from me, money by inflation, children by the Nazis"). What Rossellini called a "constatazione serena dei fatti" ("serene statement of facts") continues in this way: "Avrei dovuto ribellarmi, non ho fatto nulla come tanti della mia generazione. Oggi paghiamo dei nostri errori. Dobbiamo essere consapevoli." ("I should have rebelled; I did nothing like so many of my generation. Today we are paying for our mistakes. We must be aware"). However, for now, the awareness is the director's. "Sii buono" ("Be good"), the father admonishes his son who, in the meantime, has prepared the poison for the parent who is guilty, among other things, of not resisting Nazism. It is instead the feckless eldest son, whose responsibility the father never stops talking about, who lets himself be arrested in order to redeem himself after his parent's sermon, and perhaps even to prevent his sister from prostituting herself to the Allied soldiers—wealth's representatives who act like neo-colonizers. The tram appears to come and go from one sequence to another, carrying a plot whose background is always the ruins of the city. The release of the older brother after his father's death has a form of mockery to it. Edmund's gesture loses any utilitarian justification. The brother/former soldier whom he wanted to rescue is saved without his cruel action. The countdown to Edmund's suicide begins; he no longer belongs to his family or to the group of vagabonds. He is already an outcast. His exclusion from all possible belonging proceeds almost pedantically. Even the Nazi pedophile beats him (the Nazis, as in *Roma città aperta*,[13] are carriers of various types of degeneration). He tries to play with the children on the street but not even they want him. There are ruins, always ruins, and more ruins. He climbs on ruins, and he looks down on ruins and funerals. The funeral is that of his father. The child's composure is impressive and remains constant. Before that, however, there is a somewhat ambiguous, mystical passage. Edmund sees a priest playing an organ and, standing outside, he listens to the music that the priest is playing inside the roofless church. He stops, everyone is still: the road becomes a painting and the child looks up, a patch of sky with the church's cross in front of him. It is a glimpse of spirituality that perhaps invites Edmund to redemption—maybe an un-Christian one, because suicide is not condoned by Christianity—or perhaps the vision is not strong enough to stop him. Edmund runs away from this call too. He finds an old gun that he points at himself—it is difficult to say whether he does so seriously or as a childish joke.

As noted, *Germania anno zero* is a film with a thesis. The causes of the disaster are those mentioned during the sermon of the religious father: economic crisis, departure from Christian and traditional values, Nazism, and the responsibility of the generation of "fathers" who did not put up necessary resistance. Now a new narrative is urgently needed, a new proposal within the cultural-political discourse of neorealism. A city project and two levels of discourse (as in the ideological dualism of the director looking for a synthesis): one concerns the re-establishment of tradition; the other is concrete, specific, and made up of daily needs. It is the second that has real grip. Neorealism takes the discourse on the human being to a concrete plane and puts it on the level of needs, almost on a level of urban sociology.

Return to Rome

Europa '51 was presented in Venice in 1952 and won an International Award. It further clarifies the intentions of Rossellini in *Germania anno zero* and shows how much of Rome and Europe there was in that movie. Edmund seems to have survived for another 20 cinematographic minutes but only for the sake of inexorably committing suicide. There is no escape. A thick, black, toxic cloud envelopes the new generation that grew up in war. Their dramatic future, that is *the very future*, is severely compromised. It is in the idea of the human being, in the education of children, and in the expectations for their future that nothingness lurks. *Europa '51* is another urban trip. One at a time, and never at random, the camera shoots precise spaces within the city. It starts where *Germania anno zero* left us: the suicide of a child. However, there are no ruins. We are in the most beautiful part of the eternal city. Michel, like Edmund, is 12 years old. He is the son of a rich couple (his mother is English, while his father is a wealthy businessman who works overseas) and he is the scion, this time, of the winners of the war. In the early sequences of the film, Irene, the distracted mother, does not listen to Michel and leaves him in the company of attendants all day. Michel is always unhappy and jealous of his mother. The construction of the child's unhappiness is inconsistent and clichéd. Michel grew up during the war, and his days were punctuated by the bombing that took place against an apocalyptic backdrop that makes the articulation of the upcoming drama feel superfluous and the deep malaise appear deliberately spiritual. The parents distract themselves by playing with a toy train that they bought for their son but which they use to entertain guests. An apparent Oedipus complex takes hold of Michel and he flings himself down a stairwell. He does not die immediately. He survives for the time necessary to give us useful insights into the development of the film after his death. His mother goes on an investigative journey through the Rome and Europe of the 1950s, fueled by the energy that mourning the death of her child has unleashed in her. "Dobbiamo cambiare tutto nella nostra vita" ("We must change everything in our lives"), she proclaims shortly before her son dies. The descent to the outskirts of the city occurs in stages, proceeding downwards step-by-step to the furthest reaches and states of suffering. In spatial terms, Irene's trip coincides with a progressive distancing from the center of the city towards the outskirts, towards the factories, and thence towards the stretches of the river where the buildings of the city's peripheries are located. In the end Irene arrives in an inaccessible hidden area where the psychiatric hospital houses the poorest of the poor. The only exception to this progressive trip is a brief stop in the center that reveals a world of prostitution. As in the most famous descents into hell, there are plenty of guides who first introduce, and then are confronted by, the increasingly radical vision of Irene. Her metamorphosis brings about a final "chorus" of ordinary people to call her "santa" ("holy"). The guides, and their social discourses, change from time to time, depending on the precise context. Andrea, a communist and a cousin of Irene's, brings her closer to the outskirts where, for the third time, Rossellini stops in overcrowded apartments, as he did in *Roma città aperta* and *Germania anno zero*. Once more the scene is of a small room, of persons cold and in poverty, and of accommodation with too many inhabitants. Irene, deprived of other motivational impulses, attends to their needs and finds sustenance in their suffering. "Per dare amore" ("To give love"), the woman will say. "To effectively improve the human being based on their conditions," we could say. Poverty and suffering become a reservoir of spirituality that allow Irene (and her director) access to a timeless dimension with her missing son ("Il mio paradiso non è in terra perché Michel non e qui" ("My heaven is not here on earth, because Michel is not here"), the woman will say.

In the early stages of the journey, Irene limits herself to observing and listening. Andrea, however, by starting with the Roman suburbs, says that the poor must be given a "coscienza" ("conscience"), speaking in Marxist rhetoric that is quite similar if not identical to the Soviet one of the "new man." But, in contrast, Irene speaks of "speranza" ("hope"). Thereafter, the discourses begin to gradually diverge. Through the needs of a poor, hospitalized child, Irene begins to find direction. She focuses firmly on the boy's needs and remains in the suburbs, where 10–12 people live in one house: "Se lavorassero come operai vivrebbero meglio" ("If they worked as laborers they would live better"), says a Communist suburban neighbor, "ma sono braccianti..." ("but they are farm workers ..."). The themes of urbanization and Russia covered in the 1930s by Alvaro return to Rome 20 years later within this film.

The guide to the second space, the one that is still empty and whose horizon is the expanding suburbs, is a mother of six children, (her own and adopted). The importance of adoption is central in the discourse on love, both Rossellini's and his future saint's. The death of a poor anonymous person and a meeting with children mark Irene's path towards the house of Masina, and this house, if not the same, is very similar to the house of Fellini's future Cabiria, another character who was played by Fellini's wife, Masina. At this point there is a quick nod to the changing status of women and their emancipation. The woman/mother interpreted by Masina is, here, single by choice. This is quite a strong turning point, considering the period. Andrea, who appears and disappears, provides the ideas that are reflected upon, and states that "serve una coscienza di classe" ("a class consciousness is needed") for "un continuo progresso, in cui l'uomo si fa padrone del proprio destino" ("a steady progress in which the human being becomes the master of his fate"). Such a world will be the real paradise. Irene, then, through a very weak narrative pretext—she must stand in for her friend whom Andrea had given a job to because this woman has to meet her lover—ends up working in a factory. This, in turn, opens up a new level of analysis in the film. In her eyes, work is not the solution, and she gives the opinion that "... il lavoro è una condanna. ... Nel paradiso in terra non c'è posto per Michel. Io cerco quello eterno" ("...work is condemnation. ... In heaven on earth there is no place for Michel. I seek the eternal one").

The societal photograph is completed by the figure of a prostitute who is known in the city outskirts and who we see, in this case as well, at the same Roman city center locations which Fellini will show Cabiria. The prostitute falls ill because she is poor, and dies. In so doing, she leaves Irene in an unconvincing narrative situation. A neighbor who has become a deviant due to poverty commits a robbery and Irene helps him to escape, convinced that "il libero arbitrio" ("free will") will lead him to turn himself in to the police. Her action is enough to land her in trouble with the law and, while the trial takes place, she is confined to a psychiatric hospital; the last space of suffering—one that is also spiritual—examined by Rossellini in this film. Irene is not a Communist, nor does she want to enter a convent; there is, resultantly, no predetermined space for her spirituality in society. The people believe that she is "santa" ("holy"), but society must lock her up with other outcasts of various kinds. "Dovremmo difendere la società così come è anche se oggi non c'è più una verità'" ("We should protect society just as it is even though today there is no longer one truth"), concludes the judge.

Conclusion to Part One

Italian society, like many European societies, aims to shape human beings mainly by focusing on current needs but without a definitive concept of humanness. These societies tend to modify the current profile of human beings, moving from one draft to another as contextual needs change; however, they do preserve elements from previous drafts. In the following chapters I show what these elements are. The constant thread running through the main discourses, in Italy as in Germany and Russia, seems to be that the human being must be malleable and, consequently, transitional.

The city (whether Moscow, Berlin, or, Rome), functions as a laboratory where "The 'Transitional' Human Being" is formed. The Soviet Union's experience represented the biggest urban breakthrough and was a variant of the left-wing totalitarianism that governed half of Europe and many other countries for so many years. Spatial control was essential for the production of the "new man." The control of the human being's mobility was a crucial element shared not only by the different totalitarian systems. As is shown in Part II of this work, it remains a characteristic exploited according to specific contextual needs by contemporary societies. Nothing like this would have been possible without the technological means of our time. The isolation of individuals and groups of individuals, as well as the freezing of their mobility are essential conditions for exercising a control that is so powerful that it can strip a set of basic cultural, political, emotional, linguistic, social and professional constructs that are the core of what is intended for humanity in specific historical and geographic contexts. From this point of view, Agamben's reading of Levi and Arendt's analyses of the errors of the French Revolution that became apparent with the experiences of stateless persons during the early-twentieth century show that being "simply men" without being legally protected by political affiliation to a state opened the way to making the human being superfluous. Hannah Arendt, analyzing the birth of the national state order, underlines how, in the name of national sentiment, rights were increasingly recognized for citizens belonging by birth and origin to a given national community. In this way, the nature of the state changed from an instrument of law into an instrument of the nation. The divine origin of a nation's people was the claim that legitimized its sanctification. The divine origin of the individual, however, was no longer in itself sufficient, as in the framework of the Christian religion. The individual could boast the divinity of their origin exclusively through belonging to the "divine" people. The (national) state was no longer an instrument of (universal) human rights but turned into an instrument of national interest. Only through belonging to a given nation were those rights protected by the state, but they were protected as a consequence of the national interest.

Along with the bulldozers and mechanical arms described in Alvaro's reportage on Agro Pontino, modernity has enormously improved and enhanced the control instruments that are available to those in power. The social engineers put in place are as effective as heavy industry. The levels of organization, along with propaganda and cultural discourses that made possible the shaping of a "new man" had never before been seen. In the process of making the human being superfluous, totalitarianism targeted the human being's will, uniqueness, and individuality; as clearly shown in the works of Levi, Alvaro and Rossellini. Their perspectives, however, have different departure points. Levi seems to start from the Enlightenment and a very Italian form of secular humanism, while Alvaro and Rossellini both make direct references to the (Christian) tradition and its interruption. Despite these differences, all of them seem to attribute a human being's profile to a cultural-political discourse. Through hard work, this kind of discourse has created a positive model of human beings, which Auschwitz and the gulag ended. There is no longer a "universal man." While it is said that possible remedies could come from an alteration in the address of this discourse, something seems hopelessly irretrievable. This something is the idea of an unchanging and durable profile of the human being. Now that the great narratives are over, articulations describing the human being are ever more important. Individuals are trapped within the world's

Conclusion to Part One

actual realities with which they have to deal. This is all we have: economic conditions, health, housing, employment, and social relationships. What is now needed is a broad view, a far-reaching projection of the future, a reassembling of the fragments. A new narration is needed; but, this does not seem possible. The absence of narration has been accompanied by an absence of a concrete design for the human being; and in any case, improvement seems to be what is required. It follows, that nothing else is to be done but focus on the problems, on a critique of what was wrong, and improve little by little. The human being has, at least theoretically, been conceived out of the rejection of the non-human of Auschwitz. It is the human being who feels cold, who is hungry, who suffers, who plans to not feel cold and hunger, and to not suffer. It is from the horror of Levi's non-human that we begin to reimagine the human being. Starting from their rights: those rights define them. The relevance of material conditions that slowly sneak into the conception of the national human being becomes clear. Now the human being's profile, instead of mirroring an alleged universality, is articulated by a set of rights; the specificity of which vary according to e context. It starts with what are commonly recognized as the basic rights necessary for living with dignity in our time. It starts, then, from people's needs. After the war ended, those needs were many and very evident. The needs of the citizen became part of the discourse of cities. Filming the ruins of post-war Italy and Europe, as Rossellini did, meant also highlighting how urgent it was to rebuild the country and its infrastructures. Exposing the failure of the "new men" as drafted by totalitarian systems—see, for example, Edmund's suicide—also meant highlighting the need for a new citizen who mirrored a different system of values. Rebuilding the country, its economy, its infrastructures, its political culture, and its cities became the (re)starting point. Cinema and literature adapted to the historical context. While Fascist cinema was a powerful propaganda tool, neorealism contrasted with the old cultural discourse and elaborated a new one. A new Italian narrative was urgently needed; a new proposal within the cultural–political discourse of neorealism. The latter includes a city project and two levels of discourse (as in the ideological dualism of Rossellini looking for a synthesis): one concerned with the re-establishment of (the Christian) tradition, and the other made up of daily needs. It is the second that prevails. A new project, a new city, a rebuilt reunified country, and a new human being were all possible and, in Italy, a "new" Italian was made. The "new" human being does not have the same traits everywhere. His Italian post-war profile mirrors closely the contextual needs of the country and, in the next chapter, I examine what those needs (and through that the traits of the "new" Italian) were, and how literature and cinema became part of that process.

In the early-twentieth century, as de Grazia reminds us, European nation-states were engaged in a competitive system. Education, military training, and public rituals were used to shape the profile of citizens and nationalize the masses. After nationalizing male subjects, the focus began to include women who, in Italy, under Fascism, were given the profile of mothers of the race. Population size, military demands, the need for cheap labor, and declining fertility rates within the ideological framework of Nazi-Fascism and its biopolitics all informed gender policies. Demographic concerns, along with the inclusion (during WWI) or the exclusion of women from the workforce (after 1919) became key factors in gender politics. The biological politics of Fascism polarized gender profiles and excluded women from the labor market and relegated them to the role of child-bearers. Fascist cinema represented mobility, idleness, and affairs as negative aspects typical of "impure" "biracial" women, while motherhood and a lack of mobility were positive features that described Italian women. Men, on the other hand, in times of imperialistic war, were represented as fathers, settlers, heroes, soldiers, aviators, and "modern knights" of steel empowered by uniforms, weapons, and loud engines. The need and the possibility to "redo man" along the above lines, as Gentile puts it, became a central aspect of Fascist propaganda. Once the war was over, "men"—meaning human beings—needed to be "redone" so as to mirror the different demands and values of another kind of state. Pina, the positive character in *Roma città aperta,* bore the new values that, in Rossellini's view, were auspicious for women. She blends traditional traits like their love for their children, husband, and family with progressive active participation in the public arena as workers, members of the resistance and, ultimately, as heroines. A few years later, in post-war Rome, Rossellini also represented women, mothers, and workers who remained single by choice. This signaled a strong

Conclusion to Part One

turning point especially when one considers the period. Nevertheless, as historians like de Grazia observe, it was only in the 1970s that the repressive Fascist laws on gender policies were completely erased. The cultural and political struggle that led to the referenda on abortion and divorce are discussed in Part Two.

The twentieth-century experiences of stateless persons examined in Part One, demonstrated how vulnerable the "simple man" was when not accompanied by national adjectives (such as German, Italian, American or Russian). The universal and natural human being was substituted by the national human being. Racism, which can be a complement to nationalism, emphasized alleged ethnic differences. The urgent task for totalitarian states was to homologate and continuously adapt their citizens to the changing needs of the state. The differences were frightening. This is why the migrations of yesterday and today were, and are, good indicators of the idea of the human being and citizen that is being elaborated. Migration and minorities contained, and contain, something subversive in the eyes of totalitarian elites. This aspect did not disappear with their fall. It resurfaced in new forms after the end of the Cold War (which had frozen international mobility and, with it, imposed a negotiated world order and economy)—when migrant waves reached Italy and Europe starting from the 1990s, as is discussed in Part Three.

Part Two

The Urban Explorer

Federico Fellini's film *La dolce vita* is much more than a phenomenon in the universe of the media. It ended up becoming an important event in the same context that it sought to represent. It became part of a long cultural and political turmoil that possibly culminated with the referenda of the 1970s on divorce and abortion. The main Italian institution that contrasted the new concept of life that accompanied the economic boom and the student protests of 1968 was undoubtedly the Catholic Church:

> Esaminando la sterminata letteratura giornalistica, critica e storica prodotta, si ha l'impressione che il film di Fellini sia stato preso a pretesto per uno scontro di estrema durezza, in un momento particolarmente delicato della storia nazionale: la Chiesa, con papa Giovanni XXIII, si stava avviando verso il rinnovamento dopo gli anni dell'integralismo di Pio XII; nel Palazzo si andavano creando le condizioni di un'alleanza tra cattolici e socialisti per avviare una politica riformistica; gli stili di vita conoscevano profonde trasformazioni per effetto dell'industrializzazione e dello sviluppo delle comunicazioni di massa.

> Looking at the vast journalistic, critical and historical literature it has produced, one has the impression that Fellini was used as a pretext for a clash of extreme severity, at a particularly delicate moment in national history: the Church, with Pope John XXIII, was heading towards renewal after the years of Pius XII's fundamentalism. There would be the possibility of creating the conditions for an alliance between Catholics and Socialists in the Vatican to initiate a reformist politics; lifestyles would undergo profound changes as a result of industrialization and the development of mass communication. (Costa 7–8)

Part Two

This important shift was immediately represented from different angles and with different sensitivities by protagonists of Italian literature and cinema such as Pasolini, Calvino, and Fellini. Postwar Italy, recounted by neorealism and affected by unemployment, emigration, and housing problems suddenly became aware of the economic boom that was experienced predominantly in industrialized and urban areas, and its profound implications on the country's life. If there is both a single moment or period when this happened, and a single cultural representation that made it broadly known, they are, respectively, the year 1959, and the movie *La dolce vita*. The release of the movie coincided with, and instigated a cultural earthquake. "Tutti sentivano il bisogno di intervenire sul film: per cercare di bloccarlo o per proteggerlo da interventi censori, per condannarlo o per assolverlo, per vituperarlo o per adattarlo alla propria prospettiva ideologica." ("Everybody felt the need to intervene in the film: to try to block it or to protect it from attempts at censorship, to condemn it or acquit it, to berate it or adapt it to their ideological perspective") (Costa 8). From the Rome of De Sica's *Ladri di biciclette* (The Bicycle Thieves), to the city of Via Veneto it seems that far more than 11 years passed. The image that the country had, of itself, had not yet been updated; this is why the *Roman Observatory*, among others, re-titled the film *The Disgusting Life*, as Fellini himself mentioned in an interview. "Sono miserie che non è opportuno portare sullo schermo" ("These are misfortunes that shouldn't be brought to the screen"),[14] yelled the priests and the journalists of the Catholic press. "Mi fa molto piacere che l'organo vaticano gridi Basta! Questo, per gli uomini di buona volontà, non può significare che Continua!" ("I am very pleased that the Vatican's forum shouts Enough! This, for men of good will, cannot but mean Continue!") (De Santi 21) replied Pasolini, who put at the center of his own creativity of those years what he used to call, with great lucidity, "mutamento antropologico" ("the anthropological shift"). As indicated by Pasolini himself, *Accattone* was the movie that mainly targeted these problematics, but they can also be found in many of his other works and are also well-articulated in *Lettere luterane* (*Lutheran Letters*). The change of the mood of production, alongside industrialization, urbanization, and the gradual entry of the Italian masses into the new system were accompanied by deep transformations and sharp contradictions. New and better railroads, highways, television, newspapers, universities, literature, and cinema brought the country together under a new and unified national consciousness, as well as a new vision of the world from both scientific and cultural points of view. The city functioned as a physical and cultural laboratory where the new Italian was formed, and in which innovative kinds of cultural expression were developed and promulgated. Many of these aspects impacted on and are part of Italo Calvino's works. The question that concerns the type of relationships that individuals have with their city is focus of this section, as it was central to the entirety of Calvino's work and was also in several of Fellini's films—*Le notti di Cabiria, La dolce vita* and *Roma*; all set in Rome.

Chapter Seven

Excluded and Transformed

The transformation of vast areas of Russia "into a bread factory" (as noted in Part I with regard to Corrado Alvaro's reportage) was accompanied by a desire to make proletarians of the farmers; a process that also involved the massive deportation of landowners. In the city, in an attempt to regulate the lives of individuals, the state applied very strict controls on the mobility, employment, and time management of all citizens by creating interlocking standardized routines. The Western responses to similar problems varied, at least on some points. Standardized temporal coordinates are apparent here, too, but not with the same rigidity; leaving the way open to new dynamics. An extreme territorial mobility (one that, for Calvino, meant that the city dweller was always considered to a traveler/migrant), a relatively less-mediated approach to knowledge, and systemic responses to ever-more-technological hyper-environmental problems were the major points of divergence.

The gradual entry, without alternatives, of the entire population into the new system was not so dissimilar in terms of the mutation of the individual's profile. The writer who, more than anyone else, spoke of an anthropological turning point was Pasolini. He did so in such apocalyptic terms as to end up perhaps devaluing the disclosed news. Italy's process of modernization coincided with strengthening its internal cohesion, beginning at the linguistic level. In a television interview on 22 February 1968, released to RAI, Pasolini analyzed the process the Italian language's formation which, unlike the development of other European languages, was born through literature. The dialects which he loved so much as expressions of popular culture suffocated by modernity remain potential languages. They were never realized because they were excluded by the literary prestige of the Florentine dialect. Contemporary Italian no longer owes its unitary aspect to literature but, instead, to television, and the linguistic capital is not Rome but technological Milan. During the interview, Pasolini noted the change, and affirmed with unusual caution that it could not be judged as a positive or a negative. However, in the final analysis it was a negative trend for Pasolini and was not a mystery at all. In a polemic letter dated 8 July 1974 and addressed to Calvino he wrote: "I dialetti (gli idiomi materni!) sono allontanati nel tempo e nello spazio: i figli sono costretti a non parlarli più perché vivono a Torino, a Milano o in Germania." ("Dialects (the maternal idioms!) are removed in time and space: their children are forced not to speak them any more, because they live in Turin, Milan or Germany") (Pasolini, "Limitatezza della storia e immensità del mondo contadino" 67). In the same letter, he clarified his longing for the pre-modern and pre-national world: "È questo illimitato mondo contadino prenazionale e preindustriale, sopravvissuto fino a pochi anni fa, che io rimpiango (non per nulla dimoro il più a lungo possibile, nei paesi del Terzo Mondo, dove esso sopravvive ancora, benché il Terzo Mondo stia anch'esso entrando nell'orbita del cosiddetto Sviluppo)." ("It is this limitless pre-national and pre-industrial peasant world, which had survived up to a few years ago, that I long for) (it is not for nothing that I live as long as possible in Third World countries, where it still survives, although the Third World is also entering the orbit of so-called Development)" ("Limitatezza" 66).

In one of his latest works, *Lettere luterane*, he outlined the new individual, starting from the national profile (Italian), tendentiously of the middle class, bourgeois and, therefore, economically speaking more affluent than before. In this profile, bourgeois and Italian are part of the same adjective. For him, this profile is not only cultural and economic but, literally, also material, biological, of the flesh.[15]

The novelty is epoch-making; the break interrupts a millenary tradition. The gap that has been created between the generations of fathers and sons is as unbridgeable as ever:

> Da quando sei nato, quei modelli umani e quei valori antichi non son serviti più al potere: e perché? Perché è cambiato quantitativamente il modo di produzione delle cose. La verità che dobbiamo dirci è questa: la nuova produzione delle cose, dà

> a te un insegnamento originario e profondo che io non posso comprendere (anche perché non lo voglio). E ciò implica una estraneità tra noi due che non è solo quella che per secoli e millenni ha divisi i padri e i figli. (*Lettere luterane* 18)

> Since you were born these human models and those ancient values have no longer been useful to those in power. And why? Because the mode of production has changed quantitatively. The truth we must tell ourselves is this: the new mode of production of things—that is to say, the change in things—gives you a basic and profound training which I cannot understand (also because I do not wish to do so). And that implies an estrangement between the two of us which is not merely that which for centuries and millennia has separated fathers and sons. (*Lutheran Letters* 35)

Pasolini also criticized the Church which, considered as an historic institution of pre-modern Italian society, has now come to terms with bourgeois consumerism. In a famous 1973 article in the *Corriere della sera* ("Analisi linguistica di uno slogan" 20) Pasolini was inspired by an advertising slogan for a brand of jeans called "jeans Jesus" which stated: "Non avrai altri jeans all'infuori di me" ("You shall have no other jeans but me"). This slogan, for Pasolini, became an indication of a deeper phenomenon that concerned the role of the Church in Italy during those years. Compromise with the new system of values would be fatal for the Church for religion would lose authority and survive only in a folk or consumer form. For Pasolini, nothing escaped the conformist assimilation of new Italian capitalism. Even Fascism had not gone so deep. "Nessun centralismo fascista è riuscito a fare ciò che ha fatto il centralismo della civiltà dei consumi." ("No Fascist centralism has been able to do what the centralism of the consumer civilization has done") ("Limitatezza" 31).

In an essay dated 1962, Italo Calvino reserved a frontal attack for Pasolini. For Calvino, too, the industrial civilization engulfed everything, even the stirrings of rebellion. According to Calvino, Italian literature and the economic system that surrounded it was in need of rebels.

> Così povera di ribelli è la letteratura italiana che i nostri ben pensanti avevano bisogno che ce ne fosse almeno uno per additarlo all'esecrazione pubblica, hanno scelto il più classico, il più virgiliano, il più appassionatamente professore di tutti noi. Pier

Chapter Seven

> Paolo Pasolini, l'unico per cui la tradizione è carne della sua carne, l'unico che riporta ad onore proprio le forme letterarie che erano solo i ben pensanti ad amare ancora—la poesia delle odi civili e quella del popolaresco dialettale—, l'unico che in fatto di morale ancora crede che tutto sia questione di peccato e di redenzione. (Calvino, *Una pietra sopra: discorsi di letteratura e società* 78)

> So short of rebels is Italian literature that, when our conformists required at least someone to single out for public loathing, they chose the most classic, the most Virgilian, the most passionate professor of us all. Pier Paolo Pasolini, the only one for whom tradition is flesh of his flesh, the only one who honors precisely the literary forms that only the conformists still loved—the poetry of the civil odes and that of folk dialect—the only one who still believes that, in moral issues, everything is a matter of sin and redemption.

Pasolini too polemized with Calvino on several occasions. In October 1975, shortly before his death, he published in the journal *Il Mondo* a "Lutheran Letter" addressed to Calvino. The arguments were the same. A new monoculture had been created by changing the ways of production that had destroyed earlier cultures belonging to the old middle class and poorer social classes—those that were popular in the first place. For Pasolini it was literally a question of cultural genocide. The contrast between two of the greatest literary figures of the Italian twentieth century was reinterpreted and raised to a critical paradigm towards the end of the twentieth century. Within this paradigm (see Benedetti, *Pasolini contro Calvino*), Calvino was considered as pro-institutional, and Pasolini an emblem of the committed and free writer. This paradigm, however, experienced alternative fortunes. Calvino and Pasolini, although belonging to the same political area, at least at the beginning, represented two different interpretations of modernity which, in turn, tells us about the profound political and cultural mood of a country with perhaps the most complex articulated history in Europe. Italy was a country both agricultural and industrial, laic and religious—with a very polarized recent political past, trying, with great difficulty, to amalgamate those diversities. Calvino's and Pasolini's feelings were not random, and nor were their different approaches to criticism. To a certain extent, the discourses and counter-discourses that their works represent had to deal with the discourses and counter-discourses of the criticism. Calvino, who, in 1956, left the ranks of the Communist Party, seemed obsessed by the relationship with literary criticism to the point of writing and rewriting several forewords and afterwords to address, or prevent, unwelcome critical interpretations.

If it were not for the deep passion and the continuous and consistent program that stand out in the themes he dealt with following the publication of *La giornata dello scrutatore* (*The Watcher and Other Stories*), he might appear to have taken voluntary refuge in literary heights less accessible to the ideological readings of either of the critiques.[16] More recently, this paradigm has been reintroduced by Alessia Ricciardi in *After La Dolce Vita*.[17] Ricciardi explains the cultural circumstances that led to Berlusconi's rise, tracing in Calvino, Vattimo, Bonito Oliva, and other writers, artists, and philosophers of the first order a gradual withdrawal from the non-conformist fight conducted and represented by Pasolini and Fellini.

On closer inspection, the distance between Calvino and Pasolini at the beginning of their careers was not so evident. Events that occurred in Italy in the 1950s and 1960s suffered from unpredictable acceleration and major changes followed one another. Literature and the cinema record them and often participated directly. The first Calvino, the young writer, is seen by critics as a neorealist; while the mature one, the Calvino who has left his imprint on European and Western culture, is a symbol—if not the *very* symbol—of postmodernism. Fellini began working as an assistant to the father of neorealism, Rossellini, but his films have pointedly outstripped the concept. Pasolini, instead, retains his profile as a radical critic of the economic and cultural system that took root in Italy after the war. The dominant economic and cultural project revolved around the profile of a national man (the Italian)[18] who was middle-class and urban. Pasolini focused on those who were excluded; whereas Calvino appeared to be more interested in those who were transformed. The latter, however, also had the same concerns. In *La speculazione edilizia* (Calvino, *The Construction Speculation*), Quinto, a former partisan, returned to his village on the Ligurian coast and recorded the same, as it were, anthropological mutations:

Chapter Seven

> [...] la coscienza d'essere un cattivo proprietario, che non sa far fruttare i propri averi e che in un'epoca di continui avventurosi movimenti di capitali, millantati crediti e giri di cambiali se ne sta mani in mano lasciando svalutare i suoi terreni. Così egli riconosceva che in tanta sproporzionata cattiveria della nazione contro una famiglia priva di redditi agiva con logica luminosa quello che in linguaggio curiale suole chiamarsi "l'intendimento del legislatore": colpire i capitali improduttivi, e chi non riesce o non ha voglia di farli fruttare ben gli sta.
>
> [...] the awareness of being a bad owner, who does not know how to profit from his own assets and that in an age of constant adventurous capital movements, influence peddling and remittances, is sitting idly by letting his land lose its value. So he recognized that, in such disproportionate wickedness of the nation against a family with no income, he acted with clear logic in what, in curial language, is usually called "the intention of the legislator": attacking the unproductive capital, and those who cannot or do not want to make a profit must put up with it. (*La speculazione edilizia* 26)

Calvino spoke of the new man—already an ex-partisan—but not without irony. His temporary militancy in the Communist Party and his undoubted familiarity with Soviet events and the prototype of their new man must certainly be taken into account when seeking to understand thoroughly his bitterness for the drift of events in Italy. "La squallida invasione del cemento aveva il volto camuso e informe dell'uomo nuovo Caisotti" ("The squalid cement invasion had the flat and shapeless face of the new man Caisotti") (*La speculazione edilizia* 27), wrote Calvino. Quinto and Caisotti were both partisans. Caisotti was a new unscrupulous capitalist, whilst Quinto wanted to leave the ranks of the old bourgeoisie and the intellectual dynasties of the Ligurian province that, according to him, were about to go to pieces. He wanted to sell to Caisotti and, to avoid succumbing to xxx, reinvest quickly. The winning model was the scheming capitalist, corrupt and unscrupulous; an expression of a new bourgeoisie "antiestetica" and "antimorale" ("unaesthetic" and "amoral"). Calvino wrote that, after the war, part of Italy had experienced well-being; the result of industrial production. It was, however, a well-being that was dissimilar in an unbalanced national economy that was full of contradictions, and especially with regards to the geographic distribution of income. The owners of small industries in the north—corporate executives, bank managers, traders, and so on—an intermediate class between the holders of large blocks of shares and simple employees, now poured onto the Ligurian coast. The richest were only passing through, whilst the army of typists and accountancy employees stayed longer in small local hotels. However, after the holiday period, the old people spent the winter there: parents, grandparents, and in-laws.

De Gasperi had died, and the bourgeoisie who, though never finding him sympathetic, had found him useful for a while and who "pochi anni innanzi lo salutava suo salvatore, restauratore dei suoi facili agi" ("only a few years before had greeted him as a savior, restorer of its easy comforts") (*La speculazione edilizia* 108), had already forgotten him. The post-war period with its uncertainties and fears is finished. Italy has turned the page and is coping with the contradictory well-being, and with the amorality of the new bourgeoisie that has cast aside even those "virtù" ("virtues") that the elderly believed in, "conservatrice," "onesta," "senza slanci" and "senza fantasia" ("conservative," "honest," "without impetus" and "unimaginative").

The debate triggered by Pasolini over the new technological language and dialects obviously also involved Calvino, whose net positions clearly explain a point of view that was consistently held throughout his work. Pasolini, who at first denied the existence of Italian as a spoken language in general use, as we have seen, changed his opinion. For him, Italian has now begun to exist as a language "di produzione e consumo" ("of production and consumption") which privileges communication at the expense of expressiveness. Calvino did not hold back and responded with two articles: "L'italiano, una lingua tra le altre lingue" and "L'antilingua" ("Italian, a language among other languages" and "The anti-language") (*Una pietra sopra* 119–20). For Calvino, the Italian situation must be considered alongside other languages. It is the linguistic framework, with respect to the needs of modern civilization, which is problematic. This is also true for many languages—from Russian to Spanish, from French to German—while other language areas such as Africa and Asia face deeper problems. Italian, for Calvino, was an isolated language; untranslatable, and one which, in popular speech, wanders off immediately into localism and dialect and which, as a written language, when "uno va più forte nell'usare termini provenienti da "codici" diversi (come Pasolini che ne fa un minuzioso "collage" nazionale e internazionale) per farsi tradurre avrebbe bisogno d'una nota a ogni parola." ("one goes too far with the use of words coming from different 'codes' (as Pasolini, who makes a detailed national and international 'collage') to be translated would need a note for every word") (*Una Pietra sopra* 119). According to Calvino, anyone who wrote to communicate must take into consideration the degree of translatability, that of communicability (does the "technological" Italian mentioned by Pasolini exist?). The adaptability of Italian, Calvino responds, its terminology that "vuol essere specialistica senza riuscire a essere univoca, e una sintassi ramificata e sinuosa fanno di questo linguaggio uno strumento utile più a non dire che a dire." ("wants to be a specialized one without being unique, and a branched and sinuous syntax, therefore making this language a useful tool, with more to not say than to say") (*Una pietra sopra* 120). The Italian language should develop as a "concreta e precisa" ("concrete and precise") language. Otherwise, over time, it would disappear. It will not survive if it fails to become "una lingua strumentalmente moderna" ("an instrumentally modern language"). This is precisely the point. It is their attitudes towards the country's modernization that separates Pasolini from Calvino. Calvino insisted that modernity outstripped the functionality of the dialects which were once perfectly organic to their contexts:

> Mi si può obiettare che il linguaggio—diciamo così—tecnico-meccanico è solo una terminologia; lessico, non lingua. Rispondo: più la lingua si modella sulle attività pratiche, più diventa omogenea sotto tutti gli aspetti, non solo, ma pure acquista "stile." Finché l'italiano è rimasto una lingua letteraria, non professionale, nei dialetti (quelli toscani compresi, s'intende) esisteva una ricchezza lessicale, una capacità di nominare e descrivere i campi e le case, gli attrezzi e le operazioni dell'agricoltura e dei mestieri che la lingua non possedeva. La ragione della prolungata vitalità dei dialetti in Italia è stata questa. Ora, questa fase è superata da un pezzo: il mondo che abbiamo davanti,—case e strade e macchinari e aziende e studi, e anche molta dell'agricoltura moderna—è venuto su con nomi non dialettali, nomi dell'italiano, o costruiti su modelli dell'italiano, oppure d'una inter-lingua scientifico-tecnico-industriale, e vengono adoperati e pensati in strutture logiche italiane o interlinguistiche. Sarà sempre di più questa lingua operativa a decidere le sorti generali della lingua.

> It can be argued that language, so to speak, as much as it is technical-mechanical, is only terminology, a lexicon, not a language. I say that the more language is modeled on practical activities, the more homogeneous in all respects it becomes, not only this but it also acquires "style." For as long as Italian has remained a literary, and not a professional language, there was a rich vocabulary in dialects (including those from Tuscany, of course), and an ability to name and describe fields and houses, the tools and operations of agriculture and trades that the language did not have. This has been the reason for the long-term vitality of dialects in Italy. For some time now this phase has been surpassed: the world before us—houses and roads and machinery and companies and practices, and also a lot of modern agriculture—has produced names not in dialect, Italian names, or built on Italian models, or on a scientific-technical-industrial inter-language and are used and designed in logical Italian or interlinguistic structures. This will increasingly be the operating language that will decide the general fate of the language. (*Una pietra sopra* 124)

In this passage, published in 1965, the *ars poetica* that accompanied Calvino throughout his life is found. An instrumentally modern inter-language, concise, accurate—as the Calvino of *Le lezioni americane* (*Six Memos for the Next Millennium*) would say—does not deal with dialects "but [...] foreign languages." Calvino was perfectly aware of the phenomenon's contradictions, so he resorted to a solution that, in today's terminology, we call "*glocal.*" "Le mie previsioni sono queste: ogni lingua si concentrerà attorno a due poli: un polo di immediata traducibilità nelle altre lingue con cui sarà indispensabile comunicare, tendente ad avvicinarsi a una sorta di interlingua mondiale ad alto livello; e un polo in cui si distillerà l'essenza più peculiare e segreta della lingua, intraducibile per eccellenza, e di cui saranno investiti istituti diversi come l'argot popolare e la creatività poetica della letteratura." ("These are my predictions: every language will focus on two poles: a pole of immediate translatability into other languages which are indispensable for communication, inclined to get closer to a kind of high-level world inter-language, and a pole where the most peculiar and secret essence of language is distilled, untranslatable *par excellence*, and in which diverse institutions such as popular slang and the poetic creativity of literature will be invested") (*Una pietra sopra* 125). This is the horizon that Calvino

Chapter Seven

longed for. The international perspective was, moreover, essential in the aims of Communist thought that had characterized his youth. Even his cosmopolitanism was a natural consequence of that, while modernization's support for the urgent redemption of the backwardness of the old agricultural economy, as we saw in the previous chapter, was the approach energetically (and dramatically) embarked upon, not surprisingly, by the same Soviet camp. Calvino's enlightened and modern sensitivity was the deep impulse of all his work.

Pasolini's attitude with respect to modernity was very different. He, for his part, devoted a large portion of his work to the density of these changes. In *Lutheran Letters* there is a summary of his thinking and second thoughts. In this summary his conclusions about the new prototype of Italian are fairly clear. The selection of the new cultural profile, according to Pasolini, occurred on different bipolar levels: center–periphery, north–south, middle-class–workers, and developed countries–third-world citizens—farmers. The center of the city, the north, the west, the middle class are the today and the tomorrow. The rest are the past, the yesterday.

> Fuori dall'Italia, nei paesi "sviluppati"—specialmente in Francia—ormai i giochi sono fatti da un pezzo. È un pezzo che il popolo antropologicamente non esiste più. Per i borghesi francesi, il popolo è costituito dai marocchini o dai greci, dai portoghesi o dai tunisini. I quali, poveretti, non hanno altro da fare che assumere al più presto il comportamento dei borghesi francesi. E questo lo pensano sia gli intellettuali di destra che di sinistra, allo stesso identico modo. (*Lettere luterane* 35)

> Outside Italy, in the 'developed' countries—especially in France—the game has been up for some time. For some time, people have not existed anthropologically. For the French bourgeoisie the people consist of Moroccans or Greeks, Portuguese or Tunisians, who, poor things, can do no other than assume the behavior of the French bourgeoisie as quickly as possible. And that is what intellectuals—whether of the Right or the Left, think in an identical way. (*Lutheran Letters* 51)

Pasolini started from the outskirts of Rome and turned his gaze to the entire city, and thence to the whole of Italy, and finally the whole world. The judgment was unique: it was genocide on a global scale. It was, at the beginning, a cultural genocide that then turned into a veritable genocide. Pasolini seemed to be convinced that the tragic contradictions of the last World War were still in place, and that all were chargeable to imperialism. It was through this lens that the first decades after the war in Italy were read. The genocide of the Second World War, according to him, continues. Although in mitigated form, the goal has not changed. He was straightforward about this. "Lo Yemen non è ancora che un piccolo, anzi infimo, mercato per le industrie occidentali. Quindi è disprezzato e oggettivamente ridicolizzato. Il suo sfacelo pare naturale. Il fatto che esso richiede un'abiura da parte degli yemeniti pare agli speculatori tedeschi e italiani qualcosa di perfettamente naturale: gli yemeniti devono essere del tutto consenzienti a proposito del loro genocidio: culturale e fisico, anche se non necessariamente mortale, come nei lager" (*Lettere luterane* 19; "Yemen is still only a small, a tiny, market for Western industries. Therefore, it is scorned and ridiculed. Its disintegration seems natural. The fact that this requires a renunciation on the part of the Yemenites seems perfectly natural to German and Italian speculators; the Yemenites must agree without reservations to the propositions of their cultural and physical genocide—even if it is not mortal—just as in the concentration camps"; *Lutheran Letters* 32). Not only did Pasolini draw a parallel with the concentration camps, but he used the precise terminology that we saw in the previous chapter. "[…] i sergenti e i militari di carriera in genere, sono "esseri umani come gli altri": ma qui c'è una petizione di principio. I cosiddetti "altri" sono davvero "esseri umani"? Il mutamento antropologico in atto non ne sta facendo per caso dei "sottouomini"?" (*Lettere luterane* 39; "I suppose that regular sergeants and soldiers in general are 'human beings like the rest'," but here he begs the question "Are the so-called 'rest' really 'human beings'? Is the anthropological mutation which is taking place not turning them by chance into '*subhumans*'"; *Lutheran Letters* 57).

There were, in Agamben's analysis, the concentration camps that gradually stripped man of all his layers. However, the concentration camps were nothing more than a horrible laboratory for the manufacture of non-humans, which suggests that the intention of applying, later, the results on a large scale. It is the same Pasolini who was the first to draw a parallel between what he called "cultural genocide" and Nazism:

Chapter Seven

> In Accattone tutto ciò è rappresentato fedelmente (e si vede soprattutto se si legge Accattone in un certo modo, escludendo la presenza del mio estetismo funebre). Tra il 1961 e il 1975 qualcosa di essenziale è cambiato: si è avuto un genocidio. Si è distrutta culturalmente una popolazione. E si tratta precisamente di uno di quei genocidi culturali che avevano preceduto i genocidi fisici di Hitler. Se io avessi fatto un lungo viaggio, e fossi tornato dopo alcuni anni, andando in giro per la "grandiosa metropoli plebea," avrei avuto l'impressione che tutti i suoi abitanti fossero stati deportati e sterminati, sostituiti per le strade e nei lotti, da slavati, feroci, infelici fantasmi. Le SS di Hitler, appunto. I giovani—svuotati dei loro valori e dei loro modelli—come del loro sangue—e divenuti larvali calchi di un altro modo d'essere e di concepire l'essere: quello piccolo borghese. (*Lettere luterane* 78)

> In *Accattone* all this is faithfully reproduced (and one sees it above all if one reads *Accattone* in a certain way that excludes the presence of my gloomy aestheticism). Between 1961 and 1975 something essential changed: a genocide took place. A whole population was culturally destroyed. And it is a question precisely of one of those cultural genocides which preceded the physical genocides of Hitler. If I had taken a long journey and had returned after several years, walking through the 'grandiose inhabitants' had been deported and exterminated, replaced in the streets and blocks of houses by washed-out, ferocious, unhappy ghosts. Hitler's SS, in fact. The young boys, deprived of their values and their models, like their blood right, have become ghostly copies of a different way and concept of life—that of the middle class. (*Lutheran Letters* 101–02)

Pasolini seems to suggest here, that the men of yesterday were not those of today—and that men are only those of today. In other words, men are the sons and not the fathers. History has, in this view, suddenly accelerated, and the concept of man becomes a concept of time. Post-war changes were so profound that the new generation, brought up differently, fed differently, dressed differently, speaking differently, and with new cultural and political beliefs, appeared to be the zero generation of another species. Even men in the West, albeit with different features to Eastern men, seem new. Pasolini, who called himself part of the generation of fathers, felt excluded. The pain and trauma were profound.

The ideological perspective on these issues, anthropological so to speak, has a very profound and lasting importance, more than one might suspect. It is about a vision that starts from the outskirts of Rome and then extends to Africa, to Yemen, and to all the rest of the world. It implies the denial of the right to certain implicit standards of life to entire populations that, in the name of respect for others, are treated as natural reserves of diversity and plurality (Pasolini, for example, calls his contemporary Yemenis "clowns").[19]

Pasolini should certainly be recognized for the great merit of having raised the issue. The sustained rhythms of change triggered by the processes of modernization caused an unedited fracture. The transformed generation was so different from the previous one as to seem, and to be in fact, profoundly 'other'. To Pasolini, Italian did not seem to be both Neapolitan and Italian but simply Italian. In the USSR, however, the question became really dramatic. It was the farmer (and not only he) who became a new man, not his son. The fracture happened between today's self and yesterday's self. The significance of the question remains of great importance if one considers that this tension between modern and non-modern, along with other cultural and religious differences projected on a global scale, was problematically categorized in the 1990s as the "clash of civilizations" by Samuel P. Huntington.

The new post-national dynamics taking place, and the devastation of the space and time categories are open to different possible scenarios. In the third part of this work, dedicated to the issues of globalization, today's articulated reading of modernity in Italy is compared with the different approaches and expectations of modernity of migrant groups from different backgrounds. Pasolini's influence in Amelio's and Celati's filmic and written representations are highlighted.

Chapter Eight

Different Readings of Pasolini

Pasolini's assassination and the interpretation of his late work

Pasolini was murdered near Rome on 2 November 1975 on the beach at Ostia. Giuseppe Pelosi, a male prostitute then 17 years old, confessed to the murder but, in 2005, retracted his confession. The circumstances of Pasolini's murder continue to be a matter of heated debate in Italian society. Pasolini's tragic death caused a deep and lasting impression in Italy and somehow merged into perceptions of his own work and especially his unfinished novel, *Petrolio* (*Oil*) (published 17 years later, in 1992), and the movie *Salò o le 120 giornate di Sodoma* (*Salò, or the 120 Days of Sodom*) which was released three weeks after his death. Carla Benedetti, also author of *Pasolini contro Calvino, Per una letterattura impura* and, with Giovanni Giovanetti, in *Frocio e basta: Pasolini, Cefis, Petrolio* (*Just a Faggot: Pasolini, Cefis, Petrolio*) investigated both the meaning of Pasolini's work and the mystery of his death in the light of his tragic assassination in 1975. This latter book is divided in two, and most likely written in this order by, respectively, Benedetti and Giovanetti, with the first half investigating perceptions of the late Pasolini's work, both the posthumous novel *Petrolio* and the film *Salò o le 120 giornate di Sodoma* among Italian scholars, writers and journalists. The second half is written as a pure journalistic investigation within the political and judicial events of contemporary Italy—its conclusion supports the suggested paradigm of how to read the Pasolini of the first half: "Pasolini non è stato quindi ucciso da un "ragazzo di vita" poiché omosessuale, bensì da sicari armati dai poteri, occulti o meno, in quanto oppositore a conoscenza di verità scottanti, per di più in grado di divulgarle con autorevolezza anche dalle pagine di un quotidiano nazionale" ("Pasolini was not killed by 'a street kid' because of his homosexuality, but by hired killers by obscured forces, as an opponent who had learned important truths and who was in a position to authoritatively make them known on the pages of any national daily") (Benedetti and Giovannetti 89).

The first part of the book gives a detailed account of essays, articles, and other writings by Italian scholars, writers, poets and journalists who downplay the importance of Pasolini's late work by highlighting the fact that his sexual (homosexual) life had deeply impacted upon his work and was the reason for his violent death. "Lo scenario sessuale affascinò e continua ad affascinare molti anche per ragioni simboliche e estetiche. Al movimento gay conveniva di fare di Pasolini l'emblema della violenza subita dagli omosessuali nella nostra società. A gran parte del mondo della cultura permise di tessere molti bei ricami sia sullo 'scandalo' dell'omosessualità, sia sulla morte sacrificale del poeta..." ("The sexual scenario fascinated and continues to fascinate many, also for symbolic and aesthetic reasons. For the gay movement it allowed Pasolini to be turned into an emblem of the violence suffered by homosexuals in our society. For a large part of the world of culture it enabled the weaving of many beautiful embroideries both on the 'scandal' of homosexuality, and on the sacrificial death of the poet ...") (Benedetti and Giovannetti 9–10).

One of that list of scholars, journalists, and writers is Giuseppe Zigaina, for whom "It was a 'liturgical death' organized by Pasolini himself to build his own myth" (Benedetti and Giovannetti 11). For the poet Eduardo Sanguineti, the movie *Salò o le 120 giornate di Sodoma* and the novel *Petrolio* were "documents" of a private despair, whose "sadomastic depth" had now exploded into a clear pathology (Benedetti and Giovannetti 13). According to Benedetti and Giovannetti, important critics and intellectuals like Alberto Asor Rosa and Toni Negri aimed their critical remarks at "delegittimare la sua voce, a renderla ideologicamente sospetta ('reazionario,' 'nostalgico del passato,' 'nemico del progresso,' affetto da 'populismo estetico')" ("delegitimizing his voice, making it ideologically suspect ('reactionary,' nostalgic for the past,' 'the enemy of progress,' 'suffering from aesthetic populism'") (Benedetti and Giovannetti 31). The long list of Pasolini's detractors mentioned in this book includes Pietro Citati, Emmanuele Trevi, and Marco Belpoliti. Bendetti and Giovannetti do not mention other critics of Pasolini outside of Italy—most importantly Foucault and Barthes—who considered Pasolini's last film "a conceptual failure" (Annoni 176). However, there are many of Pasolini's supporters who are also important scholars, critics, filmmakers, and writers who are not mentioned in the list. The study reconstructs the political battle led by the former leader of the Italian Democratic Party and former Mayor of Rome, Walter Veltroni, who sought to reopen the investigation into Pasolini's death. It goes on to talk of the movie *Pasolini, un delitto italiano* (*Pasolini, an Italian Crime*) which was dedicated to Pasolini's assassination and directed by Marco Tulio Giordana.

Someone who provides a different opinion on Pasolini's late work and its perception is Armando Maggi who, in *The Resurrection of the body*, laments that, in Italy, critics tend to underestimate the importance of homosexuality in Pasolini's work. "If a study published in Italy does mention Pasolini's homosexual identity, it is almost exclusively in connection to his love for the men of the borgate. His homosexuality is an objective, biographical datum, not something worth critical investigation" (348). Maggi intended to fill this gap with his book which, as the author suggests, goes beyond Pasolini in investigating the context of a contemporary debate where "the subject himself" (253) becomes the new *political* battlefield (the italics are Maggi's). Maggi points out in the Introduction that, in his study, he "investigates the myth of Sodom through an analyses of the Italian artist's final creations" (3). The subject as a new *political* battlefield is relevant for the context of the transitional human being. Maggi means specifically the subject's sexual orientation while, in this work, I continue to discuss the subject from different points of view. Before looking into the insights provided by this debate, it is useful to position my work within the simplified reading paradigms of Pasolini's work. "The insistence on Pasolini's political prophecies is especially evident in the studies published in Italy, whereas the Anglo-American academy tends to see Pasolini primarily as an original filmmaker who also wrote books. For some scholars less familiar with the Italian culture, Pasolini is the author of one and only one film, *Salò*. I do not believe Pasolini's legacy lies in his troubled Marxist views" (Maggi 4).

Categorization of the approaches to Pasolini's work provides an opportunity to clarify the lenses through which I read Pasolini.

Chapter Eight

In my reading of Pasolini I move close to the first two paradigms mentioned and criticized by Maggi which, in my view, are not so different. Pasolini as a filmmaker is still the same anti-consumerist and apocalyptical Pasolini as he is in his writings. Since urbanization and its deep impacts on post-war Italy and the West are a central aspect for this book, I read both Pasolini and his interpretation from this perspective. Italy's double soul as both a rural and one of the world's most advanced industrialized countries is mirrored perfectly in Pasolini's work. His deep affection for the rural countryside, both for the past and the present, for a way of life, for its culture, for dialects, for beautiful landscapes, for concrete people, and for friends and relatives, (all of which suffer from the expansion of urbanization which has been associated in the recent historical phase with capitalism and consumerism) monopolizes the reading of Pasolini's work, and transforms it into a vantage point from which to criticize the excesses, the dysfunctionalities, and all the negative sides of contemporary Western modernity.

This aspect is easily extendable beyond Italy, as Pasolini did, sometimes creating misunderstandings and ideological barriers when facing other cultures and contexts; especially non-Western ones. The impact of his work on Italian culture, because of Italy's and many other countries' dual natures, is important. If there is a new suggestion about another perspective to consider while reading Pasolini in my book, it may be found in that (utopian) part of his ideology of representation which goes beyond Italian geography and culture. This perspective, however, moves close to what Maggi calls, in reading Pasolini, "the main Italian paradigm" and can be seen as an extension that involves a reverse point of view. Pasolini looks with hope to the "extra-modernity," i.e. to what is geographically and culturally a territory outside modernity, and feels very disappointed when the people of this territorial extra-modernity are attracted by modernity. This perspective of reading Pasolini is of particular help in explaining the logic that inspires the third part of this volume.

The subject as the new political battlefield

My interest in *Salo' o le 120 giornate di Sodoma* is related to the focus of the debate on the subject as the new *political* battlefield through this movie and Pasolini's late work interpreted mostly from this perspective. Armando Maggi's *The Resurrection of the Body* and Mario Mieli's *Elementi di critica omosessuale* are central to discussing these topics.

Pasolini's *Salò o le 120 giornate di Sodoma* (*Salò, or the 120 Days of Sodom*), which is usually referred to simply as *Salò*, is a loose adaptation of the book *The 120 Days of Sodom, or the School of Libertinage* by the Marquis de Sade, and was set by Pasolini during World War II at the time of the Fascist Republic of Salò (1943–1945). Four wealthy Italian libertines kidnap 18 teenagers—nine males and nine females. The film, structured as a Dantesque hell, narrates four months of rape, sadism, torture, and murder. Four women tell stories to inflame the fantasies of the present, while a series of rapes (among which sodomy dominates), tortures and humiliations—like defecating and eating excrement—are performed on the young victims. The release of this dystopian and, for many, horror movie, coincided fatally with the last tragic episode of Pasolini's life, overlapping the lasting deep impression that the author's death had on his contemporaries, with the perception of his late work as also being very dark and tragic. According to Sergio Citti, who contributed to the screenplay, and quoted in Benedetti's and Giovannetti's *Frocio e basta*, a possible reason for Pasolini's presence at Ostia at the time of his assassination is that Pasolini could have been looking for some stolen footage from his movie.

Salò o le 120 giornate di Sodoma investigates a continuity between historical Fascism and contemporary consumerism, individualizing a sort of techno-Fascism which makes the movie land into a dystopian territory—not quite historical, and not quite contemporary. Whilst this dystopian territory is perfect for the movie-essay that Pasolini wanted to create, it also creates many ambiguities which do not adequately represent either of the contexts. As Barnaba Maj, in the article "Old and new fascism and the 'question of sadism' in *Salò*" correctly observes, using "this historical material as a vehicle for understanding the so-called new fascism is an excess, which unfortunately produces a double opacity, both on historical facts and on the contemporary universe to which the allegory alludes" (59). Pasolini's film, concludes Maj, ends up by not departing from the traditional lines of both Italian literature and cinema that elude the problem of the relationship between Italian society and its Fascist past, that is, "the profound

Chapter Eight

questions on its historical—and mythological, ideological, social and political matrices" (62).

This film shares many of the coordinates of Pasolini's thought as expressed in the 1970s. Pasolini's radical critique of modernity is in need of a distant (mythical) territory, both geographically and/or temporally speaking, in which to postulate and project a different reality, a Pasolinian utopia where desire, young bodies, and violence are articulated in a radically different way compared to the consumerist present. His "movie-essay," as Fabio Benincasa in his "The Bibliography of *Salò*. Eros, Sadism and Avant-Garde in Pier Paolo Pasolini's Last Work" defines it, displays at its start an "essential bibliography" the main questions of which are answered and debated within the movie. Trying to understand how Pasolini's film interacts with this "essential-bibliography" is a straightforward interpretation suggested by Pasolini himself. At the core of Benincasa's reading of *Salò* is the so-to-speak mainstream understanding of the movie, the thesis of which resembles the Foucauldian notion of bio-power (145). The article highlights the Pasolinian belief that consumerism is annihilating free human subjectivity more radically than ever before (145). Sexuality, desire, joy, neurosis, possession, and violence compose the current political battlefield for shaping and controlling subjectivity. The continuity with Nazi-Fascism on the one hand and the postulation of a remote, mythical society where desire and nature enjoyed greater closeness on the other, are the polarities of Pasolini's analysis. Benincasa reads the movie as a hypertext. The list of authors starts with de Sade and his novel which inspired the movie and, includes among others—literally indicated at the start of the film as "essential bibliography"—: Barthes, Blanchot, de Beauvoir, Klosowoski and Sollers. Pasolini's intended debate with them proves helpful in clarifying the theoretical coordinates of this "movie-essay." In the pre-historical societies imagined by Pasolini, myth was not separated from history (Benincasa 134), could reconcile with desire, and control its disruptive force. "Pasolini's mythical and religious horizon is, if not irrational, at least a pre-rational dimension, related with an unconsciousness seen as an internal force of the human mind" (Benincasa 135).

Pasolini imagined an ideal escape from the modern world. He was attracted from rural archaic civilization, the destruction of which, for Pasolini, meant the destruction of desire and youth.

Conformism today, in Pasolini's view, invades the sphere of sexuality and desire, falsely free, and is now articulated only in quantitative forms of enjoyment. Eros, once the absolute joy of the lumpenproletariat, is now pervaded by neurosis and possession (Benincasa 145).

Salò o le 120 giornate di Sodoma and all of Pasolini's later works are also considered as hypertexts by Armando Maggi. However, several titles of this "essential" bibliography taken into consideration are different, just as the territory of this new *political* battlefield is different and more specific. In *The Resurrection of the Body* the sexual orientation of the subject is in sharp focus. Pasolini, who is undoubtedly one of the most important figures of twentieth-century Italian culture, was not just openly gay but put sexuality at the center of his creativity, especially in the last years of his life, including within important works published or released posthumously. An important aspect of Maggi's book is its ability to connect Pasolini's abstract theories with historical contexts and to translate them, so to speak, into specific events of those years. Reading Pasolini through such a lens becomes an opportunity by which to consider the context of the gay movement in 1970's Italy. Indeed, Maggi who, to some extent, went beyond Pasolini, dedicates the conclusive part of *The Resurrection of the Body* to a comparative reading of Pasolini and Mario Mieli's *Elementi di critica omosessuale*.

"The new human being of Mieli's utopia will be pansexual" (Maggi 18), and sexual liberation, according to Mieli, will lead to a social revolution. *Elementi di critica omosessuale* was published in 1977. I discuss it briefly here because it is relevant both in the context of this volume, and for better understanding Pasolini's later work. Mieli, in his book, analyzes the homosexuals' condition under what he calls "patriarchal capitalism." The main concept of Mieli's analysis and utopia is transsexualism, even though, as Maggi suggests, it should be understood more as pansexualism. Mieli's idea of transsexualism refers to "l'originaria ricchezza polimorfa dell'Eros" ("the original polymorphic richness of Eros") (Mieli 42) which individuals have at the beginning of their lives. The child, according to Mieli, who frequently refers to Freud and Jung and taking critically from their work only the necessary parts of their analyses, has a basic plurality of Eros' tendencies repressed by the system and the education of the new generations. "Il termine transessualità mi sembra il più adatto a esprimere, a un tempo, la pluralità delle tendenze dell'eros e l'ermafroditismo originario e profondo di ogni individuo." ("The term 'transsexuality' seems to me the most suitable to express, at the same time, the plurality of Eros' tendencies and the original and profound hermaphrodism of each individual.") (Mieli 8).

In the context of the sexual revolution of those years, Mieli and the Italian gay movement found inspiration in the United States' Gay Liberation Front of 1969. It was thanks to this movement that an historical awareness of past gay movements was acquired. Although Mieli's target remains capitalism and its alleged generic condition of alienation and repression, he looked back to the Bible and quoted the episodes of Sodom and Gomorrah (59). "Quello che è certo è che tramite il cristianesimo la condanna giudaica dell'omosessualità è giunta fino a noi." ("What is certain—writes Mieli—is that it is through Christianity that the Judaic condemnation of homosexuality has reached us.") (61). The dogma of procreation is, according to him, one of the main reasons for the stance taken by anti-homosexuals. This dogma is, in his view, the only authentic end of sexuality, and is "parte della religione e della cultura patriarcali. È quindi espressione di società maschili, in cui la donna, che è il vero soggetto della riproduzione (l'uomo non genera, scopa), viene repressivamente vincolata a un ruolo subordinato." ("part of the patriarchal religion and culture. It is, therefore, an expression of male societies in which the woman, who is the true subject of reproduction (man does not generate, he fucks), is repressively tied to a subordinate role.") (Mieli 41). Closely related to the dogma of procreation is the demographic aspect which, as shown in Part 1 of this volume, was also very important during Fascism. In the Italy and the West of the 1970s, when Mieli's book was published, it was still seen as a key factor in gender politics. "In ogni caso, possiamo osservare fin d'ora quanto sia assurdo continuare a rifiutare l'omosessualità perché è estranea alla procreazione, quando il pianeta soffre, tra l'altro, a causa della sovrappopolazione. La sovrappopolazione è soprattutto determinata dal repressivo persistere del tabù antigay" ("In any case, we can observe as of now how absurd it is to continue to reject homosexuality because it is extraneous to procreation, when the planet suffers, among other things, due to overpopulation. Overpopulation is mainly determined by insisting the repressive anti-gay taboo") (Mieli 41).

Different Readings of Pasolini

Mieli's main polemical target remains capitalism as a system in which alienation is the term most used to describe, generically, the contemporary human condition. Nevertheless, he continuously looked backwards to make historical statements. As is well known, Fascism, Nazism, and Stalinism exercised brutal persecutions against homosexuals. During Fascism, the Italian island of Ventotene was used as a place of confinement for gay people (72) while, in 1934, Russia, (which had initially adopted a different approach), introduced a law that punished homosexual acts with imprisonment of up to eight years (Mieli 81). Russia's repression of gay people is a major disappointment for Mieli whose ("revolutionary") ideology is a blend of communism and what he calls "transsexualism." The author nevertheless admits that, in the 1970s, the situation in the Soviet Union, Cuba, or Poland was far worse than that it was in England, France, and Italy (82); all of the latter were countries which showed degrees of tolerance towards the rights of gay people. Tolerance, however, is not what Mieli was looking for. The homosexual movement, he explains, was then composed by groups of either revolutionary or integrationalist homosexuals who always contrasted themselves with each other (92). Social tolerance was seen by the former as an unsatisfactory purpose: "la lotta omosessuale rivoluzionaria non ha come obiettivo il conseguimento della tolleranza sociale per i gay, bensì la liberazione del desiderio omoerotico in ogni essere umano." ("The homosexual revolutionary fight—observes Mieli—does not have as a goal the achievement of social tolerance for gay people but, rather, the release of homoerotic desire in every human being.") (63). Heterosexuality, in his view, is determined by the repression of what he calls transsexuality, a sort of richness of sexual impulses in the child that societal repression channels towards heterosexuality (19).

It is within this analytical context that Mieli's concept of schizophrenia should also be understood. Neurosis, according to Mieli's reading of Freud, is what distinguishes human beings from animals (Mieli 169). Our society today, he notes, is both neurotic and schizoid because individuals are "alienato da sé, dal mondo e dagli altri ad opera del capitale." ("alienated from themselves, from the world and from the others by capital.") (Mieli 170). From this perspective, schizophrenia becomes normal, and normality becomes schizophrenic. In the condition of schizophrenia "i falsi

Chapter Eight

confini si disintegrano... gli schizofrenici soffrono della verità." ("false boundaries are disintegrated ... schizophrenics suffer from the truth." (Mieli 173). This truth, signaled by the condition of neurosis, seems to be the perception of transsexuality by individuals themselves and 'others' (Mieli 180).

Mieli often refers to Pasolini and to Pasolini's sources, including de Sade. He published his book—*Elementi di critica omosessuale* in 1977 and it closely reflects the political and cultural climate in which Pasolini produced his later works. The episode of Pasolini's death is used conveniently, as Benedetti and Giovannetti observe, quoting exponents of the Italian gay movement to highlight the conditions in which many homosexuals found themselves in 1970's Italy. The clamor of Pasolini's assassination also exposed to public attention some lesser-known aspects of that situation. "Pasolini è stato ammazzato in quella *situazione* perché era omosessuale, perché soltanto gli omosessuali possono trovarsi in situazioni del genere. E—come dice il comunicato del Fuori!—in situazioni *del genere*, di omosessuali ne vengono uccisi ogni giorno." ("Pasolini was murdered in that *situation* because he was homosexual, because only homosexuals put themselves in such a situation. And—as it is written in the statement of Fuori!—in *such* situations, homosexuals are killed every day.") (Mieli 152).

Besides the episode of his assassination, Pasolini's work and his being one of the most important exponents of twentieth-century Italian culture who was also openly gay were important to Mieli. Armando Maggi places the figure of the mother at the center of Pasolini's later work paradigm. This is why it is important to consider another interesting aspect of *Elementi di critica omosessuale* that revolves around the figure of the mother. Mieli refers to the Freudian interpretation of male homosexuals' puberty and their identification with the mother. He remains skeptical about this conclusion because his transsexualism considers their identification with both the mother and the father important for homosexual individuals. Nevertheless, the Freudian interpretation reminded him of Pasolini's poem of 1964, "Supplica a mia madre" (Prayer to my Mother) (Mieli 43), without trying to interpret it. According to Mieli, whose ideology is transsexualism, one thing was certain: "l'amore vero per la madre impedisce a un uomo di accettare la norma eterosessuale che è offesa, aggettivazione e oppressione della donna." ("true love for the mother prevents a man from accepting the heterosexual Norm that is an offense, objectification and oppression of the woman.") (46).

Pasolini, on the other hand, denounced the 1968 movements as being too close to power. Even the sexual revolution should be seen through the lens of consumerism because, according to Pasolini, it contributed to the turning of the human body into a field of possession. He went so far as to consider the new freedom to approach young men that women enjoyed as a form of prostitution. "The new female prostitution, according to Pasolini's dubious idea, prevents heterosexual men from 'exploring' with other men, namely homosexuals, who used to get some sex thanks to the seclusion of women. The homosexual now sees his identity challenged and jeopardized by the alleged sexual revolution" (Maggi 336). These ideas can be directly traced in *Salò o le 120 giornate di Sodoma*. Pasolini himself, in a television interview of 1975 on the film set of *Salò*, considered his movie as a metaphor of what power can do to the human body, commodifying and transforming it into a thing—"Il Manifesto di Marx dice proprio questo: cioè il potere mercifica i corpi, trasforma il corpo in merce." ("Marx's Manifesto states precisely this: the power commodifies the bodies, transforms them into goods.") (Pasolini in Benedetti and Giovannetti 13). However, Armando Maggi considered the interpretation of the film as simply a metaphor for the universal objectification produced by capitalism (the young bodies used for pleasure and then discarded) and invites us to give the right importance to the "apocalyptic nature of his ideas" (257–58). The apocalyptic nature of many of Pasolini's stances is related, for Maggi, to the myth of Sodom. Maggi, who borrowed from Rocky O'Donovan's short story *Reclaiming Sodom*, considered Sodom "the land of gayness, the place to which gay identity must return to get in touch with its roots" (1). Sodom, however, remains a "burned down place, a landscape of desolation" (3). For Maggi, Pasolini was an ambassador from "this original land of total destruction" (3). However, Pasolini's ideas on sexuality, which endorse a rigorous Freudianism—as we are reminded in *The Resurrection of the Body*—are "questionable and unpersuasive." This rigorous Freudianism also seems to be part of Pasolini's theorizing of the figure of the mother. Past and present, so much polarized in Pasolini's work, come to also signify mother and father. Simply put, what is most positive in Pasolini's perspective, the past, the

Chapter Eight

pre-modern, nature, the men of the borgate—they are the sons—orbit around the figure of the mother; whilst what is corrupt—the present, consumerism, capitalism, the death of dialects and expressive languages—according to Maggi, compose the symbolic order of the father in which the mother is erased. *Political*, in Maggi's reading of Pasolini, describes "the gaze the homosexual subject directs at himself" (253). This "(homosexual) subject who is split" between longing for the mother (the utopian past) and accusing the father (the corrupt present) then becomes the site where the symbolic erases the mother. But it is the absent mother who "reigns in the subject who longs for her" (253). The longing for the pre-modern, dialects, nature, and the young men of the Roman borgate (who, as Maggi reminds us, are the "sons of the mother") takes place in this *political* battlefield. As seems clear at this point, to the usual interpretation of Pasolini—which denounces what can today be called bio-power and also rejects consumerism, and instead longs for a distant utopian time and place—Maggi adds a new *political* layer. The latter discusses the myth of Sodom and opens up the late Pasolini's hypertext to new meanings which are able to connect abstract theorizing to concrete aspects of the historical context of the 1970s. Maggi, for example, finds in the final scenes of *Salò* that are about the completion of a mass murder a direct reference to Pasolini's critical position towards the sexual revolution. The last scene focuses on the young guards. "The two guards flirt a little before dancing, because in any case their brief flirtation does not make them into perverts. These are the men who, before the sexual revolution, let homosexuals please them sexually. These are the men who can engage in homosexual acts without being tainted by them. And of course these men have fiancées, like the Shit in *Petrolio*" (Maggi 338).

In further comparing Mieli's stance with Pasolini's analysis, other significant differences are found. An important part of Pasolini's hypertext which Maggi reads is the unfinished novel *Petrolio*, published in 1992. It is not only its incompleteness that makes this novel hard to interpret. This novel is the critical edition of a lost original and, for Pasolini, neither "lost" nor "original" were casual terms. The aim is not the construction of a story but rather the depiction of a form (Maggi 162), as Pasolini had already done in other works such as the novel *Divina*

Mimesis (*The Divine Mimesis*), and the documentary *Appunti per un'Orestiade Africana* (*Notes for an African Orestes*). Carlo 1 and Carlo 2, the protagonists of *Petrolio,* go through a transsexual transformation. The form of *Petrolio,* according to Maggi, is that of a "textual" fetus, a prebirth form that reveals itself in its perfect "opacity" (160). As we saw in *Salò,* the utopian past is, in some form, always an important part of the representation. The point of convergence—and separation—between past and present in Pasolini's hypertext is, according to Maggi, the condition of schizophrenia. The characters of the novel are schizophrenic; and schizophrenia, in Pasolini's view, is the very condition of the modern human being cut from the past (Maggi 167). Maggi observes that schizophrenia is the form of *Petrolio* itself—"A schizophrenic division, metamorphosis, and loss of the original identity are the essential traits of *Petrolio*" (167). If we follow Maggi's reading, schizophrenia in Pasolini should be seen as a claustrophobic condition, a wall between the subject and reality. In contrast, for Mieli, schizophrenia signals, as previously noted, the perception of transsexualism, of the truth: it *is* the truth.

In looking beyond Pasolini, Armando Maggi historicizes this debate (including Mieli's work), and notes how many concepts have evolved since the 1970s. Among many gay men, identifications such as gay = effeminate or gay = woman—which seem to have somehow influenced, in different and critical ways, Pasolini's and Mieli's stances—are, according to Maggi, a relic of a past culture, as is Mieli's belief that sexual differences matter. "It is simply a fact that, today, "difference" as mental illness or homosexuality has no mysterious or profound meaning and this must be erased. Ours is a time of no negations" (344).

Chapter Nine

Literature as Re-Representation: Calvino and the Encyclopedic Novel

The demystification of literature led Calvino to reconsider its potential, and its role as an important human tool. To borrow a term from Daniel Dennett,[20] literature is one of those "re-representative" techniques that intervene effectively in human perceptions. The peculiarity of Calvino's prose is its open display of literature's nature as a model of possible models; literature is the means by which the human being "experiences" the world's possibilities. Calvino's unique intuition is found in this multi-dimensional and multi-disciplinary representation of a world that should be considered far and wide, at micro and macro levels, in history, and in possibilities. Through his project, Calvino gave his literary discourse two or three major coordinates, as is clear from various interventions: a cosmic speech[21] recalling the fate of the species, as well as an accompanying detailed map which describes the labyrinthine context in which human beings happen to live. According to *Le lezioni americane*, how to transform this vertiginous content in literature and investigate the human condition by means of it is the ultimate ambition that only writers have.[22]

This view of literature is peculiar to Italy and the West after the 1950s. On the one hand, knowledge has exploded in many fields and is, more than ever before, at the disposal of a cultural elite. On the other, the Italian masses need to be educated and provided with a new vision of the world from either a scientific point of view or from the point of view of a new and unified national consciousness. Intellectuals like Rossellini, who used the last part of his life to create a rich body of television productions, felt a strong urge to reach a wide audience and offer pedagogically-determined encyclopedic knowledge.[23] During those years, the centralizing power of the new medium was thoroughly exploited. The beginning of space exploration shook not only the cultural elite but also the full range of public opinion. Intellectuals felt a renewed sense of responsibility and often intervened in the newspapers. Starting in 1968, and inspired by the happenings in Paris, Calvino—along with Gianni Celati, historian Carlo Ginsburg, and the French studies scholar Guido Neri who was the translator and consultant for the Einaudi editions—began planning an interdisciplinary journal that was to be called *Ali Babà*. Although the project was discussed for a long time, it never came to fruition. Calvino intended to reach the general public and feared that *Ali Babà* would not be successful, as has been noted in a monographic edition of the magazine *Riga*.[24] Calvino felt a strong need to include multidisciplinary and encyclopedic knowledge[25] in his literary work. In his non-fiction productions, one notices an avid interest in twentieth-century philosophy, combined with scientific readings ranging from biology to astronomy, and botany to urbanism. A momentous event like the landing on the moon so strongly affected him that he became passionately involved in a debate with Anna Maria Ortese conducted through the newspapers. Despite being a harsh critic of modernity, Calvino also regarded it with unconcealed hope.[26] Not surprisingly, next to Leopardi and Ariosto, in the literary canon that he promoted as a critic and perhaps also as a publisher, he gave most attention to Galileo;[27] a figure also very much loved by Leopardi. Meanwhile, his most beloved city was New York. As with few other writers, the best that the scientific and anthropological disciplines of the period produced (Calvino had, in his family, four university professors, all in the sciences—his father in agronomy, his mother in botany, his brother in geology, and an uncle in chemistry) was transferred to the field of literature, thereby challenging the conventions of existing genres and creating experimental hybrids between non-fiction and fiction. Calvino's stated preference for the short story, which dominated the entire second phase of his career, including *Se una notte d'inverno un viaggiatore* (*If on a Winter's Night a Traveler*) which was composed of blocks of stories), seems to find an explanation in its flexibility, since it is simultaneously open to both non-fiction and fiction.[28]

The short story does not exclude the novel. On the contrary, and as theorized by Calvino, the novel that uses the short story sews together a network of representations and possible parallel universes, thereby shaping a kind of network novel. The network novel, which consists of real and possible worlds, seems to be the best way of holding together an encyclopedic re-description of the world and its potentialities. It is not by chance that Calvino focused time and again on Gadda's *Quer pasticciaccio brutto de via Merulana* (*That Awful Mess on the Via Merulana*). In *Le lezioni americane,* he opened the lesson dedicated to *multiplicity* with a long quotation from *Quer Pasticciaccio.* For Calvino, this novel represented the contemporary novel, which he defined as an open encyclopedia, a "rete di connessione tra i fatti, tra le persone, tra le cose del mondo" ("network connection between the facts, between people, between things in the world") (*Le lezioni americane* 113). But Calvino's open encyclopedia was not a typical encyclopedia born etymologically under the pretense of exhausting knowledge. Today such an approach is no longer possible, which is why the novel exploits the form of an open encyclopedia. "Quella che prende forma nei grandi romanzi del XX secolo è l'idea d'una enciclopedia aperta, aggettivo che certamente contraddice il sostantivo enciclopedia, nato etimologicamente dalla pretesa di esaurire la conoscenza del mondo rinchiudendola in un circolo. Oggi non è più pensabile una totalità che non sia potenziale, congetturale, plurima." ("What takes shape in the great novels of the twentieth century is the idea of an open encyclopedia, an adjective that certainly contradicts the substantive encyclopedia, born etymologically from the claim to exhaust the knowledge of the world shutting it up in a circle.

Today a totality that is not full of potential, conjectural, plural is no longer thinkable.") (*Le lezioni americane* 113). What a great ambition! The world should not be represented simply as it is, or how we think it is. Nor should it be re-read through only one of its aspects. The world can only be represented in the interdependence of its many dwelling facets, to which must be added a field of possible pasts, presents, and futures. The best representation of this interdependent multiplicity for Calvino is the city;[29] the best representation of the latter is the network novel.

While topics like re-representation, the open encyclopedia (which makes possible the re-representation), and the city are constants in his work, Calvino liked to preserve some polarities so that he might use their tension to reach a different dimension and produce new meanings, in addition to "mapping" problematics and not giving in to the "labyrinth" or the "sea of objectivity." The incomplete human being vs the complete human being, the

Chapter Nine

short story vs the network novel, and the fragmented subject vs the network subject are some of the topics that are discussed in this chapter.

The incomplete human being in the city

A warehouse worker, presumably of the Einaudi publishing house where Italo Calvino worked, found mushrooms in the street, ate them, and was poisoned. This relatively unremarkable event prompted Calvino to start drafting *Marcovaldo*, with the subtitle *Le stagioni in città*. The warehouse worker/Marcovaldo/Charlie Chaplin/Candide is a "laborer, father of a large family" who feels foreign to the city. As the author informs us, the city is sometimes Milan, sometimes Turin, but always "the city, any industrial metropolis," and Marcovaldo's origins do not matter. What matters is that all of the city's inhabitants are migrants. "Da dove egli sia venuto alla città, quale sia "l'altrove" di cui egli sente nostalgia non è detto; potremmo definirlo un "immigrato," anche se questa parola non compare mai nel testo; ma la definizione è forse impropria, perché tutti in queste novelle sembrano "immigrati" in un mondo estraneo dal quale non si può sfuggire." ("Where did he come from to the city, what is the 'elsewhere' that he feels nostalgia for, these are not mentioned; we could call him an 'immigrant', although the word never appears in the text; but the definition is perhaps improper because, in these stories, they all seem to be 'immigrants' in an alien world from which there is no escape.") (Calvino, *Marcovaldo* vi). The migrant, alien to the city, is "the citizen par excellence," whose extraneousness is an essential element in this and many other of Calvino's books. Embodying the different layers of this condition, and forming correlates from time to time with some specific phenomena are famous characters: from Charlie Chaplin and *Pinocchio*, to Camus' *L'Etranger* to Marco Polo. Marcovaldo/Marco Polo/Charlie Chaplin/Pinocchio is the contemporary human being who "ha perduto l'armonia tra sé e l'ambiente in cui vive" ("has lost the harmony between himself and the environment in which he lives") (*Marcovaldo* vi). The adjective "incomplete," presents Calvino in the role of a critic of himself, and explains these reflections that had already reached full development in the so-called first part of his work. This is a preface that introduces the collection of works entitled *I nostri an-*

tenati (*Our Ancestors*). The conception of *Il visconte dimezzato* (*The Cloven Viscount*) is driven by the incompleteness of the contemporary human being. The plot of the human's action is an attempt to overcome this disharmony. The "where" is the city. The "how" is, among other things, knowledge (literature, too, has a role). The feature that distinguishes them is obstinacy, not resignation—and this despite Calvino's various bitter observations in other stories that the artificial human being, a resident of our cities, would no longer chafe over anything.

What type of relationship exists between the individual and his or her city is central throughout Calvino's work. "Era sicuro e impenetrabile: in quella specie di sussiego della sua forza, e della sua adesione a un ordine che aveva fatto di lui quello che era" (*La giornata* 83; "He was confident and impenetrable: in that sort of smugness at his strength, his belonging to an order that had made of him what he was"; *The Watcher* 72), writes Calvino in *La giornata d'uno scrutatore*. "La città che moltiplicherà le mani dell'uomo, si chiedeva Amerigo, sarà già la città dell'uomo intero? O l'homo faber vale proprio in quanto non considererà mai abbastanza raggiunta la sua interezza?" (*La giornata* 83; "'Will the city that can multiply man's hands', Amerigo asked himself, 'be already the city of the whole man? Or is *homo faber* valid because he never considers his wholeness sufficiently achieved?'"; *The Watcher* 72). The city that enhances the individual,—whose constitutive incompleteness opens to an unlimited metamorphosis—can thus be seen as an extension of the human being. This double layer remains unresolved in Calvino. As the industrial town can be the extension of the human being, so the human being can become so programmed to resemble advanced machines that, in the end, it becomes superfluous, as in *Il castello dei destini incrociati* (*The Castle of Crossed Destinies*). The relationship between history (knowledge) and the city remains central to the never-resolved relationship that exists between incompleteness and completeness. With regards to question of whether the human being has achieved wholeness, Calvino gives an answer that is more certain than previous ones: the human being has, indeed, not achieved wholeness. It is their very incompleteness that really distinguishes the human being today. Incompleteness and dissatisfaction amount to desire, to a plot of contemporary existence. "E poi: l'umano arriva dove arriva l'amore; non ha confini se non quelli che gli diamo" (*La giornata* 83; "And then: 'Humanity reaches as far as love reaches; it has no frontiers expect those we give it'"; *The Watcher* 64).

Literature, too, has an auspicious role in the dynamic and relentless process of completing the incomplete human being. In the article "Il mare dell'oggettività"—first published in 1959, the year *Il cavaliere inesistente* was published (see Calvino, *Una pietra sopra*), Calvino, faced with the hyper-analytic and hyper-objective trends of our time, passionately defended the preservation of subjective awareness. He dealt with a recent turning point concerning not only literature, but also all cognitive activities, and contemporary dispositions toward the world: "Da una cultura basata sul rapporto e contrasto tra due termini, da una parte la coscienza la volontà il giudizio individuali e dall'altra il mondo oggettivo, stiamo passando o siamo passati a una cultura in cui quel primo termine è sommerso dal mare dell'oggettività dal flusso ininterrotto di ciò che esiste." ("From a culture based on the relationship and contrast between the two terms—on the one hand, the individual awareness, will, judgment and, on the other, the objective world—we are going towards or we have passed to a culture in which the first term is submerged by the sea of objectivity, by the uninterrupted flow of what exists." (*Una pietra sopra* 39). Calvino placed Sartre's novel *La Nausée* (*Nausea*)[30] and the loss of the "I" almost at the start of this turning point; the face in the mirror becomes a thing, and inaugurates a descent into a sea of undifferentiated objectivity. "Ma questa rappresentazione, già completa del processo è compiuta da Sartre restando al di qua, dal punto di vista della coscienza, della scelta, della libertà. Oggi si è dato il giro: il punto di vista è quello del magma" ("But this already complete representation of the process [writes Calvino] is accomplished by Sartre remaining on this side, from the point of view of consciousness, of choice, of freedom. Today things have changed: the point of view is that of magma") (*Una pietra sopra* 40). That is exactly what Calvino rejected through a rapid reading of many novels, including Gadda's *Quer pasticciaccio,* in which Rome is a melting pot of peoples, dialects, civilization, and magnificence and is, accordingly, described with an avalanche of details, though not without a sense of dismay that, to Calvino, is the starting point of a judgment. The representation of the magma, of totality and history, must continue to be possible in literature. "Dalla letteratura dell'oggettività alla letteratura della coscienza: così vorremmo orientare la nostra lettura d'una ingente zona della produzione creativa d'oggi, ora secondando ora forzando l'intenzione degli autori" ("From the literature of objectivity to the literature of conscience, so we would like to direct our reading of a large area of today's creative production, now sometimes favoring it and then sometimes forcing the intention of the authors" (*Una pietra sopra* 45). Representation containing a desire for contrast, a non-acceptance of the given situation, remains a mission for Calvino. As such, part of the human tension between incompleteness and completeness seems to be the problem of representation and the relationship with history, knowledge and truth. Many questions about the relationship between the individual and history are discussed by Sartre in *Critique de la raison dialectique* (*Critique of Dialectical Reason*). "Sartre ripercorre le vie della dialettica di Hegel," writes Gianni Vattimo (14), "il vero è l'intero; e la formazione autentica dell'uomo consiste nel porsi nel punto di vista del tutto." ("Sartre follows the paths of Hegel's dialectic, the true is the whole, and the authentic formation of man consists in taking on the point of view of everything as one's own."). Vattimo argues that today's understanding of "the true" and "the whole" passes through the practice of the critique of ideology. This criticism is not so much a work of uncovering what is hidden but, rather, an effort to reconstruct a non-partial point of view which is able to grasp the totality as such. Ideology is partial thought:

> La Critica della ragion dialettica è una critica nel senso kantiano del termine: cerca di chiarire a quali condizioni è possibile, concretamente, la costituzione di un punto di vista totale, non ideologico. [...] quel che importa dell'analisi di Sartre è il fatto di aver chiarito una volta per tutte (pare a noi) il carattere mitologico delle altre soluzioni del problema della dialettica; anzitutto quella lukacsiana, che attribuiva, con Marx, la capacità di una visione totalizzante del senso della storia al proletariato espropriato in quanto espropriato…
>
> *Critique of Dialectical Reason* is a critique in the Kantian sense of the term: it seeks to clarify under what conditions it is possible, in practice, to establish a total point of view that is not ideological. [...] What matters in Sartre's analysis is the fact of having made clear once and for all (it seems to us) the mythological character of the other solutions to the problem of dialec-

Chapter Nine

> tics; first of all Lukacs' who, with Marx, attributed the ability of a totalizing vision of the meaning of history to the expropriated proletariat because expropriated... (Vattimo 14)

Sartre's essay was published in 1960 but debates over dialectics and history continued for many years. If there is a literary form capable of investigating such issues, that form was, for Calvino, the encyclopedic novel. If there is also a physical space where one tends to place a possible perspective on the total, that space seems to be the city. As Joseph Francese states in *Narrating Postmodern Time and Space*, Calvino's "faith in the capability of reason to encyclopedically embrace the knowable caused him to place the subject at the center of all experience" (17).

If on a Winter's Night: The network novel

Literature has the essential function of re-representing the world; it enlarges and transforms our perception by manipulating the pace of events and finding the correct balance between reinforcements and messages, in order to give attention to the new possibilities offered by the world. Each of our interpretations may be unique because of what we know and what we believe can change. Because, according to Calvino, every story has already begun, and because every story continues, no moment can be isolated from others. Each fragment is part of a set, and everything points to something else. Homer has already existed. *The Book of the Thousand Nights and a Night*[31] as well. In like manner, Dumas has already lived, as has Dostoevsky. Therefore, *Se una notte d'inverno un viaggiatore* consists of 10 unfinished novels to be continued. An unfinished story, like life, like the human being, is to be continued. Each subsequent incarnation of Homer is different but nothing that has previously existed has been lost. The difficulty lies in identifying the extent to which any given part contributes to the unique cultural structure that has delimited the possibilities of perception for individuals. It is simpler to say that the "Father of the stories," the old Indian, seeks to alter his perception by consuming hallucinogenic mushrooms. "Ogni nuovo libro che leggo entra a far parte di quel libro complessivo e unitario che è la somma delle mie letture. Questo non avviene senza sforzo: per comporre quel libro generale, ogni libro particolare deve trasformarsi, entrare in rapporto coi libri che ho letto precedentemente, diventarne il corollario o lo sviluppo o la confutazione o la glossa o il testo di referenza." ("Every new book I read comes to be a part of that overall and unitary book that is the sum of my readings. This does not come about without some effort: to compose that general book, each individual book must be transformed, enter into a relationship with the books I have read previously, become their corollary or development or confutation or gloss or reference text.") (Calvino, *Se una notte d'inverno* 255–56).

Whilst the Calvino of *Se una notte d'inverno* is the Calvino of *Le città invisibili* of *Il castello*, he is also something more. The novel of a thousand and one shades, of a thousand and one messages, is the repetition of every novel already written, from Homer to Dostoyevsky. Yet it is also, ultimately, the novel of re-reflection and re-representation; a circumstance resulting in a new reflection, a new representation, and a new novel. Before reaching the last episodes, the reader often stops; lost between one episode and another. The crisis of perception occurs due to its location on this side of an event horizon that is technically irrepressible from the reader's modest (human) parameters or because it does not find a mainland, as it finds nothing that does not link to something else, which in turn links to something else yet again. The democratization of multiple boundaries pushes the individual to immediately encounter the totality of the world or, at least, evicts them from their familiar environments and throws them into the much promised global village. In the last unfinished novel of this hyper-novel—a very fitting genre for the new hyper-environment!—facing the *Perspective*, the subject decides to thin out his world and reduce it to his own size. Since a starting point is needed as an anchor, not even Calvino can do better than rely on the oldest artifice of human nature: love. Love is both a motivation to start again, and a guarantee of continuity that is more than a new beginning. It does not matter that Guglielmi and Ferretti have accused Calvino of wanting to seduce the average reader with Ludmilla and her marriage; Calvino intended to reach the general public. The appearances of Ludmilla and her stunt women in the unfinished novels intersperse conceptually dense traits, creating stimuli that strengthen attention. Calvino does not hide this technique of writing by any means: through the successive revelation of the readers' affairs, many things gradually evolve, including a complete theory of the novel.

Chapter Nine

When *Se una notte d'inverno* defines the novel as "un ponte nel vuoto che nessuno sa dove conduce" ("a bridge into the void that no one knows where it leads"), Calvino was evidently thinking of the crisis of identity and meaning that occurs in a larger pluralistic context which exceeds and confounds an individual's understanding. Because its logic gives back to us a world made to our measure, a book becomes a good refuge on the "winter nights" when the world is shut out. A coherent logic coming from the reading—even if its specific content does not matter—is transformed into a lifeboat amidst a chaotic sea of ideas and events. For Calvino, such a reading yields both loneliness and an estrangement from the world in which we live. The failure to perceive reality as such due to the hyper-environment, the shattering of individual contexts, and the crisis of meaning are the premises of that sensation of relief that is felt upon reading a book that asserts itself by imposing its logic. This is what must be borne in mind when Calvino defined the novel as "a bridge into the void that no one knows where it leads." We are at the point where what is important is not so much a specific logic, but rather "a" logic; precisely because it is a fiction among fictions. The importance it has for the reader is to be a bridge, a bridge that gives that impression of order and meaning valued by Ludmilla. Calvino alluded to all of this when he defined reading as the absence of the world and loneliness. Beneath this bridge lies a chaotic promiscuity of fragments, dizzy with indiscriminate possibilities, all lethal to the size of our individuality. No one knows, however, where this bridge leads. In an attempt to create a personal balance made up of several ingredients, and in an attempt to escape and live more existences in literature than the world offers, a reader prefers "letture diverse per diverse ore del giorno e letture parallele per evitare delusioni" ("different readings for different hours of a day and parallel readings so as to avoid disappointment") (*Se una notte d'inverno* 308). The book becomes the happening of the world in a possible environment chosen from a vast range of possibilities; an environment habitable by the reader. Let us remember that, in the article "Il mare dell'oggettività," Calvino passionately defends the preservation of subjective awareness. He did not change his mind in this novel. Calvino's reader achieves awareness (only) after journeying through something like *One Thousand and One Nights,* a network novel where all the strange titles compound a logical phrase but one whose full sense lies in an episode not yet read; it is to be found in the following one, in another book. We must keep reading.

Different readings of Calvino

In addition to a large number of American critics, Italian critics such as Ceserani and Berardinelli consider the Calvino of the period after *La giornata d'uno scrutatore* to be a mainstay of postmodern literature. Given that they all find in Calvino a rational and clearly enlightened severity, their observations are followed by many qualifications. Ceserani considers him modern in style and writing but postmodern in themes, like the centerless city, the weakening of subjectivity and even lightness. Although, while treating lightness, the Calvino of *Le lezioni americane* praises as its expression the second industrial revolution, namely computer sciences. In his praise of lightness, Calvino refers directly to science. It is the same Ceserani who recognizes the Enlightenment matrix of Calvino's thought:

> D'altra parte è forse proprio la consistency, a cui doveva essere dedicata la lezione mancante, che ci segnala come la posizione di Calvino restasse, alla fine, peculiare e i irriducibile a tante delle teorie postmoderne correnti: dietro all'idea della coerenza, della fermezza, dell'armoniosa compatibilità fra elementi logici e morali, si intravede il fermo ancoraggio di Calvino a una concezione che potremmo chiamare variamente razionalistica, illuministica, habermasiana, della vita umana e del pensiero.

> On the other hand it is perhaps the consistency, to which the missing lesson was to be dedicated, that shows us how Calvino's position was ultimately tested as unique and irreducible to many of the current postmodern theories: behind the idea of coherence, of firmness, of the harmonious compatibility between moral and logical elements, Calvino's firm anchoring to a concept that we call variously rationalistic, Enlightenmentian, of Habermasian, of human life and thought can be seen.
> (Ceserani 173)

Alessia Ricciardi, in *After La dolce vita: A Cultural Prehistory of Berlusconi's Italy*, makes the Calvinian idea of lightness the pivot of her criticisms. To Ricciardi, Calvinian narration since the time of

Le cosmicomiche propagates an idea of literature as a pleasant show obtained through stylistic variation, from the serial travel stories of *Le città invisibili* to the phenomenological descriptions of *Palomar*. According to Ricciardi, Calvino never broke with modernity.[32] For Joseph Francese (11) as well, Calvino is a late modernist (as is John Barth), and his subject-centric work has more in common with Pirandello, Svevo, and Pessoa; while Elena Gremigni refers to Mark Augé's *Non-lieux* (*Non-Places*) and sees elements of supermodernity, especially in *Marcovaldo* (Gremigni 101–02) and globalization (Gremigni 10), via Bauman, who quotes *Le città invisibili* (*Liquid Life* 4).

Another writer and essayist seen as a symbol of Italian postmodernism is Umberto Eco. Driven by the outcry over the publication of *Il nome della rosa* (*The Name of the Rose*), Eco published *Postille a "Il nome della rosa"* (*Postscript to "The Name of the Rose"*), a text which, from the very start, was intended to enter the debate on postmodernism. The penultimate paragraph of *Postscript*, entitled "Postmodernism, Irony, the Enjoyable," attracted especial attention. For Eco, the postmodern was more a spiritual category or, rather, a *modus operandi*. Each era, he affirmed, had its own modern and its own postmodern. In moments of crisis in history—for example, those described by Nietzsche in the second *Untimely Meditations*—the historical avant-garde attempts to deal with the past.

However, the time comes when the avant-garde (the modern) can go no further because it has produced a meta-language that speaks of its impossible texts (conceptual art). The postmodern reply to the modern consists of recognizing that the past, since it cannot really be destroyed because its destruction would lead to silence, must be revisited—but with irony, not innocently.

Eco borrowed the idea of "l'enunciazione al quadrato" ("double-coding"[33]) from architecture and, adapting it to literature, elaborated a metaphor later taken up by John Barth. The postmodern attitude became the one that says to a lover "I love you desperately," a phrase that both of them knew had already been written and previously used: "Come direbbe Liala, ti amo disperatamente" (*Postille* 38–39; "As Liala would say, I love you desperately"; "Postmodernism" 227). By avoiding false innocence and not ignoring what preceded them, the past, they can thus talk about love "in an age of lost innocence" whilst also participating in the game of irony consciously and with pleasure. According to Eco, if, with the modern, one who does not understand the game refuses it, then with the postmodern it would also be possible to understand the game and take things seriously.[34] Additionally, John Barth's resumption and interpretation of Eco's metaphor in *Postmodernism Revisited* seems to say something more. In the English version of Eco's essay, Liala becomes Barbara Cartland: "If for 'Barbara Cartland' we substitute 'the history of literature up to the day before yesterday', it is the very point of my essay 'The Literature of Exhaustion'" (Barth, "The Literature of Exhaustion" 123). The use of the notes from a double-coding viewpoint was, in fact, pointed out by Barth himself in his essay, the extended title of which he said was meant to be "the literature of exhausted possibility."[35] Both Umberto Eco and John Barth attempted to indicate an acute problem in the historical context—one that Calvino articulated very well in his idea of the encyclopedic novel. Indeed, according to Rocco Capozzi (303) in his "L'iper-romanzo di Calvino ed Eco: Molteplicità, enciclopedia e poetica dell'eccesso," writing, for both Eco and Calvino, means rewriting "the already done, said and written" from a linguistic, fabulistic, structural, and combinatorial perspective.

John Barth returned to these topics in another essay, *The Literature of Replenishment,* in which he explained that literature cannot actually be exhausted and that many have misunderstood him. Barth believes, as does Borges, that literature will never run out. As for the relationship between being modern or being postmodern, both Barth and Eco are open to a form of coexistence. Eco, perhaps to better explain his own path and intellectual production, asked himself a somewhat similar question: "Se il post-moderno è questo, è chiaro perché Sterne o Rabelais fossero post-moderni, perché lo è certamente Borges, perché in uno stesso artista possano convivere, o seguirsi a breve distanza, o alternarsi, il momento moderno e quello post-moderno" (*Postille* 39–40; "If 'postmodern' means this, it is clear why Sartre and Rabelais were postmodern, why Borges surely is, and why in the same artist the modern moment and the postmodern moment can coexist, or alternate, or follow each other closely"; "Postmodernism" 227).

Barth also uses Calvino's work to liberate his own work from any claustrophobic definition. In another essay, he strove to draw parallels between Borges and Calvino. Citing a story by Borges,

Chapter Nine

Barth saw in each writer, but especially in Calvino, a combination of "algebra and fire"—that is, of form and emotion—and called Calvino "the very model of a modern major Postmodernist."[36]

Given Barth and Eco's assumption that the modern and the postmodern can coexist, different readings of Calvino on specific aspects should be considered, for example on the matter of the subject. Calvino undoubtedly wanted to defend subjective awareness but, in order to defend it, subjective awareness must be threatened by a "sea of objectivity," incompleteness and the labyrinth. If the preface to *I nostri antenati* had been written in the 1990s, added to "Marx lo disse 'alienato'" ("Marx defined him 'alienated'"), "Freud 'represso'" ("Freud 'repressed'"), would have been "Jameson called him fragmented," and yet the final line, "a una nuova completezza s'aspira" ("to a new completeness we aspire!") (*I nostri antenati* XII), would not have been changed. Indeed, Calvino's idea of this incomplete process seems to echo Habermas' position on modernity. Linda Hutcheon revisited this very debate on modernism and postmodernism in the section 'Postmodernity, Postmodernism, and Modernism' in *The Politics of Postmodernism*. At the core of the debate is a seemingly irreconcilable exchange on the topic of modernity between Habermas and Lyotard. "Both agreed that modernity could not be separated from notions of unity and universality or what Lyotard dubbed 'metanarratives'. Habermas argued that the project of modernity, rooted in the context of Enlightenment rationality, was still unfinished and required completion; Lyotard countered with the view that modernity has actually been liquidated by history ..." (*The Politics of Postmodernism* 23–24).[37]

Borrowing from Eco and considering Cavino's *modus operandi* postmodern, if we look for an ideology of representation[38] behind Calvino's work, we will find it in the impulse of modern completion. The same can be said when it comes to both the city and the narrative of the city. There are fragments, in the city, just as there are in the narrative of the city—in Gadda, precisely—but the fragments are connected and the writer investigates these connections. This is why, according to Calvino the (open) encyclopedic novel was needed as a method of knowledge and, above all, as "rete di connessione tra i fatti, tra le persone, tra le cose del mondo" ("a network of connection between facts, between people, between the things of the world") (*Le lezioni americane* 103). Furthermore, as he stated in his latest work, the last *Lezione americana* (117), classification as modern or postmodern does not even matter with the most representative contemporary novel (*l'iper-romanzo*), like *Se una notte d'inverno un viaggiatore* and *Il castello dei destini incrociati*. Instead, what matters is the thread that runs implicitly through novels by authors like Flaubert, Gadda, Musil, Proust, and Calvino: knowledge as multiplicity. "La conoscenza come molteplicità è il filo che lega le opere maggiori, tanto di quello che viene chiamato modernismo quanto di quello che viene chiamato il postmoderno, un filo che—al di là di tutte le etichette—vorrei continuasse a svolgersi nel prossimo millennio." ("Knowledge as multiplicity is the thread that binds together the major works both of what is called modernism and of what goes by the name of the *postmodern*, a thread—over and above all the labels attached to it—which I hope will continue into the next millennium.") (*Le lezioni americane* 113). It is exactly this passion for knowledge that leads, for example, Gadda "dall'oggettività del mondo alla sua propria soggettività esasperata" ("from the objectivity of the world to his own irritated subjectivity") (*Le lezioni americane* 106). It is also this passion for knowledge that brought Calvino to postulate the network novel. In this effort to re-represent his context, its variants, its impulses, and its possible futures, one can say that Calvino was modern, postmodern, pessimistic, critical, inspired by science, and intrigued by the future and so much more, because a mixture of elements and genres also provided his context.

The network subject

It is as if Calvino had found himself faced with equal choices between thinning out the perspective, in the sense of making the world end, and consulting science and technology, and between the subject reduced to a robot in the city of machines and the subject alleviated and strengthened by recourse to science. This is a subject part Kublai Khan and part Marco Polo, part lone emperor and part sedentary traveler. Calvino tried to break the impasse and offer a detailed representation open to possibilities. It was a representation that added the chessboard, the map, and even computer science to the network novel. The lost and weakened subject gave way to Kublai Khan, to the emperor visiting everything that exists in the garden of his palaces, in front of a chessboard. The subject who uses technology and mathematics to represent the world is the emperor subject, a literary delirium of the contemporary individual. For Calvino, the world had to be reconstructed from the perspectives of knowledge, geographical representation, sense, and the reader/subject, before it could be reconstructed from the perspective of literature. This was the intention of his encyclopedic novel.

The domain of urbanization and spatial categories has, amongst others, been examined by Fredric Jameson in his important essay on postmodernism. Jameson pointed out that, in an era of multinational capitalism, the topic of discussion should be the subject's ability to represent the whole. His paradigm of postmodernism, which was very influential in the cultural landscape of the late-twentieth century, showcased the present domain of spatial categories against temporal categories, as well as the transition from a centered to a fragmented subject. The postmodern subject finds that it is difficult to represent the multiplicity of time and organize it into a coherent experience. In *Raccontare il postmoderno*, Remo Ceserani privileges the fragmentation of the subject lost in hyperspace when reading Calvino. In fact, in the last unfinished novel of Calvino's *Se una notte d'inverno un viaggiatore* (a hyper-novel adapted to the new hyper-environment), the subject thins out his world in order to bring it back down to size in front of the Perspective. I believe that this is not the only possible reading. Calvino denied wanting an ending for his last books. In Calvino's characters, subjects tend to identify themselves with the city, inhabit hyperspace, live more roles and embody different "identities," as Marco Polo does in *Le città invisibili* or Ludmilla in *Se una notte d'inverno,* each going on (living) from one novel to another. Yet, these experiences do not remain as disconnected fragments, unorganized or heterogeneous. Instead, they are thought out and held together in a kind of network experience, by analogy with the network form (*forma rete*) suggested, as we saw, by Calvino.

Moreover, the Calvinian hyper-environment is not only made of hyperspace. The main characters are readers who try to coordinate, build a cognitive map, read and represent the world, dominate the chaos, and experience it as a container of possibilities. In his model of political culture, Jameson (54) himself focuses on the need to build what he calls cognitive cartography, in order "to enable a situational representation on the part of the individual subject to that vaster and properly unrepresentable totality." This is precisely the deepest impulse of Calvino's work: a new cultural map; a map, geographic, scientific, economic, philosophic, and a re-representation of the world (even for political purposes, in the highest sense of the term), all in the conditions of the new hyper-environment made up of space and knowledge. The map is literally and physically present almost everywhere in his work, from the rewriting of Ariosto to *Le città invisibili*. In this light, another much more sophisticated map, then, is the chess board, which goes significantly further in trying to calculate the combinations of all possibilities. Along with the explorer Marco Polo, its user is Kublai Khan, who is not by chance a kind of hyper-subject; the emperor subject. The very idea of the network novel suggests a map, a continuity between episodes and fragments, almost a place that is inhabited by a kind of network human being who is capable of stitching together his or her own fragments, of holding together the proper plurality. Although a setting displaying a touch of the fairy-tale manipulates temporality, Calvino chose to represent a world broad, in both time and space, now starting from the first moments of life on earth and, at another time, roaming throughout space. It is a world of interconnections, of long chains of events, and not a baroque world made up of isolated fragments. It tells us about Marco Polo, a "network" human being who was perhaps able to hold together episodes of self, in both spatial and temporal senses.

The ideal sense of life, then, is, in Ludmilla's words, reading/living all the novels/possible experiences. In her search for a very complex equilibrium, Ludmilla is, in a very lucid way, "lettrice di più libri in una volta" ("reader of several books at once") (*Se una notte d'inverno* 147), trying to rule her indwelling multitude, "per non lasciarsi sorprendere dalla delusione che può riservarle ogni storia, tende a portare avanti insieme anche altre storie." ("so as not to let herself be surprised by the disappointment that every story can hold, tends to bring other stories together"). And, as we saw, she does not simply accumulate readings, but instead leads a rich, stimulating life in which all feelings and emotions are carefully measured out, alternated, and combined. There is no sense of loss for Ludmilla. There is nothing schizophrenic about her. Instead, she seems to have found completeness in her incompleteness, as incompleteness is dynamically possible to complete, to bridge, without ever being definitively completed. This is her life's plot. Ludmilla seems to have understood the lesson of monocellular Qfwfk "deathly in love." She falls in love but not enough to die. The openness toward the other is controlled to the point of safeguarding a kind of continuity. Calvino's pair of male and female readers immediately follows the Kublai Khan-Marco Polo couple. Ludmilla is the heir to the emperor subject, but wisely transplanted to the educated middle class. "You, too, lawyers, teachers, journalists, and publishers," Calvino seems to say, "You can all have access to an even cheaper plural dimension." The low cost of travel to the manifold will be open to you, too. Ludmilla, then and, with her, all of them, always expects something from the world. The ideal of Ludmilla's life seems to be an exploration of the multiplicity of the world and the properly paced continuous enrichment of experience; a process which always needs to be fulfilled but never is. It seems that the new meaning of life is to experience the world. The richer the experience, the fuller the life. "Potrebb'essere un lineamento importante che s'aggiunge al tuo ritratto: la tua mente ha pareti interne che permettono di separare tempi diversi in cui fermarsi o scorrere, concentrarsi alternativamente su canali paralleli. Basterà questo per dire che vorresti vivere più vite contemporaneamente? O che effettivamente le vivi? Che separi ciò che vivi con una persona o in un ambiente da ciò che vivi con altri e altrove?" ("It could be an important feature which is added to your portrait: your mind has interior walls that allow the separation of different times in which to stop or scroll, alternately focusing on parallel channels. Suffice it to say that you would like to live several lives at once? Or you actually live them? That you separate what you live with a person or a place from what you live with others and elsewhere?") (*Se una notte d'inverno* 147). From this there emerge two distinct possibilities for reading Calvino: the fragmentation and weakening of the subject, and the strengthening of the subject who aims to incorporate diverse identities. Calvino provided sufficient evidence to support the second option—though the options are not opposites but, rather, two sides of the same coin. The fragmented subject highlighted the need[39] to begin thinking about some type of network, plural, and multibelonging subject.

Chapter Ten

Fellini's Invisible Cities

The symbols of *La dolce vita*

In this movie, the representation of the night life of Via Veneto is one of the most striking aspects. Yet today, the Via Veneto has become a caricature of itself,[40] the showcase of a simulacrum which reflects a past that has become strangely mythical and only useful for selling at triple the price of a coffee, soft drinks and illusions to dreamers and tourists. Its sidewalks are no longer trodden by provincial journalists, ambitious actresses, writers, poets, swindlers, paparazzi, lawyers, clerks, southern dreamers, thieves, maids, hawkers of roses, and music and call girls because it is true of the whole city. Via Veneto has invaded Rome and Rome has emptied it; turning it into a museum of artifact memories. The now-ordinary events of yesterday, immortalized by Fellini's film, have gained access to that timeless dimension that great cinema is able to create. It was perhaps the shock novelty, the eruption of the event, the deep upheaval of a social earthquake to come, and the fear of the social guardians of all types and levels committed to preserving structures and hierarchies that provoke those long-lived emotions whose boost still shake us today. However, the novelties were more than one, with the result that their symbols immediately disputed the true meaning of the film. On the one hand, the novelty was Via Veneto, the impending lifestyle yearned for not only by bored decadent nobles, wealthy Americans and children of the new middle class but also young provincials, starlets in search of opportunity, southern migrants and even people of an advanced age (see Marcello's father); it was the sweet superficiality,[41] a preview of happy hour, the glittering cocktails that filtered rationality and responsibility, it was the thoughtlessness of a walk into the void. On the other hand, the novelty was Sylvia, the diva, Hollywood that plunged into the classic symbols to revive them in a new light: its own, the profane corrupting the sacred, the paparazzi, the society of the spectacle determined to dominate the scene. Today, we see no dichotomy in the symbols of *La dolce vita*. However, in the 1960s, the social metamorphosis was not entirely complete. Nor was Fellini himself fully aware of what his representation was bringing to light, considering that, in the struggle between these two symbols to excel, he lined up. It was Anita Ekberg who was to Fellini the very symbol of the film. Instead, for critics and audiences, the symbol of this film was the Via Veneto.[42] In fact, Fellini intended even a third meaning, not new, indeed structural, or rather essential, which emerges slowly through the transformation of Sylvia or more precisely with the transformation of the perception of Sylvia that will occur during that irresistible wandering in the Roman night. The reference to Dante is the most significant indicator of Marcello's intuition. However, there are at least two Beatrices in this film. When the first, Sylvia, leaves the scene, another figure enters, this time really angelic: the young waitress "dal profilo simile a quello dei quadri delle chiese umbre" ("with a profile similar to that of the paintings of the churches of Umbria") (as Marcello defines her) who calls in vain for Marcello in the film's ending. He gets sucked in by the anonymous calls of his flock, and does not have the energy to cross the water and follow the Umbrian Beatrice onto her shore. Via Veneto seems to win out in this last comparison with *La dolce vita*, when understood in Fellini's and Dante's terms. "Il film è una sintesi—as Italo Moscato points out—di una trasformazione della società italiana" ("The film is a summary"—as Italo Moscato points out—"of the transformation of Italian society") (6).

Marcello as "the self-confessed sinner" male in Celati's reading

The transformation of Italian society in Fellini's movies is also Gianni Celati's take; he considered his cinema an "anthropological telescope." However, Celati selected from among the findings of his anthropological analyzis, the transformation of the Italian male for his Binder Lecture at The University of California, San Diego (2006) entitled "Fellini on the Italian male"—later further elaborated and published as an essay (2009). In his essay, Marcello is almost an end result of a history of male characters portrayed in Fellini's cinema. The writer starts from *Roma* (Italy,1972), and a scene of relaxed young people on a Roman night where Fellini's voice over states that sex does not seem to be a problem for them. At least not anymore. This sequence opens the chapter on Roman brothels during WWII. "The comparison with the 'flower generation' serves to measure the distance between old and new sexual mores," writes Celati who finds the "aging flash" of females' bodies in the brothel to be indicative of an "amorous longing" of male characters whose eroticism is not related to 'female beauty' but much more of an elementary urge. There is, then, an essential difference with the group of young 'flower generation' Americans who sit on a flight of steps in Rome at the start of the episode and whose eroticism, according to Celati, is external, like a cinematographic spectacle. "In the new sexual climate with its different sexual attitudes, eroticism is confused with sex as advertising, where sex no longer poses any problems because everything is resolved in the outward appearance of human behavior" (224). The scene of the brothel on the other hand, since it is unrelated to female beauty, is more of a 'mental obfuscation' than a judgmental gaze. The same goes for the Baraconda theater episode, which again highlights a model of a woman who attracts more for her carnal materiality than for the shape of the body—"in other words, a woman who eludes the rationalized forms of the Greek model of beauty" (226). Fellini's male characters show an expression of desire that is not related to evaluations of female form and which are not resolved in the conquest of beautiful women. They are instead a vision filled with phantasm of our needs thanks to the contribution of our imagination. This is the "territory of the cinematic industry aspires to claim for itself, above all in relation to the imperatives set by the spectacularity of American cinema" (226). In American cinema, a class of female characters that corresponds to Fellini's "culona" (which could be translated to the so-called 'broad'), always play secondary roles—and are generally from the poorer classes. In contrast, official 'beauty' is associated with money. "The mingling of the impulse to satisfy 'amorous longing' with images of wealth is a given in the plots of 1930s Hollywood" (226). Love is associated with consumption. Celati uses Fellini's early cinema and his male protagonists to talk about the traditional Italian background and its major influencers: namely the Church, Fascism and Cinema. Ostentation, lie-telling and private repression are part of the Italian tradition dominated by the myths of the 'Latin lover', Mussolini and the Catholic culture. "Fascism proposed a similar idea of the male sex, in bellic form, as a national symbol" (245). The 'Latin lover' icon was generated by Hollywood and especially by an Italian American actor, Rudolph Valentino, whose origins played a crucial role in the exotic images linked to the stereotypes put about by the American tourist industry. "It also had a great impact on Italian sexual fantasies during the Fascist period, developing into the specialized male type we call the 'Latin lover'" (232). In Italy, a set of rules in life predispose everything towards ostentation, even with regard to the smallest concerns of everyday life and create a social conditioning that differs "noticeably from that of modern America and Europe" (231). In association with the precepts of the Catholic Church, even the separation between sexes has assumed a more rigid form in Italy. "This might help to explain the lust that circulates amongst a crowd of Italian males when fixing on a woman, as if they see her across an insuperable distance" (243). Fellini's characters are entirely defined by their appearance; for example in *I Vitelloni* (*The Bullocks*, Federico Fellini, Italy 1953)—filled with 'libidinous infantilism' and automatisms of both male seducing and family drama repression which, with Bazin and Deleuze, Celati calls a cinema of dispersion. The walks of the five friends in the movie are images "of the beginning of this dispersion of the male, or of one of his fantasies of dispersion far from the protective network of the family" (235) ... and far from its traditional repression one could add. For Celati, Marcello and *La dolce vita* are the next episode of *I Vitelloni*. The small-town male now moves in the big city. In his view, Fellini's movies are filled with (male) dreams of escaping domestic normality. Marcello is, therefore, "the self-confessed sinner," a certain kind of Italian male raised with a catholic background and *La dolce vita* is all about the collapse of religion. "And we understand that everything is profane, that everything boils down to mere spectacle and commerce—even the bells of the Vatican, even the statue of Christ with his hand raised in blessing flying over the faithful in St. Peter's Square"(238).

In my reading, however, Fellini's "anthropological telescope" examines much more, and reveals a very articulated picture. The history of the profile of the Italian male is, of course, part of the complex transformation of society as a whole.

Homo eligens

> Emma—Di che cosa hai paura?
>
> Marcello—Di te. Del tuo egoismo. Dello squallore dei tuoi ideali. Non lo vedi che quello che mi proponi è una vita da lombrico. Non sai parlare d'altro che di cucina e di camere da letto. Ma un uomo che accetta di vivere così... lo capisci che è un uomo finito? È veramente un verme. Io non ci credo a questo tuo amore aggressivo, vischioso, materno. Non lo voglio, non mi serve. Questo non è amore. È abbrutimento. Come te lo devo dire che non posso vivere così?
>
> *Emma*: What are you afraid of?
>
> *Marcello*: Of you. Of your selfishness. Of the squalor of your ideals. Can't you see that what you propose to me is the life of a worm. You can't talk about anything else except kitchens and bedrooms. But a man who agrees to live like this ... do you understand that he is a finished man? He is really a worm. I don't believe in this aggressive love, viscous, maternal. I don't want it, I don't need it. This is not love. This is brutalizing. How can I tell you that I can't live like this?" (Taken from dialogue between Emma and Marcello in *La dolce vita*, 1959).

The dialogue between Marcello and Emma—the only moment in the film where we see Marcello really passionate about something, (and the only moment of utter certainty and sincerity), is a sort of cultural manifesto. What Fellini knows, what Marcello embodies, is the certainty that the social organization model has exploded. It is not just a male rebellion, as is evident from the figure of the rich, bored, and unhappy Maddalena. Something new and strong has happened.

Along with the vulgar society of the spectacle, and a kind of American cultural and economic colonization (in the vast majority of episodes in the film they are constantly talking in English), a strong demand emerges for an authenticity that is as new as it is murky.[43] Marcello knows what he does not want, but he does not know what he wants. A potential Marco Polo, who would like to entrust his existential fulfillment to the journey and an exploration

Chapter Ten

of the world's horizontal plurality, he limits himself to travelling to all the corners of the city as well as to all ranks and trades in an exploration that is as anthropological as it is existential. Marcello has been considered to be an undeveloped character; exactly the same from beginning to end. In fact, towards the end of his journey, and especially after Steiner's death, Marcello gives up. By then he has renounced his ambition and slips inexorably towards the most degrading emptiness. One social model is over but a new one is not yet in sight.[44]

Marcello seems to be the prototype of an incomplete human being; the new transitory human being. The reading of this film can be facilitated by focusing on the city of Calvino's work. It was not by chance that *La dolce vita* was built on a large number of episodes that capture different urban realities and that are, at times, completely independent. Fellini apparently had a hard time stopping and desisting from including further episodes. The protagonist, Marcello, again a provincial journalist, is the only constant in all the scenes and is almost always accompanied by Paparazzo, conceived sometimes as a modern variant of the chronicle reporter who attends various events, sometimes as the hurried, cynical, jaunty and scandalous eye of society. He says little, takes a lot of photos and, when needed, figures opportunistically in the cruelty, as in the outdoor scene with Steiner's wife who is unaware of her husband's suicide.

Calvino's *Le città invisibili* are the possible cities. Possible cities shape possible existences. The realization of one does not have the strength to exclude the others. In the cities, the individual first learns a trade, then renews himself and makes another, and then again another:

> Entrato nel territorio che ha Eutropia per capitale, il viaggiatore vede non una città ma molte, di eguale grandezza e non dissimili tra loro, sparse per un vasto e ondulato altopiano. Eutropia è non una ma tutte queste città insieme; una sola è abitata, le altre vuote; e questo si fa a turno. Vi dirò ora come. Il giorno in cui gli abitanti di Eutropia si sentono assalire dalla stanchezza, e nessuno sopporta più il mestiere, i suoi parenti, la sua casa e la sua via, i debiti, la gente da salutare o che saluta, allora tutta la cittadinanza decide di spostarsi nella città vicina che è lì ad aspettarli, vuota e come nuova, dove ognuno prenderà un altro mestiere, un'altra moglie... Gli abitanti tornano a recitare le stesse scene con attori cambiati; ridicono le stesse battute con

accenti variamente combinati; spalancano bocche alternate in uguali sbadigli. (*Le città invisibili* 56)

> When he enters the territory of which Eutropia is the capital, the traveler sees not one city but many, of equal size and not unlike one another, scattered over a vast, rolling plateau. Eutropia is not one, but all these cities together; only one is inhabited at a time, the others are empty; and this process is carried out in rotation. Now I shall tell you how. On the day when Eutropia's inhabitants feel the grip of weariness and no one can bear any longer his job, his relatives, his house and his life, debts, the people he must greet or who greet him, then the whole citizenry decides to move to the next city, which is there waiting for them, empty and good as new; there each will take up a new job, a different wife [...]. The inhabitants repeat the same scenes, with the actors changed; they repeat the same speeches with variously combined accents; they open alternate mouths in identical yawns. (*Invisible Cities* 64–65)

Invisible Cities at times has only one character, which doubles appropriately for the dialog that allows different points of view, and sometimes no character at all. As the extremely enhanced power of subjectivity that comes and goes, appears and disappears, in the individual, who therefore exists and doesn't exist; and when he believes he exists does not know why or how to exist. However he decides to exist, but since he decides how (in what city), he becomes a self-referential, self-produced individual. No necessity threatens the ideal model of the Western individual. No longer a village, a neighborhood, a family, a language, a city, an economy, a culture, capable of transforming the birth's initial contingency in destiny. The non-necessity, the non-choice seen as a horizontal choice: more cities, ideally all cities, all roles, all partners for a serial existence that tries to consume all that the city offers. Marcello's trip, too, is a journey into the possible existences that Rome offers. It is also a journey into Marcello. City and resident are reflected in each other.[45] The first of his possibilities is Maddalena; the decadent woman who cannot escape the social control present in all forms of monitoring, including the tabloid press. For Marcello, the petty anonymous bourgeois of the boom years finally free from the elementary necessities of life, Rome is a quiet jungle where one can easily hide and build, or extract from the pack, temporary identities which are useful even for a one-

Chapter Ten

night-only adventure. From a man of the province one would expect a certain willingness and precise opportunism to seize the opportunities of undeserved wealth—but this is not Marcello's case. Rather, the sensitivity to hear the sirens of the sweet life makes him not quite identifiable with the only social model that he embodies. Although both a cunning well-connected journalist as well as an unsuccessful novelist with buried ambitions, Marcello shows the strange wisdom of a worldly man. He and Maddalena approach a prostitute who imagines a *ménage à trois*, but they definitely surprise her (and it takes a lot to surprise a prostitute!) by borrowing her squalid bed on the outskirts of the city to stimulate their erotic fantasy away from the prying eyes of the paparazzi.[46]

Waking up, daylight brings headaches. Marcello's headache is called Emma, another variant of Marcello's possible existence: the traditional one. Emma, a Southerner and wildly jealous partner hysterically offers the dominant model of life based on marriage, family and children, and has tried to commit suicide because Marcello is neglecting her. He is attracted by her, and even says he loves her, but he cannot stand her dullness, the suffocating pattern that she tries to impose. There is little that can be imposed on Marcello.

In Steiner's house, the figure of the woman returns to the center of reflection through a journalist's extravagant sallies of praise of the Oriental woman, "ancora vicino alla natura come Eva" ("still as close to nature as Eve"). Here Marcello, who never has enough of the world, in a certain sense a "horizontal" explorer of possibilities, quantitative, accumulator, who instinctively avoids the depths so as not to anchor, shows us another fundamental feature of his philosophy. "Anche a me piacerebbe tanto viaggiare. Si ha la possibilità di fare incontri eccezionali, conoscere le donne di tutte le razze. A me piacerebbe avere figli di tutti i colori: rossi, gialli... pensi che soddisfazione! Come un mazzo di fiori di campo!" ("I too would love to travel. To have the opportunity of making exceptional encounters, to know women of all races. I'd like to have children of all colors: red, yellow ... imagine what satisfaction! Like a bouquet of wild flowers!"). Then a kind of new ideology of life is announced, again at Steiner's house, in Fellini's film. It is a poetess talking, unsurprisingly, American. Two loves? Journalism and literature? "Non scelga mai!" ("Never choose!"). Chooses to not choose Calvino's Ludmilla as well, in an even more lucid way, looking for a very complex equilibrium, "lettrice di più libri in una volta" ("a reader of several books at once") (*Se una notte d'inverno* 147), trying to rule the multitude that lives in her.

The discourse of "no choice" or, rather, that of the temporary choice, transitional, serial, is easy to imagine at this point. The sociologist Zygmunt Bauman has placed this phenomenon at the core of his analysis, dubbing this trend "liquid life." Bauman takes up Calvino's idea regarding the case of Eutropia's inhabitants: "Their ideal horizon is likely to be Eutropia, one of Italo Calvino's invisible cities whose inhabitants, the day they 'feel the grip of weariness and not one can any longer bear his job, his relatives, his house and his life', 'move to the next city' where 'each will take a new job, a different wife, will see another landscape on opening the window, and will spend his time with different pastimes, friends, gossip'" (*Liquid Life* 4). The potentials of this trend are easy to imagine. All that is fixed, defined, local, and even territorial becomes a limit, as does mono belonging. This leads to the debate on extra territoriality, on the non-belonging together, with the options of a necessarily hybrid culture, and on multi belonging. Bauman understands it fully. A global elite, he says, looks into the hybrid culture for the possibility of being part of extraterritorial networks, thereby distinguishing himself from those who do not have the same freedom of choice and movement that is from the "locals." Before Bauman, Fellini and Calvino had noticed this new trend, and that the "non-choice" would become a dominant feature, especially in the upper classes of Western cities. The same thing could also be said of the "incomplete human being." Bauman puts them together. "The sole 'identity core' which one can be sure will emerge from the continuous change not only unscathed but probably even reinforced is that of *homo eligens*—the 'man choosing' (though not the 'man who has chosen'!): a permanently impermanent self, completely incomplete, definitely indefinite—and authentically inauthentic" (*Liquid Life* 31).

The open form

Neither Fellini nor Calvino choose. Fellini's episodic films,[47] the many cities and the incomplete novels of Calvino seem to reflect this content. Calvino, in the preface to *Invisible Cities*, denied that his novels had an ending. "Ma questo è un libro fatto a poliedro e di conclusioni ne ha un po' dappertutto, scritte lungo tutti i suoi spigoli..." ("But this is a book made of a polyhedron shape"—he writes of *Invisible Cities*—"and it has conclusions spread out a little bit everywhere, written along all its edges ...") (x). The same goes for all his later novels, and this also applies to Fellini's films.[48] A few years after the international success of *La dolce vita*, Fellini told a writer for *The New Yorker*: "Movies now have gone past the phase of prose narrative and are coming nearer and nearer to poetry. I am trying to free my work from certain constructions—a story with a beginning, a development, an ending. It should be more like a poem with meter and cadence" (Fellini, cited in Bondanella, *The Films of Federico Fellini* 71). Calvino and Fellini sensed, whiles choosing different genres and media, a more suitable solution for the new individual they described. Besides being among the most representative artists of twentieth century Italy, they also shared the same neo-realist past and became important protagonists of its surpassing. André Bazin, in a stimulating reading of *Le notte di Cabiria* (*Nights of Cabiria*), analyzed in a singular way just this passage and provided a possible explanation for the formal choices derived from it ("The Voyage to the End of Neorealism"). *Realism* is defined by him not in terms of aims but in terms of means, while the *neo-realism* relies on a particular relationship of means and aims. De Sica and Rossellini did not share with Fellini the deep meaning of their works, but the emphasis on the representation of reality by sacrificing the dramatic structures. According to Bazin, Italian cinema has replaced the "realism"—whose contents came from the naturalism of the novels and whose structure was due to the theater—with what he calls "phenomenological" realism that never "fixes" reality to meet the needs of a drama's psychology. Now it is almost exclusively appearance that matters, along with the documentation of all its details. In this sense, Fellini, according to Bazin, went much further in this neo-realist aesthetic, so far as to end up in the territory of the "surreal" or "magical."[49]

Fellini, therefore, did not oppose either realism or neo-realism,[50] but reached the same goal through "a poetic re-organization of the world." What happens on a formal level also affects the narrative level. De Sica and Zavattini, Bazin recalls, favored the incident as far as plot was concerned, in order to leave room for micro-action based on the complexity of even the most ordinary of events. The choices did not favor any more dramatic pre-existing organization. Fellini pushed this to extreme lengths. His screenplays are not held together by dramatic wires, and his characters are not revealed in the dramatic moments but in their restless wanderings. This reading of *Nights of Cabiria*, seems particularly appropriate for *La dolce vita*. What Cabiria begins, Marcello carries forward. She starts the exploration of Rome not without a certain neo-realist inspiration. Her house, a ruin in the middle of nowhere is her constant boast and even becomes the engine of the plot. Oscar, the last swindler of a lover, aspires to money from the sale of the house/ruin equipped, as Cabiria points out with pride, with light and water. In one episode of the film, Cabiria—during her wanderings that have no justification in terms of the plot—takes us to the caves inhabited by the homeless. Then, in the shoes of the silent reporter, Cabiria also takes us to the Via Veneto which is still portrayed to us in this film as a contrast to the wretchedness of the suburbs. The poetic veil that Fellini talks of,[51] (the magic/surrealist touch mentioned by Bazin), is inspired by Cabiria's irreducible vitality which slips into the young woman's oneiric world: a kind of "*eppur si muove*" ("and yet it moves") of life that, when it is contained and checked by reality, overflows into the oneiric. It is this same irrepressible vitality that gives brio to the film where it is less expected—the "archaeological walk" where the girls prostitute themselves. Even the final solution, that has a fairy-tale flavor and is set, not surprisingly, in the very middle of a forest, tells us of the young Cabiria's stubborn vitality. Her final gaze, mysterious and enchanted, anticipates the same light and the same movement as Paola's gaze that ends *La dolce vita*, while the desperate vitality of the girl who makes her living that way in the former, becomes the almost irresponsible joy of living in the latter. Cabiria's wandering, too, although for different deep reasons, is continued by Marcello—at this point a professional reporter like the young Fellini just arrived in Rome from Rimini (Marcello changes little: he was born in Cesena).

Considered from the perspective of this continuity, *Nights of Cabiria* can be seen as a "bridge" movie in the process of stylistically surpassing neo-realism. With irony and sarcasm, a reporter asks a question about neo-realism that falls precisely on the deaf ears of the ignorant diva, Sylvia, almost as if Fellini had wanted to mark that surpassing. In *La dolce vita* can be found all the

Chapter Ten

elements noticed by Bazin: the open form,[52] the importance of wandering, the very detailed description of appearances in various episodes, and the search for an improbable synthesis in the "surreal" or "magic" or, rather and especially, the will to reorganize the representations of the world into a new key. Many of these elements were also noted by Pasolini, who was Fellini's adviser for some of the scenes in the film. What seems more interesting to me, in Pasolini's reading, is the mention of the similarities with Gadda's novel set in Rome,[53] *Quer pasticciaccio brutto de via Merulana* (*That Awful Mess on the Via Merulana*): "In fact, like Fellini, Gadda sometimes delights in phonic pleasures, even if ironically. Like Fellini, Gadda violates the word-roots, always in the service of a meaning that reinvents those terms within a language that is altogether subjective, grotesque, violent, visceral and distorting, and yet combined with passages of veristic realism angrily slapped into the text. Like Fellini, Gadda possesses a lexicon that is the greatest pastiche imaginable" (Pasolini, "The Mature Auteur: La Dolce Vita and Beyond." 104–05).[54] It is not by chance that, in Gadda and in the same novel set in Rome, Calvino also focused. It is the case to recall here that, for Calvino, this novel represents the contemporary novel seen as an open encyclopedia.

At a time when filmmakers were inspired by poems (Fellini can also be considered a writer, as an author of screenplays) and novelists by directors, what Calvino called the form of the open encyclopedia was as much about literature as it was about cinema. The point remains the re-representation of the world, the need for which was due to the urgency of broadening the perspective. Bazin, referring to Fellini, talks of the re-organization of the world in a poetic way. The references in *La dolce vita* to *La vita nuova* (Dante Alighieri 1295; *The New Life*, 1899—with Rossetti) are much more than mere mentions. In the original title, the film had as a subtitle "2000 years after Christ." The reference to Dante is used, as John Welle ("Fellini's use of Dante in *La dolce vita*.") explains to us, to signal a radical turning point. The final call of Paola-Beatrice this time remains unheard. The world has veered. Marcello is sucked from the tribe that he did not choose. The incurable rupture with the past is resumed by Fellini several years later, in *Roma*. It is not by chance that the excavations for the construction of the subway made a fresco vanish that the Roman underground had preserved for 2,000 years. The city with eight layers, the city of churches, of squares, of the Colosseum, of monuments from all periods is reviewed in the end without any comment from the fast and noisy perspective of a tribe of "modern barbarians" who cross it on their bikes.

The incomplete human being is young

After the arrival of the diva in *La dolce vita*, Marcello—likeable rogue and happy connoisseur of the value of the contingent—finds the time to take aside two solitary hostesses. Soon after, a fair of stupid questions takes place on the stage, during which the diva is exalted in an unrivaled sensual superficiality. "Una bambola. È una grossa bambola" ("A doll. She is a big doll"), says Marcello to tedious Emma, who bothers him on the phone with her jealousy. For Emma there is nothing else in the world but Marcello. To Marcello, the world is simultaneously full and empty. He is often accompanied by a background of anxiety, as emphasized by the disquieting musical motifs that Fellini, in *Roma*, associates with the scenes of the clergy. The profane diva is exalted and appropriates, with apparent superficiality, even the Vatican's sacred places. The total ignorance betrayed in the dialogues is forgiven and ends in enhancing the exuberant candid beauty in the format of a billboard. Fellini, in a double movement of fierce criticism and unprejudiced openness to the novelty, captures in the eyes of Marcello the beauty of the soul of his time in that luminous layer of appearances spread over the Rome of the economic boom. The surrender to the sweet call of this vital foam composed of simple and immediate enjoyment is, however, voluntary. Marcello often displays a wise smile, a smug desire to indulge in the present's waves. The tone of the narrative often suggests a certain degree of complicity between Fellini and Marcello. The viewer is prompted to walk in Marcello's shoes and live the episodes in the first person. Director and protagonist at least seem to understand each other and, at times, to identify in each other.

La dolce vita flows softly and lovely again in the evening. Here begins Sylvia's metamorphosis. "Tu sei tutto Sylvia. Ma lo sai che tu sei tutto. You are everything. Everything. Tu sei la prima donna del primo giorno di creazione. Sei la madre, la sorella, l'amante, l'amica, l'angelo, il diavolo, la terra, la casa... Ah! Ecco che cosa sei! La casa..." ("You are everything Sylvia. But you know that

Chapter Ten

you're everything. You are everything. Everything. You are the first woman on the first day of creation. You're the mother, sister, lover, friend, angel, devil, earth, home ... Ah! That's what you are! Home ...") whispers a tipsy Marcello to her, with skillful lightness, wrapped into the luminous softness of the enchanted woman while dancing embraced, as if the profane was the deep secret of the sacred. "Ma perché sei venuta qui? Torna in America... fammi il favore. Lo capisci? Che faccio adesso io" ("But why did you come here? Go back to America ... do me a favor. Do you understand? What do I do now?"), whispers Marcello, again in prey to a happy torment which cannot and does not want to resist. Marcello speaks to Sylvia and Fellini speaks to us. Sylvia and a new way of life have come from America. It is of the new West that Fellini is telling us, of the social mutation that crosses the capitals of this new vision of the world. Seen from a religious perspective, this lifestyle is both seductive and sinful. It is, from an anthropological perspective, the start of a profound crisis of traditional society. Fellini adopts both perspectives.

Marcello is, in other words, a worldly man. When his paparazzo friend makes him an offer with attractive earnings, he prefers instead to take Sylvia around at night with a clear intention. "Non ti posso portare a casa mia. C'è quella matta. Non capirebbe!" ("I can't take you to my house. That crazy woman is there. She wouldn't get it!") Marcello says surprisingly, and his philosophy begins to be more and more articulated. What is it that the traditional Emma wouldn't understand? The sweet life perhaps, or something that, if articulated, would not be able to explain everything? It is a vision of life that Marcello and Sylvia share with superficiality, lightness, and profoundness. The decadent Maddalena, too, seems to be, in Marcello's eyes, a person able to understand, because he calls her when looking for a place to make love to Sylvia. Once again, the night turns out to be an enchanting opportunity for enjoyment; endless and inconclusive. The striking of bells alludes to a new subversion. The music softens and prepares one of the most familiar sequences in the history of cinema. After the profane appropriates the sacred, the jarring and desecrating modern plunges into the classic under Marcello's enchanted gaze. The Trevi Fountain adorns the luminous forms of the blonde diva. "Ma sì! Ha ragione lei, sto sbagliando tutto. Stiamo sbagliando tutti!" ("Yeah! She's right, I'm doing it all wrong. We are all wrong!") Marcello exclaims as she enters the water. Sylvia, in his eyes a plump woman and a natural eternal mystery of life, seems much more beautiful even than the monuments. A mystical sensuality enshrouds Marcello's face. It is here that Sylvia, Beatrice, angel, reaches the peak of her beauty. It is here that the timeless essence of *la dolce vita* exceeds the new looming anthropology of the Via Veneto. That is why Fellini regretted when the deafening scene-change of the social model stifled the soft suave song of *la dolce vita*. It is here that the Hollywood doll extracts, from beneath the cloak of superficial modernity, her mystical essence as woman. It is here where we realize that, despite the ignorance manifested up there in the Vatican, that sacred place, the woman also climbed, together with the doll, equally angelic and tempting. It is perhaps from this point on in the film that the anthropological aspect dominates with regard to the mystical dimension of the Fellinian reading. There is a difference between the lyrical evasion in the Sylvia episode and the routine, organized entertainment, transformed into the Via Veneto lifestyle.

It is the visit of Marcello's father that reveals a particular aspect of the Via Veneto. The father, willing to imitate his son, whose life style seems to exude the known fascination of the urban life, adopts the behavior patterns of his repertory and conceives everything as a planned escape. In a temporary escape from the "dark province," he is prepared to exhaust the savings he had set aside with a difficulty typical of the retired petty bourgeois and plunge into the lively urban life that could make him feel to be both young, and an accomplice and a teacher to his son. The father–son conflict is revealing. What, for Marcello and his friends, has little value is priceless to the father. Marcello instructs Fanny, a call-girl who performs in the night club. She flirts willingly and is even fascinated because she is worth champagne to Marcello's father, whereas to Paparazzo she is only worth a can of coca-cola. What, for the man of yesterday was an exception to the rule is, for the young men of the Via Veneto, just banal routine. Then Marcello's father suffers a heart attack and abandons Rome in a hurry, leaving the scene to its lawful inhabitants: the young.[55] That is exactly the point—Fellini caught something that now dominates our social landscape. The improvement to the conditions of life, the lengthening of life expectancies, and the extension of youth have greatly expanded the social landscape,

Chapter Ten

and have resulted in an organizational earthquake that, today, weighs on the economic equilibrium between generations and causes unprecedented economic crises.

Fellini's insights seem to be completely true almost forty years later. We have looked for them in a television phenomenon, and pop culture. It's *Sex and the City*. In this series of episodes set in New York or, more significantly, in an economically and socially filtered Manhattan, there are four women protagonists who may somehow fit Marcello's contemporary variants. All of them dream of having serious relationships that are mature and enduring. No relationship, however, seems to stick in Manhattan. Perhaps because after the end of one, the beginning of another comes quickly; an almost continuous network of relationships that systematically explore the entire residential area. Even in Manhattan, the disease of youth seems to be an unwillingness to choose. The flow of life looks like a river of possibilities, whose energy galvanizes their existence. Inebriated with the enormous potential of the world's most exclusive urban container, the characters of the TV serial appear unable and unwilling to extract just one. Choosing means eliminating all others. Not choosing means renouncing the form. The latter would give them an identity, a project, a route in which the roles are already established by a society, as Steiner said in *La dolce vita*, where everything is rigidly organized, and in which the only subject is society itself. However, the new urban individualism apparently refuses to delegate to society the formal decisions of its own life, longing for an open form which is fluid and circular and perpetuates youth. In fact, the four protagonists of *Sex and the City* surrender to the form only when their youth threatens to leave them for natural reasons. So to choose not to choose is the equivalent of prolonging youth for as long as possible. Late-modern well-being has prolonged youth, causing a new range of problems that affect families and the economic model, and explode the balance between generations (we have passed from the coexistence of three to the one of four generations, as pointed out by Marc Augé, *Non-Places*). This has caused the unprecedented economic crisis that today exists in Europe and the US. Via Veneto can, therefore, be metaphorically considered to have been one of the first European interfaces with Manhattan. The New Yorker protagonists, too, give up form only because of physical causes. The form of one of them becomes the disease while, to the other two, it becomes the departure, albeit temporary, from Manhattan (to Brooklyn and to Paris). This plot evidently represents a reality that is easily found today in most developed Western urban centers. A rich cultural program, spiced with cocktails, happy hours, meetings, opportunities, and multitudes, attracts and entertains even the progressively less-affluent urban masses. In the night in Rome of the first episode of *La dolce vita*, Maddalena points out to Marcello that, despite their considerable distance from each other in economic terms, they happen to share the fight against boredom in the late hours of Rome. Something similar happens in many, if not almost all, the episodes, including the final one in the rich producer's villa. There they meet actresses who had never become such, transvestites, lawyers, and journalists. They all celebrate together, not by chance, the divorce of one of them. Everything then becomes an entertainment for the present, an existence in tokens for the bus, tram, subway, cinema, drinks, exhibitions, meetings, evening relations to get on and off the entertainment's daily carousel to which the rest of the peripheral country yearns. Then the residences become smaller to make room for more people in the city. The rents go up and the houses become rooms, where there is space only for one: the individual. The carousel spins faster and faster and, in order to get on, one must work all day. However, what is earned during the day is immediately spent at night. The capital has become smarter. Society is not less, just differently organized. The new urban anthropology of fluid form, about which Bauman writes, now exists in its fullness. This, including the economically weaker groups, becomes another trap for the traditional system of the family, especially with regards to younger people. The relationship between earnings and the minimum necessary standard required to live, does not easily admit new families into the developed urban landscape. For this reason, after forming a family, a character from *Sex and the City*, Miranda, is forced to leave Manhattan and get off the carousel. There is another reason, this time not specifically urban. The traditional model of society is jeopardized, by the improvements in living conditions, by the prolonging of youth, and by the inadequacy of traditional family roles to fill the existence that they had formerly. The only plausible alternative seems to be the non-choice even though it is unable to turn off existential anxieties or fill the

Chapter Ten

void created by the circular infinite. This is why the Via Veneto dominates the other features of the film of Fellini; he evidently got it right. He did so several decades in advance, as often happen to artists with a very acute view.

New representations, new geographies

In both Calvino and in Fellini, the new approach to urban space is a determinant feature for their characters. The contemporary domains of urbanization and spatial categories have been examined by, amongst others, Fredric Jameson his important essay on postmodernism. As mentioned, Jameson highlights the present domain of spatial categories over the temporal, and the transition from centered to fragmented subject. He also focuses on the disappearance of personal style in favor of pastiches, and refers to analyses on the control of exchange value over use value. The postmodern subject finds it difficult to represent the multiplicity of time and to organize it into a coherent experience. Their cultural products are therefore "heaps of fragments" not dissimilar from "a practice of the randomly heterogeneous and fragmentary and the aleatory" (Jameson 25). Here Jameson refers to schizophrenia in Lacanian terms; a discontinuity between signifiers. For Lacan, and based upon one of the principles of Saussurean structuralism, the meaning is not constructed by a two-way relationship between signifier and signified but is generated by the movement from signifier to signifier. "When that relationship breaks down, when the links of the signifying chain snap, then we have schizophrenia in the form of a rubble of distinct and unrelated signifiers" (Jameson 26). It is the isolated distinct signifier that interests Jameson. Time itself, divided into past and future but united in the individual's present (by providing them with a personal identity), is a chain of signifiers which, when broken at the linguistic level, does the same on a personal level. Breakdown in the signifying chain causes a series of pure and unrelated presents in time. This break in temporality transforms the present in the isolated Signifier. In terms of art criticism, it implies emphasizing the discontinuity of the work of art, no longer unitary or organic. "The former work of art, in other words, has now turned out to be a text, whose reading proceeds by differentiation rather than by unification" (Jameson 31). The postmodern spectator faces an impossible task: "to look at all the patterns at the same time, in their radical difference" (Jameson 31). Many of these nodes taken from Jameson find a complex synthesis in the impossibility of representing and imagining our world. In search of a synthesis, Jameson mentions again the concept of the sublime in Kant. In him "the object of the sublime becomes not only a matter of sheer power and of the physical incommensurability of the human organism with Nature but also of the limits of figuration and the incapacity of the human mind to give representation to such enormous forces" (Jameson 34). Kant is, of course, introduced to explain our present difficulties with the new hyper-environment. For Jameson, "there has been a mutation in the object unaccompanied as yet by any equivalent mutation in the subject. We do not yet possess the perceptual equipment to match this new hyperspace" (Jameson 38). The architectural example of the Bonaventure Hotel in Los Angeles, too, as a self-sufficient mini-city which excludes the rest of the city, was regarded as both a symbol of postmodern and of the problem of the difficulty of the contemporary subject representing the hyperspace.

As we saw, Calvino's work deals thoroughly with these aspects. The main characters are readers who try to coordinate, build a cognitive map, read and represent the world, and dominate the chaos in order to experience it as a container of possibilities. His re-representations offer a new cultural map—geographical, scientific, economic, and philosophical—in the conditions of the new hyper-environment (made up of space and of knowledge). In Calvino's characters it is certainly possible to see, as we have done, subjects who tend to identify themselves with the city, who live the hyperspace, who live more roles, who embody different, as it were, "identities." Marcello does the same. In his way, he goes in and out of one episode to another, as Marco Polo and Ludmilla do, in respectively, *Invisible Cities* and *If on a Winter's Night*, going through (living) from one novel to another. The very idea of the network novel, as we saw in the previous section, suggests a map, a continuity between episodes, in which a kind of network human being is capable of stitching together its own fragments, of holding together the proper plurality. It is a world of interconnections and long chains of events, rather than a baroque world made up of isolated fragments. Ludmilla, then— and, with her, all of them—expects something from the world,

Chapter Ten

always, while Marcello, already middle class, seems to be the first prototype of this line.

From the network novel there emerges somehow the need for what we called in the first part of this, a multibelonging individual. The equivalent of non-belonging (of the non-human) would, in this case, be the disconnected subject, schizophrenic, lost in the impossibility of representing the multiplicity of the world. However, both the network human being (who gives a more spatial and more horizontal impression) and the multibelonging being (who adds a temporal sense, open even to that part of the hyper-environment composed of cultures and knowledge) need a cognitive world map through which to build a sense of self. Calvino worked hard to re-represent the new environment. Fellini also worked, though differently, in the same direction. The mystical dimension of his work, which took into account the religious element in the various episodes of his films, answers to the same need. The suicide of the religious intellectual, Steiner, the spectacularization of Madonna's fake appearances, and the inability to follow Paola-Beatrice's call in a Rome now "Babylon 2,000 years after Christ" deprive Marcello (the early prototype) of a definitive cognitive map. This prevents him from finding the ultimate meaning, the strong thread that holds the fragments together. There are different ways to hold together the plurality of the individual. One is to follow the current of the system itself; another can be the individual project. The individual project of Marcello, the writer, fails. Then, the new system provides him with the necessary thread that transforms him from explorer/reporter/aspiring writer, to an advertising agent, an anonymous presence in the herd of the new urban bourgeoisie. The press agent is an assimilated role through which Marcello, while living the multiplicity, as Calvino would put it, does not conflict with anything at all. He becomes a systematic automaton who lives the multiplicity as an organized seriality. A similar solution can be considered almost a comfort offered by the system. It is not the only one.

While writing about the Hotel Bonaventure, Jameson noticed another important aspect. It is not the individuals who are moving but the hotel itself, and it is the latter which transports them through elevators and escalators. The individual is helped and guided in experiencing the small labyrinth. Today, this mechanism has taken significant possession of the entire city. The

Fellini's Invisible Cities

contemporary city, often built around a center to attract tourists, as highlighted by Marc Augé (*Non-Places*), is a major mechanism for handling the continual import and export of people, as well as goods and information through railways, motorways, and airports. Escalators, moving walkways, trains, buses, and taxis all seem to be moving entire cities around the individual who, to a certain extent, reminds us of *Modern Times*' Charlie Chaplin; sucked in by cogs in the transmission, and thence fed, washed, used, and transported mechanically. The same traumatic relationship of the contemporary individual with their hyper-environment stimulates different considerations in the work of the French anthropologist Marc Augé. The individual of today, equipped with mobile phones and computers, can be in constant contact with the remotest parts of the world, and is therefore able to be somewhat independent of its most immediate physical context. This abstraction trend produces so-called non-places, spaces of circulation, consumption, and communication.[56] According to Augé, who intends to mark the difference with the paradigm of postmodernism, history is accelerating. Almost every decade of an individual's life quickly becomes a part of history (world wars, the 1960s, 1970s and so on ...), while the revolutionary improvement of transportation enables humans to interact with wider and wider territories. A superabundance of events and space, as well as the individualization of references trigger circumstances that stimulate the rethinking of issues such as identity and culture. He rejects the decadent aspect that is implicit, in his view, in postmodernism and emphasizes and privileges instead a certain historical continuity. We live in societies too complex to be interpreted in a unique way. The term that best describes the present condition is "excess": excesses of time, space, and ego. It is the latter, the excess of ego, which pertains to the individual and is somehow the real terminal of his discourse. An entire advertising apparatus, together with a system of consumption on the one hand, and individual freedom and civil rights on the other, has focused on empowering the individual's ego to levels never seen before. Individuals now build the cognitive map by themselves, tailored on themselves.

Augé's reflection on personal history that quickly ends up belonging to collective history[57] helps in a reading of a film like Fellini's *Roma*. The city's history becomes the history of the city

Chapter Ten

as lived by Fellini. All the layers of his experience become history: Fascism, bombings, theaters, brothels. It is Fellini's Rome that was represented. But Fellini's Rome is part of the true history of Rome. In *Roma* there is also another picture of excess—this time, a spatial one. Fellini and his film crew's entry into the capital was memorable. It was the 1970s. Fellini was on the screen as himself, trying once again to merge his experience with the then current history of the city. The entrance into the city's express way was an effective representation of excess in spatial, visual, and sonic terms. Cars, animals, military wagons, the busloads of fans, rain, prostitutes, and everything else made this experience a challenge—first physical and then psychological. The sonorous and visual multitude was an aggregate of isolated units which only seek to get through and come out on the other side of the tunnel. Augé notices an important disparity between the perspective of the whole in today's global world—supplied by the media and film industry as one long-continued filming, often from above, and more and more often also from satellites—and the individual's gaze which is lost in the city crowd and captures discontinuities and difficulties. Fellini's gaze in this long sequence deconstructs the sense of continuity. He critically photographs a chaotic multiplicity, which is very difficult for the individual, and to the limit of his possibilities. Fellini, however, does not hide even a certain fascination, a certain less-articulated expectation that mitigates the suspicion of a conservative attitude. The final perspective on Rome and its monuments viewed with the thrill of the speed of a large group of motorcyclists seems to refer to this expectation, re-establishing continuity in the young and accelerated pace of new, modern Rome.

    Calvino provides an image of continuity in *Invisible Cities* but the critical sense is evident here too. He does so with Trude, the second of the continuous cities. When Marco Polo approaches Trude, he already knows everything, even though it is the first time that he has visited the place. Trude is a city like many others, with the same hotels, the same shops, the same streets. Trude, then, can be found everywhere—it seems in fact to occupy the entire globe. Trude's idea crosses five continuous cities and Polo cannot ever get out. The airports, too, change only in name; they remain equal.

    Marguerite Waller highlights an innovative approach of Fellini's mounting techniques in relation to space. "One of the most striking, as theoreticians of the kind of editing known in this country as 'montage' have emphasized, is that visual images that are not contiguous with one another geographically or chronologically, and are not shot in the same lens, from the same angle, or in the same light, may become intimately related to one another—much more intimately and dramatically related than images within the same frame" (109).

The putting together of different shots ignores geography as we have considered it thus far. It is the very existence of cinema that manipulates perceptions of distances, and suggests a different geography of representations. "But what the cinema portrays today is not the concept of distance; it conveys the irrevocable feeling that everything is near to us, surrounding us, on top of us," writes Calvino in "The Autobiography of a Spectator" (25); an essay dedicated to Fellini. Cinema, alongside other media, has made an effort to represent and accompany a deep pulse of our society in this ultramodern condition. There is a new emerging geography. Aircraft quickly connect distant objects in space, creating individual maps in which Rome and New York are much closer to some than Rome and Reggio Calabria. Calvino went beyond the vision of the Fellinian individual as horizontal urban explorer, pulling the world's metropolis out of their original geography. Before Marco Polo, Calvino had begun exploring with Marcovaldo. With the ironic and enchanted lightness of this first Marco—the urban explorer, a kind of modern Pinocchio—and written approximately in the same period as *La dolce vita*, Calvino alluded to possible changes caused by the revolution in transportation:

> Entrò, sbatté gli occhi abbagliato dalla luce. Non era in una casa. Era, dove?, in un autobus, credette di capire, un lungo autobus con molti posti vuoti...
>
> Qualcuno in uniforme passava tra i sedili.—Scusi, signor bigliettaio,—disse Marcovaldo,—sa se c'è una fermata dalle parti di via Pancrazio Pancrazietti?
>
> —Come dice signore? Il primo scalo è Bombay, poi Calcutta e Singapore. Marcovaldo si guardò intorno. Negli altri posti erano seduti impassibili indiani con la barba e col turbante. C'era pure qualche donna, avvolta in un sari ricamato, e con un tondino di lacca sulla fronte. La notte ai finestrini appariva piena di stelle, ora che l'aeroplano, attraversata la fitta coltre di nebbia, volava nel cielo limpido delle grandi altezze.

Chapter Ten

> He entered, blinked, his eyes blinded by the light. He wasn't in a house. He was—where? On a bus, he thought, a long bus with many empty places...
>
> A uniformed man passed among the seats. "Excuse me, conductor," Marcovaldo said. "Do you know if there's a stop anywhere near Via Pancrazio Pancrazietti?"
>
> "What are you talking about, Sir? Our first stop is Bombay, then we go on to Calcutta and Singapore." Marcovaldo looked around. In the other place were seated impassive Indians, with beards and turbans. There were also a few women, wrapped in embroidered saris, a painted spot on their brow. The night beyond the windows was full of stars, now that the plane had passed through the thick blanket of fog, and was flying in the limpid sky of the great altitudes. (Marcovaldo 72–73)

Today it is enough to get on a city bus to get close to similar neighbors—or to get on the subway which, like an aircraft, shortens and recreates urban maps, quickly connecting non-contiguous areas of a city. The internet, similarly, albeit virtually, connects people instantly on different continents, and makes it possible to have hitherto unthinkable interactions. Spatial elements are extractable, ignoring the so-called real succession. The turmoil of contemporary spatial coordinates is a technological answer to the problems of hyperspace, and make it easier for the individual to experience the new space whilst also making it easier to represent. The cinema and literature have quickly adapted. The side effects of this are not indifferent to the possible transitional answers to the question "Who is a human being?" It is clear that overcoming geographical, mono-cultural, and national contexts is the most evident consequence.

Conclusion to Part Two

Post-war Italy went through deep transformations. Overcoming Fascism and its difficult legacy, facing the urgent needs of the population, and projecting the image of a different modern and Western country required many sacrifices and intense efforts. Reorganization involved every aspect of the life of the country: the economy, legislation, infrastructure, the education system, the media, literature, the national language and, from a broad perspective, a new scientific, political and cultural world vision. In the context of the Cold War, the new Italian Republic reunified the country better than ever before, sharing the system of production and organization of the rest of the Western Camp. The impact that all this had on the population was so deep that the important writer and film director Pasolini described the historical moment as an anthropological turning point. This anthropological shift as he called it was, according to him, first and foremost a consequence of the change of the mode of production that impacted on the people, their culture, the urban landscape, and the Italian national language—which suffocated local dialects. According to Pasolini, the new Italian citizen, who spoke Italian instead of a dialect, was a middle-class bourgeois whose appearance, dress, and even sexual life conformed to the collective trend. The profile of the new Italian, in Pasolini's terms, tended towards the middle class, therefore showing a higher level of wealth. Italian—as opposed to a non-national singular local identity such as, for example, Neapolitan—and bourgeois, have the same meaning. The relationship between wealth and the new (national) profile of the human being was highlighted in Part One. The (new) Italian, however—and this is what Pasolini felt the most passionate about—was successfully controlled to such a deep extent by consumerism that, in Pasolini's eyes, it seemed

Conclusion to Part Two

to be a continuation and evolution of Fascism. The bio-politics of the totalitarian system had not only survived in the Italian and Western society of the 1970s but, according to Pasolini, reached a level of effectiveness never seen before. Modernity was seen by him as, firstly, capitalistic consumerism and consumerism; with both being a continuation and an evolution of Fascism. The geography of this consumerist modernity has spatial, temporal and conceptual coordinates. It includes the center of the city, the North, the West, the middle class, today and tomorrow; all of these are opposed to the excluded (or to the to-be-excluded): the South, the periphery, the workers, people from third-world countries, farmers, the past, and uncontaminated nature. From an apocalyptical (Pasolinian) metaphoric point of view the excluded are closed in a virtual *lager*.

The outside world of Pasolini's utopian geography of modernity, however, and its ideological perspective on these issues, started from the outskirts of Rome and then extended to Africa, to the Yemen, and thence to the rest of the world. He was openly disappointed when the idealized people from as-yet-unmodernized countries appeared to be attracted by modern standards of living. This kind of perspective has survived Pasolini. It still informs and inspires, today. Representations about countries that belong to this ideological geography and, sometimes—as we will see in Part Three—also extend to the migrants who leave these countries to reach Europe.

Although, initially, Calvino and Pasolini belonged to the same political area, they represented two different and complementary sides of a country which was both agricultural and industrial, laïc and religious, something that is reflected in the paths that they both subsequently took. It is the vision of the country's future that divides the two writers and conditions their readings of its past. Although very critical in many aspects and particularly sensitive to the excesses of consumerism and to the environmental impact which the surge in construction was having on the beauties of the Italian coast and, more generically, in urban areas, Calvino looked at modernity with unconcealed hope. Like many prominent Western intellectuals, he openly criticized the authoritarian nature of the Soviet Union and, in the 1950s, decided to leave the Italian Communist Party. The communism that inspired the Eastern camp, however, was characterized by an irresistible attraction to science and knowledge—seen as a deep source of redemption and hope as well as being a lifestyle marked by materialism. Calvino's sensitivity or ideology of representation, although dealing with, and including in his perspective, the critical stances of postmodernism, did not really depart from this kind of modernity and, as Cesarani puts it, can be glimpsed "il fermo ancoraggio di Calvino a una concezione che potremmo chiamare variamente razionalistica, illuministica, habermasiana, della vita umana e del pensiero" ("that Calvino remains firmly anchored to a concept that can be called variously rationalistic, Habermassian and Enlightenmentian of human life and thought") (Ceserani 173). The subject-centric Calvino, who empowers Kublai Kahn, providing him with a chess board—a symbol of science and technology conceptually close to the present most powerful (quantistic, one might say today) calculators—has, in the cultural imprint of his beginnings, the original hope of empowering (completing, in his terms) the "new man" with knowledge, education and culture. Pasolini and Calvino, then, seem to be two different mutant heirs of communism. Pasolini inherited mostly anti-Fascism and the critique of capitalism, and amalgamated them with many other elements in his singular ideology. Calvino, on the other hand, while breaking away from an authoritarian ideology and maintaining a sharp critical attitude towards the present, looked forward to not giving up the utopian sensitivity of modernity's potential. Their different takes on the Italian language, for example, is a clear indication of their varying sensitivities. The evolution of the national language, which is very important for strengthening the internal cohesion of the country, became a terrain for debate between the two of them. Their confrontation is helpful in providing an understanding of the cultural and political stakes at play. The contemporary Italian language was, according to Pasolini, no longer based on the prestige of literary works, as happened after the unification of the country, but on the new media, on television, and on the industrial and economic capital of the country—on Milan. Calvino, instead, longed for an instrumentally modern language. According to him, modernity had outstripped the functionality of dialects. This instrumentally modern inter-language, concise and accurate, must be oriented not towards dialects but towards foreign languages. Nevertheless this language, he suggested, should nurture both its local and its international dual nature.

Conclusion to Part Two

Instead of the "new man," Calvino wrote about the incomplete human being. The "new man," defined by Corrado Alvaro, as we saw, as "transitional," implies a human being who needs to change. The incomplete human being is always changing, always being completed without ever reaching completion, always in transition. This aspect gained a new dimension in the contemporary hyperspace inhabited by Calvino's characters, who embody different roles, and exhibit degrees of fluidity. The chance of a disconnected and chaotic fragmentation of their experiences is averted by a different kind of completion, by a higher degree of organization. In response to contemporary big cities—to their mega-urban environments, to the plurality of information required to adequately navigate them, to the multitude of differences, to contemporary hyperspace—the answer seems to be a new kind of experience which enables them to be kept together, and to assemble these fragments and plurality. According to Calvino, a feature of contemporary literature is the network novel whose protagonist seems to be a kind of network subject. It is as if the new man is already old. Their mutant heir is the incomplete transitional human being. Their multidimensial heir, who lives in a plural hyperspace, is the network human being able to navigate our multicultural, and maybe relationship-fluid, hyperspace. However, as Kublai Kahn and Marco Polo do, this subject uses technology and mathematics to represent, and live in, the world.

Cinema and literature have important roles to play in these elaborations. In an essay dedicated to Fellini, Calvino observed that cinema uses techniques of representation that convey the feeling that everything surrounds us, everything is on top of us. The putting together of different shots ignores the geography experienced individually by each of us. From this there emerges a different geography of representation practiced by the cinema, alongside other media, which attempts to accompany a deep impulse of our time. The revolution in transportation has changed geography as it is experienced by contemporary travelers. A technological answer to the problems of hyperspace makes it easier for the individual to first represent and build a cognitive map, and then to experience the new interconnected context. Cinema and literature have quickly adapted, exploring, representing, and elaborating our lives at a time of the internet and the transportation revolution. The map of high-speed transportation transcends our local maps. The most

Conclusion to Part Two

connected world cities of the traveler's network are closer to each other for some than national localities. Clearly the profile of the traveler matters. A huge part of the world population is cut off from this alternative world map and experiences mobility in a very different way, as we will see in Part Three. In the West, however, the relatively low cost of travel opens, to the many, experience of this new (polarized) geography. The impact of this new dynamics is not indifferent to the possible transitional answers to the question "Who is a human being?"—the tendency to overcome geographical, mono-cultural, and national contexts seems evident.

Literature and cinema accompany all the phases of this process and frequently anticipate or detect the early stages of what is about to come. Fellini's Marcello and Calvino's Ludmilla are different to Marco Polo and Kublai Kahn, who are the first to play chess (experience new technology, travel, and knowledge) with the world. They are both middle-class and manage to live the mobility and multiplicity of the city and/or literature almost happily (at least in Ludmilla's case). Critics noticed that the likeable Ludmilla was a middle-class character and accused Calvino of applying commercial strategies in order to seduce his readers. The truth is that Ludmilla's and Marcello's profiles expose the situations and experiences that make many readers and viewers identify with them. They explore a world of interconnections and long chains of events, not one made up of isolated fragments. They are "network" human beings able to hold together episodes of the self in both spatial and temporal senses. Using Calvino's terms, they seem to have found completeness in their incompleteness, as incompleteness is dynamically possible to complete, to bridge, without ever being definitively completed. Living in our hyper-environment requires not only fast connections, both for travel and virtually, but also an adequate knowledge of this plural hyper-environment. The need for this dynamic knowledge is highlighted by Calvino in the concept of the (open) encyclopedic literature, in Calvino's idea of interlanguage, and in the concept of a contemporary open form of art which is also applied by Fellini and Pasolini. Reading/living all the novels/possible experiences, and moving fluidly from one episode of the experience to the next while maintaining a complex sense of continuity seems to be a possible privileged and implicitly promised plot of life. This is a type of network, plural, and multibelonging subject who speaks interlanguages, is

Conclusion to Part Two

encyclopedically educated, and is willing to explore and experience the world. This is an ideal and, let's highlight it again, privileged subject who experiences a rich world of opportunities—the *homo eligens* in Bauman's (*Liquid Life*) rereading of Calvino's terms, who keeps choosing without making a final choice, or the individual who prefers not to (definitively) choose, as Fellini's Marcello is advised—while the real one navigates confusion, difficulties, and a lack of adequate opportunities; looking through mobility to expand their chances for better opportunities and to find their little spot in the sun.

In this regard, Fellini offers other hints. The incomplete human being who chooses not to choose in Fellini's *La dolce vita* is young. The economic development of the country had other consequences. The episode with Marcello's father highlights the differences between the two generations. The prolonging of youth and increased life expectancy has altered the demographic aspects of Italian and Western societies, and has evidenced—under the new circumstances—the inadequacy of traditional family roles in continuing to fill existence as though nothing had changed. These demographic aspects, and specifically the composition of the workforce and its needs, usually also impact on both gender and migration policies, as we will see in Part Three when discussing the movie *Cose dell'altro mondo* (*Things of Another World*). Along with social, cultural and political fights, and the 1968 movements, the change in the inner equilibria of Italian society was mirrored in the referenda of the 1970s on abortion and divorce. The years between 1968 and 1978 were, indeed, one of the most intense intervals of post-war Italy. Generally known as the leaden years, they were packed with important political and social events such as the already mentioned movements of 1968, the various domestic terrorist attacks of both the extreme right and the extreme left, and the increase in the Mafia's interference in political matters. The leaden years also saw an increase in feminist activism, the promulgation of important laws such as "The Reform Law on Jurisdiction of the Family" (1975) and the "Law on equality at work for men and women" (1977), a divorce law approved in 1970, a 1974 referendum that upheld the law, and the abortion law of 1978 which was upheld by a referendum in 1981. Besides Fellini's *La dolce vita* and its cultural impact, Visconti's *L'innocente* (*The Innocent*), Germi's *Divorzio all'italiana* (*Divorce Italian Style*)

Conclusion to Part Two

and *Alfredo, Alfredo* approach many of the gender-related aspects of the cultural and political debate (see Cottino-Jones 142). Lina Wertmüller's comedies also focus on the battle of the sexes as well as on political and social issues. The gender-related aspects of her work are presented as a part of a very articulated context where political, economic, social, historical, and environmental aspects are interdependent and closely intertwined. This is particularly true in *Travolti da un insolito destino nell'azzurro mare d'agosto* which discusses—as we will now see briefly—class, geography, and gender issues of 1970s Italy. In 1977 Wertmüller, who was Fellini's assistant for *Otto e mezzo* ($8^1/_2$), became the first woman to receive an Academy Award nomination for best director. *Travolti da un insolito destino* was a big commercial and international success and starred Giancarlo Giannini and Mariangela Melato. In 2002, Guy Ritchie's remake (*Swept Away*) was released, interpreted by Madonna and Giancarlo Giannini's son, Adriano Giannini.

Travolti da un insolito destino starts with an intense and neurotic dialogue that accurately describes its historical context. Elements that emerge from Fellini's, Pasolini's, and Calvino's work are here enriched with additional analysis. First of all, the historical background. In the context of the Cold War, the fear that the communists would seize power and push the country towards the Soviet Union camp guaranteed decades of Christian Democratic power. In the 1970s, as already mentioned, social and political antagonism and unrest were very high and domestic terrorism produced some of the darkest events of post-war Italy. The so-called historical compromise, which was intended to include the Italian Communist Party (PC) in the government of the country, was being discussed; however, this culminated with the terrorist assassination of the Christian Democrat Prime Minister Aldo Moro who was trying to achieve it. The role of the Church in the intense dialogue is very much emphasized and criticized because the main topics of the discussion were abortion and divorce. The protagonists are Raffaella Pavone Lanzetti, a rich industrialist woman from Milan, and Gennarino Carunchio, a sailor, cook, waiter and general factotum from Sicily. His first name, Gennarino, recalls the teenager from Naples whom Pasolini idealized in a *Lutheran Letter* which was dedicated to him. This time, Gennarino is from Sicily but what does not change is Gennarino's alleged pureness, which in this film also recalls (somehow comically) the classic good savage. As Pasolini and many other directors and writers have done—such as, for example, De Carlo and, more recently, Celati, as we will see in Part Three—Wertmüller looked for a utopian place outside modernity which, in this movie, is an island off the Sardinian coast. In the civilized world, the rich, racist lady has the power to exploit and continuously humiliate Gennarino. On the deserted island, where they end up marooned after a shipwreck, Gennarino is far more powerful, and there are no obstacles to them falling in love. This island, however, is a temporary stay that serves as a negative mirror for the Italian context. What emerges is a polarized country with a polarized geography and society. In urban areas, in the north, in the rich strata, women are more emancipated and live, almost freely, the life which they choose to live. In suburban areas, in the south, in the poor strata, women are prolific mothers, and the patriarchal culture dominates. From Gennarino's perspective, rich women are "whores" who take part in orgies where any kind of sexual experience is practiced, including homosexual ones (Gennarino calls the upper-class males who allegedly participate in these orgies "ricchioni" or "faggots"). "Gennarino non capisce che il sessismo è una forma di oppressione equiparabile allo sfruttamento del proletariato" ("Gennarino does not understand that sexism is a form of oppression comparable to the exploitation of the proletariat"), while "Raffaella, d'altra parte, è politicamente conservatrice e razzista, anticlericale ma anche sessualmente emancipata" ("Raffaella, on the other hand, is politically conservative and racist, anticlerical but also sexually emancipated") (Frau, "La Bottana industriale e il Signor Carunchio"). Demographic and ecological aspects are also highlighted. Raffaella would like to protect natural paradises by making them inaccessible to "mass civilization." The yacht, where she sunbathes topless, and spends the nights playing cards and animatedly discussing politics, the blue sea, the wonderful Sardinian coast and its islands, should all, in Raffaella's view, only be accessible to the wealthy. The rich woman who is not a mother thinks that the prolific poor strata of the country would push the population towards 100 million inhabitants, almost doubling its actual size and causing the cementification of *Il Bel Paese*. Once again, the emancipation of the female condition is read against a demographic backdrop. The return to the modern (present) reality causes the end of the love story and the separation of the unusual couple. The heartbroken instinctual Gennarino, ready to give up his family, remains on the ground facing the rage of his wife, while the melancholic Raffaella, after the affair, returns to her husband and flies away aboard a helicopter. Class differences were, and remain, the most important. Gender relations seem to adapt to class, geography, and demography. It also looks as though their emancipation finds a better terrain in a wealthier context. This is why the improvement of the economic conditions and the auspiciously always larger middle class become the focus for social, political, and cultural changes, and attract the attention of film directors and writers. As Pasolini states in *Lettere luterane*, the "Italian" profile (and, implicitly, its project) is a bourgeois, middle-class one. The becoming of the Italian middle class did not happen by chance. Elisabetta Bini in her *La potente benzina italiana* (The powerful Italian Oil, 2013) points out that the strategical spread of mass consumptions and related improvements to quality of life were a form of political legitimization and national belonging in Europe and the Transatlantic block. The United States through the Marshall Plan pushed Italy and Western Europe towards the replacement of carbon with oil; a source over which they had better control (24). The powerful Italian oil companies also imported from the US an idea of society within which a certain model of masculinity featured. The ostentation that has been highlighted as a feature of the traditional Italian male—which we saw in Gianni Celati's reading of Fellini, was now reinforced within the profile of the male consumer. The message that passed through advertisement campaigns was that cars that ranupon oil were driven by strong men; with growing authority linked to consumption. Their advertisements "raffiguravano corpi 'americanizzati'—alti, sorridenti—alla guida di una italianissima Alfa Romeo" (they depicted "Americanized"—tall, smiling—bodies, driving a very Italian Alfa Romeo") (124). If the strong men in uniform—that we saw in Part I—were primarily pilots who flew with military airplanes as depicted by the Fascist Cinena, now, the male consumer drove a car and belonged to the middle class. Along with this model, however, came the idea of "gite domenicali" (Sunday rides) to distant locations where one could enjoy intimacy with young women; a scenario that provoked strong reactions especially from the catholic world which intended to defend young women's morality. The ads were prepared by specialized agencies in the United States and highlighted the consumerism and identity of the middle class (126).

Ludmilla and Marcello are also middle-class characters who live in developed urban areas which remain the main sites for experimenting transformations. The two of them look less like Gennarino and more like Raffaella, stripped of her racism and other conservative excesses. Fellini and Marcello seem to be aware that, in the wake of the economic boom, the old social organization model has exploded. This is not only male awareness and its consequent reaction, as Marcello's counterpart, the rich and bored Maddalena, shows. The "non-choice" suggested by a female American poet and a dominant feature especially in the upper classes of Western cities, is also embraced by the middle-class Marcello and, as already mentioned in Part Two, by the female protagonists of a more recent TV show, *Sex and the City* set in New York. This cultural battle interested the whole of the West. In the USA, according to Ross Douthat who, from the pages of the *New York Times* in February 2019, intervened in a recent debate on the issues raised by the Me Too era, "there was a clear liberal-led attack [between the 1960s and the 1980s] on the institutional form of marriage as it existed then, on the legal and cultural structure that privileged heterosexual wedlock, pushed couples toward its rules and rituals, and then constrained them from divorce." All this happened in the name of personal empowerment and female equality. The old legal and moral structures were considered oppressive. There was no longer a need for normative models of partnering. In more recent years, points out Douthat, support for no-fault divorces and legal abortions have continued, and sexual fulfillment has begun to be regarded as an essential good. Nevertheless, there has also been a degree of reconsideration of the advantages of monogamy as well as of the disadvantages of divorce.

Many of these aspects are shared by the Italian context. In *La Dolce Vita*, Marcello attacks the traditional Emma and the model of life that she represents. He rejects this model without being able to indicate a new one. The fluidity of his experience sounds like an unsuccessful search for a fulfilling alternative; resultantly, the fluidity itself becomes the alternative. The perpetual transitional human being is the perpetual incomplete human

Conclusion to Part Two

being. The fluidity of the experience could also hint at current debates on gender fluidity. The discussion from this perspective of Pasolini's later work, which includes Mario Mieli's stand for pansexualism in his *Elementi di critica omossessuale* and the connection with the US gay movement of 1969, clearly represented these problematics which are also part of today's cultural debate.

There is an important difference between the model of a fluid human being and what Calvino really suggests. Marco Polo is an enhanced subject as it were, the Soviet "new man" utopistically designed as an enhanced human being from the point of view of knowledge and culture. The fluidity in Calvino's stories should be read more as a trans-identitarian subject who does not lack a center, rather than as a centerless liquid subject. The very idea of the network novel—let me repeat and emphasize it—suggests a map, a continuity between episodes, a world of interconnections. I have provided in Part Two evidence in support of this reading. To this subject is offered an open and continuously updatable encyclopedia to help them interact with and interpret the world and the necessary technology. Calvino was writing before the digital revolution, which saw computers entering everybody's lives and internet connections virtually covering the whole world. Nevertheless he feels the need for it. Kublai Khan and Marco Polo see in the chess board a powerful calculator to help them imagine, know and interact with a wide extended environment. Calvino's re-representations are much more sophisticated because they offer the individual a new cultural map—geographical, scientific, economic and philosophical—in this new hyper-environment (made of space and of knowledge).

Using Calvino's reflections, I see today's network (trans-identitarian) individual as an individual who uses mobility to search for better opportunities and who belongs to more than one context in need of a cognitive world map (spatial and temporal, physical and of knowledge). The equivalent of non-belonging (of the non-human in Levi's terms), in this case, would be the disconnected and fragmented subject, schizophrenic (in Jameson's sense, who refers to Lacan's terms), lost in the impossibility of representing the multiplicity of the world. This culturally, legally, and geographically auspicious multibelonging individual is discussed in Part Three.

Part Three

The Geographic Human Being

Control of the human being through the control of space is a characteristic that assumed its clearest features, as we saw in the first part of this book, in the Soviet Union, where individuals were embedded by the state in spatial-temporal coordinates. The Soviet Union had to standardize the spatial-temporal profiles of individuals in order to dominate such a wide territory. The communist form was not the only totalitarian one that comprehended the real importance of managing mobility. Fascist Italy, for example, perfectly understood its importance when it enacted a specific law in 1939. There is, then, a very clear thread about the relationship that exists between power, space, and the individual that goes from the national state to totalitarian ones (like Communism, Nazism and Fascism), and to current flows of migration; as different readings from scholars such as Parati (*Migration Italy*), Carr (*Fortress Europe*), and Mezzadra ("The New European Migratory Regime") suggest. In analyzing the laws of migration in Italy and referring to Miriam Mafai's work, Parati examines the laws of the Fascist years relating to the residence of Italian citizens. In 1939, a Fascist law was passed that took a stance against urbanization in favor of a rural economy, and did not acknowledge the right of Italian citizens to choose freely where they resided. This law became unconstitutional in 1948 but remained enforceable, impacting on the lives of internal Italian immigrants in the 1950s and 1960s. In the same way, using other technicalities, current Italian laws on migration impact on the mobility of immigrants by connecting strictly labor contracts to residency permits. The fall of the Berlin wall and the end of the Cold War which had frozen international mobility posed new mobility challenges for Italy and Europe as both started to face new waves of migration. "The Bossi-Fini bill leads the discussion on migration back to terms very familiar to the restrictive 1939 laws on mobility that Fascism had embraced and post-war Italian industrialists had exploited" (Parati, *Migration Italy: The Art of Talking Back in a Destination Culture* 149). The limitations imposed on the mobility of migrants are, as we shall see, the focus of Sandro Mezzadra's article, which highlights the relationship between mobility and different levels of European citizenship. The borders of the European Union have become more and more mobile, projecting different degrees of citizenship and related rights. Within national territories, mobility rates translate into different levels of inclusiveness. The inclusiveness of European citizenship is a distinctive feature discussed directly and indirectly in Part Three. If Pasolini and Calvino were the referents of the debate on the (national) profile of post-WWII Italian, Part Three is a reflection on the geographic human being that will mark this passage. The new emerging geography that was related to the important improvements in transportation and communication seen in Part II will now coexist with a different geography that is made of borders and many obstacles along with sharp inequalities.

American Dirt (Jeanine Cummins) was published in the US in 2020. It is a thriller that narrates the story of a Mexican mother who crosses into the US with her son. As Alison Flood reported for *The Guardian US*, the book has "sparked debate about the legitimacy of who gets to tell which stories" (Flood, "Publishers Defend American Dirt as Claims for Cultural Appropriation Grow"). Though acclaimed by many writers including, for instance, Stephen King, Jeanine Cummins' novel was accused of stereotyping and faced scathing criticism from Latinx writers. In question was Cummins' right to tell the story. According to Alison Flood's report published on 24 January 2020, the Mexican-American author and translator David Bowles called the novel "harmful, appropriating, inaccurate, trauma-porn melodrama" (Bowles cited in Flood). In Kate Horan's view (cited in Flood), the "numerous inaccuracies in her story are clear evidence of the white gaze, capitalizing on hurtful stereotypes and cashing in on human suffering." Everybody is entitled, of course, to choose a subject and write about it. The problem is how much knowledge a writer has about their chosen subject, which narrative will become mainstream, and how it represents groups of people and their difficult stories. What is wrong, as David Bowles (cited in

Flood) put it, "is erasing authentic voices to sell an inaccurate cultural appropriation for millions." It is this "millions" imaginary that matters the most. It is the imaginary of public opinion that impacts on the quality of the integration of new arrivals. This imaginary also impacts the policies and the laws of the country with regard to its borders, immigration, and the very idea of national identity. The discourses and counterdiscourses that feed such an imaginary create a political battlefield where borders, or the lack of them—the already mentioned different degrees of citizenship and its related rights—are discussed and projected. In Part Three I raise similar questions with regard to the representation of realities to which mainstream Italian directors and writers have no direct knowledge. The Italian imaginary is, nevertheless, built on mainstream movies, books, and other media representations. Many of these directors, who are very much appreciated and beloved by viewers and readers, enter this difficult terrain with the best of intentions. The problems they face are similar to those raised in the US with regard to narrating the southern border-crossing: the lack of direct knowledge and their "white" gaze or, more precisely, their deep ideology of representation that, metaphorically speaking, never (and, maybe, cannot) leave(s) Italy, and always offers a local point of view when representing migrants. The stereotyped mainstream discourses often highlight different traits of otherness which, as a negative mirror, defines what Italians are and are not (supposed to be).

The terrain of the imaginary is also crucial for migratory dynamics. The context of the technological developments that have revolutionized the circulation of information has an important impact. TV, cinema, sporting events, and the internet are key factors in shaping and projecting life trajectories. It is well known how important cinema, music, literature, and TV were during the Cold War in creating an alternative, often idealized, reality which first became an important element in sabotaging the maniacal control of information, and later a factor in bringing down the Eastern European totalitarian system. After the downfall of the internal walls, it also fueled the motivation of many and caused the massive migration waves towards the West. If we looked for a similar mechanism today with regard to African migration, we would not be disappointed.

Part Three

The imaginary, geography, mobility, and discourses are all key factors that shape our contemporary world. In order to investigate many of these aspects, I have taken into consideration a good amount of mainstream and not-so-mainstream recent films, documentaries, and novels. One of the most difficult aspects in dealing with these cultural products is the relatively scarce availability of secondary literature, especially with regard to both the most recent and the non-mainstream titles. This is fortunately not always the case for the most well-known among them, like, for example, Amara Lakhous' successful novel (*Scontro di civiltà per un ascensore a Piazza Vittorio*) set in Rome. Part Three, then, has also been built as a geographic trip. It starts with the Southern Italian borders and slowly reaches the urban centers. The geography, as we shall see, also has an evident impact on the representations. The aspects in play are, however, more articulated and complex. I investigate, in this section, how different imaginaries are formed and how they impact on various subjects as well as the trajectories of their projects.

When this geographic trip reaches its destination, (larger urban areas such as Rome), the focus shifts to the "gated" communities—to say it like Bauman—that inhabit them. Many of the aspects considered in Part II are still valid but happen now in parallel, protected, and isolated social bubbles or closed communities that characterize our current urban realities. All analysis concerning globalization, from Bauman to Augé, converge in highlighting the idea that the world's elite, considered cosmopolitan, live in standard places wherever they happen to be. These are considered non-places, although what seems increasingly obvious is that, even among non-places, there is very clear stratification: for some, resorts are equipped with the most advanced technology; for others—the majority—they are no more than refugee camps. The production of non-places with different levels of standards is not very distant from the Soviet artifice. They are, however, more sophisticated. Tourists can visit a country, for example, without ever meeting poor people. The face that Italy shows specifically to Western visitors, and to the wealthy in general, is an abstraction of selected places—a cocktail of history, art, and squares polished for visitors but which are often far away from the everyday life of the country. Cities are now built on different levels that represent the economic layers of their inhabitants.

The Geographic Human Being

This is true all over the world; this is repeated (systemic) uniformity—spread more than anything else that is understood to be globalization. Rome itself, very central in this work, presents an implicit urban geography: the center is Western, the suburbs Maghrebian. The urban space is somehow dilated to allow different groups to co-exist. Rome has an international historical center—where English, French, German, Japanese and Italian are spoken—and Southern, East European, and North African suburbs. Rome is the Mediterranean face of globalization, of course, a classist and problematic one that cannot, however, stop the contamination. In Rome, one can begin to tell a different story, that of Piazza Vittorio, the most multiethnic central neighborhood, the one that brings Berlin closer to Cairo and that can keep Europe linked to the Mediterranean. The agents of this plurality are migrants. If the city's spaces are set up by ethnic communities, wealthy social classes, and voluntary and involuntary ghettos, it is the individuals who are delocalizing themselves, and decolonizing and rebelling by creatively creating proximities which are able to slowly redraw the urban map. Along these lines, it becomes clear how the national human being is transformed more and more into a geographical human being.

Chapter Eleven

The Italo-Albanian Cinematographic Confrontation on Fascism and Immigration

The nation-state model has been exported around the world via colonial expansion that made the economic motive a central aspect of the world's reorganization. Hannah Arendt identified the first elements of making humans superfluous as arising from the colonial experience, and considered totalitarianism to be the most advanced stage of imperialism. Italy, meanwhile, had its own colonial forays that were often minimized because of an almost double sense of shame: on the one hand, theirs were "modest" deeds compared to those of others; on the other, the colonial experience left a guilty conscience. For these reasons, dealing with a colonial past always becomes complicated. Immigration is, to some extent, the flip side of the colonialism coin, a reaction to the unfavorable global economic *status quo,* especially if the provenances are precisely those countries that were once colonized. This is why the event which broke the Italian mono-ethnic balance—the arrival of fleets of rusty ships full of Albanian migrants on the coast of Apulia in the early 1990s—activated a series of cultural complexes that are not easy to address. Gianni Amelio tried in the heat of the moment with a striking film, *Lamerica.*

Lamerica and the controversy on its release

Quite often the choice of a subject has an important impact on the kind of reception an artistic product will get. For example, Rossellini's choice, fresh from the success of *Roma Città Aperta,* to show Berlin at the end of the Second World War, implied a great responsibility and guaranteed attention once released. Gianni Amelio, too, before going to Tirana, had just finished a successful film—*Il Ladro dei Bambini* (*The Thief of Children*) which convinced the producer Cecchi Gori to grant him important resources for his next film. In Albania, a totalitarian regime that had lasted half a century had just fallen; this attracted a lot of attention because it was the last to do so in eastern Europe and because of the spectacular exodus that followed. Recounting this historical passage was as important as it was delicate. Amelio was sufficiently aware of this to say that he wanted to avoid filming a sort of *Tirana Open City*[58] but, among many references to Rossellini's films, the missing one, curiously, is *Germania Anno Zero*. *Lamerica* (Amelio), as we shall see, was intended to be a reportage filmed amongst the ruins of Albanian communism.

The protagonists are two Italian entrepreneurs who, in neocolonial style, go to Albania right after the fall of communism. The film opens with footage from the archives that glorifies the Fascist occupation of Albania and, halfway through the film, there is an historical summary presented through the words of an Albanian doctor who, in inaccurate Italian, tries to explain why the real name of Spiro—the third protagonist of the film in order of appearance and a survivor of 50 years of communist prison—is Michele, who is in fact Italian and not Albanian. "Prima di guerra, Albania era colonia di Mussolini ... Prima di guerra, qua tanti italiani. Comandano gli italiani in Albania, con il fascismo. Dopo di guerra venuti i comunisti. Italiani o in prigione o fucilati." ("Before the war, Albania was a colony of Mussolini ... Before the war, many Italians were here. Italians in command in Albania, with Fascism. After the war came the communists. Italians in jail or shot.") Narrated in this way, communism and 45 years of the regime seem to be a mere anti-Italian vendetta, so much so that this historical reading was the first element to excite controversy on release of the film. It was Ismail Kadare, author of the novel, *Gjenerali i Ushtrisë së Vdekur* (1963; *The General of the Dead Army,* 1991) who inspired three films on the Fascist experience in Albania—one Italian (Tovoli, *Il generale dell'armata morta*, 1983), and two Albanian (Anagnosti, *Kthimi I Ushtrisë së Vdekur,* 1989; Prifti, *Gjenerali i Ushtrisë së Vdekur,* 1975), which started the polemic:[59]

> Le faccio un esempio. Come reagirebbe lei se si dicesse che durante la Seconda guerra mondiale gli ebrei hanno perseguitato

i tedeschi? Ci sono verità che non si possono cambiare neppure nella fiction. E il regista di *Lamerica* mette sempre in primo piano l'ex soldato italiano ammattito nei decenni passati nelle prigioni albanesi. Il personaggio diventa un simbolo. È la vittima. La sua costante presenza finisce col far credere che i colpevoli sono gli albanesi. Non gli italiani invasori... Nel 1920 l'Italia ha tentato invano di occupare l'Albania, e il 7 aprile 1939 l'Italia fascista ci è riuscita. Ed è stata una doppia tragedia, perché in seguito all'invasione, attraverso la resistenza organizzata dalla Jugoslavia, è stato preparato il terreno al regime comunista. Senza l'occupazione italiana sarebbe rimasta una monarchia, senz'altro arretrata, ma con radici in Occidente.

Let me give you an example. How would you react if you were told that, during the Second World War, Jews persecuted the Germans? There are truths that cannot be changed even in fiction. And *Lamerica's* director Gianni Amelio (1994) always puts in the foreground the former Italian soldier who went crazy in previous decades in Albanian prisons. The character becomes a symbol. He is the victim. His constant presence ends up making the viewer believe that the culprits are the Albanians. Not the Italians, the invaders. ... In 1920, Italy tried unsuccessfully to occupy Albania and on 7 April 1939, Fascist Italy succeeded. This was a double tragedy because, after the invasion, through the resistance organized from Yugoslavia, the ground was prepared for the communist regime. Without the Italian occupation it would have remained a monarchy, certainly a backward one, but with roots in the West. (Valli, "Lalbania contro Lamerica")

Andrea Porporati, co-writer of the movie, answered Kadare, saying that "non avevamo l'ambizione di fare un film sull'Albania, ma piuttosto sull'Italia in relazione a quel Paese martoriato" ("our ambition was not to make a film on Albania, but rather on Italy in relation to that tormented country") (Grassi 35). *Lamerica* contains, in a sense, two stories, two films—a cinematographic debate on the twentieth century on Fascism, communism, and immigration; and the history of the region. This debate was anticipated at a distance by other films based on Kadare's novels—two Albanian and one Italian, as indicated above, and has continued with two documentaries on immigration that were produced in Italy in 2012, Vicari's *La Nave Dolce* (*The Sweet Ship*) and Sejko's *Anija: La Nave* (*The Ship*).

Chapter Eleven

A novel, two sets of propaganda, three films

In 1963, Ismail Kadare made his narrative debut with his novel *Gjenerali i Ushtrisë së Vdekur* (*The General of the Dead Army*). It is the story of a mission truly accomplished ten years after the end of the Second World War by an Italian general, and a colonel, (a chaplain in the army), to return to Italy the bodies of the 2,842 who fell in Albania during the Fascist invasion. The subject was sensitive and politically of great importance. It took many years for the novel to be translated into Italian, whereas it was published almost immediately in France where Kadare is held in high regard. In 1975, Albanian television produced a TV show. The year of its production leaves a recognizable brand on the film. All the hot topics of the moment, from isolation to the pro-Chinese Cultural Revolution, find space in the televised version of the book. The film opens with a speech by Mussolini and the slogan "Believe, obey, fight" interrupted and followed by images of a Catholic cemetery as the symbolic outcome of Fascism (not without a hostile allusion to the association between religion and invaders), and closes with a military parade in which the Albanian army flexes its muscles with Soviet and Chinese weapons. The freshly constructed bunkers are not shown yet, but the reason for them becomes ubiquitous.

During their mission the general and the chaplain encounter the general of another army accompanied by a mayor. Although it is clear that he is a German general, this fact is never made explicit. The vagueness of the general's origin has a function that is evident from what is said by the Albanian companion to the Italian general: "Now we lack only a general accompanied by a '*hoxhe*'"—a Muslim priest. This was like saying: "Generals of all origins, accompanied by priests of all religions." Other thematic strands of the film remain ideologically functional. Of primary importance among the remains of Italian soldiers in Albania are those of a colonel whose noble and rich family put pressure on both the Italian government and on the general and the chaplain directly. The elderly mother of the colonel and his young wife try very hard to ensure his recovery. This strand is central to the plot of the movie because the colonel was at the head of a notoriously punitive unit of the army known as the "blue battalion"; responsible for heinous crimes. The search for the body of the colonel allows for the reconstruction of his story, describing him as a murderer and a rapist of minors. It was in fact the mother of the raped girl who committed suicide and, at the same time, the wife of the husband hanged by the blue battalion, who killed the colonel. Everything is uncovered during the celebration of a wedding, in which the general and the chaplain participate without being invited. Albanian traditions are celebrated in the foreground of this scene, its music, the dances, and its youth, along with the uncommon hospitality; an important part of Albanian culture. The Albanians are seen as terrible enemies in war and exceedingly generous guests in times of peace, to the extent that they accommodate yesterday's enemy with all honors. This aspect is contradicted by the words of the chaplain, who describes Albanians as doomed to destruction and war, as are all Balkan peoples (these are words that end up on the back cover of the Italian edition of the novel—Kadare, *Il generale dell'armata morta* 1970). The chaplain is contrasted with the Albanian companion who finds this reading very hostile. This description, he explains, uses some obscure parts of Albanian tradition, like that of blood feuds, and seek "the elimination of the Albanian individual." But feuds and religion, he concludes, have always been instruments of invaders. Some 20 years later, albeit in a less peremptory tone, Kadare reproaches Amelio with the same hostility. For the writer, the film takes the idea of a "paese di cui non vale la pena occuparsi, perché è così lontano dall'Europa, così barbaro. Ieri si trovò come pretesto il comunismo e ora si assiste a un nuovo isolamento di questo Paese, a una sorta di ostracismo contro l'Albania. Un film come questo aiuta a giustificare l'ostracismo" ("country that is not worth dealing with because it is so far from Europe, so barbaric. Yesterday communism was seen as a pretext and now we are witnessing a new isolation of this country, in a kind of ostracism against Albania. A film like Amelio's *Lamerica* helps to justify the ostracism") (Grassi 35).

The wedding scene is the climax of the movie. The general decides to dance with the Albanians and, in the eyes of the widow—silent up to that point—this is unacceptable. The widow stops the wedding and, to the great astonishment of those present, goes to dig up the remains of the colonel from under the door-step of her home. The end of the story definitely has a macabre taste to it. The Italian general, with an ambiguous gesture that leaves room for interpretation, kicks the bag with the remains of the colonel and throws it in a river. Why does he do this? Does he distance himself from the figure of the criminal colonel or is this condemnation for having lost the war and humiliated the homeland? The film leans more towards the latter interpretation. When the widow silences him as a friend of the colonel, he explains to the chaplain that he despises the commanders who, instead of fighting, hid in tents with minors. The colonel is despised for the military defeat.

The farce that ends the film seems to be the fate of the heirs of Fascism. The colonel must be replaced. It is necessary to find another corpse of a soldier who is 182cms tall. This story overlaps another one. The German general who lost an arm in the war, accidentally unearthed some unknown soldiers and sent them to the wrong country. Who will replace the colonel? The German general proposes a deal: the corpse of a German soldier 182cm tall in exchange for money. In Kadare's novel, and in the two Albanian films by Anagnosti and Prifti, the deal will stop at a remark. The chaplain only wants to avoid the body of a deserter soldier murdered by the blue battalion ending up with all honors in the colonel's tomb. No break with Fascism. No respect for deserters.

In the same year that the TV show was released (1975), Kadare granted the royalties for making the novel into a movie to "Film 66," a French company related to the well-known French actor Michel Piccolì. The director, Luciano Tovoli, (former director of photography, writer and collaborator of Antonioni and Argento), said in an interview in 2006 on the occasion of the distribution of the DVD of *Il generale dell'armata morta* (*The General of the Dead Army*), that he had received a first suggestion from the film producer Ferreri. After another conversation with Marcello Mastroianni, who had read the French edition of the novel, Tovoli involved Piccolì, whose participation as a co-writer, producer and actor had a primary influence on the film.

Piccolì tried to shoot the film in Albania with the consent of the authorities and the assistance of the Albanian film institution. It was disagreements over the script that, above all, derailed the collaboration and put the film on a different track.[60] The film was then shot in Italy, in Abruzzo, in the mountains of Aquila and Gran Sasso. According to the film's producer, Enzo Porcelli, who was also a producer of several of Amelio's movies, this was what, together with Piccolì's excessive interventions in the direction, almost caused the failure of the film. The choice of Abruzzo curiously coincides with the amnesia and metaphorical overlapping that represents Michele, the former Fascist soldier and protagonist of *Lamerica*, who wrongly takes Albania for Abruzzo. Michele's loss—Michele who compares and confuses geographies, historical periods, Fascism, communism, and immigration—is a structural element of great importance in *Lamerica*. Amelio and his writers had definitely seen and consulted with the Italian version of *The General*, the vagueness of which—partially the result of the inability to film in Albania, and the slipping of Tovoli's film, as we shall see, towards a form of abstract Orientalism of the Albanians more suited to the relationship that the Italy of the 1980s had both with its own traumatic past,[61] and with the Eastern countries—contributed to a first cinematic imagery of contemporary Albania. Another episode, one of many that mark the movie's bumpy ride, speaks volumes about Italy's political mood at that time. The producers forced Tovoli to change the title as the original could have frightened the public and kept people away from the theatres. The new title was *L'armata ritorna* (*The Army Returns*).

Tovoli's film was not admitted to the Venice Film Festival and was, because of bankruptcy, not even distributed by the producer. Six films, including this one, were not distributed. Nearly two years after its shooting, the film was broadcast by RAI 2, the second network of Italian public television and the co-producer of the film. Kadare's novel—translated from the French by Augusto Donaudy—was subsequently published by Longanesi in 1970. However, in the note printed on the cover of the book, there is a hostile positioning of the reading.[62] According to this reading, the focus of the novel is the pride of a people "per il quale la guerra sembra essere una condizione di vita" ("for whom war seems to be a condition of life") and it is the Albanians who love the war. There is no mention of Fascist war crimes.[63] There is also no trace of self-criticism. Instead, it highlights the absurd condition of war "che unisce vincitori e vinti nella medesima desolazione" ("that unifies winners and losers in the same desolation"), and thereby suggests an abstract reading that does not focus on concrete events.

A few years after Tovoli's film, whose title was changed, as mentioned, into *The Army Returns*, the cinematographic (1989) Albanian version of the *General*, entitled *Kthimi i Ushtrisë së Vdekur* (*The Return of the Dead Army*) appeared. It was directed by Dhimitër Anagnosti. If we consider that the time between the first publication of Kadare's novel (1963) and the third film (which coincided with the fall of the Berlin Wall) was an interval of 30 years that covered a large part of Albanian communism, the political importance of the story becomes clear. Anagnosti, unlike Tovoli, favors a dramatic, political, and ideological narrative.[64] If Mastroianni's general was over the top—ridiculous, a womanizer and full of phobias—the general impersonated by Bujar Lako was "the envoy of a great state whose dignity should not be questioned."

Immediately, at the start of the movie, we see the general in the Italian Ministry of Defense building; part of a group of generals who are to be entrusted with similar missions in Ethiopia, Bulgaria, and so on. The colonial past and the sad fate of all colonial enterprises become the premise of the film. The defeat of the colonizers was what mattered most to the director (Anagnosti). It is not difficult to understand why this aspect was highlighted and why it was an implicit threat. "If you attack us, soon you will come to take back another dead army" is the clear message of the film—also stressed by the almost macabre finale when the remains of the colonel's substitute are deposited in a big black coffin, with the capital letter Z, the first letter of the Colonel's surname, emphasized, carved on the lid. The dark tones of the film, however, betray a creeping depression for the eminent end of the political system that had ruled for nearly half a century. In fact, with respect to the first version (*Gjenerali i Ushtrisë së Vdekur*, Vladimir Prifti, 1975), what was now missing were celebrations of the regime, euphoria for the present, and military parades.

The events that occurred between 1989 and 1991 deeply affected the region and the whole of Europe. Danger was expected to come from the West, from the sea and, in a sense, it did arrive from the sea. One apparently small episode marked the beginning of the end. A family of persecuted Albanians with the last name Popa (a total of six people), entered the Italian Embassy in Tirana in December 1985 and asked for political asylum. Italy refused to let the Albanian police arrest them. The gesture was considered to be a challenge that sought to discredit the communist government in internal public opinion.[65] In the official statement, the head of the family was declared to have been a Fascist collaborator during the war. Because of its isolationist policy, the retention of refugees was considered a very hostile act. The government forbade them to leave the country and, therefore, the embassy. At stake was the idea that the Albanians should not be fed with fantasies of escape and immigration. The impasse remained for several years. The event was so important that there were rumors about the involvement of other foreign secret services. The Italian archives on this matter can be consulted in 2035, 40 years after the episode took place (Luciani 93).

The episode in Albania created a very important precedent. In the summer of 1990, the so-called crisis of the embassies occurred, the first and most important crisis of dissent against the regime. Some Albanians followed the example of the Popa brothers by entering and asking for asylum first in the Italian embassy and then in others. They were imitated by thousands of people who were allowed to leave the country, mainly in the direction of Italy, Germany, and France, although only after UN intervention. This episode marked the beginning of the great exodus of Albanians. Its boom was recorded in early 1991 in conjunction with the internal rebellion that led to the fall of the communist regime. During this process, correctly reported in the film *Anija: La Nave* (*The Ship*), relations with Italy were of outmost importance. This is why Anagnosti's *Kthimi i Ushtrisë së Vdekur* (*The Return of the Dead Army*) and Amelio's *Lamerica* should be read, together with the first two "Generals," as part of this story.

Migrants, nightmares, and dreams

In 1994, five years after the production of the last *General*, the producer of Tovoli's film, Enzo Porcelli, became *Lamerica*'s executive producer. In a certain sense, *Lamerica* starts as a continuation of the *Generals*. The film opens with the so-called "unione politica, militare e nazionale" ("political, military, and national union") of the two countries, as stated in an excerpt of a 1939 Fascist documentary. In Kadare's novel, and in all three of the films adapted from his book, special attention is dedicated to the figure of the deserter who finds refuge, as did at least 6,000 of them, among Albanian peasants. *Lamerica*'s protagonist, Michele, is also a deserter of Sicilian origin who, however, is imprisoned at the end of the war in Albania just because he is Italian; he then stays there for almost fifty years. It was not just the lack of historical gratitude that triggered the controversy[66] but also the easy equation by which communism is reduced to anti-Italianism (and not anti-Fascism!). Even the infamous bunkers were anti-Italian. These aspects create the type of representation of the country presented by the film. In almost all the film, Albanians run, attack, and flee with extreme energy. It is not difficult to realize that the director, Amelio, like almost all Italian and international public opinion, was struck by the onslaught of tens and tens of thousands of immigrants on the Apulian coast in the early 1990s. In a way, Amelio remains in Italy, where the crowds arrive, projecting them like a prequel in the Albanian territory. All the cultural references that Amelio uses to read the Albanian reality are Italian: from Elsa Morante (the film's title,[67] and the concept of history[68]) to Rossellini (neorealist sensitivity and citations[69]), and from Rossellini to Pasolini (radical critique of modernity and the search for purity in the rural world and in poverty[70]). There is only one coordinate of cinematographic culture seemingly unrelated or contradictory: the fascination for Spielberg, Hollywood, and the subsequent use of Cinemascope.[71] In reality, the use of Cinemascope is much more functional to the thesis of the film than it seems. Spectacularization amplifies everything: the critique of the modern and the fear of the extramodern. The fall of Eastern European communism and the end of the Cold War radically changed Italy as well. The PCI was transformed into PDS, a corruption scandal known as "*Tangentopoli*" and the judicial inquiry that followed, known as the "*mani pulite*" or "clean hands" wiped out the main political parties (DC and PS in the first place), and paved the way for the rise of Silvio Berlusconi's *Forza Italia*. Then there followed the end of the First Republic, Mafia killings, and more and more impressive waves of migration. Suddenly everything changed. It was a lot, too much. This collective shock, and the urgent need to give meaning to everything in this film, was projected in Albania. The result is an Italo-centric movie.

The representation of Albania starts, so to speak, from the end of the film, from the overcrowded ship headed for Apulia and, before that, from the television chronicles of the landings of 1991. The overloading, and the energy of that ship require an explanation, a thread to be rebuilt in Albania. That's what the film does, showing a perpetual escape, an overflowing, desiring, distressed, energy. In each segment of the film we see men, women, and children hurrying, attracted economically,

Cinematographic Confrontation on Fascism and Immigration

physically, and psychologically to Italy as a country, geography and culture, as well as to the Italians as individuals. Language, music, pictures, clothes, shoes, cars, football are all vessels—ships to Eldorado mostly sought after, dreamed about in 50 years of enforced solitude. An attraction—which, in the film, becomes an obsession—and love which, at times, becomes almost murderous. The brutally repressed Italian passion erupts into an often aimless flight. The dreams of some become the nightmares of others. From the point of view of the desired destination, from the Italian point of view, the energy is a threat, and the attraction is a snare. (About-to-be) immigrants in the film are here and there transformed into zombies devouring Italians. In three scenes of *Lamerica, zombies* as former political prisoners, children and ordinary thieves surround, assault, undress and even burn all three of the Italian characters. Fiore, the entrepreneur impersonated by Michele Placido, who is searching among the political prisoners for a dummy to be fake president of his fake company, is surrounded and attacked by them in a dantesque scene. Gino, the young Sicilian impersonated by Enrico Lo Verso, whose car was deprived even of its wheels, is assaulted and stripped in prison, where he is locked up as a crook. Michele/Spiro, the former deserter on whose shoulders rests the History (Fascism, communism, and immigration all together) and impersonated by Carmelo Di Mazzarelli, a non-professional actor in a neorealist style, is locked up by a pack of kids and literally burned alive (though he survives with only asphyxia), not by chance in a bunker, the symbol of anti-Italian communist hostility! Then, as the zombies turn the victims into new zombies by biting them, the prisoners and the Albanians in general, after depriving Gino of his sports jeep and his passport, and stripping him of his elegant clothes in prison, turn him into yet another Albanian who has to join the crowd and attack the ships. There is a very obvious sense of anxiety from the Italian perspective, an incessant alarm of invasion that records migrating masses in perpetual movement toward Italy. A sense of alarm which, in the film, is all visual! A sense of alarm that profoundly changed the Italian imagery.

Gino, now unemployed, a beggar, an illegal migrant, meets again on the ship the multi-functional Michele/Spiro, former deserter, former political prisoner, former presidential nominee of a ghost company, and now illegal immigrant. Michele/Spiro has

Chapter Eleven

completely lost all sense of time and place to the point of confusing the Albanian coast with the Sicilian coast (having previously confused Albania with Abruzzo), the 1990s with the start of the twentieth century, and believes that the ship is heading for America, towards a new world big enough to hold migrants of all ages and of all nationalities. However, despite the Pasolinian search for purity in the poor, untouched by modernity, what remained etched in the collective imagination were the desperate crowds storming the Italian coast and the sense of impending apocalypse. It is the economic profile of the contemporary Italian who felt threatened. About six or seven years after *Lamerica*'s release, the majority of the center-right promulgated the Bossi-Fini law on immigration which ties the legality of the presence of foreigners on Italian territory largely to economic means.

Lamerica, then, is also a report on poverty. The continual amnesia of Michele/Spiro, the presidential nominee of the Italo-Albanian firm into which the scammed aid coming from Italy should have been deposited, becomes an excuse for his wandering around the north of Albania and for Gino to chase him. The central and most consistent part of the film becomes a report on the state of Chinese trains, ante-war buses, miserable suburbs, and restaurants without coffee, water, or telephones. All on a massive flight from the country. It is indeed a unique moment in history and, from an artistic point of view, a unique opportunity. The old order had collapsed. A third of the population actually left the country, while the rest coagulates in the larger cities—in some cases, as in Tirana, tripling the number of inhabitants. The process of radical change had just begun and would introduce, in fewer than ten years, a metamorphosis such that would make the country unrecognizable from many points of view. That is why, rather than *Tirana Open City*, *Albania Year Zero* seems to be a more appropriate model.

Europe first allowed the free circulation of Albanian citizens in 2010 and, thereafter, admitted Albanian candidacy for the European Union in 2014. This changed the cultural discourse. The ship that had shocked Italy and Europe in the summer of 1991 become *La Nave Dolce* (*The Sweet Ship*) in Daniele Vicari's documentary and the symbol of an important historical process in Roland Sejko's *Anija: La Nave* (*The Ship*). The emphasis now turned to human aspirations, and towards the dreamy dimensions of those events. Both films were co-productions between Italy and Albania, and both films were very well received by the public and by critics. The difference between the footage scenes shown in *Anija*, where many normal couples with children in their arms can be seen hurrying at a slow jog or accelerated walk towards the ships, and the explosive energy of a discolored crowd perpetually running in *Lamerica* is clear. If the ship in the final scene of *Lamerica*, named not coincidentally "*Partizani*" ("The Partisan," a symbol of the anti-Fascist resistance who, in Amelio's film, emigrates to Italy!!), brings together the poor of the beginning and the end of the twentieth century in a timeless and always identical journey, the *Legend* of Sejko's documentary, who had experienced that trip in the first person, becomes a dreamy modern cruise. While a kind of redemption in Amelio's film was represented by Gino's—the neo-colonizer—complete stripping of all his belongings and by his joining the poor of all times, the redemption and fullness of being in Sejko's film is sought in a tension of well-being which is as dreamy as it is modern. Clearly, the year of production allowed Sejko a calmer historical gaze. The deeply changed and modern Albania of the last part of the documentary seems also, in this case, to have been the starting point of the film. The course towards the ships and the accelerated modernization of the country appear to be the result of the same impulse, episodes of the same historical process. The cultural discourse that put together the Orientalism of stereotypes with phobias caused by immigration has dominated Italian media for at least two decades. Only recently have major newspapers and public broadcasters promoted a more positive and reassuring image. The green light towards Europe in *Anija's* final sequences explains a lot.

In 2020, the European Union finally opened negotiations with Albania for its membership. In recent years, Italy has constantly supported this process. Hundreds of thousands of Albanians currently reside in Italy, and many have acquired dual citizenship through the process of naturalization. In 2025, almost 35 years after the start of the massive migration waves to Italy, Albanian-Italians are considered to be a successful model of immigration and integration, so much so that, in an Italian Studies context, academic interest in Albanian immigration has appeared to fade. According to Serena Luciani, Director of the Italian Institute in Tirana in 1988–1990, little interest was also

Chapter Eleven

shown in the past and the reasons as to why the Italian context did not pay attention to Albania "-paese d'importanza soprattutto strategica nella dinamica della Guerra fredda—non era dovuto a una semplice indifferenza provinciale, ma era legato, in ambito italiano, al particolare processo di rimozione successivo al fascismo." ("—a country of strategic importance in terms of the dynamics of the Cold War—was not due to simple provincial indifference but, rather, to the particular process of removal following Fascism") (Luciani 86). In more recent years, even an important volume in postcolonial studies such as *Postcolonial Italy* (edited by Lombardi-Diop and Romeo), from which I discuss in this section three important articles authored by Mezzadra, Trento and Triulzi, did not include any articles about Albania, although in the book's introduction, it lists Albania as being among Italy's colonial enterprises. Mezzadra's chapter, however—which I discuss shortly—and its idea of a non-casual ranking of the immigrants' conditions and different levels of European citizenship, could implicitly tell us that the main scholarly focus is placed where the main problems are. One of the few exceptions in this regard is the volume *Il Confine Liquido* (2013; *The Liquid Border*), edited by Emma Bond and Daniele Comberiati, which debates the inclusion or exclusion of Balkan case studies under the paradigm of postcolonialism. Italian-Albanian relations should be considered, according to the authors, paradigmatic of a specific way of thinking the present categories of colonialism and postcolonialism (14). The relatively brief duration of the occupation (1939–1943), the view of colonialism as an extra-continental feature, and the absence of evident elements of exoticism and disorientation are among the aspects that have contributed to the non-application of these categories to the Balkans in general, and to the Albanian case in particular. Besides highlighting the relatively brief duration of the occupations even in the Ethiopian and Libyan cases and the decades of cultural influence exercised through the Italian media in Albania during the Cold War, Bond and Comberiati point out that, since the years immediately before the Unification of Italy, the extension of Italian national borders eastwards has been constantly discussed. "Come nel caso dell'acquisizione del porto di Assab, avvenuto prima che Roma venisse tolta allo Stato Pontificio, contribuendo in tal modo a costruire un'identità nazionale collegata fin dai suoi albori all'espansione coloniale, così il dibattito sui confini orientali della nazione si è sviluppato negli anni dell'indipendenza, facendo intravedere immediatamente come si sarebbero prospettati gli scenari futuri." ("As in the case of the acquisition of the port of Assab, which took place before Rome was taken from the Papal States, thus contributing to building a national identity connected since its dawn to the colonial expansion, likewise the debate on the eastern borders of the nation was developed in the years of independence, making it immediately clear how future scenarios would look.") (Bond and Comberiati 16).

More recently, Caterina Romeo, co-editor of *Postcolonial Italy*, in her article "Italian Postcolonial Literature," studied Albanian-Italian writers though the lens of postcolonialism. Romeo, in this article, considered the relationship between the two countries "colonial," and stressed the same elements that Bond and Comberiati had highlighted. In addition to the short-lived Italian occupation of Albania, Romeo also saw the prolonged mediatic Italian influence as "a more recent form of cultural colonialism that strongly informed the Albanians' desire to migrate" (17). Within the wider framework of postcolonial literature, too, she defined the second largest migrant community in Italy as Albanian-Italian literature.

The relatively successful experience of Albanian immigration and integration in Italy started, however, in a very dramatic fashion. The 1990s, especially, were difficult years, when a complex mix of hospitality, solidarity, discrimination, stadiums, sacrifices, hard work, criminality, and tragic shipwrecks fed Italian imaginary on Albanians in particular, and immigrants in general. Between the visually expressed nightmare of biblical invasions seen in the Amelian crowds, which contributed to a problematic collective imaginary, and Sejkos' relatively recent dreamy ship, the latter turned out to be a more appropriate representation.

Chapter Twelve

Lampesuda: The New Border

The outlook on modernity and the Italian imaginary of Africa: Pasolini, Di Carlo, and Celati

It is useful to highlight a thematic strand in Italian culture that influences representations of contemporary immigration. This strand brings together important names of the Italian twentieth century and revolves around the critique of modernity. Such criticism often ends up building an idealized elsewhere and otherwise that is also physically out of modernity.[72]

Andrea De Carlo published the novel *Due di Due* (*Two of Two*) in 1989. The protagonists are Guido and Mario, two Milanese guys with some initially anarchist inspirations. In the first part of the novel, set in the 1960s, both friends try to satisfy their need to rebel but, after many turns and adventures, one of them, Mario—thanks to a sudden inheritance left to him by the second husband of his mother—decides to move to the countryside, a move defined by his friend Guido as "the only possible salvation." In Gubbio, Mario tries to create a new small community that is in contact with nature and far from any suffocating connection with urban environments. He starts with little, first alone, then with Martina, a librarian who becomes his mate. They are joined by Chiara, her sister. Then they have two children and, finally, are joined by the restless Guido, who immediately imagines the transformation of their small community into a self-sufficient village:

> [...] io e Guido guardavamo il paesaggio, intaccato e aggredito e devastato man mano che ci avvicinavamo alla città: gli svincoli e i sovrappassi assurdi a quattro corsie, le enormi scatole di cemento dei piastrellifici e mobilifici e salumifici, gli insediamenti periferici costruiti per speculare sullo spazio e sui materiali e sulle forme e sulla vita di chi ci abita. A un certo

> punto Guido ha detto: "Noi scappiamo via e questo schifo continua a diffondersi, non c'è nessuno che prova a *fermarlo*." Ha detto che forse l'unica cosa da fare era cercarsi un'isola come avevo fatto io, proteggerla finché ci si riusciva.
>
> [...] Guido and I looked at the landscape, which appeared dented and attacked and devastated as we approached the city: the intersections and absurd four-lane overpasses, the huge boxes of cement of tile works, of furniture factories and of sausage factories, the peripheral settlements built to speculate on space, on the materials and forms and on the lives of those who live there. At a certain point Guido said: "Let's run away, this crap continues to spread, no one is trying to stop it." He said that perhaps the only thing to do was to look for an island, as I had done, and protect it until it was possible. (De Carlo 246)

This becomes the turning point, the utopian level of the whole novel. The bond with Chiara, Martina's sister, is not enough for Guido. Neither are a child, the second house next to his friend's house (where he never goes to live), or the writing of *Canemacchina* (*Dogmachine*), an antagonist novel that becomes a great success only after it has been manipulated by the system. He ends his life in a car accident, like a character from the writings of Keruak or Kundera, and leaves the second house empty and uninhabited. Mario then burns it along with the utopia of the self-sufficient countryside community. There remains only Mario's family and their agricultural and biological enterprise, more an island than anything else—this is akin to saying that there is no way out from modernity.

Seen from this perspective, the documentary film by Gianni Celati, *Passare la Vita a Diol Kadd* (*Spending Life in Diol Kadd*) is a continuation. On the possibility of transcending the imaginary of a whole life, the imaginary of one's own community, and on the potential for representation of the documentary or non-fiction, Gianni Celati, who traveled to Africa—to Senegal—where he spent three years making a documentary and writing a book, seems to place some hope. "Gennaio 2006. Quello che scriverò sono osservazioni sul modo di passare la vita in un piccolo villaggio africano, piantato nella grande savana che va dagli ultimi quartieri di Dakar al confine settentrionale del Senegal. Vorrei che tutto apparisse meno romanzesco possibile, perché non se ne può più di queste vite da romanzo a cui dovrebbe somigliare anche la nostra. Giorno per giorno passa la vita e basta" ("January 2006. What I will write about are observations on how to spend a life in a small African village, planted in the great savannah that goes from the last neighborhoods of Dakar to the northern border of Senegal. I would like everything to appear as least fictional as possible, because I cannot stand any longer these novel-like lives, which should also resemble ours. Life passes day by day and that's it") (Celati 9). This is how Celati's book—which accompanied the shooting of the documentary—starts. The novel-like lives, about which one of the most famous novelists in Italy writes, are ours, they are Western. Although taking a stand against these novel-like lives, Celati does not distance himself but, criticizing them becomes the profound motivation of the whole journey; it influences readings and filming. The contrast between "noi" ("us") and "loro" ("them"), between "qui" ("here") and "la" ("there"), between "oggi" ("today") and "ieri" ("yesterday"), where "noi," "qui" and "oggi" ("we," "here" and "today") constantly measure distances with "loro," "la" and "ieri" ("them," "there" and "yesterday"), is the gravitational core of both the film and the book. Africa becomes a land of diversity that is understood more as a contrast than a heterogeneous otherness. Celati carries within himself Italian and Western contradictions that have been caused by modernity and to which he tries to give an answer. He does so simply by trying to get out of it. He does not go to Dakar, the capital of Senegal, where the political class speaks in French but to Diol Kadd, a peripheral village without electricity, which speaks in Wolof and which seems to be located beyond or, better said, before modernity, before the infrastructures, before the capitalist frenzy, at the last border with the desert where: "la denudazione dei terreni produce effetti secondari, forme di vita impreviste. La varietà di piante che attecchiscono farebbe concorrenza anche ai più grandi giardini botanici del mondo. Isolato in una pianura che va dai sobborghi di Dakar ai confini della Mauritania, Diol Kadd è l'esempio più chiaro di un lungo tentativo d'adattarsi al deserto che avanza." ("the denudation of the land produces secondary effects, unforeseen forms of life. The variety of plants that take root would also compete with the largest botanical gardens in the world. Isolated in a plain that goes from the suburbs of Dakar to the borders of Mauritania, Diol Kadd is the clearest example of a long attempt to adapt to the advancing desert.") (Celati

Chapter Twelve

18). A natural reserve, in short, spatially beyond the last margin of modernity, and temporally immersed in a pre-modern agricultural past where watches are used only as bracelets by a few, and time is that of "delle abitudini mentali e dei movimenti collettivi nella vita quotidiana." ("mental habits and collective movements in everyday life.") (Celati 58). Every episode and phenomenon narrated almost always ends with a comparison with "us." This is the point of view, this is the center from which all distances are measured. If we are told that the Wolof are married between cousins by decisions of the elderly males and that marriage is used only to make children to be employed in the fields, the inevitable conclusion is that here "tutto ciò che noi consideriamo passione amorosa non si manifesta in nessun modo e di fatto non ha senso" ("everything we consider love is not manifested in any way and in fact it makes no sense") (Celati 49). As Celati reminds us, the same happened in the peasant past of our societies where "la ricchezza delle famiglie stava nel numero dei figli messi al mondo." ("family wealth was in the number of children brought into the world.") (52). Instead of the radio to entertain, there is a version of the storyteller, a tireless narrator of stories handed down from generation to generation. The younger generation, however, begins to dress following styles and fashions that the author traces in the youth of the south of Chicago, all for the benefit of a future "umanità pubblicitaria" ("advertising humanity") which arrives in Senegal and Diol Kadd.

Celati's book is all about measuring the distances between "us" and extra-modern life, even if the girl called Mam'Asta, the favorite of the Italian documentary film crew, gives going to Italy a try. The regret for our anxiety-riddled life that is turned fully towards earning, makes the well-known Italian writer appreciate a life fulfilled by small daily gains that guarantee only subsistence. The formal reason for the trip also focuses on a similar aspect. The Italian troupe films a comedy staged by the villagers. It is a remake of Aristophanes' *Pluto*, which was written about 2,500 years ago. The blind God of Wealth, Pluto, explains that, if all men became rich no one would want to do certain jobs and that wealth, therefore, leads to paralysis. Naturally no one listens and, when Pluto's blindness is healed and he distributes belongings to everyone, his predictions come true. The reconstruction of Aristophanes' writing in a modern key by Mandiaye, a local person, is a reference "alla povertà africana come una paradossale salvezza, o almeno un punto d'equilibrio associato alla necessità comune." ("to the African poverty as a paradoxical salvation, or at least as a point of balance associated with the common necessity.") (Celati 27). Celati seems to literally praise poverty and hope for the conservation of this natural reserve. At least this way, when we want to escape from modernity, there will remain an island to which to escape. In a life that simply flows, time is not meticulously divided and controlled by hyper-effective capitalistic organizations. Men and women, freed of the torment of gain, without anxiety, and without great desires, marry to multiply and multiply to face the needs of subsistence agriculture. It seems that this is almost the state of pre-modern harmony postulated by Calvino in his trilogy of the 1950s. Echoes with Pasolini's film *Appunti per un'Orestiade Africana* (*Notes for an African Orestes*) here become all too evident. Pasolini's documentary on a "film to be done" in the late 1960s in Uganda and Tanzania had as its goal, the choice of places and faces for the transposition of Aeschylus' *Oresteia*. Pasolini clearly aimed to reflect on the political, cultural, and anthropological effects of the imminent arrival of modernity in these countries, and to elaborate an analogy of African tribal civilization with the Greek archaic one at the time of the arrival of democracy.

Pasolini's readings of otherness—meant mostly as that of the extra-modern, extra-capitalistic and extra-Western—are known to scholars and readers. In his last unfinished novel *Petrolio*, in Appunto (Note) 41, Pasolini narrates the story of a British progressist named Tristram Walker, who has graduated from Cambridge University and works as a reporter for the daily newspaper *The Guardian*. Tristram visits Africa where, in a sub-Saharan slave market in South Sudan, he meets, purchases, and enslaves a local black 12-year-old girl named Giana. Giana's sexual slavery experience equals the cruelty seen in the movie *Salò*. Tristram, writes Pasolini, should have been an "inibito puritano" ("inhibited Puritan") but his "mezza cultura" ("half—(progressist)—culture") wants him disinhibited, allowing him in this way to accept and accommodate his "sadism classico Vittoriano" ("classic Victorian sadism") (*Petrolio* 160). Later Tristram sells Giana to a religious (European) mission and, on his way back home, first purchases Marx's *Capital*, and then visits Naples, where he meets a *scugnizza*, another Giana. The black-African Giana symbolizes,

Chapter Twelve

Pasolini writes, the people of the Third World and their "magica" ("magic") different culture. Tristram's and Giana's cultures, along with the *scugnizza*'s, the Neapolitan Giana's twins' culture, cannot communicate or be integrated.

Back to Europe then, back to Naples (so much idealized in Pasolini's *Lutheran Letter* dedicated to the teen Gennarino), and back to Italian problematics. "La pasta (della carne) era una pasta diversa da quella (...) della cultura dominante (...) (...) che poteva integrare la cultura popolare solo facendola sua, cioè costringendola a degenerare, a restare nei livelli bassi della coscienza così come era restata, per secoli, nei livelli bassi della società" ("The dough of her [the *scugnizza*'s] flash was a different dough from that (...) of the dominant culture (...) (...) which could integrate popular culture only by making it its own, forcing it to degenerate, to remain in the low levels of consciousness as it had remained, for centuries, in the low levels of society") (*Petrolio* 170).

Tristram understands and, like "San Paolo sulla via di Damasco" ("Saint Paul on the way to Damascus"), suddenly converts to Marxism. According to Pasolini, the only way these two cultures can meet is through domination, exploitation, and repression. In his view, non-capitalistic organized societies and peasants' cultures are universal. One year before his death, and most likely while he was writing this unfinished novel, Pasolini, in reply to Calvino, who had accused him of being nostalgic for the "Italietta," published an article in the daily *Il Paese Sera* entitled "Limitatezza della storia e immensità del mondo contadino" (08 July 1974; "Limitedness of History and Immensity of the Peasant World") where these analogies between Third World cultures and what he defines as Italian pre-industrial cultures are further explained. The peasant universe,—writes Pasolini—to which sub-proletarian urban cultures also belong, is transnational and does not acknowledge nations. Pasolini liked to spend as much time as he could in Third World countries because, as he states, he still used to find there a limitless pre-national, pre-industrial peasant universe. Apparently, it is the same world which Amelio was looking for in Albania in 1994, and Celati was searching for in Senegal in 2006.

Giovanna Trento's article "Pierpaolo Pasolini in Eritera. Subalternity, Grace, Nostalgia, and the rediscovery of Italian Colonialism in the Horn of Africa," included in the aforementioned volume *Postcolonial Italy*, adds a colonial reading to these analyzes. Pasolini's texts underline, in Trento's view, the continuity "between pre-Fascist colonialism, Fascism, and post-colonial representation of Italian colonial Africa" (140). Although Pasolini's idea of Africa was influenced by Marxist, Pan-Africanist, anticolonialist, Gramscian, and post-Gramscian discourses, Trento spots, in Pasolini's idea of Africa, Italy's self-representation and the construction of "Mediterranean Africa" that emerged during Italian colonialism (139–40). This construction of "Mediterranean Africa" is fundamental to the building of Italianness. Pasolini's Italianness, however, was influenced by the "southern" debate and his representation of Africa starts precisely "from Italian subalternity" (Trento 142). "Pasolini always paid poetic attention to national narratives and the building of Italianness, thus constructing an oxymoronic 'panmeridional Italianness'. Consequently, the fact that he also focused on the Italian colonial past in the Horn of Africa is not surprising, because colonialism was an important element in the building of Italianness after the unification of the country and remained such in the early-twentieth century for the shaping of both Futurism and Fascism" (Trento 141). It was evidently the Italian debate on the Southern Question that inspired Pasolini's "Pan South" (*Panmeridione*), a non-geographical *topos* where "traditional" values are subversively used to resist industrialization and late-capitalist alienation (Trento 140). It was evidently the idealized *scugnizza*, both the starting and the arrival point, and not the 12-year-old African of *Petrolio*'s Appunto (Note) 41.

Toward Italy

A human mass; dense, excessive, mysteriously bound together around an unseen but imagined trunk, advances slowly, paradoxically, in the nothingness of the desert. Among them there is not even a spare inch. People and their essential belongings are compacted into a unique human mass that glides forward monotonously. Where it comes from, and where it goes cannot be seen. Our imagination recalls something similar from recent memory. Human masses, even those transported, that glide through the water in what they call tramp steamers. The latter are called *boat people*. Nobody had seen the *truck people* before. The former cross the sea; the latter the desert. But all of them are migrants: crowds of humans forced by a driving energy, irresistible; no one knows whether they are moved by the need to escape wars, hunger, unemployment, drought or some kind of nightmare, or whether they are attracted by a dream, by the lights of distant cities or by both, creating a unique short circuit, an irresistible synergy in the face of which, overwhelmed and powerless, we recognize an enormous strength which we call the wind of history. The *truck people*, if they survive the desert, the traffickers, and the Libyan prisons, they, too, will become *boat people*, ready to infiltrate the liquid boundary of Europe. They come from the south of the South. They travel light, with little or nothing to lose except their lives. They are the focus of certain documentaries by Andrea Segre (with Liberti and Pastore) such as *A sud di Lampedusa* (*South of Lampedusa*), (with Liberti) *Mare chiuso* (*Closed Sea*), and (with Yimer and Biadene) *Come un uomo sulla terra* (*Like a Man on Earth*). The worlds look at each other. Segre and his colleagues, in *A sud di Lampedusa*, re-run images from a television set in a Libyan detention center for immigrants. A champion cyclist with obvious bands of muscles, large sunglasses, a bicycle, and a colored shirt, crosses the finishing line as the winner amid escort cars, cheering crowds, and photo flashes. The immigrants sleep on the ground, ten at a time shut in a small bare room, and imagine themselves in the goal of their dreams. More pictures, this time for other spectators outside the detention center. A sparkling Porsche, azure waters, sunglasses on tanned faces and umbrellas over refreshing beverages, beautiful men and women, elegant, highways, gigantic images on the facades of skyscrapers, and speed. Advertisements, film, TV or documentaries; it doesn't matter. Look at these clips in succession, in any order you like. All of them, one way or another, one from the perspective of the other, seem to be science-fiction films. The first world seems to be the post-apocalyptic version of the second, whilst the second at least at first seems literally to be another world. The first follows the second and dreams of it. The second places endless barriers to the first and is its apocalyptic nightmare. Think of the television series *The Walking Dead* for example. Modern civilization loses everything, is invaded by an extra-human mass, invaded by zombies. Fortunately, no one dares to call the migrants "zombies" but the deep fear of the loss of standards of advanced civilization—based primarily on its own ultra-modern infrastructure, on its own technology—the fear of radical difference, the fear of falling out of modernity, combined with the obscure fascination for an existence based on the ultimate instincts of survival, that fear is everywhere.

Imagining the world from a profoundly different point of view is arduous if not impossible. The multitude of immigrants surrounds our modernity not to demolish it but simply to be part of it. For this reason, the inhabitants of the South of our world, by paying high prices, walking, then by truck—going through hard times, prisons, sacrificing months, years of their life—pierce the net, come out on the other side, and then return to their places of birth by plane, covering the same distance in about an hour or two. Khouribga is a Moroccan city, from where many leave to reach Sicily. In the book reportage *Mamadou va a Morire: La Strage dei Clandestini nel Mediterraneo* by Gabriele Del Grande, Khouribga at times seems like an "invisible" city. "Khouribga è una città emigrata. Una macchina su due è targata Torino. Nel *suq* tra i banchetti di *Dolce e Gabbana, Nike e Versace made in China*, impazzano vocabolari e grammatiche per l'italiano. Qualche chilometro fuori dal centro crescono quartieri fantasma di villini pagati in euro e abitati tre settimane l'anno d'estate. Sì perché ogni agosto ritorna chi c'è l'ha fatta. Emigrare è uno status. Chi riesce a partire guadagna rispetto. La destinazione è una sola, l'Italia, soprattutto Torino e il Piemonte." ("Khouribga is a migrant city. Every second car has a make from Turin. In the souk, between stalls covered in Dolce and Gabbana articles, Nike and Versace made in China, many Italian dictionaries and books on grammars are available. A few kilometers outside the center, there are ghost districts of villas paid for in euros and inhabited three weeks a year in the summer. Every August, those who have succeeded come back. Emigration is a status. Who can leave earns respect. There is only one destination—Turin and Piedmont") (Del Grande 20). The desire to reach Europe is a desire for modernity and its standards of life. Their anguishes are different. So too are the distances that they travel, the means of transportation they use, in territories of uncertain sovereignty, without rights, in survival conditions, where a certain idea of humanity related to rights and to a minimum level of wealth is absent to the point whereby men and women of different origins are bought and sold as in times of slavery. All this is clearly shown in *A sud di Lampedusa* and in

Chapter Twelve

Come un uomo sulla terra. It seems clear, then, that outside the legal framework, outside a rule of law with appropriate economic means to guarantee it, the condition of human beings regresses to the level of survival laws. It seems clear, too, that the ability of a nation state to produce, among other things, the condition of legal, economic and cultural belongings depends on its economy. Looking closely at these films, one realizes that many of these states are not able to offer minimum conditions of habitation to their own people. The model of the nation state is the model of a corporate state that can fail, and its failure can cause the creaking of all the structures of belonging of individuals. The migration fluxes show us that third-world people can become, in reality, stateless people. Their communities of origin are not able to make them stay by offering an acceptable quality of life, and are also not able to intervene in their citizens' favor outside of their own territories. All the problems mentioned in the first part of this work, when we spoke about stateless people, reappear now as threatening. "In arabo c'è scritto "campo di deportazione" ma non è un campo di deportazione." ("In Arabic it is defined as 'deportation camp' but it isn't a deportation camp"), says a young man interviewed in *A sud di Lampedusa*, filmed in Niger in 2006, "È una vera e propria terribile prigione. Una di quelle che in altre parti del mondo sarebbe riservata a chi commette crimini gravi come ammazzare o stuprare qualcuno. Cose pesanti, insomma." ("It's a real and horrible prison. One of those that, in other parts of the world, is used for those who commit serious crimes like killing or raping somebody.")

Come un uomo sulla terra is another documentary film that was released in 2008. It had three authors: Andrea Segre, Riccardo Biadene, and Dagmawi Yimer. The latter is an Ethiopian immigrant who tells his own story and that of others like him. Compared to *A sud di Lampedusa*, and almost to prove the impossibility of an impersonal and autobiographical narration at the same time, there is an attempt, in *Come un uomo sulla terra*, at a more thoughtful and less immediate reconstruction, given also that the witnesses, now in Rome like Yimer himself, reconstruct completed events. The author often narrates in first person, privileging—in the Italian part—stations, roads, and places of circulation. The sad notes of the narrated story are also constantly emphasized by the soundtrack which, at times, accompany the images of the desert crossing with Morricone's music as used by Leone in his famous

Westerns, thereby drawing parallels and hints at allusions. The witness and the images of immigration here, too, form a core of contents, as simple as they are strong and indispensable. The film, which begins with a reference to Italy's colonial past in Libya and Ethiopia, continues with the narration of the recent past of the protagonist and other migrants. The narrator, describing the civil war in his country, states: "Io non credo in quella (nella politica etnica ndr). Se uno mi chiede di quale etnia sei, io rispondo sono etiope e basta, sono un uomo" ("I don't believe in that (the ethnic politics). If I am asked what ethnicity I belong to, I answer that I am an Ethiopian and, that's it, I am a human being"). He would like to make the dignity of being a human being count in his present, perhaps especially in Italy. His words want to recall a universal idea of a human being but end up underlining the contemporary unsustainability of the national profile of the human being and its obvious weakening, especially when it comes to nation states being completely unable to protect their own members. For how they are treated inside and out of their states, these individuals are, in fact, stateless. After suffering violence from smugglers while crossing the desert, they have to suffer other brutalities from Libyan smugglers on their way to Benghazi and, finally, the mistreatment of the Libyan police. Maps, itineraries, and geography dominate the film. There is a precise path of the immigrants' ordeal in Africa that the converging reconstructions of the witnesses give back to us in a raw and dense manner with problematic content. Immigrants of different origins, once they have crossed the desert, reach the coast for the first time but are arrested in the house of intermediaries in Benghazi and taken to prison without ever appearing in court. These movies focus intensively on Libyan prisons because the expulsions are often sustained economically by Italy and the European Union. Thus begins an odyssey that starts from Tripoli's and Benghazi's prisons and continues towards the peripheral prisons of the country that turn into markets for buying and selling human beings. Officially, migrants are expelled in Sudan. In reality, they are sold to new intermediaries for 30 or 50 dinars (local currency). Then, through a well-organized network, sums of money go from migrant families to trusted men among the intermediaries in the states of origin. Thanks to a perfected system that allows these exchanges, the migrants are resold to Libyan intermediaries for

Chapter Twelve

400 dinars in exchange for reaching Tripoli. None of these steps is guaranteed. Often the migrants are left halfway to their destination by the same intermediaries who demand more money. They are then arrested again by the police and the same chain of events is activated once more. From prison to prison, from expulsion to expulsion, from being sold to being sold, from betrayal to betrayal—sometimes this chain of events goes on for years. One of the witnesses says that he was arrested seven times and sold five times; always for 50 dinars. Years after their desert crossing, time in Libyan prisons and crossings of the Mediterranean Sea, the individual survivors reach Italian territory. Here, however, a new cycle begins which is made up of centers for temporary detention, expulsions, and escape. This is the European border. This is what individuals do to change their geographic coordinates and belong to a new territory. This is what Africans have to do to become European residents. Nevertheless, once in Europe, the trip continues.

With another documentary, Andrea Segre, the Italian director most dedicated to immigration issues and his co-director, Stefano Liberti, also cover the last part of the migration route: the marine crossing that African immigrants have to make to reach Lampedusa. In this film, too, is the immediacy of the contents, the facts that happened to be the primary objective of the work. The political urgency of spreading the contents is the mission of this documentary. The film's title is *Mare chiuso* (*Closed Sea*) and it narrates the pushing back of immigrants into the Mediterranean Sea. In 2009, the Italian authorities started to intercept migrants' boats in international waters, taking the immigrants first aboard Italian ships and then back to Libya, where they were subject to imprisonment and torture. A group of 11 Somalis and 13 Eritreans denounced Italy to the European Court of Human Rights for violating their rights—guaranteed by the European Convention on Human Rights (CEDU). Following sentence on 23 January 2012, on the case "Hirsi Jamaa e altri contro l'"Italia" ("Hirsi Jamaa and others against Italy," the court"): "…ha duramente condannato l'Italia per violazione del divieto di tortura sancito dall'articolo 3 della CEDU, perché i ricorrenti sono stati esposti al rischio, da un lato, di subire maltrattamenti in Libia e, dall'altro, di essere rimpatriati arbitrariamente nei loro paesi d'origine (Somalia ed Eritrea) senza beneficiare di alcuna forma di protezione." ("…strongly condemned Italy for violation of the prohibition of torture enshrined in Article 3 of CEDU, because the applicants have been exposed to the danger, on one hand, of suffering mistreatment in Libya and, on the other, have been repatriated arbitrarily to their countries of origin (Somalia and Eritrea) without benefiting from any kind of protection") (Lana and Saccucci 38–39).

The mobile border and European citizenship

In 2003, the Italian government, following a model tried out in previous years in another ex-colony—Albania—began to allocate tens of millions of euros to assist the Libyan government in preventing illegal immigration. Meanwhile, ENI, the Italian public oil company, signed agreements with Libya for billions of euros. After the signing of a friendship treaty with Ghaddafi's Libya in 2008, the then Italian Prime Minister Silvio Berlusconi commented: "Da oggi avremmo più petrolio e meno immigrati clandestini" ("From now on we will have more oil and fewer illegal immigrants" (Liberti and Segre 16). Franco Frattini, meanwhile, interviewed in his role as European Commissioner in the (2008) documentary *Come un uomo sulla terra*, argued that Europe invested to improve repatriation conditions and not to build centers of temporary permanence—"Se gli stati membri lo hanno fatto, bisogna chiedere loro." ("If member states have done it, you should ask them."). Frattini subsequently became the Secretary of State of a member-state—Italy—and the assistance to Libya continues. Official opacity is functional to the internal discourse on the human being because, in this case, discourse and facts clearly do not match. It follows, that it is better to pretend not to know. An external discourse on the human being which is different to the internal one is not possible, as we are far from the efficacy of an external discourse, that of universal rights. Bauman (*Globalization: The Human Consequences*) makes it clear that the transfer of real power towards extraterritorial and economic entities substantially restricts the function of the nation state that has a mandate only to control its own territory. Only the economic power of the nation state, in its neocolonial form—naked, raw, without perspective, and without long-range action—does what is possible. However, it ends up trampling on human rights both externally and indirectly because the information and internal

Chapter Twelve

discourse on the human being restrain it. More creatively, within its territory, centers of temporary permanence (once CPT now CIE—Centers for Identification and Expulsion), and also known as refugee camps (the refugee camps seen as non-places as or states of exception, or both) greatly extend the actions of nation states without a real legal mandate.[73]

The European Union philosophy, then, is not to deal with any issues directly at its borders, where practical, legal, or cultural problems arise but, using its economic influence, to do this in origin and transit countries. As Matthew Carr reports in *Fortress Europe, Dispatches from a Gated Continent*, the Libyan situation has extended along all European borders. Among the most significant accidents, Carr mentions the battles of Ceuta and Melilla, inheritance of the Spanish colonial experience, where 1,600 men engaged by the Moroccan government and 480 Spanish soldiers openly confronted immigrants from 12 different countries who wanted to cross through the border. The Spanish media called them "human avalanches." The migrants were pushed back or left to their own devices in the desert, as described by Carr (3):

> The "battles" at Ceuta and Melilla were the most dramatic expression of a nightmare that has haunted the European imagination ever since the end of the Cold War. From Ceuta and Melilla in the south to the 1,800-mile frontier that marks Europe's new eastern frontier [...] and the English Channel, from the Mediterranean to the Adriatic and the Aegean, European governments have reinforced their borders with police, soldiers, border guards, naval patrols, physical barriers, and detection technologies in the most sustained and extensive border enforcement program in history [...] The result is a tragic and often lethal confrontation between some of the richest countries on earth and a stateless population from some of the world's poorest, a conflict that has been unfolding for more than two decades at Europe's territorial borders and which also extends inside and beyond them.

Major Di Gregoli of the Italian Cost Guard also sees it as a conflict. Interviewed by Maria Pace Ottieri (14), Di Gregoli considers it "una guerra pacifica che il Terzo Mondo sta conducendo contro il mondo sviluppato, l'ingresso clandestino resta un non reato e per loro, dopo la morte, non c'è danno peggiore che quello di rimandarli in patria." ("a pacific war that the Third World is leading against the developed world, the clandestine entrance remains a non-crime and, for them, after the death, there is nothing worse than being repatriated"). However, the word "war" is very misleading. The dramatic or even tragic aspects that accompany migration attempts only partially justify its use. It is neither about a hate assault, nor is it an assault to destroy. The migrants want to be part of this way of life instead, they want to access better resources, and they simply want a different quality of life.

In *European policies on migration*, Sandro Mezzadra tries to track down a coherent logic—that is, racist strategies functional to the nationalism of the new state in the process of formation. His analysis is based on an idea by Foucault that considered racism as a functional aspect of the modern state. "European migration policies have profoundly racist origins without simultaneously dismissing as mere rhetoric the discourse of European institutions today, characterized by antidiscrimination programs, "antiracism," and an insistence on social cohesion" (Mezzadra 39). Racism, understood by Balibar as an "internal supplement to nationalism," is traced by Mezzadra in all its implicit stratifications, starting from border policies and, step by step, progressing up to the emerging European citizenship. It is exactly the latter's emergence that requires new forms of nationalism and racism. From this perspective, the mobile border, both external and internal (the so-called CPT and CIE are internal borders), is useful not only in interrupting political and juridical continuity but also for inserting all the necessary stratifications that separate the human being of the Global South from the European citizen. Europe projects various degrees of interiority and exteriority through the deterritorialization of its frontier, and places migrants, in this way, in spaces distinct from those of "civil society"—that is from spaces associated with a constitutional state and from the order of law and citizenship.

While within the territory, in addition to the aforementioned CPT and CIE, existing policies must also be taken into account—those with residence permits that link residence to work and end up checking, limiting, and diversifying the migrant's mobility. In conclusion, racism, according to Mezzadra can be traced in the hierarchization of the cohabitation of different bodies within the same territory; a process which promotes a different and selective degree of inclusiveness.

Chapter Thirteen

The Modesty of Representation

Media and migration projects

There has been much talk about the role of television and cinema in East European migration. There were insinuated degrees of ingenuity on the part of populations who let themselves be enchanted by the artificial splendor of advertising. However, the phenomenon is far more complex. Since the 1970s, Italian television has been captured on the other Adriatic coast thanks to proximity and to intentionally powerful antennae, while American cinema was regularly scheduled by the televisions of Tito's ex-Yugoslavia which, as one of the countries not aligned with any of the two camps, enjoyed greater opening on the world. The role of radio (the medium that took Western music everywhere), television and cinema, first in the fall of Eastern dictatorships and then in migration movements, was anything but secondary. Here is how the influence of Italian television is described during the years of the communist regime in Vlorë, Albania, a city that is around 60 miles from the Apulian coast:

> Più della metà delle famiglie avevano acquistato ormai il televisore. Tutti avevano paura, ma tutti seguivano i programmi italiani. Il Partito non lo poteva tollerare. Si organizzarono riunioni nelle fabbriche e in tutte le aziende per mettere in guardia la parte sana del proletariato verso il rischio di avvelenamento ideologico che tale fenomeno poteva causare. Seguirono arresti di persone sospette in tutte le città per dimostrare che si faceva sul serio [...] Nonostante tutto, gli uomini salivano sulle terrazze a sistemare le antenne. Stava per iniziare il Festival di Sanremo ed era ormai un evento che contagiava grandi e piccoli. Sebbene quell'anno le prime due serate vennero trasmesse solo alla radio, le voci di Al Bano, Nicola di Bari, Little Tony, Domenico Modugno, Milva, Gianni Nazzaro e Iva Zanicchi

Chapter Thirteen

> entrarono con furore nelle case di Valona. Sabato sera le strade si svuotarono come se ci fosse il coprifuoco. I bar chiusi, gli autobus fermi, le luci spente, i vetri oscurati con coperte di lana per paura della polizia.
>
> More than half of the families had already bought a television. Everyone was afraid, but everyone followed the Italian programs. The Party could not tolerate it. Meetings were organized in factories and in all companies to warn the healthy part of the proletariat about the danger of ideological poisoning that this phenomenon could cause. Arrests of suspected people followed in all the cities to prove that they were serious about it… Despite everything, the men climbed the terraces to fix the antennae. The Sanremo Festival was about to start and it was now an event that infected adults and children. Although that year the first two evenings were broadcast only on the radio, the voices of Al Bano, Nicola di Bari, Little Tony, Domenico Modugno, Milva, Gianni Nazzaro and Iva Zanicchi entered with fury in the houses of Vlorë. Saturday night, the streets emptied as if there were a curfew. The bars closed, the buses stopped, the lights were turned off and windows were dimmed by wool blanket out of fear of the police. (Guaci 74)

The ship which became the iconic image of the overcrowded fleet of Albanian immigrants who reached Italy after the fall of communism in the summer of 1991 was named after the city of Vlorë. To that event is dedicated Daniele Vicari's movie *La Nave Dolce* (*The Sweet Ship*). Telling of this experience, Artur Spanjolli, another Albanian writer, highlights the collective imaginary nurtured by television images. "Io vedevo per la prima volta l'Occidente, il sud di Albano Carrisi e di Anna Oxa, vedevo i palazzi, i semafori, i negozi, i giardini che avevano immaginato chissà quante volte negli anni feroci del comunismo." ("I saw for the first time the West, the South of Albano Carrisi and Anna Oxa, I saw the buildings, the traffic lights, the shops, the gardens that I had imagined who knows how many times over the years of the ferocious communist dictatorship") (Spanjolli 141). The eloquence of images, and the standards of life sabotaged the unique model of reality imposed by the monism in power. The Western "Elsewhere" nurtured a sort of "Metaphysics of the Otherwise" that lit up the imaginary of the masses, making many generations dream. Mark Fisher in his final lectures published in Postcapitalist Desire (2021), refered also to Jean—François

Lyotard's *Économie Libidinale* (1974, Libidinal Economy, 1993), and maintained that the Soviet bloc tried to inhibit and block desire (38). They did not succeed. "There is no outside. There is no Soviet realm where people don't want Levi's" (196). According to Fisher, after the sixties and the seventies, this clearly became the problem: "the immersion into capital", "the lack of any outside", "the difficulty of thinking from and outside capital" (196). This historical impact turned out to be important because "da un lato le narrazioni emesse dai mezzi di comunicazione di massa italiani in Albania mettono in circolo uno spazio narrative controcorrente rispetto a quello ufficiale" ("on the one hand, the narratives issued by the Italian mass media in Albania put in circulation a narrative space that contradicted the official one"), and, on the other, once the walls came down, stimulated "una mobilità non più solo immaginaria" ("a 'mobility' that is no longer just imagined") (Moll 127).

If we try to understand whether the same mechanism influences African immigrants, we will not be disappointed. From stories told by migrants in Segre *et al.*'s film *A sud di Lampedusa*, it emerges that the migrant flows from Libya have become the important phenomenon that we have come to know in the last 20 years. The suspicion that, besides the extreme conditions of poverty, this phenomenon has much to do with the far better circulation of information from the West in the years of global media, is easily confirmed by other readings. As Mathew Carr (153) points out in *Fortress Europe*: "Today such information is more available than ever before as a result of all-pervasive global media and the Internet ... the cafés of Tangier daily transmit Spanish TV channels that provide a constant reminder of these differences to young jobless Moroccans, and the backstreets of the Kasbah are dotted with Internet cafés and Skype booths that enable prospective migrants to cross virtual borders and stay in contact with friends or relatives on the other side of the Strait. The same information is available in even more distant countries."

The information makes it conceivable to outline the elsewhere, and the elsewhere becomes the dreamed-of territory, becomes the space of rebirth, the space of an otherwise that changes the dark destiny assigned to the individual in his or her state of birth. Stories embellished by those who have made it in the West, and pieces of colorful life seen on TV alongside photographs and films from the internet promote a dreamlike, almost spiritual element, where the escape from hell and the spark of the elsewhere turns on the dream of the otherwise.[74] The work of Arjun Appadurai, the anthropologist born in India, is particularly relevant to these aspects of this book. Technological development has profoundly changed the migratory dynamics and established close links between globalization and modernity. In a world of planetary interconnections, the first to change is "the imagination," a category with a potential that is not easily measurable but involves an unpredictable development of subjectivity. The imagination, no longer the prerogative of artists only, becomes, according to Appadurai (*Modernity at Large*), a collective factor which is also a transnational one (global events like the Olympiads help to generate it). It is as if the inhabitants of the aforementioned Calvino's Eutropia desired new lives, new jobs, and new houses because they are able to imagine other houses, other occupations, and other lives. They are able to do this thanks to an increasingly interconnected world where the mass media circulates transnational information. This aspect profoundly affects the formation of modern subjectivity. "The first step in this argument is that electronic media decisively change the wider field of mass media and other traditional media. This is not a monocausal fetishization of the electronic. Such media transform the field of mass mediation because they offer new resources and new disciplines for the construction of imagined selves and imagined worlds" (Appadurai 3).

According to Appadurai, the nation state will not be able to manage the relationship between globalization and modernity for a long time, and an emerging post national system will have to deal with heterogeneous elements. For him, globalization does not automatically imply homogenization or Americanization. On the contrary, its main characteristic seems to be the tension between cultural homogenization and cultural heterogenization and the nature of this process, for Appadurai historical, would be even localizing. Today's landscape is quite jagged, and the processes put in motion remain fluid and unpredictable. But what is most interesting in this context is the close link that exists between imagination and immigration. This is obviously not a new bond, as first literature, then cinema, and later television have anticipated (as in the case of migrations from the ex-communist camp area) the deeper and immediate role of the internet (think for example of the changes triggered by it in the complex events of the so-called "Arab Spring"). This imaginary that circulates in a thousand ways between cinema, TV, and the internet obviously transcends the space of the nation state that progressively loses control of these aspects within its territory. Nevertheless, we can point out that the declination of this imaginary takes on different angles both when it is adopted by a given community and when it is individually processed. Part of this non-homologous slant is the combinatorial characteristic of the imagination that mixes local or individual elements with what is perceived through the mass media. The collective or individual yearning, the otherwise dreamed about that offers trajectories on which to stretch the collective and individual projects, does not create, at least for now, a homogeneous planetary imaginary. The Western otherwise, for example, does not move on the same trajectory as that of other collectives. Different fears generate different dreams. Different pasts trigger different futures.

On this side of the sea

Edward Said *(Orientalism)* saw orientalism as a discourse but now we need to see the discourses that govern and produce the imaginary as mutated and updated forms of orientalism. Behind the flat and homologated perception of the migratory phenomenon in Italy, there is an imaginary nourished by the standard clichés of a media discourse that crosses and dominates the whole of society. It is an imaginary that produces and maintains strong power and subjection relationships within the host society. Maria Pace Ottieri's inquiry book entitled *Quando sei nato non ti puoi più nascondere* (*Once You're Born, You Can No Longer Hide*), inspired a film to which it lent its title and some themes. The first, to not grasp the importance of imaginary, of the yearning for the West, or at least its contents, are the authors of this film, the director Marco Tullio Giordana and the scriptwriters Sandro Petraglia and Stefano Rulli. The authors of the film, perhaps also because of the vibrant polemics coming from the Albanian community when *Lamerica* was released, were nevertheless fully aware of these potential limits: "Comunque, entrando in questi mondi, la cosa più dura è stata vincere la tentazione—che sarebbe stata presuntuosa e sbagliata—di raccontare il film dalla parte dei diseredati,

Chapter Thirteen

degli emigranti. Il film parla di *noi* più che di *loro*, parla dei nostri sensi di colpa in quanto occidentali. [...] I viaggi per mare dei clandestini hanno dei livelli di tragedia quasi non rappresentabili. In qualche modo anche *Lamerica* di Gianni Amelio aveva lo stesso pudore, anche Amelio ha messo al centro del racconto un personaggio 'di qua del mare.'" ("However, entering these worlds, the hardest thing was to overcome the temptation—which would have been presumptuous and wrong—to tell the film from the point of view of the dispossessed, of the emigrants... The film speaks of us more than of them, speaks of our feelings of guilt as Westerners. The journeys by sea of the illegals contain almost non-representable levels of tragedy. Somehow even Gianni Amelio's *Lamerica* had the same modesty, even Amelio put at the center of the story a character 'from this side of the sea.'") (Petraglia in Giordana et al. 18–19).

In reality, *Lamerica* did not have this modesty because the representation of the Albanian context was the main goal of the film. Amelio tried to penetrate the Albanian context but he represented it amplified through the wide and frightened eyes of those from "this side of the sea." From the point of view of those "this side of the sea" in Giordana's film, the origins of the individuals disappear, and the nationalities do not matter; they all become *others*, migrants, poor, while the sidewalk seems to be a hateful but ineluctable destiny for migrant women. The director, Giordana—very much beloved in Italy and associated mostly with his highly inspirational films *I 100 passi* (*One Hundred Steps*) and *La meglio gioventù* (*The Best of Youth*)—auditioned many actors of various nationalities for the part of the migrant protagonist Radu.[75] Finally he chose a Romanian, simply because the actor was the most convincing. Here is the homogenizing look that, from the top (Western), captures and represents continuities while leaving out details. In the second part of the movie, when the migrants land in Apulia, they are placed in a center of temporary stay (then CPT, today CIE). Migrant faces and names are shown while they are being registered through a long series of close-ups. Giordana has put in the same boat, cinematically and metaphorically, immigrants from Kosovo, Syria, Burundi, Albania, Croatia, Bosnia, Sudan, Jordan, Pakistan, India, Montenegro, Sri Lanka, and Romania. Giordana, in the comment accompanying the film, says that the generality of the faces shown are authentic. Here there is also an unclear moment: it is not certain whether, in the statements of nationality, Giordana is referring to the newly landed people—a scene preceded by the migrant boat docking—or to the same ones plus those of others in the CPT who arrived via other routes, not shown in the film. The director used regular migrants but that does not mean that they arrived on that boat, via that route. They are, yes, authentic generalities in life but, in the film, they are actors, and the boat becomes global because Giordana puts them together. Again, to underline the very immediate level of the symbols in the film, the Italian child's second name, son of wealthy Brescians, is Lombardi.

The film, from many points of view, becomes *Lamerica 2*; a continuation. Its true development begins at sea, where *Lamerica* ended. The points of contact, as we will see, are many. In his film, Giordana—who, in an interview, said that he was inspired by the Rossellinian model of Edmund—an Italian child who falls from the boat of his wealthy father, a Brescian industrialist, and is rescued by a migrant boat. As they say, "all in the same boat," a global one in this case, Italian and immigrants, that in the film physically crosses the Adriatic from Greece to reach Lecce, and metaphorically continues towards a common future that remains open, like the ending of the film. The nationalities of the migrants who, in the same boat, have crossed the Adriatic, already indicate that little attention has been paid to geographical routes that are anything but superfluous. As a result, both Indians and Croatians miraculously cross the Adriatic (probably leaving from Greece or Turkey, not from Dubrovnik) together with Africans and Romanians. One of the protagonists of the film, the teenager who saves the Italian child, is a Romanian. The film was released in 2005, the year that Romania and the EU signed the Treaty of Accession. The Romanians fast turned into the largest immigrant community in Italy thanks to their free circulation in Europe. Accordingly, it makes little sense to have just one Romanian in the illegal migrant's boat. As members of the largest immigrant community, they soon became the target of public opinion, like the Albanians were when *Lamerica* was shot in 1994. The author of the book that inspired the film, Maria Pace Ottieri, commented: "È strano come, nonostante le migliaia di persone approdate sulle banchine del porto, le idee geografiche dei funzionari siano ancora così vaghe, come se a parte l'Occidente, il resto del mondo fosse un immenso serbatoio di poveri, uguali e intercambiabili." ("It's strange how, despite the thousands of people landing on the docks at the port, the geographical ideas of the officials are still so vague, as if, besides the West, the rest of the world were an immense tank of poor people, identical and interchangeable.") (23).

The gaze "from this side" of the sea seems, then, to be able to represent only internal frontiers; those inhabited only by Italians. However, even in this case, it is the media that nourishes the imagination of the authors who, evidently because of their lifestyle as part of an economically privileged class, seem to have few direct experiences. The crossing, as we will see, is a journalistic line-up and nothing more. Borrowing from Verga's novel, *I Malavoglia* (*The House by the Medlar-Tree*), Giordana considers the Apulian smugglers as just two wretches looking for a fluke that will redeem their condition.

The artistic plot of the film focuses on Sandro who, having fallen in the water one night from his father's sailing boat, is saved by the young Romanian, Radu, and taken aboard the migrants' boat, where he catches the eye of the smugglers who suspect the wealthy nature of his parents. He then risks being kidnapped so that the smugglers may extort money from his family but is saved in an unlikely fashion by Radu's intervention; the latter fakes Sandro's Kurdish origins and tells the smugglers that Sandro speaks Kurdish and is not worth kidnapping. Radu, a polyglot who speaks English in addition to Italian, also has an alleged younger sister, Alina. A good part of the film is based on the complexity of the two young migrants, and especially on the sensual girl. The use of the female body for survival is the territory on which the authors dare to intrude and they give more emphasis to it. Friendship, solidarity, exploitation, and love fill and overlap in the grey space of the triangle, where the codes are undefined, as if navigating in international waters. Here, then, is the main theoretical effort of the authors: the possible meeting is that between the young generations without the cultural and ideological superstructures to prevent the meeting. This is like saying that the meeting between our generations is not working; we hope it will be better among the new generations, we hope it will be better tomorrow. Sandro's efforts succeed where the Italian imaginary fails to understand Alina's and Radu's reasons, in particular, and the migrants' reasons in general, because it is a lazy imaginary that is made up of us and them, made up of comfortable prejudices, and unable even to make the most basic distinctions like nationalities. The 18-year-old Radu does little to be understood—he first escapes in order to not be repatriated, then he steals to get away. He also seems to push the sister/girlfriend into prostitution, exactly in the way that the Italian media present Eastern European immigrants, creating the profile in which robberies and prostitution are part of the standard menu offered to the Italian collective imaginary. Even the ambiguous relationship between Alina and Radu is actually very offensive. Giordana, in a commented version of the film, says of Radu: "Forse un fratello, forse un amante. Forse tutti e due!!!" ("Maybe a brother, maybe a lover. Maybe both of them!!!"). It is feared that the basic family and emotional ties that are fundamental to the functioning of Italian society, are not respected or adhered to by migrants.

The brother or the boyfriend turns into his sister's or girlfriend's pimp. This is the real nightmare of the host society: the insidious threat of the barbarizing of its social life. This is the Italian point of view which describes the country's deep fears towards the stranger. Giordana explains in the film's commentary that the prostitutes we see in Brescia at the beginning of the movie—approaching Sandro alongside the car door—are a warning, a first sign of what he will later discover. Incredibly, in a scene in the migrants' boat, the director states that the migrant women are not aware of the kind of life that is waiting for them: "Sandro sa che troveranno il marciapiede..." ("Sandro knows that they will find the sidewalk ..."). About Alina, he says: "Il destino che aspetta Alina una volta sbarcata." ("The fate waiting for Alina once disembarked."). In short, the bitter reality, according to the director, is that prostitution is the fate of all migrant women. Alina becomes its symbol! The film is in fact just this: a journalistic stereotype spread in a cinematographic representation with intentions of denouncement. A representation that, however, reproposes the clichés and perhaps also reinforces them.

Sandro, the child, strives to understand; the father does not; the generations line up. The merit of the film is its recognition of the need to make a new Italian—that is, a new profile that goes beyond that discussed by Pasolini and Calvino, the making of the post-Italian, the making of the Italian European, the making of the Italian Mediterranean. Fulvio Orsito, in his article "Percorsi Mediterranei" (Mediterranean Routes) dedicated to this film, after highlighting the continuity between *Lamerica* and this movie, organized his work around the meaning of the Mediterranean as "uno spazio metaforico di transizione" ("a metaphoric space of transition") (213). With regard to the need for a different education for Sandro, he wrote: "È infatti attraverso questa immersion forzata nella liquidità mediterranea che Sandro riuscirà a comprendere che di questi tempi l'interazione con l'Altro è un dovere morale, e che concetti come *classe* e *nazione* (il riferimento è all'italianità, ma anche alla nordità provinciale a cui va ascritto il *milieu* sociale della sua famiglia) sono altrettanto porosi, liquidi e mutevoli come lo spazio mediterraneo che, seppur brevemente, si trova costretto ad occupare." ("It is in fact through this forced immersion in Mediterranean liquidity that Sandro will be able to understand that, in these times, the interaction with the Other is a moral duty, and that concepts such as *class* and *nation* (the reference is both to Italianness and to the provincial northness to which the *social milieu* of his family belongs) are just as porous, liquid and changeable as the Mediterranean space which, even if briefly, he is forced to occupy.") (Orsito 214).

Orsito places emphasis on the importance of the meeting with the Other because this is what the film does. It is striking, however, that Radu, a young citizen of the European Union, is still seen as the abstract Other or that, going beyond this movie and this article, after many years of immigrant arrivals, we still resort to the excessive use of abstract and limiting generic categories and metaphors that do not offer much-needed insight. Articulations are important. They describe identities and offer specific knowledge. This is precisely what the movie does. It is an abstract fairy tale that teaches, in Orsito's words, "un dovere morale" ("a moral duty"), as fairy tales usually do. Orsito's correct conclusion that "il *Bildungsroman* di Sandro sembra evocare quello che (su una scala più ampia, è il *Bildungsroman* dell'Italia" ("Sandro's *Bildungsroman* seems to evoke what, on a larger scale, is the *Bildungsroman* of Italy") (219) is clearly the undeniable merit and scope of this film. Elena Dalla Torre, in her article "Accordi globali: gioventù europea e immigrazione femminile nei film dei fratelli Dardenne e di Marco Tulio Giordana" ("Global Agreements: European Youth and Female Immigration in the Films of the Dardenne Brothers and Marco Tulio Giordana"), along with highlighting the need for a more thorough representation and treatment of the abuse of illegal migrant women (Dalla Torre 237), seems to complete and bring to its logical conclusion Orsito's reading. Giordana's film and *La Promesse* (*The Promise,* by Jean-Pierre and Luc Dardenne), are two movies about intercultural friendship that represent, in Dalla Torre's view, a process of restructuring Europe politically and socially (Dalla Torre 221). The idea of a "post-Europe" or "New Europe" is suggested as a way of overcoming nationalisms and colonial pasts. Both these movies, observes Dalla Torre, describe a path of maturation for their young protagonists based on the need for them to deal with the multicultural dimension of the European context (240). This is why, in Giordana's film, Sandro is a child who becomes a teenager in this almost multi-ethnic *bildungsfilm* and who, in a deeply changed national context, lives in the transition from childhood to adolescence. There is an ambiguity to growing up on many levels: the affection for Alina, the Romanian girl for whom—from a fraternal affection (he asks his parents to adopt her)—he silently slips into another feeling. It is he who seeks for Alina, and it is he who saves her from a possible life of prostitution. More than saving her, in reality, Sandro "can no longer hide" from the changed world.[76] He needs to open up, and to break with the closed, monoethnic, national bourgeois mentality of the previous generation. Alina, from her side, with make-up on her face, partially reveals herself, a little at a time at the end of the film, through the door which is ajar in the underground shed. Her complex condition becomes a call that Sandro cannot but answer. Openings involve risks. The director seems to be aware of this to the point whereby he chooses the children for the meeting of different cultures. However, another imaginary must soon be provided to the children, which nobody is doing. The female body of Alina, transformed from a child to a very young woman is, despite the strong mass-mediatic stereotype that inspires it, the most disturbing synthesis of the whole film, the nightmare of a society that is afraid of seeing the end of the minimum conventions of cohabitation. It is the stranger, the unknown, the bearer of this peril. Sandro, trying to understand Radu's reasons, asks an African worker in his father's factory if he ever stole. The worker answers that he did so when he was hungry. Once he found employment, he stopped. Here, then, are the

Chapter Thirteen

migrant's reasons according to this generalizing fairy tale. They are poor, like in *Lamerica*. Their nationality does not matter; they are not Italians, so they are poor. The internal border, therefore, even before being cultural or linguistic, is economic, classist. The spaces where migrants are represented are eloquent: a shabby boat, a center of temporary stay (detention), and an industrial warehouse. When they briefly enter Sandro's beautiful house (an illegitimate space for them, evidently) they end up stealing. The only space in which they are represented as happy is a transitory space, a non-place, the train which, in some way, represents their expectations in life, that dreaming, with an amazed look on their faces, of the possible next stop, of a possible new life. Unfortunately, their next stop is an underground shed in Milan, where the present and the future are dark and squalid. Sandro will try to rescue Alina but, of Radu, now clandestine, nothing is known. During the crossing of the Adriatic, all the well-known standard moments are present, one after the other: the crowded conditions, the lack of food and water, the abuse of women, the dead thrown into the sea, the technical failures of the battered vehicle, the boat abandoned by the smugglers, the arrival of the coastguard, and the accompanying of the migrants to a detention center. The representation of the external border has no element of novelty, no particular analysis but sets out, in linear fashion, what is regularly already communicated by the media. Sea tragedies, the real ones, those where boats sink and nothing else is known anymore, are not represented, nor those crossings full of unexpected events. A successful crossing has been represented, so to speak, in which there is little that is new, or of considerable interest. The authors underlined in various interviews that they did not want to deal with the tragedies of the sea and that they only wanted to give their point of view. The external border, then, seems to remain unexplorable from an artistic and Italian point of view. However, at the same time, it is still represented by the mainstream media, and the collective idea of the external border is mediated by these representations. The documentary, on the other hand, offered very different results. As we will see in the next section, the role of the documentary in dealing with immigrant sea crossings has been fundamental in the quality of its representation, and with regards to the number of films produced.

The representation of sea crossings and the role of the documentary

In recent years, some documentary film productions have shown better results regarding the representation of the external border. The documentary as a genre is perhaps the main instrument that has investigated and tried to represent the sea crossings. According to Angela Angelone, "the website for the Centro Studi Immigrazione (CESTIM) lists 63 documentaries that have dealt with the topic from 2006 through 2012, but over half of these (36) were made in 2011 and 2012 alone" (69). According to the same website (www.cestim.it), 33 documentaries that focused on immigration were produced in Italy between 2013 and 2017. The reasons for such a phenomenon should be looked for at a political and cultural level that addresses the difficulty of assuming different points of view and is therefore pertinent to divergent imaginaries. Within the representation of the point of view of the protagonists, a first aspect of great importance is the irreplaceable role of testimony. When, for example, a documentary deals with the aforementioned migrant sea crossings, overcoming the infinite terrestrial, political, marine and meteorological barriers makes the migrants survivors. The ZALAB producer Alessandro Triulzi, stated that analyzing the film *Come un uomo sulla terra*—produced by ZALAB—drew a link between limited experiences and the importance of testimony:

> Migrants' testimonies, particularly those by sub-Saharan people, are to be considered in many ways "survivor" narratives: their trekking through forest, desert, and sea to reach the southern European shores is in itself a survivor's achievement, one for which irregular migrants who "make it" are, in Primo Levi's words, either "drowned" or "saved." Those who make it only do so at tremendous human, psychological, and physical cost and, like war, genocide or drought survivors, they often come back voiceless [...] Thus the "speaking out" of the migrants, when it occurs through persuasion and internal self-awareness, is a consciously voiced testimony that is made possible by a listening context, which makes the actual reenacting of the experience the only possible way to elaborate it and transmit it to others. (Triulzi 104–05)

Chapter Thirteen

Documentary productions also count on relatively faster times, cheaper productions, and the irreplaceable and hardly imaginable point of view of the migrant protagonists. This is especially true in times of, emergency, of transition, and great political confusion. In "Imagining Lampedusa," Áine O'Healy compares the representation of the mainstream media with documentary representation. "Mainstream television reporting is invested in representing Lampedusa and Linusa as sites of crisis ... in mainstream reports, the voices and perspectives of the migrants themselves are almost never heard" (O'Healy 154). The work of the director Andrea Segre such as the aforementioned *Mare Chiuso* (*Closed Sea*)—dedicated to the push backs in international waters operated by the Italian navy and to the consequent condemnation of Italy by the European Court—seems to fit perfectly into this uncertain territory. The film not only tells this story but is an integral part of it. The central core of the film is footage shot by the migrants themselves, with a smartphone, which shows the migrant boat and the arrival of the Italian navy ship. It is around this footage and the story told by the protagonists that the film, winner of many prizes, including the Rossellini Prize, was built. A story of great political importance, footage shot by chance by the protagonists with the technology available, gave life to an artistic product which, with incredible immediacy, became part of a judicial process. "Questo è il senso di *Mare chiuso*: un lavoro collettivo che non sarebbe mai stato possibile senza l'adesione entusiastica e fortissima dei protagonisti; senza l'impegno e la sensazione di costruire insieme qualcosa che potesse arrivare ad avere un'influenza sull'opinione pubblica del Nord e un peso sulle decisioni politiche." ("This is the meaning of Closed Sea"—state the authors, Liberti and Segre—"a collective work that would never have been possible without the enthusiastic and strong support of the protagonists; without the commitment and the feeling of building together something that could have an influence on the public opinion of the North and a weight on political decisions.") (21).[77]

Reading the history of the making of this documentary, one can clearly understand both how important the use of internet has been for the exchange of visual material and the power of new technology that allows even a smartphone to shoot images of great content relevance. In the same way, it is easily realized that relatively low costs facilitated the journey from the idea to the actual realization of the visual product. When the visual medium, is no longer—because of accessibility costs—exclusively in the hands of the great film and television producers, products of this kind are facilitated. "Although documentaries, like feature films, provide highly mediated constructions of the social realities to which they allude," points out O'Healy, "their directors are generally not subject to the tight controls of commercial film production or hindered by considerations of substantial profit making" (161).

A reflection on how to objectively approach difficult themes is one of the representation strategies in Segre's documentaries. Anita Angelone, in "Italian documentaries and immigration," 2016, states that Segre's strategy was inspired by the work of the French sociologist Luc Boltanski and the concept of distant suffering. Boltanski (*Distant Suffering: Morality, Media, Politics*) questions the relationship of the spectator with the media's representation of suffering, and claims that the spectator is cut off and cannot act to alleviate suffering. Andrea Segre, however, "states in an interview, his main concern in his films is to document a reality of suffering that somehow transcends the distance between the spectator and the reality viewed" (Angelone 71). The director of *Mare chiuso* conceives, for all the reasons mentioned up to now, a form of authorial sharing which he calls "participatory." The point of view of migrant-witnesses is included not only through the massive use of interviews, but also through the sharing of the entire production process of the documentary. Segre attempts to short-circuit the gap between film-maker, subject, and spectator. The footage is mainly shot by the people who had experienced the border-crossing and not by the director. Teresa Fiore, in a recent essay, also analyzes Segre's way of working. "Because of this interconnection, this visual work plays off trans-individual relations via participatory modalities with fluid perspectives: multiple directors and writers are involved whose roles are flexible and complementary, as well as migrants who are both in front of and behind the camera" ("From Exclusion to Expression in *A Sud di Lampedusa* and *Come un Uomo sulla Terra*" 51). The difficulty of representing distant, complex, and extremely dramatic contexts, both because of the limits of the knowledge of this reality of Italian directors and because of the different political will of the mainstream media, has created a void filled mainly by an engaged audio-visual production which is open to the participation of subjects who are

Chapter Thirteen

often protagonists of the events recounted. "Taken as a whole, this audio-visual work sheds light on the complex imbrications of Italy in and outside its borders in a geographical and cultural area that spans from Italy to the sub-Saharan region" ("From Exclusion to Expression" 51).

Like Segre's *Mare chiuso*, Gianfranco Rosi's *Fuocoammare* (*Fire at Sea*) aimed to have, and indeed had, a political impact. Rosi, who spent one year on Lampedusa and was allowed to film on board military ships during rescue operations, decided to use captured footage with no interviews when representing migrants, as well as a neorealist storytelling when representing the islanders. These choices confirm again the problematics of representation when dealing with border crossings. Rosi arrived on Lampedusa with the intention of making a short film. He immediately realized that he wanted to tell a lot more, and remained on the island for more than a year. There are two aspects of this film that are relevant to this chapter: the hybrid genre documentary fiction, and the geopolitical context. The political urgency of this story had an important impact on the final product. "The most-well-used and the most dangerous route for undocumented migration into Europe continued to be the Mediterranean. [...] In 2013, 60,000 migrants arrived in Italy at Lampedusa or Sicily, or were rescued at sea. The following year the numbers had more than doubled to 170,000. This increase was accompanied by a shocking death toll as smugglers in Libya packed migrants into overcrowded and unseaworthy boats even outside the normal 'migration season' when seas were calmer" (Carr 279).

On 3 October 2013, more than 350 migrants drowned less than a quarter of a mile from Lampedusa. In the wake of this disaster, the Italian navy and coastguards conducted a year-long search-and-rescue operation which covered more than 27,000 miles. Between October 2013 and October 2014, *Mare Nostrum*, a naval and air operation by the Italian government, saved more than 130,000 people. The International Organization for Immigration reported that 3,072 migrants died in the Mediterranean in 2014. Italy could no longer afford *Mare Nostrum* and asked for help. The message was that the migrants approaching Lampedusa were not only an Italian problem but a European one. With the slogan "Europe starts on Lampedusa," many manifestations took place on the Sicilian island which sought to draw international attention to this ongoing drama. The British government was very critical of *Mare Nostrum*, and considered the rescue operations a "pull factor." Instead of answering Italy's call, Europe replaced *Mare Nostrum* with the reduced *Operation Triton*, under the direction of FRONTEX, the European border agency. *Triton* was more a border enforcement service than a rescue operation. In the first months of 2015, the death toll was 50 times higher than it had been in the same period of the previous year (Carr 280). In April of that year, in a single week, 900 migrants died, and the European Union decided to reinstate a search-and-rescue operation. The British Prime Minister, David Cameron, promised to send the British navy to help but "he also declared that rescued migrants would be taken to the nearest safe country, which was most likely to be Italy" (Carr 281). Unlike Segre, and the footage captured with a smartphone in *Mare chiuso*, Gianfranco Rosi was allowed to film the rescue operations on board an Italian navy ship. The Italian government did not want to deal alone with the migrant crisis. On 23 February 2016, the British newspaper *The Guardian* ran an article entitled "Italian PM to give Migration Film to Heads of State at EU Summit: Matteo Renzi says he will bring 27 copies of Gianfranco Rosi's award-winning documentary Fire at Sea to Turkey meeting," and *The Economist*, a few months later on June 9th, said of the movie: "Beautiful cinematography and searing images, but also odd choices and murky priorities in the award-winning film." *Fuocoammare* was immediately given an award at the Berlin Film Festival which recognized both the quality and the urgency of the message conveyed by the movie; it starts by showing on the screen the numbers involved in the ongoing tragedy: "L'isola di Lampedusa ha una superficie di 20 km2, dista 70 miglia dalla costa africana, 120 miglia da quella sicialiana. Negli ultimi 20 anni circa 400 mila migranti sono approdati a Lampedusa. Nel tentativo di attraversare il Canale di Sicilia per raggiungere l'Europa, si stima che siano morte 15 mila persone." ("The island of Lampedusa has a surface area of 20 square km, and lies 70 miles from the African coast and 120 miles from that of Sicily. In the past 20 years 400,000 migrants have landed on Lampedusa. In the attempt to cross the Straits of Sicily to reach Europe, it is estimated that 15,000 people have died."). For this low budget movie, Rosi was sponsored by RAI Cinema, the Italian public television company. However, in order to cut costs, he worked almost alone, handling sound and camera duties himself. Focusing on the parallel happenings of the arrival of the rescued migrants and the everyday life of the people of Lampedusa, Rosi composed a hybrid of captured footage and storytelling. The documentary style of representing the migrant tragedy was mixed with the (fictional) narrative of the lives of the islanders. Powerful moments like the migrants singing rap music and recounting the crossing of the desert (it sums up all that we already know through Segre's films), the dead bodies lined up on board the Italian ship, and the incredible footage which captured close-ups of real tears of blood was mixed with the normality of the old-fashioned way of life of the inhabitants of Lampedusa who almost turn a blind eye to what is happening. An old lady listens to a program on the radio about 260 shipwrecked people, with many dead among them, and mutters "poor souls" but keeps on preparing lunch for her family without changing any tiny little detail of her normality. A grandmother recalls the bombs of World War II while talking to her grandson, Samuele, and the way in which the bombs made it look like the sea was on fire, forcing the fishermen to stay at home—in just the same way that the stormy weather does during the film. The title song *Fuocoammare*, after which the movie is named, tries, then, to establish historical parallels. Twelve-year-old Samuele Pucillo, like the neorealist iconic characters Edmund and Bruno, spends his time innocently wandering around the island. Samuele's lazy eye cannot see the migrant crisis that is shocking the world. However, his anxiety, along with the pain of Pietro, his doctor, who takes care of the wounded migrants and often deals with dead bodies, tells us that we cannot accept this kind of new normality. The doctor's authentic monolog about his real work with migrants on board the ship is another striking moment. Something must be done urgently. The blood-crying faces of sad, wounded, just-saved migrants on the Italian military ship fill the screen and our imaginary of these events.

Like a documentary: *Terra* di mezzo (1997), and *La mia classe* (2014)

Ascending geographically, and entering the periphery of the internal border inhabited by mostly illegal immigrants—therefore in the last layers of the territorial human being—fiction tries to imitate the documentary as a more credible artistic form. This is what Matteo Garrone does in *Terra di mezzo* (*In-Between Land*).[78] One day the director, as he reveals in the interview "La finzione del reale" ("The Fiction of Reality"), happened by chance to see a suburban Roman road and was visually struck by what he saw. *Terra di mezzo* "è nato dall'atmosfera un po' surreale delle campagne romane tra le prostitute dai vestiti fantascentifici, i pastori che giravano con le pecore e i ciclisti che sfrecciavano con le loro tute colorate" ("was born from the somewhat surreal atmosphere of the Roman countryside among prostitutes in sci-fi clothes, the shepherds who walked with sheep and cyclists who darted about in their colorful suits") ("La finzione del reale" 195). The film did not have a script, and Garrone decided to dig deeper. The camera moves in the suburbs as in the days of neorealism and, as then, along with the sheep on the side the road, not even the crane building the first row of houses of the beginning (or end, depending on the perspective) of the city is missing. The African prostitutes, by the edge of the road, sit on old high chairs, the young Albanian construction workers, and the Egyptian gas-station worker at the center of the three episodes of the film are not professional actors and, in life, most probably do similar work. The Italians who interact with them are professional actors. This hybrid cast reveals the reasons for Garrone's choices. The different trajectories of the two groups of characters are also interesting. The first group stays in the suburbs and shyly approach the city—Rome—with its surrounding villages which, in 1997 when the film was released, had already started to show signs of the multiethnic condition that today dominate. The Romans, impersonated by some well-known faces of the Italian screen, make incursions into the suburbs, looking only for prostitutes and workers. The acting of the first group is mixed with testimony, as the characters actually perform these activities in real life. The plural meeting takes place, not by chance, in a fluid and transitory space like a suburban road. It gradually, step-by-step, enters the city, starting from gas stations. The roles in these meetings are defined and polarized: on the one hand there are prostitutes and workers; on the other, mostly (but not only) males who buy sex, labor, and petrol. There is more. The difference for the umpteenth time is in the economic conditions of the people. The Albanian workers, young and white, penetrate the city but remain outside the window, looking at their peers participating in a classical dance class or swimming in the pool. They are outside; the others are inside. The host community has established the roles, while the newcomers are exploring. Garrone captures this very early phase of transition (at least from a territorial point of view) through a film composed as a documentary; a mixture of testimony and fiction. The big news that is about to change the ethnic face of the country happens on the way to the city, and makes its first entry into the suburbs. In this film, photography, the documentation of a condition, of a state of things, is especially important and remains a fundamental mark in Garrone's work, so much so as to be the distinguishing feature of his multi-celebrated film *Gomorrah*. "I shot it like a documentary," explains the director, "but there were many people behind the camera, and it was all done on set. But I wanted the audience to think it was a documentary, which many people did, so that means I've done good work. I have made documentaries, and my work has always mixed two genres" (*Cinema Today* 124). The hybridization of genres is not only a stylistic marker but, first of all, a necessity dictated by the author's goal; it is dictated by the context taken into consideration.[79] "In his filmography, Garrone focuses on stories which emerge from the periphery of Italian life, gleaning ideas from everyday reality and adding his own input in such a way that his screen fiction appears more real and possible than the absurdities of life itself" (d'Arcangeli 176). Garrone feels that the representation of difficult-to-penetrate worlds could have problems of credibility. The documentary register sounds like a promise of high-fidelity representation. The thesis in a film represents a point of view "on this side" of the sea (in Giordana's and Rulli's eyes), of the periphery, of the marginalization; a point of view imposed on the represented matter, a point of view constructed by an often collective, standard, imaginary that has been generated by the discourses of wealthy classes as, often, the experience of life of directors and screenwriters is limited to the selected environments of urban centers. The documentary register, at least in the intentions of the director, tries to break down this barrier, and penetrate this imaginary in order to understand the lives of those who experience these difficult-to-penetrate world in the first person.

The Modesty of Representation

In other words, it seeks to penetrate the real places where things happen, often putting the real characters at the center, whether they be migrants, prostitutes, or members of the Camorra; thus it touches on and aims at the testimony instead of the representation. Real faces, real locations, as in the times of neorealism. Almost feeling the same need that Segre felt when he decided to involve different subjects in the film-making process, Garrone considers the writing process as an open construction site. "Depicting credible emotional and cognitive responses from characters who circulate in abnormal social contexts requires considerable technical expertise, and the writing process sometimes continues during filming when the actors may contribute to it, or ideas may evolve from comments by bystanders" (d'Arcangeli 180).

In *Silhouette*, the short that opens *Terra di mezzo*, there is—deliberately—a repeated and long close-up of the sad face of a prostitute. While she is being used from behind, a silent and immense sadness emanates from her eyes, whilst the man's face is not shown, as if it were an impersonal brute force that overwhelms her. However, the music that accompanies it creates a metaphorical short circuit which enhances the synthesis power of the representation. Through an African melody there is an almost territorial, geographical overlap. The suburbs of Rome taste of Africa, but a suffering Africa, an Africa as a disregarded possibility in a sad, melancholic Rome. This choice, however, involves many problems. The music we listen to should take us into the inner world of the characters, taking it for granted that they actually listen to these melodies. That a similar choice is problematic is suggested by the rest of the soundtrack. The respective episodes of the film are accompanied by African and Albanian music. By choice or by oversight, the Albanian side is associated with the music of the Arbëresh communities who have lived in Italy, mostly in Calabria, for several centuries. However, this music is barely a part of the emotional language of Albanian teenagers and cannot give us back their inner world. This juxtaposing confirms the difficulty of penetrating and representing distant worlds. The perspective, therefore, remains that of the Italian director.

Shortly after the afore described scene, in the *Silhouette* episode, the idea of the geographical human being becomes limpid. When the client and the woman enter the village invaded by a group of

Chapter Thirteen

Japanese tourists, the external looks intimidate the prostitute, forcing her to not leave the car. This is suggestive of the kind of globalization we live in: the tourists are Japanese, the prostitutes are African. However, if the prostitutes seem obliged to stay out of the city, or at least outside of its central areas, having the young workers of the second short film wait at the side of the road is like showing us a second level of the road—that is, a road that penetrates the city. From this perspective, the road seems to be another liquid space that prepares a reality that is a part of urban centers. On this road, the first polarized groupings are formed: Italian clients and African prostitutes, Italian clients and, again, Albanian workers. This polarization causes individuals to regroup immediately in small communities in which they share their condition and seek a minimum of protection. Precisely, too, because the road is a pre-urban territory, polarization, divisions, submissions, and community logics are part of urban centers. The last short in the film is set in the city, but in a space that appears to be a non-place. The focus is on one individual only, an Egyptian immigrant. The area where everything is concentrated is a gas station in which the man seems to be locked up and isolated by an invisible fence, welcoming, as he can, Romans of all kinds, even the inevitable racist thugs. He is insulted, mistreated, entertained, and given advice, showing us a gallery of interactions that immobilize him in an isolated space while the city moves around him, varied and unpredictable. The film, as the title *Terra di mezzo* also suggests, is mostly about transitory spaces inhabited by migrants—almost wanting to draw the path that would be ideally taken after the first overcoming of the outer borders and to document the first part of the internal border, a stretch still fluid, not organized, where the interactions are improvised but not too much.

The representation of difficult topics, and specifically those that deal with migration, are the main focus of a metacinematographic film by Daniele Gaglianone, *La mia classe* (*My Class*). There are aspects that it shares with *Terra di mezzo* and several other films that have been considered in this work: from the themes to the specific contents and to the ways of representing them. The protagonist is an Italian teacher impersonated by an Italian film star, Valerio Mastandrea. It is set in an Italian language class for migrants living in Rome. They, again, are not professional

The Modesty of Representation

actors but play themselves. From this point of view, the film is close to the documentary in style. However, the different forms of hybridization that we have seen so far are somehow also present in this film—whose genre remains deliberately uncertain. The lines between documentary and feature film, facts, and fictions are intentionally blurred. The different levels of representation of the migrant reality strongly influence the structure of the film. The migrant class deals with the real problems that they encounter in Rome—the search for work and a home—and with problems arising from the passing of the 2002 Bossi-Fini law. Then, on another level, we see a group of filmmakers who are continuously present during the shooting and, towards the middle of the film, a Pirandellian raid of a level of reality that exceeds the representation thus far narrated. Meantime, the mock class—but with migrant protagonists and real problems—scrupulously sums up everything contemplated up to now (a bit like in Giordana's 2005 film *Quando sei nato non ti puoi più nascondere*), from legal problems with residency permits to the difficulties of finding a home, to nostalgia for the country of the origin, to the difficulties of integration and the extreme conditions of the countries of origin. Finally, there is even the desert crossing, with that narrated by Segre et al.'s *Come un uomo sulla terra* summarized here in a woman's monologue. Nothing is missing: there is abuse, there are dead bodies, glasses of pee instead of water, signs of torture on the body, and many extreme conditions—of which we have been informed by the films analyzed thus far. The geographical representation is accurate and carefully distributed. It represents the major migrant routes and also integrates the most important recent historical events—such as, for example, the Arab Spring. All in one class. As Giordana's boat was metaphorically global, so is Gaglianone's class. Each one represents something, be it an historical event, a nation, or a specific problem. The class is very well organized. Mastandrea, who relies on different experiences in these roles, is particularly credible. However, it is the rupture of this plane of representation that justifies and redeems the film. One of the characters, Shadi—the young Egyptian man who experienced the Arab Spring—is found to have no valid documents, a fact to which the teacher turns a blind eye in order to keep him in the classroom. However, something happens out of fiction and in real life, or at a higher level of pretense of reality

Chapter Thirteen

(we cannot know, doubt survives at the end of this metafilm): Issa, a migrant actor, has problems with his documents and the director forces him to leave the class and the film. In the first level of representation, the fictional part, the young Egyptian man is helped to stay in the classroom. In the second level of representation, the other young African man, called Issa, born in the Ivory Coast, is ousted from the film. The rest is the parallel and dramatic development of these two stories. In the first level, Shadi is found without documents by the police, ends up in jail and, probably close to his fatal repatriation, hangs himself with his trouser belt. However, the film ends with the police raid on the film's location, where they arrest Issa who, if deported, would risk losing his life. We cannot see if he hangs himself like his avatar in fiction or not. We do not know if something else happens that we do not see. This part of "real" events shirks away from representation. What we do not see, what is not represented, is the real theme of the film which ponders—with mastery—on how representable the migrant phenomenon is in general, and in real life, in particular. We remain uncertain about many things, including the genre of the film, which turns into a very particular docu-fiction.

Chapter Fourteen

On Communities

> The community is seen as an army of armed guards that control the entrance; predators and hunters lurking in, replacing the pre-modern figure of the ogre of the mobile vulgus, both promoted to the rank of new public enemy number one; reduce public spaces in enclave, "defensible" with selected access; separation, rather than bargaining, of the life in common; criminalization of any difference. (Bauman, *Community: Seeking Safety in an Insecure World* 112)

It is no coincidence that, in Zygmund Bauman's analysis of globalization, it is the fear of the loss of security that is one of its most important aspects. Behind a phenomenon that he calls the "desire for community," there is the uncertainty, the hidden danger of a uniform mass, the need to rule out the threat. According to Bauman, behind the need for walls in any sort of community within our metropolises, the trauma of uncertainty is to be found. Any kind of voluntary enclosure in a community, seen from the perspective of this Polish-born sociologist as a form of auto-ghettoization, can serve the purpose of examining the danger of the unpredictable magma that crosses our cities. From this perspective, Bauman writes, "community means *sameness*, and 'sameness' means exclusion of the other" (*Community* 112). Not unlike Bauman, Paul Virilio also bet everything on insecurity, entitling his book *Ville Panique* (*City of Panic*). The emphasis in Virilio's work is the rapid pace of technological and scientific progress that eludes political control. All the insidious phenomena of our world, in the contemporary era, take the suffix "hyper" and "mega": hyper-concentration, megalopolis, and hyper-terrorism. It is precisely the city, the megalopolis, the space of economic globalization, where the revolution of the media has made obsolete the idea of territorial sovereignty as the basis for the rule of law. The decline of the nation state, according to Virilio, has given way to the advancement of what he calls the new city-state—a hyper-concentration of this kind brings about the hyper-accident and causes disproportionate collective anxieties.

Closed communities: *Io sono Li*, *La Giusta distanza* and *Cose dell'altro mondo*

After many documentaries on immigration from Africa and the social and economic structure of the Veneto *(Marghera Canale Nord [Marghera North Channel]; Pescatori a Chioggia/[Fishermen in Chioggia]; La malombra/[The Bad Shadow])*, Andrea Segre returned to a cinematic treatment of immigration topics with *Io sono Li* but, in dealing with the complex issues of (urban) integration, he used the metaphors of artistic fiction, a clearly perceived change in his stylistic methods. Segre offers a very careful and aesthetic photography that is well able to articulate the moods of the characters. Both protagonists come from complex realities, closed and distant. Contrary to the process in the documentary, the information is reduced to essentials, leaving plenty of room for imagination and states of mind, painted like a craftsman even in the most specific nuances, echoing the same attention to detail as in *Le conseguenze dell'amore* (*The Consequences of Love*) by Paolo Sorrentino, perhaps thanks to the collaboration of the director of photography Luca Bigazzi, who also worked with Sorrentino. Much is said through metaphors, poems, letters, silences, camera angles, colors, and light; it gives rise to a highly lyrical film. Then, when the protagonist Shun Li appears on the screen, the ethnic red of the lanterns, as well of the passionate poetry of Qu Yuan—the traditional Chinese poet (340 BC–278 BC) who is linked with the Dragon Boat Festival and remembered by floating candles and lanterns in rivers—almost always dominates. This color theme is literally a red thread that runs through the film because Shun Li never misses an opportunity to put small candles and lanterns in water to the point of being constantly associated by viewers with poetry, colors, water, and mystery. During this uninterrupted communication through metaphors, the girl is also associated with the lagoon, which she defines as "sostantivo femminile, calmo e misterioso" ("a feminine noun, calm and mysterious"), in contrast to the sea, a masculine noun, "mai in pace, e sempre in movimento" ("never at peace, and always in motion"). The juxtaposition of genders is a sub-theme of the film, put on the screen, clearly, sharply, and without solutions. The Chinese males are always bosses or mobsters, and often vulgar. The women are victims, offended both morning and evening (as recited in the verses of the Chinese poet) but also gentle, delicate, and dreamy. The only Italian female figure who appears in the film is the angry wife—who is also a mother, tired, and submissive—of Devis the bully from the city of Chioggia. In contrast, the Italian men are less schematic and represent different themes in the film. These parallels, perhaps too simple, appear functional to the issues of a globalization—among other things, also male chauvinism—which is central to the film itself.

Shun Li is a young Chinese girl who works in a textile factory in Rome, where she sews 40 shirts per day; ten more than needed to pay her debt and bring her eight-year-old son to Italy as soon as possible. From the very beginning, we are catapulted into a world of darkness, where there is little talk and where what is said sometimes perplexes us. Shun Li is in a situation of temporary semi-slavery, held hostage by a group of compatriots who totally resemble a mafia organization. Her arrival and subsequent occupation in Italy seem to be their concern. The son has remained in China with his grandparents and joining his mother depends on the willingness of this organization, even though the details of how and when are not clear in the film. Only they (the organization) decide and communicate what they call "la notizia" ("the news") at some point, as if it were an administrative and bureaucratic act that decreed the payment of a debt and the freeing of the person. How they technically control the movements of her son in China and across national borders is not known. The extreme opacity of the organization makes the unexplained believable. Shun Li is transferred to Chioggia at their will.[80] There she will work in a tavern just purchased by the Chinese and predominantly frequented by old local fishermen. This choice is the first weakness of the plot. It is not clear, in fact, why Shun Li cannot continue to pay her debt in the company in Rome—also run by the Chinese—and why she has to move to the north-east. Her Italian, with its strong Chinese accent (it will eventually be a source of sympathy and genuineness thanks to the beautiful interpretation of the expert actress Zhao Tao) in an environment where the local dialect is spoken almost exclusively, makes this choice incomprehensible but, once again, the opacity that surrounds the entire Chinese community depicted in the film makes almost everything probable.

Chioggia is located on a small Adriatic peninsular area between the Venetian Lagoon and the delta of the River Po, about half-way between Venice and Ferrara. It is clear that there is a considerable distance between the world of the local fishermen and that of the Chinese community. Also noticeable, more importantly, are the reciprocal separations. It almost seems as if Segre, a native of Chioggia, wanting to talk of separations, chose to set the film where the distances between the two communities are extreme—as are also the consequences.

Shun Li, trapped in this double isolation, makes friends with an old fisherman, Bepi—a Yugoslavian immigrant who has been in Italy for the past 30 years—known as The Poet because of his versatility in composing instantly playful rhymes. The origin of Bepi[81] is another aspect that draws attention. A native of Pula—yet he does not call himself a Croatian but a Yugoslav (the film was released in 2012)—and apparently well integrated into his community, his origin is widely considered to be a minor detail. This tells us that integration takes time. Pola is the Venetian name of the city that is known as Pula in Croatia and which has, for centuries, been part of the Serenissima Republic of Venice. Nevertheless, if his friends consider him in all respects a Chioggia man, they do so by virtue of the 30 years he has spent in the city and not because of historical plots. On the other hand, his considering himself to be Yugoslav reflects a conception of time as well as the geography of the state. Bepi had lived in Tito's Yugoslavia and had left. The transient nature of the state entity seems to want to focus on the individual. Tito is dead. Mao Zedong is dead. Now Bepi and Shun Li who, apart from their pasts as citizens of communism, also have the sea in common, meet in Chioggia. Nevertheless, in his boat, Bepi offers her "Yugoslavian" grappa while Shun Li does not draw away, even for a second, from the lanterns and her poet's verses. While, Segre wants two people to meet who have gone through history and met up in Chioggia, they also remain as representatives of their communities.

The co-existence of communities remains the central theme of the film *Io sono Li*. Between Shun Li—a Chinese fisherman's daughter—and Bepi, the fisherman of Chioggia, a romantic friendship develops that immediately alarms both communities in equal measure. After a brief sequence in which the friends of the poet give their own reading of international events ("i soldi americani finiscono in Cina" ("American money ends up in China") says one of them, referring to the relocation of labor), there comes a moment when the authorial thesis and the ideology that produces the contrasts in the film are made explicit: economically triggered fears of the layers, feed distrust, closure, and discrimination. There is thus a preventable form of class hatred towards the enterprising stranger. The dark threat is known as "la mafia cinese" ("Chinese mafia") which, as in the potential *affaire*, through the marriages of their young girls with the old, targets the properties of locals. Despite the apparent banality of the statements (The Poet does not have more than a dilapidated fishing hut in the middle of the sea), the closures become dramatic. "Gli italiani parlano male dei cinesi per colpa tua" ("Italians speak ill of the Chinese because of you"), argued the leaders of the organization, successfully intimidating her to move away from the fisherman, otherwise they would punish her by preventing her son's arrival. However, not long after her child arrives, Shun Li, who has since gone to work in an import-export factory, wonders who has paid her debt. This is the second weak point in the plot. Our thoughts go immediately to her friend in Chioggia. The organization's leaders say that only a Chinese person can pay off the debt. They also say that the friend with whom she shared the room in Chioggia ran away after leaving some money. Is this the money that brought Shun Li's son to Italy? Considering that her friend was most probably working to settle her own debt with the organization, one might wonder how she got the money to help her friend. Was it Bepi who paid, through her? Difficult to know. A bitter surprise awaits the girl when she comes looking for him. The Poet, who apparently could not stand the separation, has died and, very conveniently, the problems of a difficult relationship are resolved. In short, everything fades in the poetics of the impossible, which seem to be explicit both as a metaphysical limit and as a concrete content that challenges the experience of integration in still-closed communities.

Chapter Fourteen

The visual ethnic composition of the film, the exaltation of the cultural peculiarities of both protagonists' worlds, the speaking in metaphors by Shun Li and her friend, the verses of the Chinese poet, the Venetian dialect, and the fishing world—rough, articulated, and sophisticated at the same time—lyricized even in its smallest detail, seem to want to capture and enhance the deep beauty within every culture. On the other hand, the meeting of the protagonists, both deeply rooted in their cultural systems apart from the obvious social criticism of the Chinese mafia and the racist people of Chioggia, would seem to suggest that the co-existence of cultures is possible, that life in common, and though difficult to achieve, would be beautiful; and that the multicultural model works if it is based on what we have in common (not surprisingly, as we saw above, Shun Li is the daughter of a Chinese fisherman)—that is, on some universal elements of our humanity. Behind the romantic friendship between Bepi and Shun Li is the desire to explore each other's worlds, the desire to enter each other's cultural universes. Shun Li loves to go fishing with Bepi and Bepi is so fascinated by the commemoration of the Chinese poet that he asks for a funeral that follows the same ritual. The film highlights the mutual fascination of the other that seems to intoxicate their souls. To kill, instead, are the ignorance, the phobias, the suffocating closures, the lagoon trap that, as the friend of Shun Li says, does not return to the sea a part of the water that enters it. The grey of Chioggia becomes refined when decorated by the colors of Shun Li. The multicultural model seems to satisfy the preferences of Segre but the closures, well described in the film, transform the context into an archipelago where cultures remain isolated; unable e to really interact.

From this perspective, Zygmund Bauman looks suspiciously at a multicultural model[82] that treats "culture" as "synonymous with the besieged fortress and in a fortress under siege the inhabitants are required to manifest their unswerving loyalty daily and to obtain from any hob-nobbing with outsiders" (*Community* 141). Bauman, one of the theorists most involved in debates on globalization, notes that only the new global elite succeeds in being extraterritorial. However, these cosmopolitans are not the bearers of a new synthesis of global culture. They end up living in virtually identical hotels everywhere they go. For Bauman, "cosmopolitanism" is inadequate for the role of "global culture." The cosmopolitan archipelago would be composed of many islands in which conformity, and the exclusion of the other, triumph. So, it is only a matter of "closed communities," those that we meet in every corner, and in every class of society. Insecurity leads to the closing of ranks in an attempt to avoid pitfalls. To Bauman, "closed communities" are voluntary ghettos that aim to limit space, social closure, and internal homogeneity. However, "it is only the racial-ethnic division that gives the homogeneity/heterogeneity opposition the capacity to infuse the ghetto walls with the kind of solidity, durability and reliability they need (and are needed for)" (*Community* 116). It follows, that it is the ethnic-racial division that provides the "ideal model" on whose same lines the other surrogates are formed. The difference in real ghettos lies in the simple fact that no one can get out of them. This is the individual's limitation, above all spatial, in affecting the theory of Bauman, who is critical of the current model of globalization because it tends to deterritorialize the elite and territorialize and localize the poor.

There is not much difference in the reflections stimulated by the perspective of another film set in the Veneto (in Concadalbero Veneto) that also focuses on integration issues. The North-East, in need of foreign labor for its industries, has difficulty developing a new cultural perspective that can provide cohesion in an already multiethnic context. Carlo Mazzacurati's *La Giusta distanza* (*The Right Distance*)[83] develops both the complaint against a strong cultural prejudice towards strangers and the wish for a so-called "intercultural tomorrow" in which the multiple perspectives and cultural traditions that inhabit the Venetian context should create a cultural hybridization that can provide a new cohesion. This is demonstrated by the choice of the soundtrack, where the music of Radiodervish, an Italo-Palestinian band whose members were born and raised in Bari, stands out. It is shown in the words of Hassan, the Tunisian mechanic, in love with the protagonist, Mara, who does not even like the culinary nostalgia of foreigners: "Se stai qui, stai qui e basta!" ("If you're here, you're here and that's it!"). This is demonstrated by his Moroccan brother-in-law chef who prepares the *piadine* or flatbreads as if he were born in Bologna, while Mara tries to prepare the couscous. Elements like these show that Veneto's state of contamination and miscegenation is more advanced than it appears in Segre's film—or, at least, that Mediterranean migrants in general, and Maghrebian migrants in particular, enjoy a relatively better state of integration than those from the Far East. Even the words of Hassan's public defender at the end of the film, unfortunately faithfully mirroring the clichés of his country, allude to foreigners' varying degrees of understanding of the Italian system including the weaknesses of the legal system. According to the defender, who is portrayed by the authors with open antipathy, Albanians and Romanians come to arrangements and shorten their detention. The Arabs do not. The tragic death of Hassan, who commits suicide in jail, proves this. There are other elements in the film that hint at the different levels of integration of foreigners. The country tobacconist has married a Romanian woman, probably much younger, while the Arab sister of the protagonist has married a Moroccan (and it is a much more successful marriage). On the other hand, the Chinese, generically called "orientali" ("oriental"), only appear "incatenati" ("chained") in a clandestine laboratory, about which the boy journalist, the narrator of the film, writes an article in which nobody is interested.

The collective reaction to the relationship between Hassan and Mara is a much weaker one than that seen in Segre's *Io sono Li*. There is one, however, which is unfortunately still very important. Soon after Mara begins her relationship with Hassan, she writes to her friend as if she were excusing herself ("Penserai che sono pazza!" ["You'll think I'm crazy!"]). To Hassan's marriage proposal Mara responds with silence. The director allows her a double alibi or escape. Mara says that she is not a conventional girl,[84] and that the model work, kids, and weekends spent shopping at the mall do not suit her, without letting us know if this is the reason for her refusal to marry Hassan or whether, as a non-conventional woman, she was able to have a relationship with Hassan. This is an important passage. The conventional formula of the family in the film seems to hide the dark impulses of men in the area, hidden customers of erotic telephone calls, and killers of dogs and women (such as the driver transformed into Mara's rapist and murderer) who sweep everything under the carpet by conveniently blaming foreigners. "The presence of the dead dogs carried away on stretchers or left in the dust from the very beginning gives the film a feeling of unease and the foreshadowing of more violence to come," writes Gloria Pastorino. "Not all is quiet in the apparently calm town where hidden desires are revealed violently" (137). The perpetuation of a conventional form of social organization, a hybrid of tradition and consumerism (Mara indicates the mall to be a place where families spend weekends almost as if they were interdependent models), would seem to be a source of multiple closures. The killing of that same Mara sounds like expulsion. When she writes to her friend that she does not feel that she fits into the model family—children, shopping mall at weekends—she confirms her future as a spinster that her mother foresaw for her daughter. Unfortunately, her exclusion is much more radical.

The second flight (failed) that the director grants Mara was already planned from the beginning of the film. Mara replaces a teacher who, not coincidentally, had gone crazy (and was then immediately expelled from a hypocritical context); consequently, Mara was in town for a limited period—at the end of the assignment she would have left for Brazil but her murder occurs before this planned departure. The impediments to the marriage were many. Her murder and the quick and superficial blame laid on Hassan emphasize the closure of the context. What if she had not been accidentally killed? What if she had not planned to go to Brazil? What would have been her relationship with Hassan? Seeing Bepi and Shun Li, or Mara and Hassan together in everyday life still does not seem possible in the Venetian context.

The dogs periodically killed from the beginning to the end of the film, the teacher who goes crazy, the guys who stalk and spy on Mara at night in her garden, the young reporter who spies on her e-mail account, the comfortable blaming of Hassan (seen as the anomaly who arrived from the outside), and a bus driver—the most routine presence in the town who is transformed into a killer—all outline a polarized context that is needy, and deficient of balance. It is precisely the double life of the driver—during the day an emblem of the main social model, a worker, a future father of a family, a weekend customer at shopping centers, but at night transformed into an exterminator of dogs, a rapist and even a killer—which contrasts the two sides of the same coin. Normality at all costs is opposed by the deep restlessness caused by profound ongoing changes. In a truly open context, the teacher might not have gone mad, the driver probably would not have turned into a killer, and the stranger would not be a stranger. A culturally more dynamic context would also be better equipped to respond to the economic and social challenges of globalization. The closure of these communities, however, speaks more to the fragility of a transitional phase than of loyalty to the past. The Venetian context in particular, as with the Italian context in general, is in search of new equilibria. The transformation may be delayed, but it cannot be stopped.[85]

Veneto and immigration are dealt with again in another film by Francesco Patierno which is entitled *Cose dell'altro mondo* and loosely based on the film *A Day Without a Mexican* by Sergio Arau.[86] It is a fairly ambitious work in terms of its content, with a cast of the best typical Italian comedy of recent years; the interpretations of Diego Abantantuono and Valerio Mastandrea succeed in conveying the contradictions and ambiguities with great clarity. The recitation of Abantantuono, echoing his roles in *Marrakech Express* and *Mediterraneo* which were films by Gabriele Salvatores, brings to mind the delicacy of the register of comedy when facing acute problems such as racism. In fact, the films of Segre and Mazzacurati considered in this work, take on a dryer approach which is facilitated by a different register than comedy. The latter, however, allows Patierno to adopt otherwise impossible narrative devices and, through them, to present a thorough enough authorial thesis.

The narrative device that contains the film's plot, though borrowed from the film by Arau, has its roots in some basic considerations of current Venetian reality—made up of small-and medium-sized industries created within a few decades and, as a result, still free of proper and appropriate cultural elaborations—against a backdrop of an historically agricultural context. The Venetian industrialist, from the television screens at his property and cursing heavily—as even politicians from the region and beyond often do—points the finger precisely at this entrepreneurial group. "Vorrei dire due parole a tutti quei signoretti ipocriti, che non discendono dalla borghesia imprenditoriale ma sono la m... arricchita [...]" ("I would like to say a few words to all those so-called gentlemen, hypocrites who do not descend from the entrepreneurial bourgeoisie, but that are sh .... enriched [...]"), the protagonist says, turning to those who now mourn them: "la manovalanza negra che gli ha garantito di avere trentacinque telefonini, il cambio del macchinone ogni due anni. A loro e a tutti i sedicenti intellettuali, analfabeti, disoccupati che non hanno voglia di fare niente... a loro io dico ufficialmente..." ("Negro laborers who have ensured that they have 35 mobile phones, and a change of big car every two years [...] To them and to all the so-called intellectuals, illiterate, unemployed people who do not want to do anything ... to them I say officially ...") and concludes swearing vulgarly. The character of the Magic Magician, the comments of the mayor, the rituals that close the film and such television talk explicitly and repeatedly emphasize these aspects. As in a rural past populated by superstitious rites for invoking rain, first is invoked the magical disappearance of all the immigrants, with extremes of xenophobia worthy of the Klu Klux Klan. Then, after being satisfied and after discovering that their well-being is entirely based on the work of foreigners, the return of the latter is also magically invoked. More complex analysis articulated are in this simple plot. The Veneto reality, like the Italian one, is much more rugged and contradictory than it at first appears. The daily actions and positions taken by the inhabitants are affected by different and often disparate visions of the world. The racist and hypocritical entrepreneur, Mariso Golfetto (Diego Abatantuono) is contrasted with his daughter, Laura, a leftist non-conventional, once again interpreted by Valentina Lodovini (of *La Giusta distanza* fame), who lives with his North African worker; contrasted with her ex, a cop who decides not to engage in serious relations and who feels skepticism towards "leftist" multicultural theories, is the cop's mother, who is entrusted to a caregiver originally from Eastern Europe. And then there is Marcello, the squad taxi driver, passionate about anti-immigrant patrols, and law enforcement's indifference to the disappearance of foreigners and small turncoat entrepreneurs etc.

Different are the visions of the world, and the languages. Marcello, the squadrist, tells the cop that acting with the anti-immigrant patrols is "come andare a caccia." ("like hunting"). The non-Italians, it follows, are beasts and the conception of the human being here becomes a national conception. The Venetians and the Italians are implicitly human. Foreigners, those poor people, are not. They can be hunted like animals. In the film, every time an adjective of nationality is used, it is always accompanied by something derogatory. The Islamists? "Fondamentalisti." ("Fundamentalists.") Albanians? "Fancazzisti." ("Slackers")— such comments fit the language of the average racist—but they become "di merda" ("shitty") in the language of the "hunter" squad. In addition, media references are also important. The fear of the rapist metropolitan stranger is widespread throughout the world, even in international cinema. This is the case of Pierre Morel's *Taken* and *Taken 2*, later translated into Italian and quoted as *Io vi troverò* (*I Will Find You*), in which the protagonist, a former CIA agent played by Liam Neeson, is transformed into an avenger hunting a gang of Albanian traffickers and rapists. Mariso Golfetto (Abatantuono) cites the film, and criticizes the tough Liam Neeson for being a softie. The authors' irony is obvious: the listener who hears these confidences is a young Nigerian woman, a prostitute, and mistress of the hypocritical entrepreneur. Also ironic is the broken English of Golfetto: "Take the camel and come back to home" is screamed from the screen of his TV channel. Grotesque as it is, this language is far from harmless. Just follow the political events, the language, and the vulgar shouts of the politicians in *La Lega Nord* (*The Northern League*) that rule the different cities of Veneto, when they referred to the then Minister for Education in the Letta cabinet of 2013–14, the black Cécile Kyenge, casually injured almost every day and invited to become Minister in Egypt, with all the implied meanings of the international vision of *La Lega Nord*. The photograph that the film portrays of this situation is fairly accurate. Terms such as camels, rapes, and robberies abound in the sentences whenever there is an adjective of a different nationality or a different religion.

It is not even lacking a socio-economic reading level, repeated often enough by journalists and sociologists as to become a cliché. The absence of foreign caregivers becomes an opportunity for comments by Mario's frigid wife (another count against the husband, who has a Nigerian lover). "Una badante? Da dove? Dalla Sicilia? Dalla Sardegna? Dall'Abruzzo? ... Una volta chi è che faceva le cameriere? Le italiane, no? ... Tutti dottori, tutti primari, tutti avvocati?" ("A caregiver? From where? From Sicily? Sardinia? From Abruzzo? [...] The one who was a waiter once? The Italian, right? [...] All doctors, all head physicians, all lawyers?"). In a world where an ethnic marker becomes an economic marker, an indication of class—the articulation of the problems that arose from a relative economic well-being—continues. Added to the very high and unjustified economic expectations of the younger Italian generation is the increasing length of life of their fathers' generation that brings with it high economic and social costs. In an increasingly less-young Italian society is interlocked the presence of foreigners who are able either to perform those useful job functions no longer desired by the natives, or meet the need for young labor capable of paying the social costs of the older generation. However, despite this vital dependence on foreigners, there is the additional ingratitude of discrimination: the Venetian *Lega Nord* politicians have even proposed the elimination of benches in the public parks in order to prevent homeless immigrants from sleeping there at night. This heavy discrimination seems, however, to have some functionality when viewed from the point of view of "class conflict." In this way, not only are labor costs kept low—oppressing the economic claims of foreigners, but their expectations of different employment and social integration are also dampened. In short, non-Italians should aspire to be just workers, caregivers, and farmers. Even the cultural window opened by a world vision of the "leftist" never becomes a door. Again, also in this film, the character interpreted by Valentina Ludovini, despite the arrival of an unplanned child, is not able to transform the relationship with the immigrant into a marriage. "In fondo sono uguale a te" ("In the end, I'm the same as you"), says Laura to her racist father when she betrays her absent African partner to her ex, Ariele. It almost seems that coexistence with the stranger is only possible if it is temporary and within the limits of the traditional model of the family. It can be considered an enriching experience at best but not as a life project. And that, is exactly what the film is trying to say. Patierno himself defines the integration as "un processo ancora da compiersi" ("a process yet to be completed"). It is of this "incompleteness"—narrated from the perspective of the natives—this unpreparedness, this delay, this closure that he wanted to talk about in his film.[87]

It is important to emphasize the rhythm produced by the transformations which have assailed and continue to assail Italy, particularly because of its geographic position. Within the Italian context, the Veneto is particularly interesting because of its rapid economic development which has even changed the nature of its social problems. The rapid transformation from an emigration to an immigration context has not, as of yet, been accompanied by appropriate cultural elaborations, as Segre did not fail to note at the end of *Io sono Li* (*Shun Li and the Poet*).[88] Mazzacurati, on the other hand, speaking of *La Giusta distanza*, implicitly places the phenomena of immigration and globalization within the great process of modernization: "In fondo il film è soprattutto questo: una registrazione dello scontro drammatico tra arcaicità e modernità" ("After all, the film is this above all: the recording of the dramatic encounter between archaism and modernity") ("Intervista a Carlo Mazzacurati, '*La Giusta Distanza*'"). The agents of this modernization, for the Veneto director, are people who have come from abroad—immigrants. The French anthropologist, Marc Augé, has much the same perspective on the phenomena of globalization, urbanization, and immigration. "We will rediscover the sense of history. Or at least, this is the illusion that can reawaken in the most optimistic of us the sight of the city in transformation, just as similar illusions were reawakened in the nineteenth century in the poor in rural Europe; and just as they are reawakened in the damned of Earth who prefer the risk of death in flight rather than experiencing it while waiting in their own country. Deceptive and promising, city lights still shine" (Augé, *An Introduction to Supermodernity* 21). However, in the case of Veneto it is much more specific. When we speak of Chioggia or of Concadalbero Veneto, we are not talking of large urban concentrations where aspects of globalization are very evident and much studied. Another interesting reading is offered by an important theorist of globalization, John Tomlinson (*Globalization and Culture*). Through various interpretations and reinterpretations, including Marc Augé's (*An Introduction to Supermodernity*) notion of supermodernity and non-places, and Garcia Canclini's work (*Culturas hibridas*) dedicated to Latin American cultures, shifting attention to "the margins" and taking as an example the research carried out in Tijuana—a Mexican town that, because of the internal migration of workers, has seen its population grow tremendously—he considers deterritorialization to be the cultural condition of globalization. That of Tijuana becomes, for Tomlinson, the example of a place whose local identity is generally formed through its relationship with the rest of Mexico and North America. Tomlinson concludes "the phenomenon of deterritorialization, far from being exclusive to the centers of affluence in the West, is in certain ways experienced more sharply at the margins" (141). His analysis helps us to place these phenomena even outside large urban concentrations. There is a point, relevant to this work, in which Tomlinson and

Bauman converge (the author's direct references to Bauman's work concern, instead, other aspects). This point concerns the relevance and importance of the role of fears and uncertainties. The process of deterritorialization, for Tomlinson, seems not to be a linear one but one characterized by a dialectical "push-and-pull," like globalization itself. Part of this process also seems to be examples and thrusts of re-territorialisation. "Amongst the latter are the various existential vulnerabilities that come when our lives are opened up to the wider world and our sense of a secure and circumscribed home—both literally and metaphorically—is threatened. The drive towards reterritorialization can thus be seen in various attempts to re-establish a cultural 'home'" (Tomlinson 148). The uncertainties and fears are fully exploited, even on the political plane, as shown by the polemics at the end of Patierno's film. From a formal point of view, *Cose dell'altro mondo* presents an interesting limit in neither exploiting the good start nor knowing how to proceed. This plot limit, however, hides a certain basic pessimism which can, to a degree, be traced in the melancholy tone of the narration. After the invocation of the Apocalypse on the part of the impersonal entrepreneur played by Diego Anbatantuono ("Apocalypse Now!"), and in the form of a parody of global imaginary produced by international cinema, all types of relationship become, to a certain degree, post something which, if not apocalypse, is at least an implosion of relations, codes, and ideas for the future. It is not, therefore, a limitation of the plot. Along with the awareness that overcomes the function of denouncement and analysis, it becomes difficult to imagine ready and lasting solutions.

Lakhous' closed rooms

Closures, perhaps more evident in the suburbs, often characterize cohabitation in all urban environments. Rome is no exception, as emerges from the reading of *Scontro di civiltà per un ascensore a Piazza Vittorio* (*Clash of Civilizations over an Elevator in Piazza Vittorio*) by Amara Lakhous. This novel has the merit of bringing back the true dimension of the problem, transforming the usual bi-polar focus (foreigners *vs* locals) into a multicentric mini-archipelago in which individuals of disparate origins cohabit the same building without ever meeting either in reality or on an imaginary level. The only space in which they are forced to live is not the square (despite the Piazza Vittorio being the famous square of the multi-ethnic Roman market, celebrated as a place of trade since the 1948 film by Vittorio De Sica, *Ladri di Biciclette—Bicycle Thieves*) but the elevator, the most modern symbol of classic buildings. The confrontation meetings take place, not by chance, in this unique and moving space (a non-place if we like). The murder of a grotesque individual, called the gladiator, becomes an excuse to explore the thousand different ways of living and interpreting the same context, the same reality, and gives life to a novel made of "stanze chiuse" ("closed rooms"), as Ugo Fracassa (*Patria e lettere*)[89] calls them. Fracassa, like many other critics, sees in Lakhous' novel the famous model of Gadda's *Quer pasticciaccio brutto di Via Merulana*, starting from the pretext of the crime up to the adoption of a plurality of stylistic registers, of dialectal inflections, of divergent and plural subjective instances in its attempt to represent Rome. In making this juxtaposition, Fracassa, via Barthes (*Mythologies*), underlines the author's will to adopt a realistic register and to produce "l'effetto del reale" ("the effect of reality"), through the use of the "illusione referenziale" ("referential illusion") when, for example, Lakhous tries to make the referents speak directly. A need that we have seen dominate in the cinema of these years, which prefers the documentary form to deal with complex issues and, in particular, immigration. It is as if the Italian-Algerian writer, though through the abundant use of free indirect speech, had put a microphone in front of all his characters. It is difficult to say to the extent to which the Gaddian model was an inspiration to Lakhous and to what extent, in aiming at the representation of the Roman multitude, there is something objective that attracts certain artistic forms. Is not missing here, as in Fellini and Gadda, the unique subject, whether Marcello, Ingravallo or Amedeo in our case, able to explore the perspectives and sew everything together, offering us a kind of network novel and a subject like Marco Polo, able to put all together. In the end, the value of the novel is that it has given us a detailed multi-ethnic map accompanied by imaginaries that populate Rome. The presence, then, among the many characters, of both Ahmed/Amedeo (Algerian) as the author, who is a reference figure in all the "closed rooms," and of an aspiring film director, Johan, who wants to put everything together around the crime of the elevator, offers clear metanarrative elements. Despite this, once again, the declared reference model is neither Calvino nor Gadda: Amedeo's and Johan's reports have in common a precise reference: cinema and, more precisely, Neorealism. "Sono arrivato a Roma per studiare cinema e realizzare il bel sogno che mi accompagna da quando ero piccolo. Io sono un grande amante del cinema italiano e non nascondo la mia passione per il Neorealismo, che per me è la miglior risposta al cinema di Hollywood. Adoro i film di Rossellini e *Ladri di biciclette* di Vittorio De Sica sono fra i migliori film nella storia del cinema. Alcune scene del secondo film sono state girate proprio a piazza Vittorio." ("I arrived in Rome to study cinema and bring the beautiful dream that has accompanied me since I was a child to life. I am a great lover of Italian cinema and I do not hide my passion for Neorealism, which for me is the best answer to Hollywood cinema. I love Rossellini's films and Vittorio De Sica's *Bicycle Thieves*, which are among the best films in the history of cinema. Some scenes of the second film were shot right in Piazza Vittorio.") (Lakhous, *Scontro di civiltà* 84).

Johan, however, as in one of Italo Calvino's last unfinished novels, *Se una notte d'inverno un viaggiatore*, announces the title of his future film that coincides with the title of the novel, thus offering us the perspective of the whole of these pieces of stories. In this case, too, the map of the whole is offered, but through a recourse to cinema. This is the point—it was the cinema that provided the imaginary of Rome even before the characters lived there. It is still that abstract idea of Rome that accompanies them in everyday life, and it is still that old map that guides them every day. It is the idea of living in that mythical place which is the common element of their subjectivities. It is not Hollywood, as in Appadurai's (*Modernity at Large*) case, but Cinecittà and Neorealism. Then it becomes a too-evident kind of time shift. It is the cinema of yesterday that has nourished today's migrant imaginary. There has probably been a mediation of the previous generation through the selection and circulation in the national circuits of origin of the past's cinematographic glories. This is perhaps how the characters who are inspired by Rossellini, De Sica, and Germi are explained. The same Amedeo, the author's stand-in, confirms the convergence with Johan: "Quanto mi piace il film di Pietro Germi *Divorzio all'italiana*, non mi stanco mai a rivederlo" ("How I like Pietro Germi's *Divorzio all'Italiana* (*Divorce Italian*

Style), I never get tired of watching it again") (Lakhous, *Scontro di civiltà* 88). Lakhous' subsequent novel is entitled *Divorzio all'islamica a viale Marconi* (*Divorce Islamic Style in Viale Marconi*). However, if the cinema travels with a certain delay, the case of television is different, as are the geographical areas from which the migrants come. Here, importance of the influence of television or, rather, that of cinema varies. As a result, expectations and how migrants read contexts varies. Another element of the imaginary that many characters share comes from soccer. The "mentalità del catenaccio all'italiana" ("Italian-style *catenaccio* mentality")[90] becomes the metaphor of closure with which Amedeo describes the multi-ethnic subjectivities that inhabit the condominium of Piazza Vittorio. Soccer considerations then follow which, refer to recent times—to Berlusconi's Milan and, indirectly, to a more immediate diffusion of images thanks to the medium of television and its global diffusion. The imaginary of migrants then becomes an unpredictable puzzle in which famous traditional actors like Anna Magnani and Aldo Fabrizi are in the company of the Champion's League teams, while the facts of recent news (the events are set in Rome in the late 1990s) such as the investigation *Mani Pulite* (*Clean Hands*), become a corruption metaphor to explain why the football teams of Roma and Lazio do not win like Milan, Inter, and Juventus do. The reading of this imaginary becomes fundamental for understanding today's Italy.

The community of the communities

All roads lead to Rome ... all roads lead to Piazza Vittorio. With this quote by Pasolini the documentary *L'Orchestra di Piazza Vittorio* (*The Orchestra of Piazza Vittorio*) both begins and ends. The documentary narrates the story of the formation of an international orchestra in one of the best-known squares of the capital in the first decade of the twenty-first century. The square's proximity to the largest railway station in Italy, to Termini, has caused a change in its inhabitants. Attracted to this area adjacent to the station, together with the poor, is almost a hierarchical list of the last of the earth: the homeless, prostitutes, addicts and, above all, migrants. The historical merchants sold to the Chinese and the population that used to live there changed as a result. Piazza Vittorio, already a market and exchange area, is transformed into both a challenge of coexistence and a political challenge between left and right. A closed red-light cinema and a city association—Apollo 11—tried to appropriate the space to use it for cultural activities. The township, led by the left, answered the request of Apollo 11, and purchased the building with the intention of allocating it to cultural activities. This step, together with the subsequent sponsorship of the Roma Europa Festival, is very important for understanding the cultural and political story of *L'Orchestra di Piazza Vittorio*. The collaboration of the Apollo 11 association with local institutions follows a fairly precise cultural political track. The members of the association intended to form an orchestra inspired by the Piazza Vittorio, inspired by the plural coexistence there, to oppose "un discorso culturale" ("a cultural discourse") to the 2002 Bossi-Fini law on immigration. How this cultural discourse contrasts the philosophy of the law (which "rende le persone merci" ("turns people into goods") as said in the film) is taken for granted but never articulated. The search for musicians starts from the microphones of a protest demonstration against the Bossi-Fini law, even if it does not bear immediate fruits. As the story develops, the musicians involved are all high-profile, simply international, and sometimes do not even live in Rome. For the authors of the film, and for the people involved in the creation of the orchestra, an international multicultural orchestra becomes the bearer of a discourse against the law that transforms human beings into "goods," and is automatically in favor of immigration. The orchestra seeks to mirror changes within the migrant population, and its success, besides its good artistic quality, is precisely due to its nature. It is the multicultural model that is implicitly the element of the greatest contrast to the discrimination of foreigners in Italy. The subtraction of ethnic difference as a discriminatory tool should inspire, along with a different cultural and political climate, fairer legislation on the subject of immigration. The institutional support of the center left, shown by the benevolence of the city of Rome and of an organism like the Roma Europa Festival, shows that multiculturalism is turning into a founding discourse of the Europe to come. In this regard, Teresa Fiore in *Pre-Occupied Spaces* makes an important and useful observation. In considering this docufilm as a remake of Fellini's *Prove d'orchestra*, Fiore underlines a parallel between the nation-building aspect of Fellini's film, where it explored regional diversity and the "postnational scenario of multhietnic coexistence" of this docu-musical (Fiore, *Pre-Occupied Spaces* 78). "Fellini embarked on a similar project almost thirty years earlier with *Prove d'orchestra*, an interrogation on the Italian nation from a regional perspective. Directly inspired by this film, Ferrente dialogues with a canonical auteur, but he fundamentally reshapes the terms of Fellini's project" (*Pre-Occupied Spaces* 80). The postnational scenario is, of course, important for the new European Union; it is essential to multhietnic coexistence. However, to be part of this orchestra, it is necessary to represent the culture of an ethnic community. When Italian musicians become part of the orchestra, the narrating voice of Mario Tronco, the director and founder of the orchestra, explains that, in an international orchestra the participation of Italy is also legitimate. The participating musicians, then, do not do so individually but as representatives of the cultures of the communities they represent. The orchestra, by the very nature of an orchestra, adopts one of their songs from time to time, and through so doing creates a kind of cultural community of ethnic communities. It is then a multiculturalism which tries to open passages, to create common spaces.

There still remains the question of the closed communities posed by Bauman (*Community: Seeking Safety in an Insecure World*) in whose analysis multiculturalism becomes multicommunitarism. For Bauman, belief in the multicultural model fills a void around the very idea of the human being. He refers to Russell Jacoby's *The End of Utopia*. Both Bauman and Jacoby believe that our wealthy strata have nothing to say today on the ideal condition of human beings. From these authors' perspective, multiculturalism as a paradigm is "the ideology of an era without an ideology" (Jacoby 33). Alessandro Dal Lago appears not to be distant from these positions. With his *Non persone* (*Non-Persons*), he brings these analyses into the Italian context, and identifies in multicultural or differentialist theories the cultural and political strategies of the institutions and the private-social sector which, in Italy, serve as a substitute for the state, in order to produce ethnic-cultural markers which will be useful for the control of foreigners. Migrants, according to Dal Lago, exist only as "others," as fragments of other cultures or other religions but not as subjects who do something under certain conditions (170). When migrants become invisible in the informal economy market, their presence is tolerated and ignored. However, as soon as they gain visibility, they are "etnicizzati e culturalmente segregati" ("ethnicized and culturally segregated").

Chapter Fifteen

The Multi-Belonger

> How many times, since I left Lebanon in 1976 to live in France, have people asked me, with the best intention in the world, whether I felt "more French" or "more Lebanese"? And I always give the same answer: "both". (Maalouf 1)

There are several authors *in Italian* who write in more than one language or adopt self-translation. In fact, possessing more than one passport, citizenship, or residence permit is not a merely bureaucratic issue. Stateless persons, illegal immigrants, uprooted persons, and non-belongers can equate dangerously to non-human as the concept emerges from Hannah Arendt's, Giorgio Agamben's, and Primo Levi's work. It is no coincidence that the possession of two passports speaks of Italian-Americans, French-Germans, and so on. That legal hyphen is the thread of multi-belonging that is also a cultural issue. Multibelonging can be seen as an inclusive solution which is historically circumscribed and certainly transitory. It's duration can be difficult to anticipate. In this chapter I focus mainly on Helga Schneider's *Lasciami andare, madre* (*Mother, Let Me Go*), Jhumpa Lahiri's *In altre parole* (*In Other Words*), Gëzim Hajdari's *Corpo Presente* (*Present Body*), Milan Kundera's *L'Ignorance* (*Ignorance*) and Carmine Abate's *La festa del ritorno* (*The Homecoming Party*), and their cultural strategies and other implications.

Multibelonging in literature

The protagonist of Schneider's autobiographical novel, *Mother, Let Me Go*, is the daughter of an SS functionary. She abandons her mother and her mother tongue, German, to write in Italian and build a new identity in Italy. Her identity arises from a denial: she does not want to be the daughter of a Nazi; she does not want to be crushed by an unbearable collective and family trauma; she wants to be a new person. The burning need to overcome fears, poverty, and trauma evolves into a personal plan of redemption that springs from the self and craves to overcome these constraints. Helga's very complex relationship with her mother makes Helga want to recoup her German identity. Being the daughter of a German mother entails being a German, too. "È così vecchia, così fragile. Ancora una volta, mio malgrado, mi intenerisce. Sto per andarmene, e ho paura che non riuscirò a spezzare il legame che mi unisce a lei. E dire che ho tentato di farlo mille volte, in mille modi diversi. Perfino rinnegando la mia madrelingua." ("She is so old, so fragile. Again, despite myself, I am touched. I am leaving, and I'm afraid I will not be able to break the bond that connects me to her. And to think that I have tried to do it a thousand times in a thousand different ways. Even denying my mother tongue.") (Schneider, *Lasciami andare, madre* 107).[91] Despite her choice to live in Italy, her decision not to speak German, and her willingness to condemn the horror; despite all this, a bond remains: she is still German, the daughter of her mother. That bond cannot be broken because of her history: her emotions, the imprinting of her beginnings, her pain, her first language. Helga no longer has only one single belonging. She has a bond, expressed by the hyphen (-), a sort of bridge that allows her, and every multi-belonger, to move from one belonging to another. When Helga cannot stand the pain of being the daughter of a woman who exterminated children in gas chambers, she escapes into the Italian language, speaking perhaps with a slight accent. And when her identity as a daughter makes it impossible for her to erase from her life the existence of her mother, who is now around ninety years old, Helga speaks German again, she turns German again, although a different kind of German, one that is more than a bit Italian, and not only in her attachment to coffee.[92]

Jhumpa Lahiri makes a similar choice in her memoir, *In altre parole* (*In Other Words*). Lahiri decided to learn Italian and moved to Rome, where she spent several years, as she explained an interview published in *The Wall Street Journal*:

> Yes, I've been writing in Italian now for three years. I've written not just this book, but other things—diaries, short stories, things that are piling up with time. But it all feels like a dream; there is a kind of surreal element to it. I speak English. I grew up speaking Bengali. This is the normal, the known, the obvious composition of who I am. Then there's Italian, this strange, other component of me that I've just created (Burnham Schwartz, "How Jhumpa Lahiri Learned to Write Again").

After going back to New York, she started to experience a sense of nostalgia that was precious to her. "And so strangely the point of all this is that even though the nostalgia has been crushing at times in the past three months, I'm strangely proud of it. Because the fact of having it means I belong somewhere" (Burnham Schwartz). The new language and the new belonging helped her to escape the pain of her past.

> English is loaded. In my search to become my own person, to define myself in some way and not be defined by others, English represented feelings of guilt... That is why I learned Italian, because I wanted to feel at peace, and I wanted to be in a quiet room all by myself. When I opened that door, when I went into the Italian room, it was really quiet, and all of that *dolore* of the past—the confusion, the conflict, the feeling of what did it mean for me to be reading and writing vis-à-vis my parents and their world—it just went away (Burnham Schwartz).

When she was a child, she avoided speaking in Bengali in the presence of her friends, and felt a need to hide. A double sense of shame derived from the need to hide her origins, coupled with awareness of that need caused her deep pain. She felt that the use of the language and her relationship with her parents were connected. "Non era possibile parlare in inglese senza avvertire un distacco dai miei genitori" ("It wasn't possible to speak in English without feeling somewhat detached from my parents") (Lahiri, *In altre parole* 112). Inhabiting a third language, distant enough from the meanings and emotions of her main two languages, gives Lahiri a chance to explore the possibility of another new identity. She admits, however, the triangular relationship of the three languages, of the three belongings. Living for some time "in Italian," allows her some distance from the other two belongings. It is distance, not detachment. Being a prestigious American writer when she reaches Italy functions as a passport for Lahiri. Italy extends a welcome to her that it very rarely offers to migrants; the latter have to struggle to inhabit even its cultural margins.

"Ombra di cane" ("Dog Shadow") (Hajdari, *Corpo Presente* 59) is how Gëzim Hajdari, an Italian-Albanian poet, describes his condition in both Albania and Italy. The threshold of belonging and non-belonging are themes brought by Hajdari to a new and even more evident level. The birth country is seen as feminine in his work as well. It is the mother/bad mother to be invoked, almost in the tradition of Leopardi. But, as if to underline the conceptual shift from "natural man" to "national man," now the bad mother/stepmother is not nature but the motherland. He emigrated to Italy in 1992.[93] The anguish of the individual bred in a totalitarian collectivization of consciousness is, unfortunately, extended to the exile's condition of abandonment to such an extent that it is even uncertain whether Medea—perhaps the richest metaphor and theme of Hajdari's poetry—is related exclusively to the guilty motherland. "Ti inchinerai davanti a me Medea/con senso di colpa/e troverai nei passi leggeri sparsi nel buio/la mia solitudine divenuta amore" ("You will bow in front of me Medea/with guilt and you will find in the light steps scattered in the dark/my loneliness become love") (*Stigmate* 107). Due almost to a fluke of history, the "new man," Hajdari, fled to the West like so many other "new men" in search of a context in which the utopian, modern promise of redemption of the human condition through techno-scientific progress along with democracy, freedom, and prosperity was a reality. But the burden of the past— "Portiamo nelle tasche l'elenco/dei morti" ("We bring the list/of the dead in our pockets") (*Corpo presente* 21)—is perpetuated in a condition that seems like a continuation more than anything: "Gëzim/Ombra di cane rimarrai/ovunque tu vada" ("Gëzim/The shadow of a dog you will remain/wherever you go."). Motherland as a bad mother/ stepmother, therefore; one remains tied to her, loving her, hating her, keeping her "in the pocket." Hajdari, has an almost new mother country that is similar to the bad mother and that, given the migrant condition, does not quite replace it. The poet constructs his condition through bilingual poetry, always publishing his books simultaneously in Italian and Albanian, making it difficult for everyone to understand the language of original drafts.[94] Perhaps more than the writings of any other Italian poet born abroad, Hajdari's poetry lives in the condition between non belonging and multibelonging. He knows that a precarious grip on multiple contexts is better, much better, than non-belonging at all.[95] "La nostra paura/rimanere senza sepoltura/ in Occidente" ("Our fear/remaining without burial/in the West") (*Stigmate* 121.) The abyss of non-belonging is black, dark, and fuels his poetry. "Dove fermarmi mio terrore/i sassi che ho gettato controvento/hanno aperto su di me enormi abissi" ("Where to stop my terror/the stones I threw upwind/opened an enormous abyss beneath me") (*Stigmate* 25).[96] It is no coincidence that the status of those possessing two passports speaks of Italian-Americans, French-Germans, and so on. That legal hyphen is the thread of multibelonging that, as we shall see, is also a very important cultural issue.[97] The hyphen that marks multiple belongings has important cultural implications which, in the contextualizing and re-contextualizing, and the stripping and redressing, had already appeared in the Soviet Union. In this regard, Corrado Alvaro in his *Viaggio in Russia*, provides important insights by showing how the nationality issue was addressed by the Bolsheviks:

> L'uomo sovietico è nuovo in quanto ha ottenuti uguali diritti di fronte allo Stato senza pregiudizi di razza; sono eccettuati dall'uguaglianza i figli e i nipoti dei vecchi borghesi a meno che non abbiano compiuto tali atti da meritarsi i diritti civili; alle duecento razze che compongono l'Unione è stata aperta la partecipazione alla cosa pubblica; agli Iacuti (i Sampoiedi: il nome è stato cambiato perché Samoiedi vuol dire "quelli che si mangiano fra loro") ai Chirghisi agli Usbechi ai Turcomanni, è stato largito un nuovo alfabeto latinizzato che mette ogni popolo a contatto con la cultura e la civiltà. Cultura e civiltà sono per ora quelle compiute dalla borghesia industriale dell'Occidente, o nate sotto quel segno. L'uomo sovietico si deve servire di tali conquiste non per sé individualmente, come accade in quel periodo europeo, mai ai fini della collettività, ultimamente ai fini dello Stato.

> The Soviet man is new since he has obtained equal rights in front of the state without prejudice against race; the sons and grandsons of the old middle class are excepted from the equal-

> ity, unless they have performed the necessary acts to deserve civil rights; public participation has been opened to the 200 races the Union is made up of; a new Latinized alphabet that puts all people in contact with culture and civilization has been bestowed on the Iacuti (the Samoyeds: the name was changed because Samoyeds means "those who eat each other"), on the Kyrgyz on the Uzbeks, on the Turkmen. Culture and civilization is now something accomplished by the industrial bourgeoisie of the West, or those born under that sign. The Soviet man must profit from these achievements not for himself individually, as it happened during that European period, never for the community, most recently for the state. (*Viaggio in Russia* 75–76)

Our exclusive interest here is the effort that was made to bring together many ethnic groups within a new nation-state. "Precisamente alla cultura"—writes Alvaro—"i russi affidano il compito di cementare tante diverse nazionalità e lingue che compongono l'Unione e la diffusione e la norma dei loro ideali di vita" ("To culture, precisely,"—writes Alvaro—"the Russians entrust the task of cementing the many different nationalities and languages that make up the Union and the diffusion and the norm of their ideals of life") (*Viaggio in Russia* 46). Culture and civilization seem to be artistic, scientific, technological, and social knowledge borrowed from more developed contexts and, after passing through the ideological filters of the system, carried on in Russia itself. The Bolsheviks entrusted to this knowledge not only the countrywide teaching of literacy, but also the construction of that form of cultural prosthesis that would become the characteristic trait of the "new man." In addition to belonging to an original ethnic and cultural context, the "new man" had elements in common with the new citizens in terms of certain local universals, or rather Bolshevik universals. They were literally asked to get rid of their old cultural habits in order to adhere to a new vision of the world.[98] The means for creating the "new man" were coercive, violent, and often criminal. Although the effort was immense and comparable to nothing that had come before, the belief that culture and knowledge were a means of emancipation from the mono-ethnic cultures held fast. Hand in hand with this solution, the Bolsheviks clothed their citizens in a unique legal mantle, that of the federation. Without it, and without the new common culture of the state, the abyss of non-humans that appeared in Europe between the world wars, would have been the same. That is why today the legal bridge, the hyphen of multibelonging, after having accompanied the complex and uncertain process of the building of the European state, preserves its fundamental importance throughout the world during the present time of high social mobility. In this historical phase, belonging to one, two or more countries in a concrete, non-utopian way, though imperfectly, often remaining marginal, is much more realistic and much more pragmatic than directly claiming to be a citizen of the world (or just human beings), although the latter remains the ideal horizon. But as Charles Taylor has pointed out, multibelonging requires multi-recognition: legal recognition and/or cultural recognition, more than one context recognition (Taylor, "The Politics of Recognition").[99] The nonrecognition or even the misrecognition, according to Taylor, "can inflict harm." It remains unclear whether these groups of writers are recognized properly by their contexts or not. Every case is different, but since this condition is a very articulated one, they hardly are. Multibelonging[100] can be seen as an inclusive solution, certainly transitory. Its nature cannot be merely and exclusively legal.

Cultural capital

Inclusion, belonging(s), and identities are part of an economic, political, and cultural process. It is important to specify more fully here the process of the acquisition and shaping of identity. From this point of view, Kwame Anthony Appiah's reply to Taylor on the themes of multiculturalism is illuminating: "Dialogue shapes the identity" (Appiah 154). "I develop as I grow up, but the very material out of which I form it is provided, in part, by my society."[101] It is this material from the context "offered" (or imposed) to the individual to form their own identity that is important here. Individuals compose their identity with what is available to them in their own context. Becoming a multi-belonger means also to seek to expand the choices available and to form a combination—in an identity—that was not offered by any one of the individual contexts alone. Multibelonging, then, means to expand the choices available in order to escape the limited offers of the single context. It is in this field of possibilities that the game of identity and its source is played. It is the context that provides the raw material for identities. If there is more than one context, the individual becomes the artist who, with his or her own imagination, with a project, and by investing a great deal of energy can create his/her own identity. The first to take advantage of these spaces are the translingual writers who use multibelonging by creating in their works additional cultural and anthropological values. Many other individuals use similar possibilities, finding employment, for example, as *cultural mediators* (Amara Lakhous's Amedeo/Ahmed of *Scontro di civiltá* is considered a cultural mediator by the critics for his ability to interpret different perspectives), who are professional figures created politically in the host context. Economists focus on the compared economy; lawyers seek customers with certain characteristics. It then becomes a creative way to use the context, but which, unfortunately, often produces poor results. Adding a new hyphen may to some extent help improve the combinatorial drawing from a larger number of opportunities.

The concepts of *cultural capital*[102] and *habitus* proposed by Pierre Bourdieu (*Le Sens pratique*) can help to better articulate what different contexts can concretely offer these individuals. Changes of the *habitus* of all migrant groups can be slowed down by ethnic islands. When migrants organize with each other and exclude outside influences as much as possible, the preservation of the original *habitus* is probable. Something changes with the "second generations" educated in Italy, and the 2017 proposal—that didn't make it in the Italian Parliament—for the new law of citizenship that was in part organized around the concept of *ius culturae* proves it.[103] There is also a new 2022 proposal that is being discussed in the Italian parliament called, significantly, *ius scholae*. The environment of school and work tends to prevail over that of the ethnic group, and the effort to strengthen a belonging goes somehow towards the culture of the previous generation since it is the weakest. But if the inclusion process fails, both economically and culturally, the need to recoup the origins of the previous generation becomes stronger. The first generation of migrants, those with a different original cultural capital, and those who are able to use the language properly and have the most sophisticated cultural tools, come into conflict with the *status quo* either by radically changing part of their *habitus* or acquiring educational degrees and new cultural tools. They will eventually hybridize their cultural capital by building a vision and a profile that will exceed all context boundaries, including that of their origin. This surplus creates a form of alienation and externality with respect to all contexts, even with respect to new and potential ones. A complete identification tied to a national context is no longer possible. What is possible, however, or rather what is certain, is the feeling of relative belonging for specific historical intervals, as well as for the sharing of different experienced contexts. These belongings often require the hyphen to explain an experience of life and a cultural condition. In Italy, there are many Italian-Romanians, Italian-Albanians, Italian-Algerians, and Italian-Americans (we put "Italian" at the beginning for reasons of linguistic convenience). There is also an increasing number of Italian-Albanian-French, Italian-Romanian-English, Italian-Bulgarian-Americans, and so on. If the hyphen enhances an intercultural or transcultural condition, the surplus in respect to all the contexts urges one to maintain a critical and vigilant point of view. "Sono un esule esiliato nell'esilio" ("I am an exile exiled in exile"), writes Hajdari (*Stigmate* 25). The exile in this case is the excess over all contexts, past and present. The individual who develops multibelonging, always threatened by surplus and by externality, is an individual who frequently moves between different territories, an individual with several simultaneous territorial links who is increasingly deterritorialized.[104]

The choice to write in two languages involves targeting two linguistic communities and demands belonging, albeit problematic, critical, and marginal, to both cultural contexts. With regard to this aspect, it is important to stress the experience of two other writers *in Italian* who lived in a third country for several years. Ornela Vorpsi and Elvira Dones, both born Albanian, are now living in France and in the U.S., after a period spent, respectively, in Italy and Switzerland. Both continued to write and publish in Italian, at least until recently. Vorpsi, who was born in 1968, has now published her new novel in French. It is a complex phenomenon that could be partly explained by the notion of cultural and, specifically, linguistic capital. Vorpsi emerges as an Italian writer, while Dones, a journalist born in 1960, published first in Albanian. Of the three languages, both seemed to mainly favor the second language, Italian, presumably because the acquisition of a third language required a fairly extended time interval. Indeed,

Vorpsi has been living in France since 1997, and only in 2014 did she choose French for her writings. The length of the period that one needs to be comfortable writing in another language, especially in a third one, is meaningful for the very concept of country/countries that I approach in the next paragraph when talking about Kundera's *Ignorance*. However, with Vorpsi and Dones, the public and critical success (recognition) that some of their works have enjoyed in Italy plays an important role. The various awards that they have received, as well as the attention which they have garnered from the publishing industry and the public in Italy may be the equivalent of educational qualifications and may, therefore, be somehow regarded as cultural capital. A cultural capital that can also be used from a distance. Certainly, it is a carefully cultivated form of cultural belonging. Hajdari too, who has spent recent years first in France and now in England, keeps writing bilingual poetry and spending time in Italy. For anagraphic reasons, he is not planning to use English for his writings. A similar case is Lakhous, who has spent recent years in New York without losing his ties with either Italy or Algeria. The multibelonging, if the abyss of non-belonging is overcome, can become a great advantage and privilege. To achieve multibelonging beyond the specific intercultural capital already mentioned, an individual needs economic resources and efficient and cheap transportation. The revolution wrought by the internet in this regard is perhaps too obvious to mention. Multibelonging is facilitated by the technological advantages of the twenty-first century. When it approaches acceptable levels, it becomes an enviable cultural condition that, ideally, the citizens of the West aim for as well.

Impossible returns and organized returns

The possibilities and modalities of multibelonging vary depending on the components on either side of the hyphen (-)/s and, of course, on the historical period. Milan Kundera's analysis in *Ignorance* with regard to the relationship that the émigré has with the old and the new country should be circumscribed to the historical period. This novel was published in 2002 (the French version, *L'Ignorance*, in 2000). Two decades of exile taken into consideration end together at the impassable border between the Czech Republic (the Socialist Republic of Czechoslovakia at that time) and the rest of Europe. The frontier, the important differences between the two organizational systems, the barrier of police[105] that divides two worlds, has a profound impact and makes possible the figure of an émigré:

> Europe's Communism burned out exactly two hundred years after the French Revolution took fire. For Irena's Parisian friend Sylvie, that was a coincidence loaded with meaning. But with what meaning? What name could be given to the triumphal arch spanning those two majestic dates? The Arch of the Two Greatest European Revolutions? Or The Arch Connecting the Greatest Revolution with the Final Restauration? For the sake of avoiding ideological argument, I propose that we adopt a more modest interpretation: the first date gave birth to a great European character, the Émigré (either the Great Traitor or the Great Victim, according to one's outlook); the second date took the Émigré off the set of The History of the Europeans. (*Ignorance* 30)

It was the barrier that separated two very distant political and economic systems, and made the return impossible and, even, not desired. The 20 years outside of Ithaca are those that count more than the return—they are the years that really count for Ulysses and for the protagonists, Josef and Irena. "For twenty years he had thought about nothing but his return. But once he was back, he was amazed to realize that his life, the very essence of his life, its center, its treasure, lay outside Ithaca, in the twenty years of his wanderings. And this treasure he had lost, and could retrieve only by talking about it" (*Ignorance* 34). When the Berlin Wall came down, when the Czech and Slovak Republics left behind their communist past and became part of the EU, the figure of the émigré probably disappeared. "She had never disguised her views from him, so it was certainly possible for him to know her well, and yet he was seeing her exactly the way everyone else saw her: a young woman in pain, banished from her country. He himself comes from a Swedish town he wholeheartedly detests, and in which he refuses to set foot. But in his case it's taken for granted. Because everyone applauds him as a nice, very cosmopolitan Scandinavian who's already forgotten all about the place he comes from" (*Ignorance* 24).

Chapter Fifteen

With the transformation of an émigré into a cosmopolitan the question of return also ends. There is no longer the barrier made by the police, made by obstacles, made of substantial differences of political organization or styles of life, and the years gone by have produced considerable changes.[106] There are no more nightmares that torment Irena, Josef and all immigrants (a more appropriate term when it comes to overcoming geographic, economic and political barriers because it concerns an extended multitude of people): the collective nightmares of return, the nightmares of remaining on the wrong side of the barrier.[107] It is clear that the hyphen (-) is a bridge needed more when the distance between the two sides is important. If there is nothing to bridge, if one finds universals that help him or her to live in similar cities, as in the case of Kundera's character, there is no need to become a multi-belonger. It is clear that the impossible return, the trauma of the removal of the original identity, needs the hyphen (-), but the hyphen (-) is desired, because it is not there yet.

Today, the conditions that African and Asian migrants leave behind as well as the obstacles that they must overcome in order to arrive in Europe are no less dramatic than those experienced in the times of Eastern European communism. When the differences, the barriers, the walls, and the difficult circumstances remain as such, the impossibility of the return about which Kundera writes remains a valid issue. It remains equally valid to question the concept of country. "For the very notion of homeland, with all its emotional power, is bound up with the relative brevity of our life, which allows us too little time to become attached to some other country, to other countries, to other languages" (*Ignorance* 121).

The protagonists of his novel still fail in the process of return—which turns into a goodbye to the first country not adequately said during the escape—the past recalled does not coincide, the future is in the countries where they have spent the last 20 years (France for Irena, and Denmark for Josef). Their bond was transitional, their future impossible. The concept of the fatherland[108] (in French '*patrie*' is used[109]), precisely because it concerns periods of prolonged living elsewhere, changes, becomes less rigid, leaves space for something else; as the circle of friends change and, with them, the language of the inner voice, the language of friends, lovers, affections, readings, writing, the language of work. Kundera himself wrote this novel and many others in French. The same translation of the "fatherland" into "homeland" indicates clearly the need to adapt the concept of the country to the different circumstances that reflect an increasing number of naturalized citizens. If the 20 years spent far from the "fatherland" by Kundera's characters, increase because of their decision to continue living in the new "homeland," the time to become attached to another country is now sufficient and, in some cases, leaves room (time) for more than one country.

There are new shared movie jokes, new songs to wake up to, and new languages to teach the children, the new generation. All this, of course, requires better living conditions and cultural and technological tools. All this has yet to come. All this is a reality still very imperfect. The mother tongue is the language of childhood, in which to talk precisely to the mother, to the parents, to childhood friends ("It was the music of some unknown language. What had happened to Czech during those two sorry decades? Was it the stress that had changed?"—(*Ignorance* 54), while the motherland of birth is, in the best of cases, the place to spend holidays—Christmas, Easter, summer (even when it comes to countries of non-Christian religion: the organization of work in the West for now sets the times)—to take the kids and to introduce them to relatives and cousins (as happens to many migrants today). Always at Christmas, sometimes at Easter, and maybe in the summer—as happens to the protagonist of Carmine Abate's novel, *La festa del ritorno*. Tulio, a young Calabrian (Arbëresh) goes to work in the French mines. After the loss of his first wife, and with a small daughter to take care of, he forms a family in the Calabrian village where he was born. Father and son tell perspectives of the same story around a bonfire, lit at Christmas during a feast for the emigrant's return. Almost all of the events take place precisely at Christmas and sometimes at Easter, when the Calabrian emigrant returns from France, where he is working in the construction industry. These are not the dynamics of return that Kundera talks about. In this case the only barrier is economic. The periodic return is not in doubt. The two countries somehow divide the year (France is seen as the country where he suffers and stays begrudgingly). The times of multibelonging are

Chapter Fifteen

clearly dictated by the organization of work. It is our context that provides, as said, the raw material for our identities. It is our current (political, technological, economic) context then that can decide to handle smoothly a new transnational and maybe transitory phase by supporting, both legally and culturally, multibelonging dynamics.

Conclusion to Part Three

In the 1990s, massive flows of migrants reached the Italian coast for the first time. Tens of thousands of Albanians arrived in Apulia in 1991. In 1994, Gianni Amelio represented these events in a striking movie. By establishing an historical parallel with the beginning of the twentieth century's dream destination for Italian emigrants, the Italy of the 1990s became "*Lamerica*" and the Albanians, like yesterday's emigrants, today's poor. This parallel, however, ends here. The visual alarm of previously unseen invading biblical crowds dominates the movie. The "new poor," as Amelio himself explains, also remind viewers of the Pasolinian extra modern people, "the universal and immense peasant universe" and Amelio's idea of emigrants feels like the projection of Pasolini's Italian South. In this book I have investigated the historicized meaning of the idea of the human being, focusing on his/her transition from a universal concept to a national one moulded according to the needs of each (historical) context. It is clear why, then, from this perspective, a timeless universal idea of the human being is not helpful. The current national profile relies on specific historical, legal, cultural, and economic components that are not easily exchangeable, while any universal idea of humanness not accompanied by specific legal belongings opens up to the dramatic experiences (of non-belonging) of stateless people. The economic conditions and the postulated universal features of the peasant universe, as Pasolini or Amelio put it, are the presumed common denominators of yesterday's emigration and today's immigration. More abstract categories used outside theoretical contexts where abstractions are necessary—such as, for example, that of the (distant) "other" who, in today's historical context is brought up every time and almost always happens to be poor—could be considered as similar to this discourse,

Conclusion to Part Three

which does not take into consideration the specific articulations of groups' and current individuals' circumstances. The different geographies created by the transportation revolution and its implicit different opportunities for mobility are also untold. The "pre-modern" people, like our "peasant grandfathers," travel by truck in the desert (or in empty, desert-like landscapes, as in Amelio's Albania), and on boats at sea by paying smugglers instead of plane tickets that they are not allowed to purchase. The national identity is now also linked to economic conditions and to temporal categories. Countries devastated by wars or climate emergencies, or which have economically and/or legally failed, create disastrous consequences for their inhabitants, whose condition after departure becomes similar to those of the stateless people or non-belongers discussed in Part One. The migrant, who presumably does not possess enough cultural capital to compete in the European qualified labor market, is implicitly assumed to be poor and pre-modern and is expected to work in agriculture, caregiving, or the heavy and poorly paid jobs which today's locals no longer want to do—temporal categories, as already said, are important. A layered level of inclusiveness (legal, cultural, and economic) and a layered concept of citizenship agree with a layered idea of the national human being. Being born in disadvantaged countries is often translated into a specific class belonging in the destination country. The managing of national borders, within which are applied a specific and articulated (national) idea of the human being—who becomes mobile and is pushed in other territories, as Mezzadra convincingly argues—already projects, before even entering Europe, territorial layers and layered inclusiveness. Within the national territory itself, the mobility rate then translates into different levels of inclusiveness.

The economic trait of the human being's profile is clearly present in the current legislation on migration (starting from the Bossi-Fini law, and up to 2018 and 2025 decrees). The economic means of the new arrival are important when seeking to become an Italian resident first, and a citizen, later. The relationship between the modern birth of the nation-state with colonial experiences which, according to Trento and Bond and Comberiati, are also specifically true in the Italian case, are reflected in the economic profile of the "National Man."

Conclusion to Part Three

Fascism soon grasped the powerful potential of cinema in particular, and the media in general, as did Nazi Germany and the Soviet Union. As we saw in Part Two, the postwar Italian Republic properly understood the importance of the new and old media for both shaping national identity and fighting the Cold War. The media have remained crucial for the current dynamics and have dramatically increased their impact. The influence, or even the control of the collective imaginary, is a sophisticated tool in today's context. The representation of borders and migrant mobilities is a delicate and thorny aspect, so much so that it has an impact on the very existence of the European Union, as the Brexit episode has shown. I have investigated in Part Three how these aspects are represented, and highlighted both objective difficulties (mainly related to direct experience and knowledge) and subjective ones (ideologies of representation).

The role of the documentary and its relationship with geography versus the role of featured movies and the representations of urban areas are among my findings. They need careful and disciplined interpretation to avoid any possible and easy pitfalls. A specific genre has no implicit advantage in better representing difficult-to-penetrate worlds. Some specific features, however, do help to explain the contingent and historically limited better results. The documentary as a genre is perhaps the principal instrument that has represented migrant sea crossings. In the span of only six years (2006–2012), for example, 63 documentaries were dedicated to this topic (Angelone 69). While the relatively faster making of less-expensive non-mainstream productions, along with the inclusion of migrants in the filmmaking process, seem to be the main reasons, the barely imaginable point of view of the sea-crossing' protagonists is the most important among them. It is not the case that Andrea Segre, the Italian director who is most dedicated to the representation of these difficult issues, defines the authorial sharing as a "participatory process" that goes far beyond the usual and nevertheless crucial massive use of the interview. Ascending geographically, and approaching the periphery of the internal border, fiction adopts the documentary register as a more credible artistic form. Segre's awareness of the dynamics at play in the representation of these difficult worlds is also shared by other film directors like Gianfranco Rosi, Matteo Garrone, and

Conclusion to Part Three

Daniele Gaglianone who hybridize genres to represent not only border crossing but also the last layers of the territorial human being. Here comes a not-hypothesized finding when the drafting of Part Three started. Hybridization, which should be considered contingent and as a director's creative artifice, certainly shows, however, awareness of the complexities at play when representing these difficult-to-penetrate worlds. The unexpected finding is related to two different generations of film directors. On the one hand, we have Celati (born in 1937), Amelio (born in 1945), and Giordana (born in 1950) while, on the other, we have the immediately following generation of directors represented by Rosi (born in 1963), Gaglianone (born in 1966), Garrone (born in 1968), Segre (born in 1976), and many others. If we consider these two groups we will see some convergences in the methodologies, ideologies, and topics of their representations. There is no doubt that Segre, Rosi, Gaglianone, and Garrone are much more aware of the problematics implicit in intercultural representation. I believe that, as in the case of the artistic genre, there is no easy answer and that we need to again avoid pitfalls by breaking down some of the circumstances that may have created this apparent dichotomy. These circumstances are mainly age-related and can be explained by a different historical context in which the new generation of directors was formed. When Giordana expresses the desirable different intercultural education of the new generation, it seems that it has already happened with regard to the younger and very talented Italian film directors. Segre, Rosi, and Garrone seem to have a better understanding, and to be better interpreters (of the peripheries) of today's plural Italy. Once again, these considerations are related to the specific cultural products taken into consideration in Part Three and should not be generalized.

Italian cinema and literature have a good grasp of the representation of the multiplicity of interactions of our urban environments. They can be considered as laboratories that first experimented with the living together of multitudes whose plural origins mingle in the interweavings of class, gender, ethnicity, and culture. In 2008, for example, the time frame around which these movies were produced, foreign residents represented 14 per cent of Milan's population and 10.9 per cent of Rome's, while the overall Italian percentage hovered around 7 per cent (Allievi, "Immigration and Cultural Pluralism in Italy: Multiculturalism as a missing model"). Mazzacurati, Patierno, Gaglianone, Lakhous, and Ferrente offer a complex representation of today's Italian urban centers in which reflection on communities is the shared main focus. Zygmund Bauman's concept that he calls "desire for community" is related to the fear of the loss of security. Urban communities of any kind, based on class, religion, gender, sexual orientation, culture, profession, age, ethnicity or on a combination of them, try to protect internal homogeneity within voluntary ghettos by building real or virtual walls. Ethnicity is often one of the main markers able to give to the homogeneity/heterogeneity opposition the needed solidity, durability, and reliability. Economically triggered fears—as in the case of North-East Italy, represented, as we saw, by Segre's, Mazzacurati's, and Patierno's movies—feed distrust, closure, and discrimination. There is thus a preventative form of class hatred towards the enterprising stranger, transforming the city into an archipelago where cultures remain isolated, without being able to really interact. The multicultural model seems to be the remedy for these closed communities, even though its articulation remains pretty vague. Bauman considers, for example, "cosmopolitanism" to be inadequate for the role of "global culture." The cosmopolitan archipelago would be composed of many islands on which conformity, and the exclusion of diversity, triumph. Today's landscape is composed of "closed communities," those that we meet on every corner and in every class of society. The perpetuation of a conventional form of social organization, a contemporary hybrid of tradition and consumerism, would seem to be a source of multiple closures. *La Giusta Distanza*'s protagonist, Mara, for example, indicates the mall as a place where families spend weekends almost as if they were interdependent models of a single reality in which she does not fit.

The work of Arjun Appadurai tells us that, in a world of planetary interconnections, the first to be affected is "the imagination," a category which potentially involves an unpredictable development of subjectivity. In Lakhous' novel this unpredictability is shown in the shared imaginary that Amedeo and Johan have about Rome. Their common reference is cinema and, more precisely, neorealism. It was (Italian) cinema that provided the imaginary of Rome even before the characters arrived there. It is still this abstract idea of Rome that accompanies them in everyday life, it is still that old map that guides them every day. Understanding the complex map of imaginaries that shape subjectivities and inform projects is very important if we try to build, so to speak, a map of universals that opens the closed rooms, betters communication, and transforms the lived urban space from an archipelago of closures into an interconnected, more homogenous, and shared space (*piazza*). In a wider context, at both national and transnational scales, the map of imaginaries remains crucial. The role of the Western media in the Cold War years, first, is well known; then in the post-1989 Eastern European mobilities later and, now, in today's global mobilities, although in the latter there is also an important contribution from other kinds of new media based on the internet. From Hollywood to European cinema, from national television to the streaming of transnational media like Netflix or, more recently, Disney, from Facebook to Skype or to WhatsApp, the imaginary contributors are many and the consequences unpredictable. Appadurai, for example, sees in this reality an emerging post-national system that has to deal with heterogeneous elements. According to him, it will have an impact on the nation-state model which, for a long time, will find it difficult to manage the relationship between globalization and modernity.

The demographic aspects, which we saw were very important not only during Fascism but also in the second half of the twentieth century, are once again in sharp focus when it comes to considerations of both migrant fluxes and the gender composition of the workforce. "Senza migranti l'Italia sarebbe un Paese più povero e anziano, spiega Bankitalia" ("Without migrants, explains Bankitalia, Italy would be a poorer country full of the elderly") was the title of the daily newspaper *Corriere della Sera*'s article of 03 April 2018 which referred to a study completed by Bankitalia, the central bank of Italy. If future migration flows were eliminated, and those not born in Italy who were resident in 2016 assumed demographic parameters identical to the rest of the population, the result would be devastating, according to Bankitalia's study. "Di qui l'invito dei tre curatori dello studio—Federico Barbiellini Amidei, Matteo Gomellini e Paolo Piselli—a intervenire su estensione della vita lavorativa, aumento della partecipazione femminile al mercato del lavoro e incremento nei livelli di istruzione per 'contrastare i puri effetti contabili legati all'evoluzione nella struttura per età.'" ("Hence the invitation of the three curators of the study—Federico Barbiellini Amidei, Matteo Gomellini and

Conclusion to Part Three

Paolo Piselli—to intervene in the extension of the working life, the increase in female participation in the labor market and the increase in education levels to 'contrast the pure accounting effects related to the evolution in the age structure.'") (Maurizi, "Senza migranti"). As we saw in Part Two, when discussing the relationship between generations in Fellini's film *La Dolce Vita* and in Part Three when discussing Patierno's *Cose dell'altro mondo*, prolonged life expectancy and the extension of youth have had a deep and complex impact on the structure and organization of our societies, starting, as this study highlights, with the composition of the active workforce. If the latter shrinks—the dependency ratios (the ratio between the non-working-age and the working-age population) have a strong impact on the economy—the overall economic balance of society can no longer sustain the current standard of living. Since the unification of the country, for more than a century, the percentage of the elderly population (persons over 64 years of age) has stood in Italy at levels less than half of those of the youngest population (under 15 years of age). This was no longer the case after the 1980s. According to this study, a progressive structural change led the older population to overnumber the younger one at the end of the twentieth century. "In uno scenario limite in cui non ci fossero residenti con cittadinanza straniera, nel 2061 la quota di popolazione in età 15–64 anni sul totale della popolazione, prevista pari al 55 per cento, scenderebbe a poco più del 40 per cento." ("In an extreme scenario in which there were no residents with foreign citizenship, in 2061 the amount of people between the ages of 15–64, which is expected to be at 55 per cent, would drop to just over 40 percent." (Maurizi, "Senza migranti"). As the authors of the study highlight, the majority of immigrants are young, active, of working age, and have a positive impact on national fertility rates. The inclusion in the workforce of migrants and women might be demanded by the demographics of today's Italy, as Bankitalia's study highlights, but the fight for equality should be imposed by democratic activists. Without the push of these democratic forces from within our societies, no rights would ever be granted. If Fascism responded to the demographics with certain dictatorial policies (as discussed in Part One), a democratic society has other options. Unless the process of the automatization of work opens up unpredictable scenarios in Italy and Europe then, even from a

Conclusion to Part Three

demographic point of view, an open, equal, interconnected, and plural society seems to be the best answer to the current challenges of our times.

The cohabitation of pluralities in our societies brings us back to the reflection on the need for a community; a constant aspect of urban environments. If Mazzacurati's *La Giusta distanza* shows how the protagonists Mara and Hassan find it difficult to shape their relationship within the traditional family-oriented and consumerist small-town model, the same happens to Patierno's *Cose dell'altro mondo* protagonists who, even when expecting a child, cannot fit into a long-term traditional family planning project. In both cases, it is important to highlight that the meeting happens between an immigrant male and an educated young Italian woman—in both movies she is a teacher—whose emancipated condition provides an opening for this meeting. The open attitude in this case is the fruit of a combination between a very progressive young woman thirsty to experience the world with the desirable prolonged youth condition which clashes with the main model based, in Mara's own words, "on family and spending the weekends at the mall." Mara, who loves to experience the world—she is about to move to Brazil for one year—and wishes to live thirteen different lives (an artistic reincarnation of Calvino's Ludmilla), claims that she would spend one of them with the traditional Hassan who is ready to spend the only life he projects to have with Mara. In *Cose dell'altro mondo* the (Italian) progressive female protagonist has a child from a relationship with an immigrant worker but plans to marry her Italian ex-boyfriend. The same worries regarding the reflection on communities figure in Özpetek's *Le Fate Ignoranti*. A different community is expected, on the one hand, to remedy to the absence of families since, in the (bourgeois) family model, even its marginalized (mainly because of the sexual orientation) protagonists cannot fit and, on the other, to turn it into a laboratory of a different (wide open) society. However, even this (utopian) community remains, in order to protect its members from a discriminating society, closed and hidden by necessity. In the majority of cases, as already said, it is the racial-ethnic aspect which should be seen as the most problematic and as the one which is able to solidify the closures. Ferrente's film *l'Orchestra di piazza Vittorio* sees in the multicultural model the remedy to the phobic closures that are often transformed into discriminating migration laws like, for instance, Bossi-Fini. It

Conclusion to Part Three

also sees in it the new cultural model of the new Europe where, in order to go beyond the archipelago of cultures (hyphenated from the perspective of this work), a (metaphoric) orchestra is needed in the same way that it was needed a few decades earlier when the regional and local differences had to be dealt with; as Fellini's *Prove d'orchestra*, which inspired this movie, shows. The general limit, or the danger today, is to transform multiculturalism into multicommunitarianism, as Bauman puts it. Belonging to one community and/or its culture becomes a kind of visa permit to enter—not just then as an individual with particular skills, to quote Alessandro Dal Lago—and inhabit the shared and virtual multicultural space. There is much vagueness in this concept, to the point that Jacoby calls it "the ideology of an era without ideology." According to both Bauman and Jacoby, there is an evident lack of a real, ideal elaboration on the human being's condition. Multiculturalism as an archipelago of (closed) cultures is not much help if we do not build an intercultural orchestra that is able to share them, to use the metaphor of the movie. Hyphenated cultures of multibelongers revolve around the same culture on the other part of the hyphen (-): the Italian/European culture. It is the latter that should be able to host pluralities and offer/build shared intercultural universals.

This supposedly should also be the case when it comes to hyphenated literatures. There are many writers "in Italian" who practice translingual literature and target with their work more than one (linguistic) community. Very often the condition of alienation, marginalization, and non-(complete) belonging to either of the (cultural) communities is highlighted in their writings. Nevertheless, they write in more than one language, adopt self-translation in one direction or the other, organize literary events in one or both (linguistic) communities, and are read in one or both languages. That of non-belonging, despite literary metaphors, is a very dramatic condition. The twentieth-century tragic experience, as we saw in Part One and as it emerges from Arendt's, Agamben's, and Primo Levi's work, matches, from a legal point of view, (and not only from the non-belonging condition), that of stateless persons. Today that condition can be found in illegal immigrants, uprooted or non-belongers rhyming dangerously with that of Primo Levi's non-human. It is clear why the possession of two or more passports, or even of one passport and of one residence permit, speaks of Italian-Americans, French-

Conclusion to Part Three

Germans, and so on. The legal hyphen signals the condition of multibelonging which, as we saw in Part Three, also has important cultural and economic layers. The hyphen implies a balance, a bridge, whether temporary or not, without which one risks falling into the abyss of the non-human. This human condition is, especially considering today's high rate of mobility, an important feature of our times and is well described in the literary work of (Italian) translingual writers.

The arrival in Italy of massive flows of migration in the 1990s coincided with a new literary phenomenon that saw an increase in the literary text authored by writers who were not born in Italy. The scholar who was the first and the most dedicated to the study of this new development was a comparatist, Armando Gnisci, who labeled this literature as *La letteratura italiana della Migrazione* (*Italian Literature of Migration*), which became known as "letteratura migrante" ("migrant literature") and the writers as "scrittori migranti" ("migrant writers"). Gnisci's poetics, however, exalted the decolonization and transculturalization of Europeans (*Via della transculturazione e della gentilezza*) longing for a "creole Europe" (*Creolizzare l'Europa: Letteratura e migrazione*). In the United States, the scholar who, also in the 1990s, initiated the study of this literary phenomenon was the Italianist Graziella Parati. Her book Migration Italy: The Art of Talking Back in A Destination Culture (2005) is one of most important books to which many Italian-American scholars refer. Other proposed paradigms are multicultural literature (Orton and Parati), postcolonial literature (Romeo and Comberiati) and translingual literature (Sinopoli).[110] In the 2000s, Italian writers not born in Italy were generically called "migrant writers". Many of them, who did not sign any literary manifesto but who participated in often-compensated literary events dedicated to this literature, passionately debated the label "migrant writers" for many years. Chiara Mengozzi in her article "'What little I know of world I assume.' Cornici nazionali e mondiali per le scritture migranti e postcoloniali" ("'What little I know of world I assume.' National and world frames for migrant and postcolonial writings"), recalls that the literary production of immigrants in Italy in its first phase was aimed at modifying "the representation imbalance" and therefore sought to contest the dominant public discourse and its stereotyped and alarmist characterization of immigration and immigrants. To this first phase followed the attempt of critics to find a corresponding definition for this literature. However, definitions like "migrant", "Italophone," "minor," "creole," "hybrid," "mestizo," and "nomad," to name but a few, with Mengozzi, "di fronte alle numerose e ripetute proteste degli scrittori" ("after numerous and repeated writers' protests") (Mengozzi 23), and the risks of ghettoization along with the limits of each of the adopted labels, were problematized and finally "la critica sembra aver, per così dire, allentato la presa" ("the critics seem to have loosened their grip") (Mengozzi 24) on the definition matter. It is interesting to note that "the loose definition" approach is also adopted with regard to the study of Italian emigration. Pamela Ballinger in "Beyond the Italies. Italy as a Mobile Subject" explains that "in trying to capture this field of mobilities, scholarship on Italian communities abroad has moved away from a singular vocabulary of italiani nel mondo towards a vision of altre italie (other Italies) or diasporas" (Ballinger 26). *Altreitalie* has become the most important publication of the Center for the Study of Other Italies which was created in 2005 with the support of Fondazione Agnelli and the Compagnia di San Paolo. The concept of "altreitalie" remains "under-theorized (perhaps deliberately)" (Ballinger 27).

The Italian literary canon has been slow to open and mirror the new plural composition of the country. Thirty years after the publication of *Io, venditore di elefanti* (*I, the Elephant Seller*) by Pap Khouma (1990), as Daniele Comberiati ("Lo studio della letteratura italiana della migrazione in Italia e all'estero") points out, we can agree that the relationship of this literature to the national canon is still very difficult. Some important media outlets like the daily *Corriere della sera* have defined these writers as "I nuovi italiani" ("the new Italians") but any different adjective in front of "Italian" for writers who, in many cases, have been living in the country for some time—twenty or thirty years—still sounds strange. Franca Sinopoli makes a useful observation in the context of this work by highlighting the dynamics at play from the national identity formation perspective that I discussed in Part Two. The marginality which affected this literature, according to Sinopoli, has been determined (not only in Italy) from the centrality assigned to national cultural monolinguism. The latter has long penalized the same Italian authors of literature of so-called dialectal and linguistic minorities. The presence of authors of foreign origin who use Italian as a language of literary expression, points out Sinopoli, who correctly defines these writers as "translingual," gives an aspect of transnationality to Italian literature which thus considers translingual writers to be part of the contemporary Italian literature. It is clear that the rethinking of the Italian literary canon will reflect the cultural and political project of the Italy's near future. Despite the fact that some of the most important Italian publishers like Einaudi, Bompiani, and Feltrinelli have included some of these authors in their catalogs, and the world of cinema, in a few cases, has adopted their novels, the impact on public opinion of these writers in representing either what they know best—the difficult-to-penetrate worlds—or on offering different perspectives on Italian society, remains marginal. With the exception of 1994's aforementioned polemic between the Italian director Amelio, and Kadare and Vargas Llosa who, however, are not Italian writers, there has been no debate conducted through national media, as in the recent already mentioned US case of Latinx writers who (successfully) contested *American Dirt*.

Anthony Julian Tamburri in his *To Hyphenate or Not to Hyphenate*, suggested replacing or removing the hyphen in Italian-American adjective. The hyphen, in his view, signals the dominant group's resistance of accepting the new arrival (43), and may even be seen to be a colonizing sign (44). Tamburri's concern about the use of hyphen is similar to the debate on the definition issue of Italian writers born elsewhere (any additional adjective to Italian, even *postcolonial*, could sadly be seen as a "colonizing sign"). Agreeing that a loose grip on the definition issue is a better choice, it is worth mentioning that these writers deal with heavier adjectives, in front (or after) the adjective Italian, than a "tiny" hyphen, which, however, in my book is invested with a different (legal, cultural, transnational) meaning that is closely related to the current historical context. From the point of view of this work, after reiterating that the definition issue, for the time being it is better not to be stressed, as both multicultural literature and, especially, translingual literature are the most shared perspectives, even though they somehow lack precision. It is difficult to tell how similar writers are whose origins vary and who come from all corners of the world. The hyphenated literature of multibelonging writers can concretely show their cultural contexts of belonging. We can simply talk about German-Italian writers, Brazilian-Italian writers or Albanian-Italian-French writers within the context of Italian-European literature. Today the legal bridge, the hyphen (-) of multibelonging, after having accompanied the difficult process of the building of the European Union, preserves its importance. Belonging, although imperfectly and often marginally, to one or more countries is, in this historical phase, much more realistic than directly claiming to be citizens of the world. This is why even the use of the definition of "world literature"—sometimes adopted as a wider framework for translingual literature,—while ideally very desirable, still seems to belong to a distant horizon.

Stefano Allievi, in his article "Immigration and Cultural Pluralism in Italy: Multiculturalism as a missing model" states that immigration, also increasingly important statistically speaking, undermines Italy's self-image as a monocultural and monoreligious country. His main point in this article is that the important "quantitative" presence of immigrants causes even more important qualitative changes (economic, cultural, social, political, religious) so much so that they alter the scenario completely. The articulation of the new multicultural Italy is, however, more complex than it seems, starting from the fact that a multicultural model able to drive this new phase of the country is missing. For Allievi, the Italian missing model is not necessarily a negative—it can be an opportunity. The multicultural experiences exist more at a local level than at a national one, where contrasting ideologies play a bigger role. The indicators that are changing because of the presence of immigration in Europe, as Allievi points out, are causing "new problems, new processes of interrelation, new conflicts and new solutions to them" (86). They are creating "nothing less than a different type of society which is quite different to that imagined with the rise of the nation state and its founding principles" (87). We now find ourselves in this new society without having the "rules and plans" that help us to live in it. The process of pluralization is changing society and us along with it. Allievi's conclusion, that when talking about the impact of immigration in Italy we are talking about society as a whole, is also my point. The reflection on migration in Italy is not just about migration; it is about Italy, and it is about Europe; it is the most recent new stage of the Italian contemporary history of the transitional human being.

A Final Note

Summertime is a 2020 TV streaming miniseries coproduced by Netflix and the most important Italian film producer, Cattleya. It is loosely inspired by Federico Moccia's *Tre metri sopra il cileo* (Three Meters above the Sky), whose protagonist is Summer, the Afro-Italian teenage daughter of an unmarried couple whose mother is an Italian waiter and her father, an African-Italian musician in love with Gershwin's *Summertime* (performed by Armstrong and Fitzgerald) who travels a lot. Summer's and her teenage friend's love life in Cesenatico, a port town in Emilia-Romagna on the Italian Adriatic coast, is not dominated by Summer's different appearance. While this could be discussed from the point of view of the kind of debate caused, as already said, by *American Dirt*— Summer's character, once again, is inspired by Federico Moccia's novel and not by Igiaba Scego's (*La mia casa è dove sono*) story!—I am mentioning *Summertime* mainly because of the seeming lack of problematization of this aspect that is implicitly a deliberate choice of this mainstream TV show which targets an international young adult audience. If we watch Brignone's film *Sotto la croce del sud* that we discussed in Part One, its faulted "biracial" protagonists, the hardworking honest Italian settlers, the docile indigenous population, and the muffled *Summertime* one after the other, the sense of time will be striking. From a colonial reality, made of plots directly inspired by Fascist racial laws, the viewer lands in our plural world made up of interconnections, of long chains of events, and of transnational media that intentionally produce a

A Final Note

certain kind of transnational imaginary. We realize that, between 1938 and 2020, a lot has happened from many points of view, without being able to immediately articulate everything because of the complexity of the events. That articulation, from the point of view of the discourses on the human being idea or profile, among many other aspects, was one of the goals of this volume.

Another relevant consideration that follows this reflection is the importance of historical dates. If we were to quickly indicate some important dates from the twentieth century, we would think about 1914, 1917, 1945 and 1989 to mention but a few. Of course, 1945 was a key date for Europe and for Italy. In 1989 the Berlin Wall was brought down, producing other local important dates like, for example, 1991—the fall of the Albanian dictatorship and the start of mass migration towards Italy—and 1992 for the start of the scandal of *Mani pulite* (*Clean Hands*) that brought down the main political parties and caused the end of the so-called First Republic. It is too obvious to mention that a generation, along with the adjective of national belonging, might need to specify the temporal segment of that belonging. That is of course also and first of all true, as we saw in this volume, for post-Fascist and post-Cold War Italy though with different articulations and reasons.

The dates are important for conventionally signaling major changes, but many other changes have their own pace, their own different calendar. They started long ago, they have crossed different periods, and they will maybe crystallize at some point in the near future. Today many new questions that have no specific calendar demand answers. It is, for example, still too soon to tell what impact the automatization of work trends will have on our work, employment, social life, and maybe, world order. Populisms, sovranists, and others once again seek the return of hermetic borders, of sameness, of a lack of diversity, and of old concepts of national identity (one only hopes that they would never produce nightmares of the kind of Foucauldian-Agambenian concepts of caesurae discussed in Part One). Brexit happened. Italian populists, who enjoy a great deal of consensus, are galvanized. The combination of these two trends (the automatization of work and the isolation tendency) are also producing discourses of a different kind of highly skilled labor that could become the main characteristic of the profiles of future new residents of countries like

A Final Note

England or the United States. The pressure that the past century has put on the required profiles of "new men" could increase for today's citizens who may, in order to adequately live and work in our complex societies, be required to deal with the importance of education and knowledge; now stressed like never before.

Another important date could unfortunately be 2020–2021, the years of seemingly the most important world crisis since WWII. The Coronavirus pandemic seriously threatened our societies, causing pain, fear, loss, insecurity, and unemployment. Historically all the significant events, and this pandemic of course was one of them, are followed by important turns. Many predicted a strong turn to our way of life, even when the Covid-19 pandemic was over. Some saw the end of globalization, others longed for a more just world. The truth is that the pandemic and its social distancing threatened the very essence of our times, our mobility, our connectivity, our human networking. The most important cities that are the laboratories of today's modernity, like New York, Paris, or Milan, were the hardest hit. The same goes for the wars in Ukraine and Middle East. The quick end of these new wars is what we all hope for but we could be on the brink of the third world war followed by the nightmare of a nuclear conflict. The real weight of these dramatic events and all the implications, even from the point of view of the topics discussed in this volume, however, will be better understood only a few years later.

Notes

1. Unless otherwise stated, all translations from the Italian throughout this volume are mine.
2. "There is a new decree law named after the minister, Salvini, which corrects the existing immigration law on a few points, like that of the cancellation of dual citizenship when an individual is condemned for felonies related to terrorism" (see italiapost.it/decreto-sicurezza-salvini-cosa-prevede/). The 2025 decree-law expands detention powers and allows for the transfer of migrants to Albania under a bilateral protocol, even if they've requested asylum—if the request is deemed dilatory (see https://www.edotto.com/articolo/decreto-immigrazione-ddl-di-conversione-alla-camera-le-novita).
3. It is important to highlight similarities between Orwell's *1984* and Alvaro's *L'uomo è forte*, as they are relevant to our understanding of why the latter did not enjoy the same attention as *1984*. "Lo scrittore Corrado Alvaro, oltre e ai romanzi e ai racconti legati alla Calabria, quali *L'età breve*, *L'amata alla finestra* e *Gente in Aspromonte*, è anche l'autore del romanzo *L'uomo è forte*, un libro affascinante la cui lettura riporta continuamente al più conosciuto romanzo 1984 di George Orwell. L'uomo è forte è stato pubblicato nel 1938, il romanzo di Orwell nel 1949. Quindi, tra i due libri corre un lasso di tempo, a favore di Alvaro, di circa undici anni. Ma quando si parla di regimi totalitari, di ideologie miranti a livellare ogni individualità, delle violenze fisiche e psicologiche esercitate da un potere assoluto si cita sempre *1984* e mai *L'uomo è forte*, che pure ebbe molto successo in Italia: nel 1945 aveva già toccato la quinta edizione, e fu poi tradotto in altre lingue" ("The writer Corrado Alvaro, in addition to novels and stories related to Calabria, such as *L'età breve* (*The Short Age*), *L'amata alla finestra* (*The Beloved at the Window*) and *Gente in* Aspromonte (*People in Aspromonte*), wrote also *L'uomo è forte* (*The Man is Strong*), a fascinating book whose reading continually brings to mind the most famous novel *1984* by George Orwell. *L'uomo è forte* was published in 1938, Orwell's novel in 1949. So between the two books runs a time frame, in favor of Alvaro, of about eleven years. But when it comes to totalitarian regimes, ideologies aimed at leveling each individuality and the physical and psychological violence exercised by absolute power, *1984* is always cited, never *L'uomo è forte*, which also had great success in Italy: in 1945 Alvaro had already produced the fifth edition, which was then translated into other languages"), stated Nadia Crucitti.

Notes

4. Faltrop Porta focuses on Alvaro's exile to Germany: "I motivi di questo esilio di cinque mesi sono vari: la ragione dichiarata nelle lettere a Nino Frank è finanziaria, mentre nel diario Alvaro riferisce un incontro con un assessore del Comune di Berlino, al quale espone la sua difficile situazione di oppositore al regime fascista: [...] non posso lavorare in Italia, dopo la rotta delle opposizioni [...] poiché quasi tutti i miei amici sono scomparsi, chi ucciso e chi emigrato all'estero, io sono rimasto come un bersaglio di cartone e ho finito con l'assumere un'importanza che non mi spetta e che sinceramente non merito" ("The reasons for this five-month exile are various: the reason stated in the letters to Nino Frank is financial while, in the diary, Alvaro reports a meeting with an assessor of the City of Berlin, to whom he exposes his difficult situation as an opponent of the Fascist regime: '[...] I cannot work in Italy, after the route of the oppositions [...] since almost all my friends have disappeared—got killed and emigrated abroad—I remained like a cardboard target and I ended up having an importance that I sincerely do not deserve'") (7).

5. Alvaro extends his perspective to the rest of Italy: "Chi ricorda l'Emilia, la Romagna, il Veneto, specie il Veneto ricostruito dopo la guerra, ne ritrova qui lo schema; il senso è lo stesso, quello l'aspetto, e l'uomo ha reso vecchio questo paesaggio nuovo imposto allá natura in un anno." ("Those who remember Emilia Romagna, Veneto—especially Veneto, rebuilt after the war—find the scheme here; the sense is the same, that is, the aspect, and man has made old this new landscape imposed on nature in a year.") (*Terra nuova* 47).

6. According to Faltrop Porta, there is no lack of references to the Nazi-Fascist regimes in Alvaro's novel. "I rapporti amorosi, come in Solitudine, sono segnati da "una specie di animosità gelosa e dispettosa," e la vedova che, in Stranieri, morde il polso del giovane italiano, sembra preannunci l'amante che addenta la mano al protagonista, in *L'uomo è forte*, prova supplementare che questo romanzo sulle tirannie si ispira non solo alla Russia sovietica, ma anche alla Germania." ("Love relationships, as in *Solitudine*, are marked by 'a kind of jealous and spiteful animosity', and the widow who, in *Stranieri*, bites the young Italian's wrist, seems to herald the lover who bites the hand of the protagonist in *L'uomo è forte*, providing extra proof that this novel about tyrants is inspired not only by Soviet Russia, but also by Germany.") (35).

7. "Auschwitz è precisamente il luogo in cui lo stato di eccezione coincide perfettamente con la regola e la situazione estrema diventa il paradigma stesso del quotidiano." (*Quel che resta di Auschwitz* 44; "Auschwitz is precisely the place in which the state of exception coincides perfectly with the rule and the extreme situation becomes the very paradigm of daily life."; Agamben, *Remnants of Auschwitz* 49).

8. The Italics are the author's. In Italian it is "*semplicemente uomo*"—literally "simply man."

9. Druker (*Primo Levi and Humanism after Auschwitz: Posthumanist Reflections*) refers to the analysis of Adorno, Levinas, Lyotard, and Foucault which, individually and collectively, considered the Enlightenment as an event that paved the way for twentieth-century totalitarianism, and ar-

gued with Foucault that along with liberties, the Enlightenment brought discipline. In his reading, the secular Italian tradition had a great influence on Levi's work.

10. The age of Edmund remains unknown. In the film the child says that he is 15 years old but he does so because this was the minimum in order to be allowed to work. A woman replies that Edmund does not seem to be more than 12 and she is not contradicted. Strangely, even critics like Bondanella credit him as being 15 years old. The actor who played Edmund was 12. Edmund's age is not an inconsequential issue because the suicide of a teenager is different from the suicide of a child.

11. Carlo Lizzani has published his notes on how this movie was produced. The role and the will of the PCI are of particular interest. "Antonello Trombadori, allora dirigente della Sezione Cultura del Partito Comunista, fu l'abile regista dell'operazione. Forse perché già pensava di suggerire—per il documentario in Sicilia—il nome, addirittura, di Luchino Visconti. Ma pensando anche—e me lo disse esplicitamente—che stando io accanto a Rossellini avrei potuto influenzarlo non politicamente (come è stato riportato un po' frettolosamente e tendenziosamente in una recente intervista sulla mia attività di quegli anni e sui propositi di egemonia esercitati in quella stagione da Trombadori e dal PCI, del resto con intelligenza e trasparenza, sui cineasti italiani), ma piuttosto per aiutarlo, con ricerche, documentazioni, testimonianze, a realizzare la *Roma città aperta* della Germania. Che sembrava poi essere il proposito dello stesso Rossellini." ("Antonello Trombadori, at the time director of the Cultural Section of the Communist Party, was the able director of the operation. Perhaps because he was already thinking of suggesting, for the documentary in Sicily, a name like Luchino Visconti. But also thinking—and he told me explicitly—that, standing next to Rossellini, I could influence him, not politically (as has been reported, a bit hasty and tendentiously, in a recent interview about my activities during those years and about purposes of hegemony exercised by Trobadori and the PCI in that season, moreover with intelligence and transparency, over the Italian film-makers) but, rather, to help with research, documentation, evidence, to make the *Roma città aperta* of Germany. It also seemed to be the same purpose for Rossellini.") (32).

12. "Though Rossellini's films spoke with an optimism and faith appropriate to the events of 1945, subsequent developments have proved him more a dreamer than a prophet. No leader emerged to carry out this synthesis of Marxism and Catholic humanism, and no social order arose to fulfill his political imaginings" (Marcus 53).

13. "The film looks back to *Roma città aperta* in many ways, the flanking panels of the war triptych symmetrical as portraits of cities and families, children under duress, and women using their wiles to survive (Edmund's sister, who worries about becoming 'a loose woman', recalls Marina, for instance, and one rebellious boy's exclamation—'If I had a father like that, I'd show him'—in *Roma città aperta* eerily portends Edmund's familiar eugenics in *Germania anno zero*)" (Quandt 17–18).

Notes

14. The material quoted here is taken from Pier Marco De Santi (*La dolce vita: scandalo a Roma, Palma d'oro a Cannes*). This quote is by Father Angelo Zucca, director of the "Angelicum" in Milan (19).

15. "L'educazione data a un ragazzo dagli oggetti, dalle cose, dalla realtà fisica—in altre parole dai fenomeni materiali della sua condizione sociale—rende quel ragazzo corporeamente quello che è e quello che sarà per tutta la vita. A essere educata è la sua carne come forma del suo spirito. La condizione sociale si riconosce nella carne dell'individuo (almeno nella mia esperienza storica). Perché egli è stato plasmato dall'educazione appunto fisica della materia di cui è fatto il suo mondo" (*Lettere luterane* 18; "The education given to a boy by things, by objects, by physical reality—in other words, the material phenomena of his social condition—make that boy corporeally what he is and what he will be all his life. What has to be educated is his flesh as the mould of his spirit. Social condition is recognizable in the flesh of an individual (at least in my historical experience). Because he has been physically shaped by the education, the physical education, of the matter from which his world is made"; Pasolini, *Lutheran Letters* 30).

16. See, for example, the essay by Asor Rosa written in those years and republished in a relatively recent (2001) volume. Both the words reported by Calvino, and Asor Rosa's comment (who, in this volume, defines Calvino as "lo scrittore italiano più sorvegliato e riservato degli ultimi quarant'anni" [Asor Rosa 60; "the most guarded and reserved Italian writer of the last 40 years"]), do not appear to lack hints of socialist realism. "Ma questa ci sembra una comoda formula per eludere il problema centrale dell'opera di Calvino, quale egli stesso l'ha precisato: aiutare gli uomini ad essere "sempre più intelligenti, sensibili, moralmente forti ecc.," ma non gli uomini in generale (astratta categoria), ma gli uomini nuovi, gli uomini della classe operaia, forza e motore della storia: "… è proprio a quel tipo di uomo o di donna che noi pensiamo, a quei protagonisti attivi della storia, alle nuove classi dirigenti che si formano nell'azione, a contatto con la pratica delle cose." Calvino non si può spiegare quindi con "cariche" di nessun genere, bensì vedendo come egli sia riuscito a legare, in effetti, la sua attività di scrittore agli uomini nuovi, alla classe operaia." ("But this seems an easy formula to evade the central problem of Calvino's work, as he himself has pointed out: help men to be 'increasingly intelligent, sensitive, morally strong and so on', but not men in general (abstract category), but the new men, the men of the working class, strength and engine of history: ... it is precisely this kind of man or woman we think of, of those active protagonists of history, the new governing classes which are formed in the action, in contact with the practice of things. Calvino cannot be explained in this way with 'charges' of any kind but, seeing how he was able, in fact, to bind his work as a writer to new men, to the working class.") (Asor Rosa 12).

17. It is worthwhile noting here that, among other aspects examined and criticized by Ricciardi, is Calvino's cosmopolitanism. She takes into account the 90 writers mentioned by Calvino in *Le lezioni americane* and his ars *poetica*. "These figures represent Calvino's ideal of a cosmopolitan intellectual community, from whose accomplishments he aims to extrapolate a *mathesis universalis* for the literature of the next millennium. The principle of cosmopolitanism, in fact, is a longstanding theme of his critical writing. In an essay published in *Il Contemporaneo* in 1956, he attacks the supposed anticosmopolitanism behind Gramsci's idea of the 'nazional popolare'. [...] Although he wrote these words in 1956, his antipathy toward the notion of the national-*popolare* seems to resonate in the image of literary culture set forth in *Le lezioni americane*" (90).

18. We must consider that national space was at that time a broad, extensive space, far greater than the local realities that they were intended to overcome. The unitary dynamics were modern dynamics, which required considerable development of infrastructures and new communication technologies. It is possible, albeit cautiously, to draw some parallels with the dynamics of today's European Union.

19. "Le cose moderne introdotte dal capitalismo nello Yemen, oltre ad aver reso gli yemeniti fisicamente dei pagliacci, li hanno resi anche molto più infelici." (*Lettere luterane* 20; "Modern things which capitalism has introduced into the Yemen have not only made the Yemenis physically clowns, they have also made them unhappier."; Pasolini, *Lutheran Letters* 32).

20. "The dramatic improvements in all our kinds of investigations from the foraging strategies of our hunter-gatherer days to the contemporary investigations by our police, poetry critics, and physicists, are due in the main to the explosive growth in our technologies of re-representation" (Dennett 144).

21. "Vogliamo dalla letteratura un'immagine cosmica (questo termine è il punto di convergenza del mio discorso con quello di Eco), cioè al livello dei piani di conoscenza che lo sviluppo storico ha messo in gioco" ("We want from literature a cosmic image (this term is the point at which my discourse converges with that of Eco), that is, at the level of knowledge plans that the historical development has put into play") (Calvino, *Una pietra sopra* 97).

22. Jean-François Lyotard, in *The Postmodern Condition* (*La condition postmodern*), recognizes the narrative form as the ability to weave into its fabric a plurality of knowledge, which is considered language games within his theoretical perspective: "[...] the narrative form, unlike the developed forms of the discourse of knowledge, lends itself to a great variety of language games. [...] The areas of competence whose criteria the narrative supplies or applies are thus tightly woven together in the web it forms, ordered by the unified viewpoint characteristic of this kind of knowledge" (20).

23. "Da questa utopia nasce la sua necessità di abbandonare il cinema di fiction per fare film storici per la televisione. Il tentativo di strutturare una Enciclopedia della storia dopo aver tentato, nei film precedenti, di imbastire una Enciclopedia dei sentimenti" ("From this utopia comes its need to abandon the cinema of fiction to make historical films for television. The attempt to structure an encyclopedia of history after trying, in previous films, to set up an encyclopedia of feelings") (Rossellini, "Presentazione" 11–12).

Notes

24. See issue 14 of the magazine Riga, dedicated to Ali Babà (Calvino et al. and editors Barenghi and Belpoliti, *Alì Babà: Progetto di una rivista 1968–1972*; see also Di Stefano, "Calvino, la rivista inesistente").

25. "Difficile immaginare un destino letterario più riuscito e felice di quello di Italo Calvino. Sicuramente l'autore più amato dagli italiani di tutte le età, letto nelle scuole elementari e medie, studiato all'università diligentemente analizzato e ammirato senza riserve dalla critica, Calvino ci accompagna dall'infanzia alla senilità. La sua opera costituisce uno dei più certi e accreditati breviari estetici e morali dell'italiano contemporaneo. Forse non ce ne siamo accorti, ma Calvino ha finito per avere, presso le classi medie di oggi, un ruolo di pedagogo e di moralista analogo a quello che ebbero Collodi e De Amicis un secolo fa" ("It's hard to imagine a literary destiny more successful and felicitous than that of Italo Calvino. Surely the author most loved by Italians of all ages, read in elementary and middle schools, studied at the university, studied diligently and wholeheartedly admired by critics, Calvino takes us from childhood to senility. His work is one of the most reliable and accredited, aesthetic and moral breviaries of contemporary Italian. We may not have noticed, but Calvino has ended up being, for the middle classes of today, a pedagogic and moralistic role similar to that which Collodi and De Amicis had a century ago") (Berardinelli 91).

26. Berardinelli's consideration of Calvino as a "neo classic" whose new theoretical perspective was guaranteed by the establishment has garnered praise among critics. "Si è creduto, ancora con Roland Barthes e con l'avanguardia parigina di 'Tel Quel', con Borges e con la cosiddetta 'école du regard', di trovarsi in una situazione di rischiosa vertigine, di radicalismo apocalittico, di scandalosa e provocatoria nullificazione di ogni valore ereditato. E invece si stava già passando a un regime nuovo, di modernità garantita dalle istituzioni universitarie e dalle teorie estetiche del moderno, ormai consolidate e protettivamente dedite al sostegno divulgativo di quanto, fino a qualche decennio prima, era apparso scandaloso. Ci si credeva cioè in una situazione ancora estremistica, e si era entrati invece, con la scienza strutturalistica delle avanguardie, in una situazione neo-classica" ("It was believed, even with Roland Barthes and the Parisian avant-garde of *Tel Quel*, with Borges and the so-called "école du regard," to be in a situation of risky dizziness, apocalyptic radicalism, of scandalous and provocative nullification of any inherited value. But we were already moving towards a new regime of modernity guaranteed by the universities and by the modern theories by now well established and protectively dedicated to the support of what, until a decade before, had seemed outrageous. We believed even then to be in an extremist situation, and we had entered instead, with a structuralist science of the avant-gardes, into a neo-classical situation") (Berardinelli 99).

27. In *Italo Calvino e la scienza* (*Italo Calvino and Science*), Massimo Bucciantini reconstructs a reflection of the 1970s that sees Agamben, Ginzburg, Del Giudice, and Calvino making in-depth reflections on the relationship between experience and experiment, as well as between science and story. At the center of these considerations stands the figure of Galileo;

scientist, and writer. For Calvino, science and story could coexist without depriving narration of its cognitive function. As a result, the primacy of Galileo in his canon is very significant (142–43).

28. "L'ultima grande invenzione d'un genere letterario a cui abbiamo assistito è stata compiuta da un maestro della scrittura breve, Jorge Luis Borges, ed è stata l'invenzione di se stesso come narratore, l'uovo di Colombo che gli ha permesso di superare il blocco che gli impediva, fin verso i quarant'anni, di passare dalla prosa saggistica alla prosa narrativa" ("The last great invention of a literary genre that we have seen has been accomplished by a master of short writing, Jorge Luis Borges, and was the invention of himself as a storyteller, the Columbus' egg that allowed him to overcome the blockade that prevented him, until about forty years old, moving from non-fiction prose to fiction prose") (Calvino, *Le lezioni americane* 49).

29. "Un simbolo più complesso, che mi ha dato le maggiori possibilità di esprimere la tensione tra razionalità geometrica e groviglio delle esistenze umane è quello della città. Il mio romanzo libro in cui credo d'aver detto più cose resta *Le città invisibili*, perché ho potuto concentrare su un unico simbolo tutte le mie riflessioni, le mie esperienze, le mie congetture, e perché ho costruito una struttura sfaccettata in cui ogni breve testo sta vicino agli altri in una successione che non implica una consequenzialità o una gerarchia ma una rete entro la quale si possono tracciare molteplici percorsi e ricavare conclusioni plurime e ramificate" ("A more complex symbol, which has given me greater possibilities of expressing the tension between geometric rationality and the entanglements of human lives, is that of the city. The book in which I think I managed to say most remains *Invisible Cities*, because I was able to concentrate all my reflections, experiments, and conjectures on a single symbol, and also because I built up a many-faceted structure in which each brief text is close to the others in a series that does not imply logical sequence or a hierarchy, but a network in which one can follow multiple routes and draw multiple, ramified conclusions") (*Le lezioni americane* 70).

30. It is noteworthy that, in Ihab Hassan's *The Postmodern Turn*—a collection of essays written over 20 years, this novel is placed at the beginning of postmodernism in the second chapter, which contrasts modernism and postmodernism. "If we can arbitrarily state that literary Modernism includes certain works between Jarry's *Ubu Roi* (1896) and Joyce's *Finnegans Wake* (1939), where will we arbitrarily say that Postmodernism begins? A year earlier than the *Wake*? With Sartre's *La Nausée* (1938) or Beckett's *Murphy* (1938)" (30).

31. *The Book of the Thousand Nights and a Night* (1885), subtitled *A Plain and Literal Translation of the Arabian Nights Entertainments*, is an English-language translation of *One Thousand and One Nights* (the "Arabian Nights"): see en.wikipedia.org/wiki/The_Book_of_the_Thousand_Nights_and_a_Night. I refer to the first American edition—Burton (1900).

32. "It may be argued, instead, that Calvino's idea of contemporary culture does not entail any significant break with the legacy of modernism. On this

Notes

view, he merely repackages certain features of the modernist creed, most notably insistence on the autonomy of the work of high art and allegiance to a cultural canon entirely made up of such works, by identifying these features popular with signifiers such as lightness. This gambit, however, cannot be played in the name of modernism's ideology of the new and avant-garde experimentalism. Thus Calvino's project must operate through continuous denial of its nihilist lack of convictions. What he fails to acknowledge is the need for art of the present day to re-examine modernism and its aesthetics with a critical eye" (Ricciardi 83).

33. Charles Jencks suggested the idea of "double-coding" in architecture in order to explain the need for hybrid language and style. "To this day I would define Post-Modernism, as I did in 1978, *as double-coding: the combination of Modern techniques with something else (usually traditional building) in order for architecture to communicate with the public and a concerned minority, usually other architects*" (472; emphasis in original). Jencks, commenting on the use of double-coding in literature, refers to the dialog between Eco and Barth. "Thus Eco underlines the lover's use of Post-Modern double coding and extends it, of course, to the novelist' and poets' social use of previous forms. Faced with a restrictive Modernism, a minimalism of means and ends, writers such as John Barth have felt just as restricted as architects forced to build in the International Style" (473).

34. In "P.S. 'I love you'," Diane Elam uses Eco's *Postscript* to analyze *Il nome della rosa*. Her concept of ironical temporality tries to mark the difference between modern and postmodern historical approaches, and highlights the postmodern representation of the past "with difference" (Elam 197). The ironic representation of the past is also the target of Linda Hutcheon's concept of double-coded politics. In her view, parody is double-coded in political terms because "it both legitimizes and subverts that it which it parodies" (97). The ironic reprise of the past also shows self-consciousness about our culture's means of ideological legitimation. For example, in feminist art, "the politics of representation are inevitably the politics of gender" (Hutcheon 97).

35. "Italo Calvino, on the other hand, began as an Italian new realist (in *Il sentiero del nidi di ragno*, 1947; *The Path to the Spiders' Nest*, 1957b) and matured into an exemplary postmodernist (with, for example, *Le Cosmicomiche* 1965; *The Cosmicomics*, 1968 and *Il castello dei destini incrociati*, 1973; *The Castle of Crossed Destinies*, 1976) who on occasion rises, sinks, or merely shifts to modernism (e.g., *Le città invisibili*, 1972; *Invisible Cities*, 1974). My own stories and novels seem to have both modem and post-modem characteristics, and even occasionally, pre-modern features" (Barth 196).

36. "What I mean is not only the fusion of algebra and fire, the great (and in Calvino's case high-spirited) virtuosity, the massive acquaintance with and respectfully ironic recycling of what Umberto Eco calls 'the already said', and the combination of storytelling charm with zero *naiveté*, but also the keeping of one authorial foot in narrative antiquity while the other rests

firmly in the high-tech (in Calvino's case, the Parisian 'structuralist') narrative present" (Barth, "'The Parallels!' Italo Calvino and Jorge Luis Borges").

37. Ihab Hassan lists 11 "definities" that characterize postmodernism. Among them we find indeterminacy, fragmentation ("indeterminacy often follows from fragmentation"), the unpresentable, irony, and hybridization. "These eleven 'definities'," explains Hassan, "add up to a surd, perhaps absurd. I should be much surprised if they amounted to a definition of postmodernism which remains, at best, an equivocal concept [...]" (*The Postmodern Turn* 173). In an essay of 2003, "Beyond postmodernism: Toward an aesthetic of trust," Hassan states, regarding Postmodernism, "I know less about it today than I did some thirty years ago" ("Beyond postmodernism" 199). He also openly avoids contrasting modernism with postmodernism: "Still, rather than construct bizarre tables, contrasting modernism with postmodernism, as certain critics have done, I propose to engage postmodernism in ways that may lead us through it, beyond it" ("Beyond postmodernism" 200). Even clearer in this regard is Linda Hutcheon, in the epilogue of the second edition of her *Politics of Postmodernism*. "Let's say: it's over. What we have witnessed in the last ten or fifteen years and what I'd like to explore in this epilogue is not only the institutionalization of the postmodern, but its transformation into a kind of generic counter-discourse (Terdiman 1985) of the 1990s, overlapping in its ends and means (but by no means interchangeable) with feminism and postcolonialism, as well as with queer, race and ethnicity theory" (Hutcheon 166). Jameson had pointed out that Lyotard and Habermas were working from different, legitimating "narrative archetypes"—"one French (1789) Revolutionary in inspiration, the other German and Hegelian. Rorty critics both of them, underlying 'an almost overblown sense of the role of philosophy today'" (Hutcheon 24).

38. The conceptual grounding of Hutcheon's postmodern view of the politics of representation is Althusser's notion of ideology "both as a system of representation and as a necessary and unavoidable part of every social totality" (6).

39. As Peter Carravetta points out in *Del Postmoderno,* many important contemporary thinkers showed great concern when dealing with these issues. "Al di sotto di queste dinamiche sociali si può percepire anche un'ansia causata dagli stessi concetti e rappresentazioni dei pensatori radicali, di coloro che hanno dichiarato che la Modernità è in declino e si sta frammentando (Vattimo, Derrida, Barthes, Jameson, Rorty, giusto per menzionare alcuni autori noti), che il soggetto (come è stato inteso da Descartes fino a Husserl) è privo di un centro ed è alienato, che la politica è morta o sclerotizzata al punto da non essere più riconoscibile, che la teleologia e il logocentrismo sono dannosi e possono perfino portarci all'imperialismo, alla guerra e all'etnocentrismo, e così via con una serie di previsioni apocalittiche." ("Behind these social dynamics one can also perceive an anxiety caused by the concepts and representations of radical thinkers, those who have declared that Modernity is in decline and is fragmenting (Vattimo, Derrida, Barthes, Jameson, Rorty, just to mention some well-known authors), that

the subject (as understood from Descartes to Husserl) is devoid of a center and is alienated, that politics is dead or sclerotized to the point of no longer being recognizable, that teleology and Logocentrism are harmful and can even lead us to imperialism, war and ethnocentrism, and so on with a series of apocalyptic predictions.") (15).

40. "The truth is that, in response to "*La dolce vita*," Via Veneto has transformed itself and has made a violent effort to come up to the image I gave it in the film" (Fellini, *Fellini on Fellini* 66–67).

41. "I privilegiati di tutte le Via Veneto d'Italia—diceva Alicata—erano sempre stati presentati con un'aureola di stuzzicante mistero, oppure come *eroi del nostro tempo*, rappresentanti irraggiungibili di una vita dorata e felice. I loro divertimenti, spesso insulsi e grossolani, e non di rado sfocianti nel vizio, venivano fatti passare come eleganti manifestazioni di raffinatezza e di classe; i loro insopportabili sprechi, come simpatici passatempi di spensierata gente per bene. Via Veneto era il loro mitico ritrovo." ("The privileged of all the Via Venetos in Italy"—said Alicata—"had always been presented with a halo of intriguing mystery, or as *heroes of our time*, unreachable representatives of a golden happy life. Their amusements, often silly and crude, even bordering on vice, were paraded as elegant expressions of sophistication and class, and their unbearable wastes, as nice carefree pastimes of good people. Via Veneto was their mythical meeting place") (De Santi 48–49).

42. Of those who might have become the symbol of the film, Anita Ekberg or Via Veneto, Fellini speaks briefly in an interview—see Costantini (52).

43. "So three kinds of man–woman relationships are discovered by Marcello to be unfulfilling, to give no stable sense of private self in this world of public frenzy. He rejects woman as whore, woman as goddess, and woman as mother-wife. One of the wonderfully Italianate (and Felliniesque) aspects of *La dolce vita* is that Marcello searches for purpose, beautiful women play major roles" (Costello 49).

44. "Because all remains external, Marcello fails to develop Maddalena's acute self-awareness, his idealization of Sylvia never gets beyond romantic dependency, he cannot create meaning for himself as the miracle, and he relies on Steiner as a surrogate intelligence. Inevitably, he is unable to create anything when left to his own intellectual devices at the beach" (Burke 101).

45. "I gave him the outline of the role: a somewhat cynical journalist, a witness, but at the same time implicated in what he witness" (Fellini cited in Costantini 55).

46. "The Maddalena episode ends, as do all seven episodes, with negation, with no escape or discovery. Dawn comes without bringing light. The morning after the night at Adriana's looks much like the morning after the wedding celebration in *La Strada*. The morning does not mean refreshment, it means litter and waste and exhaustion. This morning foreshadows all the mornings in the film" (Costello 41).

47. "In *La dolce vita*, Fellini presents an ordered appearance of disorder; the scenes seem fragmented because the lives of the characters are fragmented. Most of the sequences, as Gilbert Salachas points out, follow 'the same

dynamic rhythm; the adventure begins in the evening, reaches its greatest frenzy in the heart of the night, and ends in the imprecise haze of dawn. Each daybreak brings a provisory, gloomy conclusion that disperses the nocturnal spell'" (Murray 113–14).

48. "Mi sono sempre rifiutato di mettere la parola fine ai miei film… Mi sembrava una certa e propria violenza non solo contro gli spettatori ma anche contro gli stessi personaggi di cui stai raccontando la storia. Non ci può essere una fine per questi personaggi che comunque continueranno a vivere a tua insaputa, all'insaputa dell'autore." ("I have always refused to put the word 'end' to my film … It seemed to me a real violence not only against the spectators but also against the same characters whose story you are telling. There cannot be an end to these characters, who still will continue to live without your knowledge, without the knowledge of the author") (Moscato 9).

49. "It is a little as if, having been led to this degree of interest in appearances, we were now to see the characters no longer among the objects but, as if these had become transparent, through them. I mean by this that, without our noticing, the world has moved from meaning to analogy, then from analogy to identification with the supernatural. I apologize for this equivocal word; the reader may replace it with whatever the term that expresses the hidden accord which things maintain with an invisible counterpart of which they are, so to speak, merely the adumbration" (Bazin 99).

50. This turning point in the career of Fellini, even to Burke, corresponds to a change in the profile of the represented individual. "The shift in *La dolce vita* away from dramatic, realist considerations of plot and character will result in the films of 'de-individualization' and fragmented identity that characterize the latter part of his carrier" (112).

51. Robert Richardson noted that elements in *La Dolce Vita* were common to Eliot's *The Waste Land*. According to Richardson, the sequences and images of Fellini's films, as happens in the poetry of Eliot, generate impressions in the public only through a progressive accumulation and become truly comprehensible only towards the end. "The work of Fellini and Eliot is similar in ways that range from the fortuitous to the important, but beyond particular likenesses of theme, image, tone, or technique, there is, I think, an overriding similarity that has significance not only for their work but for a great deal of twentieth-century poetry and film" (111).

52. There are those who see in the open form another element that ranks consistently in our reading. Antonio Moresco, in a letter to Carla Benedetti after the publication of *Pasolini contro Calvino*, exalts in a somewhat Heideggerian way the open form as a common feature of both Pasolini and Calvino. For Moresco it is the ambition of the eternal youth of the contemporary individual and the need to keep the death at a distance that makes many artists prefer this form (44).

53. It (Gadda, *Quer pasticciaccio*) appeared for the first time in five episodes in the journal *Literature* in 1946 and was published in one volume 11 years later by the editor Garzanti in Milan.

54. In a note by the publishers, it is emphasized that Pasolini wrote on Gadda in *Passione e ideologia* 1948–1958.

Notes

55. "Anche il padre è colto nel momento in cui vorrebbe superare (sia pure per un attimo) la sua dimensione provinciale e contadina (il virgiliano fortunate senex) ma finisce pietosamente con l'evidenziare tutta la sua fragilità di vecchio che ha perso in modo definitivo (per gli altri) il diritto alla vita" ("The father, too, is caught in the moment in which he would like to overcome (albeit briefly) his provincial and peasant stature (the Virgilian fortunate senex), but mercifully ends in the highlighting all his frailty as an old man who has permanently lost (for the others) the right to life") (Bispuri 100).

56. Augé's idea of non-place contrasts with the idea of place in the traditional ethnology that sees the culture locatable in space and time. "They are spaces where crowds of people criss-cross without relating. The non-places can be both the necessary facilities for the accelerated circulation of people and goods (highways, junctions and airports), and the means of transport, the big shopping centers. And even the refugee camps." (Augé, *Non-Places* 22).

57. "We barely have time to reach maturity before our past has become history, before our individual histories belong to history writ large. [...] Nowadays the recent past—'the sixties', 'the seventies', now 'the eighties'— becomes history as soon as it has been lived" (Augé, *Non-Places* 22).

58. When interviewed by Domenico Scalzo, Amelio pointed out that he did not mean to be the Albanian Kiarostami. Amelio acknowledged that his cinema was fed by Hollywood but denied having been influenced by Spielberg for this film or wanting to spectacularize it.

59. "Lo scrittore peruviano Mario Vargas Llosa ha accusato il regista di avere trattato gli albanesi come se fossero degli insetti e lo scrittore albanese Ismail Kadaré ha detto che il film è insultante per il suo paese. Rispondendo, Amelio ha definito Vargas Llosa un 'imbecille pericoloso' e Kadaré un 'trombone.'" ("The Peruvian writer Mario Vargas Llosa accuses the director of having treated the Albanians like insects and the Albanian writer Ismail Kadare said that the film was offensive for his country. Answering, Amelio defined Vargas Llosa as 'a dangerous imbecile' and Kadare as 'a braggart.'") (Valli 27).

60. According to Tefta Cami, at that time the Albanian Secretary of State for Education and Culture, in the original script the kidnapping of the general and the priest was anticipated; an unlikely episode in the years of Communist dictatorship. See Cami ("E vërteta e 'Gjeneralit të ushtrisë së vdekur'.").

61. The themes concerning the memory and representation of Fascism are the focus of many recent publications. A good example is Ruth Ben-Ghiat's article ("Fascism, Writing, and Memory: The Realist Aesthetic in Italy, 1930–1950."). "Rather more credibly, Ben-Ghiat indicates that even highly self-conscious Anti-Fascists, who belonged to the Communist Party or fellow-travelled with it, were decidedly unwilling to confront the full implications of the 'perpetrations' of the Fascist years and thus helped to construct a memory which was at least as much about forgetting as about remembering" (Bosworth and Dogliani 4).

62. For the whole note see "Il Generale dell'armata morta." Here is the passage from Kadare's novel taken from the dialogue of the Italian chaplain, a self-proclaimed expert of the Albanian context, with the general. It is a hostile look, implicitly and clearly stigmatized by Kadare: "'Exactly. And the Albanians have always had a taste for killing or getting themselves killed. Whenever they haven't been able to find an enemy to fight they've turned to killing one another. Have you heard about their vendettas?' ['Yes']. 'It's an atavistic instinct that drives them into war. Their nature requires war, cries out for war. In peace, the Albanian becomes sluggish and only half alive, like a snake in winter. It is only when he is fighting that his vitality is at full stretch'. The general nodded approvingly" (*The General of the Dead Army* 32).

63. "By the time Mussolini's corpse was hanging by its feet in Piazzale Loreto, Italy had used conventional weapons and weapons of mass destruction to kill about a million people, and had become responsible for countless war crimes, especially in the brutal subjugation of Libya and Ethiopia, well before the alliance with Hitler" (Lichtner 193).

64. The political nature of the film is further articulated through the distinction between Fascist and anti-Fascist victims. After the capitulation of Fascism, some of the Italian soldiers joined the Albanian resistance to fight the Nazi occupation. A conspicuous number formed the Gramsci battalion, whose victims are celebrated with honors in the movie. This distinction, which is historically accurate, underlines the fact that anti-Fascism is not anti-Italianism. 'Without interference in the internal affairs of communist Albania, peaceful coexistence is possible', seems to be the message of the movie.

65. This was only the second episode of this nature that happened in Eastern Europe during the Cold War period. The first happened in 1956, right after the Hungarian Revolution. Cardinal Mindszenty entered the US embassy in Budapest and stayed there until 1971.

66. In 2012, the Albanian television channel ABC produced a documentary entitled *Partizani shqiptar që shpëtoi 20 mijë ushtarë fashistë* (The Albanian partisan who saved 20,000 Fascist soldiers; see www.zemrashqiptare.net/news/28051/partizani-shqiptar-qe-shpetoi-20-mije-ushtare-fashiste.html?skeyword=Partizani shqiptar që shpëtoi 20 mijë ushtarë fashistë). In September 1943, after the country's capitulation, about 100,000 Italian soldiers were held in Albania as it was then under Nazi occupation. The documentary tells the story of a communist officer of the Albanian army who succeeded in repatriating about 20,000 soldiers to Italy. The documentary also criticizes communist historiography which mentions episodes of tens or maybe even hundreds of Italian soldiers being executed by Albanian partisans. In 1945, the Albanian dictator Enver Hoxha and the Italian Vice Secretary of State Mario Palermo signed an agreement by which Albania could keep those Italian citizens whose profession was useful in the rebuilding of their country. The rest would have to be repatriated. According to

documents dated from 1947 there were estimated to be 952 Italian citizens still in Albania; mostly engineers and technicians. The vast majority later returned to Italy but an undefined number were held in Albanian prisons.

67. During the interview with Domenico Scalzo, Amelio informs us that the original title of the movie was *L'America*. The latter was suggested by the scriptwriter Porporati. Amelio was not happy about this title. When he was shown how Useppe, the child, one of the main characters of Elsa Morante's novel *La Storia*, transforms it into *Lamerica*, Amelio found what he was looking for.

68. "Il mio vecchio non è Albanese, né italiano, non è più niente, è un fantasma, il fantasma del contadino di una volta, che poteva essere qualsiasi cosa e che nella sua ignoranza, nel suo farsi usare dalla Storia, nel suo non essere in grado di opporsi alla Storia, nel suo essere trascinato e manipolato dalla Storia, però aveva ancora qualcosa da affermare magari anche solo il valore del pane, che vuol dire la natura, il rispetto della terra, il sacro, il necessario" ("My old man is not Albanian, nor Italian, he is nothing, he is a ghost, the ghost of the old peasant, who could be anything and who, in his ignorance, in his being used by history, in his not being able to oppose history, in his being dragged and manipulated by history, still had something to affirm, perhaps even just the value of bread, which means nature, respect for the earth, the sacred, the necessary") (Amelio, *Interview with Domenico Scalzo,* cited in Scalzo 215).

69. "La fabbrica che vogliono comprare Gino e Fiore nella sceneggiatura era un pastificio. Nel film è diventata, invece, un'industria di calzature, con un ribaltamento per nulla casuale. È il primo trauma che subisce Spiro all'uscita del campo di lavoro è proprio il furto delle scarpe. Ricorda qualcosa? Certo, ricorda "Paisà", l'episodio in cui gli scugnizzi, quelli veri, ubriacano il soldato americano e lo derubano di tutto, scarpe comprese. Che l'episodio del mio film fosse una citazione precisa, me ne sono accorto solo a cose fatte" ("The factory that Gino and Fiore wanted to buy in the script was a pasta factory. In the film, however, it manufactures footwear, with a reversal that is not at all casual. The first trauma that Spiro suffers at his exit from the labor camp is precisely the theft of his shoes. Does it ring any bells? Of course, it reminds us of 'Paisà', the episode in which the rascals (*scugnizzi*), the real ones, get the American soldier drunk and rob him of everything, including his shoes. I realized that the episode of my film was a precise quotation only at the end") (Amelio, cited in Scalzo 174).

70. "Il vecchio protagonista è un emblema di quello che è stato il passato contadino del mondo, nell'Europa in particolare forse in Albania più che altrove. Quel mondo contadino che è stato ridotto a carne da macello per le guerre, per le rivoluzioni. Diceva Pasolini che il vero genocidio avvenuto nel '900 è stato quello dei contadini. E se non c'è più il mondo contadino, non c'è più la terra, il rapporto con le stagioni, non c'è più la natura, non c'è più la radice biologica dell'appartenenza a una cultura" ("The old protagonist is an emblem of what has been the peasant past of the world, in Europe in particular and perhaps in Albania more than elsewhere. A peasant world that

has been reduced to meat for slaughter for wars, for revolutions. Pasolini used to say that the true genocide that occurred in the 20th century was that of the peasants. And if there is no longer the peasant world, there is no longer the earth, the relationship with the seasons, there is no longer nature, there is no longer the biological root of belonging to a culture") (Amelio, cited in Scalzo 215).

71. The use of Cinemascope gave rise to quite a few criticisms of Amelio. The most famous was that of Guido Aristarco, who responded to an open letter by Nicola Siciliani de Cumis. "Mi limito a rispondere, per il momento, a uno solo dei tuoi quesiti, senza peraltro argomentare. Sì, *Lamerica* è un film 'utile', utile nella accezione del nostro Zavattini, ma dove le intenzioni sembrano spesso rimanere tali, non artisticamente risolte. Ci sono momenti intensi sul piano espressivo: la sgangherata nave "Partizani" ripresa dall'alto con quel sovraccarico umano. Ma stilisticamente—e non soltanto stilisticamente—*Lamerica* non mi convince, a cominciare dall'impiego del Panavision, che rimanda a certi effetti da kolossal, al modo spettacolare ad esempio con cui Costa-Gavras tratta temi politici di grande attualità" ("I am answering, for the time being, only to one of your questions, without however arguing. *Lamerica* is a 'useful' film, useful in the sense of our Zavattini, but where intentions often seem to remain such, not artistically resolved. There are intense moments on the expressive level: the ramshackle ship 'Partizani', filmed from above with that human overload. But stylistically—and not only stylistically—*Lamerica* does not convince me, starting from the use of Panavision, which recalls the effects of certain colossal films, to the spectacular way, for example, in which Costa-Gavras deals with political topics of great current interest") (cited in Scalzo 199).

72. Norma Bouchard and Valerio Ferme investigated the idea of the Mediterranean in some of the most important European writers and philosophers such as Goethe, Marx, and Nietzsche. It is enlightening to see how close this idea of the Mediterranean in European modern thought is to the readings of Africa suggested by Pasolini in *Appunti per un'Orestiade Africana* and Celati in *Passar la vita a Diol Kadd (Spending Life in Diol Kadd)*. "Concurrently, another facet of early modern discourses about the Mediterranean emerged in this century. Northern travelers belonged to countries where the shift to Atlantic trade had led to industrialization and scientific innovations. These led to related phenomena, such as the separation between the public and the private sphere of life, the loss of the sense of community, the new rationalization of human labor and the workday, and other sociocultural transformations. In their eyes, the preindustrial Mediterranean could offer a temporary antidote to the changes brought about by modernization. This vision shapes Goethe's view of the Mediterranean as a harmony of sky, land and people, whose echoes traverse works by Shiller and Schlegel to reach Marx and Nietzsche" (Bouchard and Ferme 22).

73. For a recent history of Italian detention centers, see Fiore (52): "Expulsion and detention centers in Italy date back to the very early immigration laws in the 1990s; in the 2000s the situation only worsened since Italy resorted to both massive repatriation and a proliferation of different types of

Notes

detention centers bearing the euphemistic names of Centre of Temporary Permanence and Hospitality (CPTA), Hospitality Centers (CdA), Centre for Hosting Asylum Seekers (CARA), Centre for First Aid and Hospitality (CPSAs) or the more realistic denomination of the Centre for Identification and Expulsion (CIE) and the recent Hotspots. ... As the detention centers grow, both in number and 'quality', the suspension of the democratic law of the polity has increasingly become a norm rather than an exception, as Campesi as well as Rigo and Di Giovanni have pointed out in their work on detention and expulsion practices."

More recently (2023), Italy and Albania signed a bilateral agreement allowing Italy to transfer up to 36,000 asylum seekers per year to detention centers in Albania. These migrants are typically rescued at sea by the Italian Coast Guard or Navy, outside EU territorial waters. Once in Albania, they await decisions on their asylum claims. If granted asylum, they can enter Italy; if denied, they're returned to their country of origin. The Italy-Albania migrant center deal is facing significant delays and legal challenges. The two planned centers in Albania were supposed to open in spring 2024, but as of mid-2025, they've not yet become operational. Italian courts and EU legal experts have raised concerns about the legality and human rights implications of processing asylum seekers outside EU territory.

74. See, for example, this passage from Gabriele Del Grande: in which role of Skype and Messenger in migration towards Piedmont is important and concrete. "Dalla città dei fosfati e dalle sue campagne sono partiti non pochi degli 8.146 marocchini sbarcati in Sicilia nel 2006, più di un terzo dei 22.016 giovani arrivati via mare in Italia in tutto l'anno. I loro racconti al ritorno alimentano un immaginario già viziato da anni di studi eurocentrici, pellicole americane, telefilm italiani e francesi sui canali satellitari, pubblicità, campionati di calcio, ore e ore su internet nei *cyber caffè* sempre affollati a ogni crocicchio della città. Tutti i più giovani hanno amici della riva nord del Mediterraneo con cui chattare su *Skype* o su *Messsenger*. Bisogna partire. In fondo è molto più reale la schermata di un pc o il video clip dell'ultimo tormentone *hip-hop* che gli asini fuori o gli strilli del *muezzin* dagli altoparlanti appesi ai muri delle moschee. Nessuno più vuole tirare ogni mattina carretti carichi di arance per le spremute, o mucchi di panni e vestiti cinesi per il mercato." ("From the city of phosphates and its countryside have departed not a few of the 8,146 Moroccans who landed in Sicily in 2006, more than a third of the 22,016 young people who arrived by sea in Italy throughout the year. Their stories when they go back feed an imaginary already spoiled by years of Europe-centered studies, American movies, Italian and French TV shows on satellite channels, advertising, football leagues, hours and hours on the Internet in cyber cafés, always crowded at every crossroads of the city. All the youngest have friends from the north shore of the Mediterranean with whom they can chat on Skype or Messenger. We must depart. At the end, the screen of a PC or the video clip of the latest hip-hop torment are much more real than the donkeys outside or the screams of muezzins from the speakers hanging on the walls of the mosques. No one wants to pull carts full of oranges for juices every morning, or piles of cloth and Chinese clothes for the market.") (Del Grande 20).

75. "Nel copione era scritto che i due ragazzi erano moldavi. Non sono riuscito a trovarne di convincenti e alla fine ho allargato il campo anche ad altre nazionalità. Ho cominciato a vedere albanesi, montenegrini, kosovari, pronto a correggere la sceneggiatura. Alla fine ho scelto un ragazzo rumeno…" ("In the script it was written that the two boys were Moldovans. I could not find convincing evidence and, in the end, I expanded the field to other nationalities. I began to see Albanians, Montenegrins and Kosovars ready to correct the screenplay. In the end I chose a Romanian boy") (Giordana et al. 10).

76. "Not only is the movie a *bildungsroman* because Sandro evolves to a certain maturity, but it is also a filmic example of the construction and negotiation of the identity of a young bourgeois Italian boy whose sense of the world is constructed before and after his encounter with Otherness" (Benelli 223).

77. The story and its transformation into film was narrated in a book, published with the film itself: Liberti and Segre (21) *Mare chiuso* (*Closed Sea*). The passage comes from the introduction entitled "Un progetto lungo tre anni" ("A Three-Year Project").

78. "Con un pizzico di fantasia, ovvero quello scarto che sancisce il passaggio dal documentario alla cosiddetta finzione. Garrone si muove nelle sue prime opere sul crinale che separa l'uno dall'altra" ("With a bit of imagination, that is the waste that sanctions the transition from the documentary to so-called fiction. Garrone moves in his first works on the ridge that separates one from the other") (Pallanch 19).

79. Garrone clearly explained this aspect: "It is not a thesis where I want to say who is good and who is bad. I did not want to judge. I wanted to show this from faces, the light, the locations, so every person and location could give me new inspiration" (*Cinema Today* 125).

80. In the director's notes which were included in a press release that accompanied the release of the film, Segre explained that he wanted to set the film in the two contexts best known to him: the Roman suburbs and the Veneto, transformed, thanks to sustained economic development, from a land of emigrants into a land of immigrants. While visiting an inn in the area, Segre met a Chinese woman who fired his imagination and inspired him to make the film.

81. Bepi is played by Rade Šerbedžija, born in Bunić and not, coincidentally, one of the most relevant actors of the former Yugoslavia. His has become a familiar face in international cinema thanks to his roles in such films as Manchevski's *Po Dezju* (Before the Rain), Rosi's *La tregua* (The Truce) and Kubrick's *Eyes Wide Shut*.

82. "It works, though, as an essentially conservative force: its effect is a recasting of inequalities, which are unlikely to command public approval, as 'cultural differences'—something to cherish and obey" (Bauman, *Community* 107).

Notes

83. This movie received a L.A.R.A Award (Free association representing artists). To Giuseppe Battiston, for the role of Amos, went recognition as best Italian interpreter at the 2007 Rome International Film Festival. Mazzacurati is the author of many films. The critic Femaldo Di Giammatteo synthesizes his work thus: "Aizzato dalla *ferula* morettiana, affronta tremando *Notte italiana*. Gli va bene. Trema più ancora, senza Moretti, per *Il prete bello*. Gli va male. Peggio gli va con *Un'altra vita*, esposto a Venezia nella vetrina del cinema italiano, come si usa con i rognosi (come si usava ai tempi fascisti della Mostra volpiana) Gli va (in apparenza) bene con *Il toro*, premiato con un Leone d'argento." ("Powered by the Morettian *ferula*, he faces *Notte italiana* (*Italian Night*) trembling. It works fine. Trembles even more, without Moretti, for *Il prete bello* (*The Handsome Priest*). It doesn't work. Worse goes with *Un'altra vita* (*Another Life*), exposed in Venice in the window of Italian cinema, as it is used with the mangy (as was used in the Fascist times of the Volpian Exhibition). It works (apparently) well with *Il Toro* (*The Bull*), awarded with a Silver Lion.") (Di Giammatteo 9).

84. "What for him is a rebirth ('*Ho sentito la vita dopo tanto tempo*', he writes on a note left next to the coffee maker in the morning) for her is the beginning of an affair that in no way would make her change her plans and prevent her from seeing the world" (Pastorino 135).

85. "The Italy presented by Mazzacurati is involved in an arduous search for a new equilibrium. Corning into contact with small-town life, the new economy has stimulated local communities to reassert themselves. The interaction between internal and external forces has given rise to a new flexible identity" (Urban 184).

86. "Ha già suscitato polemiche a non finire—e un'interrogazione parlamentare, addirittura—l'opera terza di Francesco Patiemo (napoletano, classe 1964; un brillante esordio col cupo "Pater Familias" nel 2002 e una seconda prova, sei anni più tardi, stazionante fra manierismo e ritualità, "Il mattino ha Toro in bocca"): sulla scorta d'una pellicola diretta da Sergio Arau, "A Day Without A Mexican" (ambientata in una California da cui sparivano improvvisamente i messicani), il cineasta campano ha tratto un apologo intriso d'ironia, che si tinge col procedere verso la conclusione d'una sottile malinconia." ("It has already caused no end of controversy—and even a parliamentary questioning—the third work of Francesco Patierno (a Neapolitan, born in 1964, a brilliant debut with the gloomy *Pater Familias* in 2002 and a second trial, six years later, stationary between mannerism and rituality, 'The Morning has Bull in the Mouth'": on the basis of a (2004) film directed by Sergio Arau, *A Day Without A Mexican* (set in California from where the Mexicans disappear), the filmmaker from Campania has drawn an apologue imbued with irony, which is tinged with a subtle melancholy as it progresses towards the conclusion.") (Troiano, "Cose dell'altro mondo").

87. "C'è una specie di intolleranza molto sotterranea che noi non vogliamo ammettere anche in chi crede di essere più aperto di altri... nei confronti del diverso, dello straniero. Ma messo alla prova, in certe situazioni, si rende conto che forse il suo processo nei confronti dell'integrazione è ancora da

compiere. Volevo fare un film che riflettesse su questo." ("There is a kind of very hidden intolerance towards the different that we do not want to admit even in those who believe they are more open than others. However, put to the test, in certain situations, he realizes that perhaps the process towards integration is yet to be completed. I wanted to make a film that reflects on this." (Patierno, "Intervista (Venezia 68) www.rbcasting.com").

88. "L'Italia è diventata un paese d'immigrazione negli ultimi vent'anni e questo ha segnato sicuramente la crescita e lo sviluppo di questo paese. Quello che particolarmente colpisce il Veneto è il fatto che il Veneto fino a trent'armi fa era un luogo di forte povertà, di forte emigrazione, molto più che altre zone. Poi all'improvviso è diventato un luogo di ricchezza e all'improvviso è diventato un luogo di immigrazione. Questo è successo tutto in pochi anni e non ce stato il tempo di elaborare questa trasformazione che è avvenuta all'interno di un'unica generazione." ("Italy has become an immigration country over the last 20 years and this has certainly marked the growth and development of this country. What particularly strikes one about Veneto is the fact that, up to 30 years ago, it was a place of great poverty and strong emigration, much more so than other areas. Then suddenly it became a place of wealth and immigration. This all happened in a few years and there was no time to process the transformation that took place within a single generation.") (Segre, "Intervista al regista Andrea Segre").

89. "Nello *Scontro di civiltà*, invece, le voci chiamate a deporre sull'omicidio dell'ascensore, pur numerose e giudiziosamente colorite in tono partenopeo, meneghino e capitolino (la medietà standard dell'italiano parlato è prerogative dei personaggi immigrati), risuonano nelle stanze chiuse di altrettanti capitoli intitolati alla "verità" di ciascun personaggio [...]" ("In *Scontro di civiltà*, instead, the voices called to testify to the murder on the elevator, though numerous and judiciously colored in Neapolitan tone, Milanese and Capitoline (the standard mediety of spoken Italian is the prerogative of the immigrant characters), resound in the closed rooms of as many chapters entitled to the 'truth' of each character [...]") (Fracassa 85).

90. "*Catenaccio*" is from *catena* or chain: an extremely defensive football strategy.

91. "È così vecchia, così fragile. Ancora una volta, mio malgrado, mi intenerisce. Sto per andarmene, e ho paura che non riuscirò a spezzare il legame che mi unisce a lei. E dire che ho tentato di farlo mille volte, in mille modi diversi. Perfino rinnegando la mia madrelingua." ("She's so old, so fragile. Once again, in spite of myself, it softens me. I'm about to leave, and I'm afraid that I will not be able to break the bond that unites me with her. And to say that I have tried to do it a thousand times, in a thousand different ways. Even denying my mother tongue.") (Schneider, *Lasciami andare, madre* 107).

92. "È incredibile come voi italiani siete attaccati al vostro caffè' sorride mia cugina. Ai suoi occhi, oramai, io sono 'l'italiana'. 'E voi ai vostri würstel' ribatto, ma senza acrimonia: voglio bene a Eva, nonostante gli anni trascorsi, la sento vicina come una sorella." ("'It's amazing how you Italians are attached to your coffee', my cousin says, smiling. In her eyes, now, I am

'the Italian girl'. 'And you to your würstel', I reply but without acrimony: I love Eva, despite the years spent apart; I feel as close to her as to a sister") (Schneider, *Lasciami andare, madre* 20).

93. Mia Lecomte thus synthesises Hajdari's path: "Vincitore di svariati premi, tra cui nel '97 il prestigioso Montale per l'inedito, proprio grazie a quest'ultimo il poeta albanese godrà per un periodo di una certa notorietà presso "l'ufficialità" critica italiana, che nel corso degli anni tenderà poi a dimenticarsi sempre più della sua produzione poetica, relegandola nell'ambito delle scritture migranti, dove al contrario sarà sempre più studiata e riconosciuta dagli accademici" ("Winner of several awards, including the prestigious Montale in 1997 for unpublished works, thanks to this award the Albanian poet enjoys a period of a certain notoriety among the 'official' Italian critics, who over the years tend to forget more and more his poetic production, relegating it to the area of migrant writings, where on the contrary it will be increasingly studied and recognized by academics") (179).

94. According to Mia Lecomte, who refers to Hajdari's interviews, the poet writes first in Italian and then translates into Albanian (178).

95. Lecomte observes, for instance, how Hajdari, after emphasizing non-belonging to his birth country with pain and anger, later recoups and re-elaborates his relationship with it. "Dopo aver cantato la disappartenenza del suo corpus poetico, Hajdari recupera la Storia del proprio paese, la sua antichissima tradizione culturale e popolare, e su di esse rifonda eti-camente il significato profondo di un universale destino di migranza." ("After having sung the demarcation of his poetic corpus, Hajdari recovers the history of his country, its very ancient cultural and popular tradition, and ethically re-establishes the profound meaning of a universal destiny of migrants.") (185).

96. From the vast poetic production of Hajdari, two volumes of poetry were consulted: *Stigmate* and *Corpo presente*.

97. Giorgio Agamben addressed this problem in an article of 23 January 2016 which was published by the French daily *Le Monde* and was focused on the current phenomena of depoliticizing trends and increasing fear in today's France. Recalling the historical experience of Fascism and Nazism Agamben pointed out: "It is in this context that we must think about the disturbing project of cancellation of citizenship for citizens with dual nationality, which recalls the Fascist law of 1926 on the denationalization of 'citizens unworthy of Italian citizenship' and the Nazi laws on the denationalization of Jews. In November 2018, the Italian parliament passed a law that makes possible the cancelation of naturalized citizenships for individuals who are condemned for specific felonies." (*Zone Grigie che preparano dittatore*).

98. During the nineteenth and twentieth centuries, as Yuval Noah Harari points out in *Homo Deus*, "industrialized nations such as Germany, France and Japan established gigantic systems of education, health and welfare, yet these systems were aimed to strengthen the nation rather than ensure individual well-being" (30). On this ground was further developed the profile of the "new man" which took place during a large part of the twentieth

century in Eastern Europe. The Soviet Union worked with the idea of the "new man" both within the national context of its federation and within the satellite nations of the communist camp. The multiethnic federation needed the common ground offered by the supranational utopia of the new man, whose main feature was knowledge. As Harari put it, "Today the main source of wealth is knowledge" (15).

99. In the 1990s, Charles Taylor formulated the concept of recognition. It initiated a debate on multiculturalism that led to several publications involving many intellectuals, among them Habermas and Appiah. "The thesis is that our identity is partly shaped by recognition or its absence, often by the misrecognition of others, and so a person or a group of people can suffer real damage, real distortion, if the people or society around them mirror back to them a confining or demeaning or contemplatable picture of themselves. Non-recognition or mis-recognition can inflict harm, can be a form of oppression, imprisoning someone in a false, distorted, and reduced mode of being" (25).

100. Zygmund Bauman analyzes the economic aspects of belonging versus non-belonging. He maintains that the condition of multibelonging is available only to an international elite. He examines the economic aspects of non-belonging and how these translate into exclusion. Identity, in the conditions of modern liquidity, must be continuously renewed. Halting the process of identity construction results in the revocation of social status and class membership. Those who cannot maintain the process of building an identity end up among the ranks of the "sub-classes," among the ranks of the excluded. "It is the exclusion, and not the exploitation as it was hypothesized by Marx a century ago, that is today one of the main causes of the most visible cases of social polarization, of an inequality that becomes deeper and of increasing volumes of poverty, misery and human humiliation" (*Intervista sull'identità* 46).

101. It is important to consider the context of this affirmation. A longer quotation should help readers to better understand Appiah's perspective: "It seems to me that this notion of authenticity has built into it a series of errors of philosophical anthropology. It is, first of all, wrong in failing to see what Taylor so clearly recognizes: the way in which the self is, as he says, dialogically constituted. The rhetoric of authenticity proposes not only that I have a way of being that is all my own but that, in developing it, I must fight against the family, organized religion, society, the school, the state—all the forces of convention. This is wrong, however, not only because it is in dialogue with other people's understandings of who I am that I develop a conception of my own identity (Taylor's point) but also because my identity is crucially constituted through concepts and practices made available to me by religion, society, school, and state, and mediated to varying degrees by the family. Dialogue shapes the identity I develop as I grow up, but the very material out of which I form it is provided, in part, by my society, by what Taylor calls its language in 'a broad sense'. Taylor's term 'monological' can be extended to describe views of authenticity that make these connected errors" (Appiah 154).

102. For a detailed explanation of this proposed law, see an unauthored editorial note of the daily Secolo d'Italia published on 16 Jun. 2017, www.secoloditalia.it/2017/06/lo-ius-soli-spiegato-in-cinque-punti-come-cambia-la-legge-in-peggio. See also the lates proposal discussed in the Italian parliament on 21 March 2022 and called *Ius scholae*.

103. Cultural capital can exist in three forms: in the incorporated state—that is, in the form of long-term provisions (*habitus*) associated with certain types of knowledge, ideas, values, skills, etc.—in the objectified state, in the form of cultural goods, paintings, books, dictionaries, tools, etc.; and in the institutionalized state—which is a form of objectification, as the different educational degrees (see Bourdieu, *Le Sens pratique*).

104. For Fausto Pellecchia, Hajdari's bilinguism and self-translation produce a poetic language that is neither Albanian nor Italian but is fed by their relationship, and creates a dimension of extra-territoriality (Lecomte 185).

105. "What? What was that she just said to herself? 'The police barrier is pretty solid, thank God'? Did she say, 'Thank God'? Did she—an émigré everyone pities for losing her homeland—did she actually say 'Thank God'?" (Kundera, *Ignorance* 26).

106. "The gigantic invisible broom that transforms, disfigures, erases landscapes has been at the job for millennia now, but its movements, which used to be slow, just barely perceptible, have sped up so much that I wonder: Would an *Odyssey* even be conceivable today? Is the epic of the return still pertinent to our time?" (Kundera, *Ignorance* 54).

107. "Martin, her husband, was having the same dreams. Every morning they would talk about the horror of that return to their native land. Then, in the course of a conversation with a Polish friend, an émigré herself, Irena realized that all émigrés had those dreams, every one, without exception" (Kundera, *Ignorance* 15).

108. Julius Kirshner, in his *Marriage, Dowry, and Citizenship in Late Mediaeval and Renaissance Italy*, traces back the idea of the Fatherland to Roman Law and gender politics. "Justianians' *Corpus iuris* was the product of a vast empire, in which the status of a Roman citizen signified attachment to a common fatherland, not to a particular territorial community" (162). Legitimate children acquired their father's *origo*, or place of origin, whereas illegitimate children acquired their mother's place of origin. In Italian medieval communities, the legal capacities of women were, again, circumscribed. "The social reproduction of patrilineal regimes depended on sons succeeding their fathers as heads of the household and as masters of the family's patrimonial properties" (160).

109. In the French edition of this novel, Kundera uses the word "*patrie*" while, in the American edition it is translated as "homeland." "Car la notion même de patrie, dans le sens noble et sentimental de ce mot, est liée à la relative brièveté de notre vie qui nous procure trop peu de temps pour que nous nous attachions à un autre pays, à d'autres langues" (*L'ignorance* 139–40).

110. For a detailed study on the methodologies and the critical reference grids

A Final Note

through which this literature is studied, see Comberiati's article "Lo studio della letteratura italiana della migrazione in Italia e all'estero: una panoramica critica e metodologica" ("The Italian literature study of migration in Italy and abroad: a critical and methodological overview") and Chiara Mengozzi's "What little I know of the world I assume." Cornici nazionali e mondiali per le scritture migranti e postcoloniali" ("What little I know of the world I assume." National and world frames for migrant and postcolonial writings").

Material previously published from this volume

From Part 1:

Kubati, Ron (2017). "From Calabria to Russia: Southern Question and Urbanization in Corrado Alvaro" in Lucia Dell'Aia (ed.), *Soggetti e Oggetti*. Rome: Aracne, pp. 53–63.

From Part 2:

Kubati, Ron (2016). "Literature as Re-Representation: Calvino and the Encyclopedic Novel", *Forum Italicum, 50*(3): 1161–1179.

From Part 3:

Kubati, Ron (2015). "Italian-Albanian Cinematographic Confrontation on Fascism and Immigration," in Mario Domenichelli and Rosanna Morace (eds), *Translingual Italian Literature Between Emigration and Immigration: special issue, La Modernità Letteraria*. Pisa–Rome: Serra, 2015, pp.141–156.

Kubati, Ron (2013). "Comunita' Chiuse: Io Sono Li, La Giusta Distanza, Cose dell'altro mondo" (Closed Communities) in Simona Wright and Giovanni Spani (eds), *New Perspectives on Veneto. Literary and Cultural Itineraries. Special issue of NEMLA Italian Studies,* xxxv: 221–244.

Kubati, Ron (2021). "Translingual Literature and Multibelonging", in Graziella Parati, Marie Orton and Ron Kubati (eds), *Contemporary Italian Diversity in Critical and Fictional Narratives*, Fairleigh Dickinson University Press. All rights reserved.

Works Cited

Abate, Carmine. *La festa del ritorno*. Milan, Mondadori, 2004.

Agamben, Giorgio. *Homo sacer. Il potere sovrano e la nuda vita*. Turin, Einaudi, 1995.

———. *Homo Sacer: Sovereign Power and Bare Life*. Stanford, Stanford University Press, 1998.

———. *Lo stato di eccezione*. Turin, Bollati Boringhieri, 2003.

———. *Remnants of Auschwitz: The Witness and the Archive*. Translated by Daniel Heller-Roaze, New York, Zone Books, 1999.

———. *Quel che resta di Auschwitz: L'archivio e il testimone*. Turin, Bollati Boringhieri, 1998.

———. *Zone grigie che preparano dittatore*. 2016, comune-info.net/2016/01/democrazia-dittature/. Accessed 28 Nov. 2018.

Allievi, Stefano. Immigration and Cultural Pluralism in Italy: Multiculturalism as a Missing Model. *Italian Culture*, vol. 28, no. 2, 2010, pp. 85–103.

Alvaro, Corrado. *Colore di Berlino. Viaggio in Germania*, edited by Anne-Christine Faltrop-Porta, Reggio Calabria, Falzea Editore, 2001.

———. *Gente in Aspromonte*. Florence, Le Monnier, 1930.

———. *L'amata alla finestra*. Turin, Fratelli Buratti, 1929.

———. *L'età breve*. Milan, Bompani, 1946.

———. *L'uomo è forte*. Florence, Giunti, 1938.

———. *L'uomo nel labirinto nella Russia Sovietica*, Milan, Alpes Editrice, 1926.

———. *I maestri del diluvio: Viaggio in Russia*. 1935. Massa, Memoranda Edizioni, 1985.

———. *Terra nuova. Prima cronaca dell'Agro Pontino*. 1934. Milan, Claudio Lombardi Editore, 1989.

Works Cited

Angelone, Angela. "Italian Documentaries and Immigration." *Italian Political Cinema: Public Life, Imaginary, and Identity in Contemporary Italian Film*, edited by Giancarlo Lombardi and Christian Uva, Bern, Peter Lang, 2016, pp. 69–80.

Annoni, Gian Maria. "*Salò* after *Salò*: expanded readings of Pasolini's last film." *Corpus XXX, Pasolini, Petrolio, Salò*, edited by Davide Messini, Bologna, Clueb, 2012, pp. 173–76.

Appadurai, Arjun. *Modernity at Large: Cultural Dimensions of Globalization*. Minneapolis, University of Minnesota Press, 1996.

Appiah, Anthony K. 1994. "Identity, Authenticity, Survival: Multicultural Societies and Social Reproduction." *Multiculturalism: Examining the Politcs of Recognition*, edited by Amy Gutmann, Princeton University Press, pp. 149–64.

Arendt, Hannah. *Eichmann in Jerusalem: A Report on the Banality of Evil*. New York, The Viking Press, 1965.

———. *On Revolution*. New York, Viking Press, 1963.

———. *The Human Condition*. University of Chicago Press, 1964.

———. *The Origins of Totalitarianism*. New York, Harcourt, Brace and Co., 1958.

Ariosto, Lodovico. *Orlando Furioso*. 1532.

Asor Rosa, Alberto. *Stile Calvino*. Turin, Einaudi, 2001.

Attali, Jacques. *A Brief History of the Future*. New York, Arcade, 2009.

———. *Une brève histoire de l'avenir*. Paris, Librarie Arthème Fayard, 2006.

Augé, Marc. *An Introduction to Supermodernity*. Translated by John Howe, London, Verso, 1995.

———. *Non-lieux: Introduction à une anthropologie de la surmodernité*. Paris, Editions du Seuil, 1992.

———. *Non-Places: Introduction to an Anthropology of Supermodernity*. London, Verso, 1992.

Banti, Anna. *Le donne muoiono*. Edited by Carol Lazzaro-Weis, Modern Language Association, 2001.

Barenghi, Mario, and Marco Belpoliti. *The Magazine "Riga" dedicated to "Ali Baba."* Milan, Marcos y Marcos, 1998.

Barth, John. "Postmodernism Revisited." *Further Fridays*. New York, Little Brown and Co, 1995.

———. "The Literature of Exhaustion." *Postmodernism and the Contemporary Novel*, edited by Bran Nicol, Edinburgh University Press, 2002.

Works Cited

———. "The Literature of Replenishment." *The Friday Book: Essays and Other Non-Fiction*, London, The John Hopkins University Press, 1984, pp. 193–206.

———. "'The Parallels!' Italo Calvino and Jorge Luis Borges." *Context*, no. 1, 2013, web.archive.org/web/20051228221740/http://www.centerforbookculture.org/context/no1/ barth.html.

Barthes, Roland. *Mythologies*. New York, Hill and Wang, 1957.

Baudrillard, Jean. *The Perfect Crime*. New York, Verso, 1995.

Bauman, Zygmund. *Community: Seeking Safety in an Insecure World*. Cambridge, Polity Press, 2001.

———. *Globalization: The Human Consequences*. New York, Columbia University Press, 1998.

———. *Intervista sull'identità*. Edizioni Laterza, 2003.

———. *Liquid Life*. Cambridge, Polity Press, 2005.

Bazin, André. "The Voyage to the End of Neorealism." *Federico Fellini: Essays In Criticism*, edited by Peter Bondanella, London, Oxford University Press, 1978, pp. 94–102.

Beckett, Samuel. *Murphy*. London, Routledge, 1938.

Benedetti, Carla. *Pasolini contro Calvino*. Turin, Bollati Boringhieri, 1998.

Benedetti, Carla, and Giovanni Giovanetti. *Frocio e basta, Pasolini, Cefis, Petrolio*. Milan, Effigie, 2012.

Benelli, Elena. "The 'Other' from Another Shore: Identity at Sea in *Quando sei Nato non Puoi Più Nasconderti*." *From Terrone to Extracomunitario: New Manifestations of Racism in Contemporary Italian Cinema*, edited by Grace Russo Bullaro, Leicester, Troubador, 2010, pp. 219–39.

Ben-Ghiat, Ruth. "Fascism, Writing, and Memory: The Realist Aesthetic in Italy, 1930–1950." *The Journal of Modern History*, vol. 67, no. 3, 1995, pp. 627–665.

———. *Italian Fascism's Empire Cinema*. Bloomington, Indiana University Press, 2015.

———. "The Imperial Moment in Fascist Cinema." *Journal of Modern European History*, vol. 13, no. 1, 2015, pp. 59–78.

Benincasa, Fabio. "The Bibliography of *Salò*. Eros, Sadism and Avant-Garde in Pier Paolo Pasoloni's Last Work." *Pasolini's Lasting Impressions: Death, Eros and Literary Enterprise in the Opus of Pier Paolo Pasolini*, edited by Ryan Calabretta-Sajder, Madison, Fairleigh Dickinson University Press, 2018, pp. 131–48.

Berardinelli, Alfonso. "Calvino moralista. Ovvero come restare sani dopo la fine del mondo." *Casi critici: Dal postmoderno alla mutazione.* Macerata, Quodlibet, 2007.

Bispuri, Ennio. *Federico Fellini e il sentimento latino della vita.* Rome, Il Ventaglio, 1981. Boltanski, Luc. *Distant Suffering: Morality, Media, Politics.* Cambridge, Cambridge University Press, 1999.

Bond, Emma, and Daniele Comberiati, editors. *Il confine liquido.* Nardò, Besa, 2013.

Bondanella, Peter. *Italian Cinema. From Neorealism to the Present.* New York, Continuum, 1996.

———. *The Films of Federico Fellini.* Cambridge, Cambridge University Press, 2002.

Bondanella, Peter, and Cristina Degli-Esposti, editors. *Perspectives on Federico Fellini.* New York, G.K. Hall & Co., 1993.

Bosworth, Richard J.B., and Patrizia Dogliani, editors. *Italian Fascism: History, Memory and Representation*, Basingstoke, Palgrave Macmillan, 1999.

Bouchard, Norma, and Valerio Ferme. *Italy and the Mediterranean: Words, Sounds, and Images of the Post-Cold War Era.* New York, Palgrave Macmillan, 2013.

Bourdieu, Pierre. *Le Sens pratique.* Paris, Minuit, 1980.

Bucciantini, Massimo. *Italo Calvino e la scienza: gli alfabeti del mondo.* Rome, Donzelli, 2007. Burke, Frank. *Fellini's Films: From Postwar to Postmodern.* New York, Twayne, 1996.

Burnham Schwartz, John. "How Jhumpa Lahiri Learned to Write Again." *Wall Street Journal,* 20 Jan. 2016, www.wsj.com/articles/how-jhumpa-lahiri-learned-to-write-again-1453305609. Accessed 28 Nov. 2018.

Burton, Richard F. *The Book of the Thousand Nights and a Night.* Denver, Press of the Carson-Harper Company, 1900.

Calvino, Italo. *I nostri antenati.* Turin, Einaudi, 1960.

———. *If on a Winter's Night a Traveler.* Translated by William Weaver, New York, Harcourt Brace Jovanovich, 1981.

———. *Il castello dei destini incrociati.* Turin, Einaudi, 1973.

———. *Il cavaliere inesistente.* Milan, Mondadori, 1959.

———. *Il sentiero dei nidi di ragno.* Turin, Einaudi, 1947.

———. *Il visconte dimezzato.* Turin, Einaudi, 1952.

———. *Invisible Cities.* Translated by William Weaver, New York, Harcourt Brace Jovanovich, 1974.

Works Cited

———. "Italo Calvino: The Non-Existent Knight." In *Our Ancestors*, translated by Archibald Colquhoun, London, Vintage, 1998.

———. *La giornata d'uno scrutatore*. Turin, Einaudi, 1963.

———. *La speculazione edilizia*. Turin, Einaudi, 1963.

———. *Le città invisibili*. Turin, Einaudi, 1972.

———. *Le Cosmicomiche*. Turin, Einaudi, 1965.

———. *Le lezioni americane: Sei proposte per il prossimo millennio*. Milan, Garzanti, 1988.

———. *Marcovaldo ovvero: Le stagioni in città*. Milan, Mondadori, 2002.

———. *Orlando furioso di Ludovico Ariosto raccontato da Italo Calvino*. Turin, Einaudi, 1970.

———. *Palomar*. Milan, Mondadori, 1990.

———. *Se una notte d'inverno un viaggiatore*. Turin, Einaudi, 1979.

———. *Six Memos for the Next Millennium*. Translated by Patrick Creagh, Cambridge MA, Harvard University Press, 1988.

———. "The Autobiography of a Spectator." *Perspectives on Federico Fellini*, edited by Peter Bondanella, and Cristina Degli-Esposti, New York, G.K. Hall, 1993.

———. *The Castle of Crossed Destinies*. Translated by William Weaver, New York, Harcourt Brace Jovanovich, 1976.

———. *The Cloven Viscount*. Translated by Archibald Colquhoun, Glasgow, William Collins, 1962.

———. *The Cosmicomics*. New York, Harcourt Brace Jovanovich, 1968.

———. *The Path to the Spiders' Nests*. Translated by Archibald Colquhoun, London, William Collins, 1957.

———. *The Watcher and Other Stories*. Translated by William Weaver, New York, Harcourt Brace Jovanovich, 1971.

———. *Ti con zero*. Milan, Mondadori, 1967.

———. *Una pietra sopra: discorsi di letteratura e società*. Turin, Einaudi, 1980.

Calvino, Italo, et al. *Alì Babà: Progetto di una rivista 1968–1972*, edited by Mario Barenghi, and Marco Belpoliti, Milan, Editore Marcos y Marcos, 1998.

Cami, Tefta. "E vërteta e 'Gjeneralit të ushtrisë së vdekur'." *Tirana observër*, 17 Sept. 2006, p. 11.

Camus, Albert. *L'Etranger*. Paris, Gallimard, 1942.

———. *The Stranger*. Translated by Joseph Laredo, London, Penguin Books, 2000.

Works Cited

Capozzi, Rocco. "L'iper-romanzo di Calvino ed Eco: Molteplicità, enciclopedia e poetica dell'eccesso." *Tra Eco e Calvino. Relazioni rizomatiche*, edited by Rocco Capozzi, Milan, EncycloMedia, 2013, pp. 302–24.

Carr, Matthew. *Fortress Europe: Dispatches from a Gated Continent*. New York, The New Press, 2012.

Carravetta, Peter. *Del Postmoderno*. Milan, Bompiani, 2009.

Celati, Gianni. *Passar la vita a Diol Kadd*. Milan, Feltrinelli, 2011.

Ceserani, Remo. *Raccontare il postmoderno*. Turin: Bollati Boringhieri, 1997.

Collodi, Carlo. *Le avventure di Pinocchio. Storia di un burattino*. Florence, Felice Paggi, 1883. Comberiati, Daniele. "Lo studio della letteratura italiana della migrazione in Italia e all'estero: una panoramica critica e metodologica." *La Modernità Letteraria*, no. 8, 2015, pp. 43–52.

Costa, Antonio. *Federico Fellini: La dolce vita*. Turin, Lindau, 2010.

Costantini, Costanzo. *Conversation with Fellini*. New York: Harcourt Brace Jovanovich, 1995.

Costello, Donal P. *Fellini's Road*. Paris, University of Notre Dame Press, 1983.

Cottino-Jones, Marga. *Women, Desire, and Power in Italian Cinema*. London, Palgrave Macmillan, 2010.

Crucitti, Nadia. *Affinità tra "L'uomo è forte" di Alvaro e "1984" di Orwell*, www.nadiacrucitti.it/index.php?id=3.

Cummins, Jeanine. *American Dirt*. New York, Flatiron, 2020.

Dal Lago, Alessandro. *Non-Persone: L'Esclusione dei migranti in una società globale*. Milan, Feltrinelli, 1999.

Dalla Torre, Elena. "Accordi globali: gioventù europea e immigrazione femminile nei film dei fratelli Dardenne e di Marco Tulio Giordana." *Il cinema di Marco Tulio Giordana*, edited by Federica Colleoni, et al., Rome, Vecchiarelli editore, 2005, pp. 223–44.

Dante Alighieri. *La vita nuova*. 1295.

Dante Alighieri, and Dante Gabriel Rossetti. *The New Life*. Translated by Dante Gabriel Rossetti, London, Ellis and Elvery, 1899.

De Beauvoir, Simone. *Tous les hommes sont mortels*. Paris, Gallimard, 1947.

De Carlo, Andrea. *Due di due*. Milan: Mondadori, 1989.

De Grazia, Victoria. *How Fascism Ruled Women. Italy, 1922–1945*. Berkeley, University of California Press, 1992.

"De Laurentiis risponde a Fellini." Il Giorno, 27–10–1958." *La Dolce Vita raccontata dagli Archivi Rizzoli*, edited by Domenico Monetti, and

Giuseppe Ricci, Rome, Centro Sperimentale di Cinematografia, Fondazione Federico Fellini, 2010.

De Sade, Marquis. *The 120 Days of Sodom, or: The Romance of the School for Libertinage*. 1785. Translated by Austryn Wainhouse, and Richard Seaver, New York, Grove Press, 1966.

De Santi, Pier Marco, editor. *La dolce vita: scandalo a Roma, Palma d'oro a Cannes*. Pisa, Edizioni ETS, 2004.

Del Grande, Gabriele. *Mamadou va a morire: La strage dei clandestini nel mediterraneo*. Rome, Infinito edizioni, 2009.

Dennett, Daniel. *Kinds of Minds: Toward an Understanding of Consciousness*. New York, Basic Books, 1997.

Di Giammatteo, Fernaldo. "Ritratto (di Regista) Italiano." *Carlo Mazzacurati*, edited by Andrea Filippi, San Gimignano, Città di San Gimignano, 1995.

Di Stefano, Paolo. "Calvino, la rivista inesistente." *Corriere della sera*, 30 June 1998. p. 31. archiviostorico.corriere.it/1998/giugno/30/CALVINO_rivista_inesistente_co_ 0_98063012908.shtml.

Dones, Elvira. *Vergine giurata*. Milan, Feltrinelli, 2007.

Douthat, Ross. "Are Liberals Against Marriage? Debating the Decline of Wedlock, Again, in the Shadow of the Baby Bust." *New York Times*, 3 Dec. 2019, www.nytimes.com/2019/12/03/opinion/liberals-marriage.html?action=click&module=Opinion&pgtype=Homepage.

Druker, Jonathan. *Primo Levi and Humanism after Auschwitz: Posthumanist Reflections*. New York, Palgrave Macmillan, 2009.

D'Arcangeli, Luciana. "The films of Matteo Garrone. Italian Cinema is not Enbalmed." *The Italian Film Directors in the New Millennium*, edited by William Hope, London, Cambridge Scholars Publishing, 2010, 175–88.

Eco, Umberto. *Il nome della rosa*. Milan, Bompiani, 1980.

———. *Postille a "Il nome della rosa."* Milan, Bompiani, 1984.

———. "Postmodernism, irony, the enjoyable." *Modernism/Postmodernism*, edited by Peter Brooker, Longman, 1992.

———. *Postscript to The Name of the Rose*. London, Harcourt Brace Jovanovich, 1984.

———. *The Name of the Rose*. London, Harcourt Brace Jovanovich, 1983.

Elam, Diane. "'P.S. I love you': Umberto Eco and the romance of the reader." *Umberto Eco's Alternative*, edited by Norma Bouchard and Veronica Pravadelli, New York, Peter Lang, 1998, pp. 185–207

Works Cited

Eliot, Thomas Stearns. *The Waste Land*. New York, Horace Liveright, 1922.

Esposito, Roberto. *Termini della politica* Vol. I, Milan, Mimesis, 2018.

Fellini, Federico. *Aufsätze und Notizen*. Zurich, Diogenes Verlag, 1974.

———. *Fellini on Fellini*. London, Eyre Methuen, 1976.

Ferretti, Gian Carlo. *Le capre di Bikini*. Rome, Editori Riuniti, 1989.

Fiore, Teresa. "From Exclusion to Expression in *A Sud di Lampedusa* and *Come un Uomo sulla Terra*: Visualizing Detention Centers along Italy-Bound Migrant Routes." *Journal of Italian Cinema and Media Studies*, vol. 6, no. 1, 2018, pp. 49–64.

———. *Pre-Occupied Spaces, Remaping Italy's Transnational Migration and Colonial Legacies*. New York, Fordham University Press, 2017.

Flint, R.W., editor. *Marinetti, Selected Writings*. New York, Farrar, Straus and Giroux, 1971.

Flood, Alison. "Publishers Defend American Dirt as Claims for Cultural Appropriation Grow." *The Guardian*, 24 Jan. 2020, www.theguardian.com/books/2020/jan/24/publishers-defend-american-dirt-claims-cultural-appropriation-jeanine-cummins-oprah.

Forti, Simona. *Il totalitarismo*. Rome–Bari, Editori Laterza, 2001.

Foucault, Michel. *Il faut défendre la societé*. Paris, Gallimard, 1997.

———. *La volonté de savoir*. Paris, Gallimard, 1976.

———. *The History of Sexuality*. Translated by Robert Hurley, London, Penguin, 1984.

———. *The History of Sexuality. Volume 1: An Introduction*. Translated by Robert Hurley, New York, Pantheon, 1978.

Fracassa, Ugo. *Patria e lettere: Per una critica della letteratura postcoloniale e migrante in Italia*. Rome, Giulio Perrone, 2012.

Francese, Joseph. *Narrating Postmodern Time and Space*. New York, State University of New York Press, 1997.

Frau, Ombretta. "La Bottana industriale e il Signor Carunchio: 'Travolti da un insolito destino' quarant'anni dopo." *Huffington Post*, 03 Jan. 2015, www.huffingtonpost.it/ombretta-frau/bottana-industriale-signor-carunchio-insolito-destino_b_6091202.html.

Freud, Sigmund. *Three Essays on the Theory of Sexuality*. Translated by James Strachey, New York, Basic Books, 2000.

Gadda, Carlo Emilio. *Quer pasticciaccio brutto de via Merulana*. Milan, Garzanti, 1957.

———. *That Awful Mess on the Via Merulana*. Translated by William Weaver, New York, Encounter, 1965.

Works Cited

Garcia Canclini, Néstor. *Culturas hibridas. Estrategias para entrar y salir de la modernidad.* Mexico City, Grijalbo, 1990.

Garrone, Matteo. *Cinema Today: A Conversation with Thirty-Nine Filmmakers from around the World.* New Brunswick, Rutgers University Press, 2011.

———. "La finzione del reale." *L'invenzione del reale. Conversazioni su un altro cinema*, edited by Dario Zonta, Rome, Contrasto, 2017, pp. 195–211.

Gentile, Giovanni. *Manifesto degli intellettuali del fascismo.* Rome, Il Mondo, 1925.

———. *Preliminari allo studio del fanciullo.* Florence, Sansoni, 1924.

Giordana, Marco Tullio, et al. *Quando sei nato non puoi più nasconderti: sceneggiatura del film dallo stesso titolo di Marco Tulio Giordana*, edited by Lorenzo Codelli, Milan, Marsilio, 2005.

Giuliani Caponetto, Rosetta. *Fascist Hybridities, Representations of Racial Mixing and Diaspora Cultures under Mussolini.* London, Palgrave Macmillian, 2015.

Grassi, Giovanna. "Kadare attacca Amelio. 'Che razzismo in Lamerica'." *Corriere della Sera*, 13 Dec. 1994, archiviostorico.corriere.it/1994/dicembre/13/Kadare_attacca_Amelio_che_razzismo_co_0_94121314502.shtml.

Gremigni, Elena. *La realtà dell'immaginazione e le ambivalenze del moderno.* Florence, Le Lettere, 2011.

Guaci, Leonardo. "I Grandi Occhi del Mare." *Il Mare si Lasciava Attraversare: Antologia di Scrittori Albanesi sull'Esodo*, Lecce, Besa, 2012, pp. 74–98.

Guida, Patrizia. *Letteratura femminile del Ventennio fascista.* Lecce, Pensa Multimedia, 2000. Guglielmi, Angelo. "Domande per Italo Calvino." *Alfabeta*, I, no. 6, 1979, pp. 12–13.

Hajdari, Gëzim. *Corpo presente. Trup i pranishëm.* Lecce, Besa, 2011.

———. *Stigmate.* Lecce, Besa, 2001.

Harari, Yuval Noah. *Homo Deus: A Brief History of Tomorrow.* New York, Harper, 2017.

Haraway, Donna. "A Cyborg Manifesto: Science, Technology, and Socialist-Feminism in the Late Twentieth Century." *Simians, Cyborgs and Women: The Reinvention of Nature*, New York, Routledge, 1991, pp. 149–82.

Hassan, Ihab Habib. "Beyond Postmodernism: Toward an Aesthetic of Trust." *Beyond Postmodernism: Reassessments in Literature, Theory, and Culture*, edited by Klaus Stierstorfer, Berlin and New York, Walter de Gruyter, 2003, pp. 199–212.

———. *The Postmodern Turn: Essays in Postmodern Theory and Culture.* Columbus, OH: Ohio State University Press, 1987.

Hobsbawm, Eric. *The Age of Extremes: The Short Twentieth Century, 1914–1991.* New York, Pantheon, 1994.

Huntington, Samuel P. *The Clash of Civilisations.* New York, Simon & Schuster, 1996.

Hutcheon, Linda. *The Politics of Postmodernism.* London and New York, Routledge, 2002. "Italian PM to give Migration Film to Heads of State at EU Summit." *The Guardian*, 23 Feb. 2016, www.theguardian.com/world/2016/feb/23/matteo-renzi-italian-pm-fire-at-sea-gianfranco-rosi-migration.

Jacoby, Russell. *The End of Utopia: Politics and Culture in the Age of Apathy.* New York, Basic Books, 2000.

Jarry, Alfred. *Ubu Roi.* 1896.

Jameson, Fredric. *Postmodernism, or The Cultural Logic of Late Capitalism.* Durham, NC, Duke University Press, 1991.

Jencks, Charles. "The Death of Modern Architecture. What is Post-Modernism?" *From Modernism to Postmodernism: An Anthology*, edited by *Lawrence* E. Cahoone, Cambridge, MA: Blackwell, 1996, pp. 457–463.

Joyce, James. *Finnegans Wake.* New York, Faber and Faber, 1939.

Kadare, Ismail. *Il generale dell'armata morta.* Translated by Augusto Donaudy, Milan, Longanesi, 1970.

———. *Gjenerali i Ushtrisë së Vdekur.* Tirana, Shtepia Botuese Naim Frasheri, 1963.

———. "Prilli i thyer." *Gjakftohtësia*, Tirana, Naim Frasheri, 1980, pp. 176–360.

———. *The General of the Dead Army.* Translated by Derek Coltman, New York, New Amsterdam, 1991.

Kirshner, Julius. *Marriage, Dowry, and Citizenship in Late Mediaeval and Renaissance Italy.* Toronto, University of Toronto Press, 2015.

Khouma, Pap, and Oreste Pivetta. *Io, venditore di elefanti. Una vita per forza tra Dakar, Parigi e Milano.* Milan, Garzanti, 1990.

Kundera, Milan. *Ignorance.* Translated by Linda Asher, New York, Harper Collins, 2002.

———. *L'ignorance.* Paris, Grand Livre du Mois, 2000.

Lahiri, Jhumpa. *In altre parole.* Milan, Guanda, 2015.

———. *In Other Words.* Translated by Ann Goldstein, London and New York, Bloomsbury, 2016.

Works Cited

Lakhous, Amara. *Divorzio all'islamica a Viale Marconi*. Rome, Edizione E/O, 2010.

———. *Scontro di civiltà per un ascensore a Piazza Vittorio*. Rome, Edizioni E/O, 2006.

Lana, Anton Guido, and Andrea Saccucci. "La condanna di Strasburgo: Storia di una sentenza." *Mare Chiuso*, edited by Andrea Segre, and Stefano Liberti, Rome, Minimum Fax, 2013, pp. 38–48.

Lazzaro-Weis, Carol. "Introduction." *Le donne muoiono*, by Anna Banti, New York, Modern Language Association, 2001.

Lecomte, Mia. *Di un poetico altrove. Poesia transnazionale italofona (1960–2016)*. Firenze, Franco Cesati, 2018.

Levi, Primo. *I sommersi e i salvati*. Turin, Einaudi, 1986.

———. *If This Is a Man*. Translated by Stuart Woolf, London, Vintage, 1998.

———. *La ricerca delle radici*. Torino, Einaudi, 1981.

———. *Se questo è un uomo*. 1978. Turin, Einaudi/l'Unità, 1992.

———. *The Drowned and the Saved*. New York, Simon & Schuster, 1988.

———. *The Search for Roots: A Personal Anthology*. New York, The Penguin Press, 2001.

Liberti, Stefano, and Andrea Segre, editors. *Mare Chiuso*. Rome, Minimum Fax, 2013.

Lichtner, Giacomo. *Fascism in Italian Cinema since 1945. The Politics and Aesthetics of Memory*. New York, Palgrave Macmillan, 2013.

Lizzani, Carlo. "Come nacque Germania anno zero: Lettere da Berlino." *Rossellini, Dal neorealismo alla diffusione della conoscenza*, edited by Pasquale Iaccio, Naples, Liguori, 2006.

Lombardi-Diop, Cristina, and Caterina Romeo, editors. *Postcolonial Italy: Challenging National Homogeneity*. New York, Palgrave Macmillan, 2012.

Luciani, Serena. "I rapporti tra Albania e Italia subito dopo la caduta del regime." *Il confine liquido*, edited by Emma Bond, and Daniele Comberiati, Nardò, Besa, 2013, pp. 85–97.

Lyotard, Jean-François. *La condition postmoderne*. Paris, Les Editions de Minuit, 1979.

———. *The Postmodern Condition*. Translated by Geoffrey Bennington, and Brian Massumi, Minneapolis, MN, University of Minnesota Press, 1984.

Maalouf, Amin. *In the Name of Identity*. Translated by Barbara Bray, New York, Arcade, 2001.

Works Cited

Maggi, Armando. *The Resurrection of the Body*. Chicago, University of Chicago Press, 2009.

Maj, Barnaba. "Old and New Fascism and the 'Question of Sadism' in Salò." *Pasolini's Lasting Impressions: Death, Eros and Literary Enterprise in the Opus of Pier Paolo Pasolini*, edited by Ryan Calabretta-Sajder, Madison, Fairleigh Dickinson University Press, 2018, pp. 49–64.

Marcus, Millicent. *Italian Film in the Light of Neorealism*. Princeton, Princeton University Press, 1986.

Marinetti, Filippo Tommaso. "Contro il matrimonio." *Democrazia futurista. Dinamismo politico*. Milan, Facchi Editore, 1919, pp. 59–65.

———. "Marriage and the Family." *Marinetti, Selected Writings*, edited by R.W. Flint. New York, Farrar, Straus and Giroux, 1971.

———. "The Founding and Manifesto of Futurism." *Le Figaro*, 20 Feb. 1909.

Marinetti, Filippo Tommaso, and Alceste De Ambris. *Il manifesto dei fasci italiani di combattimento*. Milan, Il Popolo d'Italia, 1919.

Maurizi, Gianluca. "Senza migranti l'Italia sarebbe un paese più povero e anziano, spiega Bankitalia." *Corriere della Sera*, 3 Apr. 2018, www.agi.it/economia/bankitalia_migranti_pil_calo_demografico-3725908/news/2018-04-03.

Mauro, Walter. *Invito alla lettura di Corrado Alvaro*. Milan: Mursia, 1975.

Mazzacurati, Carlo. "Intervista a Carlo Mazzacurati, '*La Giusta Distanza*'." *YouTube*, 2007, www.youtube.com/watch?v=rZKgivZ6mNM.

Mengozzi, Chiara. "What Little I Know of the World I Assume." Cornici nazionali e mondiali per le scritture migranti e postcoloniali." *La Modernità Letteraria*, no. 8, 2015, pp. 27–42.

Mezzadra, Sandro. "The New European Migratory Regime and the Shifting Patterns of Contemporary Racism." *Postcolonial Italy: Challenging National Homogeneity*, edited by Cristina Lombardi-Diop, and Caterina Romeo, New York, Palgrave Macmillan, 2012, pp. 37–50.

Mieli, Mario. *Elementi di critica omosessuale*. Turin, Einaudi, 1977.

"Michel Foucault College de France 1976, p. 227." *Remnants of Auschwitz: The Witness and the Archive*, by Giorgio Agamben, New York, Zone Books, 1999, p. 84.

Moccia, Federico. *Tre metri sopra il cileo*. Rome, Il Ventaglio, 1992.

Moll, Nora. "Il ruolo della televisione nella communità narrative Italo Albanese: I grandi occhi del mare di Leonard Guaci." *Il confine liquido*, edited by Emma Bond, and Daniele Comberiati, Nardò,

Works Cited

Besa, 2013, pp. 117–36.

Morante, Elsa. *La Storia*. Turin, Einaudi, 1974.

Moresco, Antonio. *Il vulcano*. Turin, Bollati Boringhieri, 1999.

Moscato, Italo. "Quando l'Italia uscì dalle catacombe dei rotocalchi e della tv." *La Dolce Vita raccontata dagli Archivi Rizzoli*, edited by Domenico Moretti, and Giuseppe Ricci, Rome: Centro Sperimentale di Cinematografia, Fondazione Federico Fellini, 2010.

Murray, Edward. *Fellini the Artist*. New York, Frederick Ungar, 1976.

Nietzsche, Friedrich. *Human, All Too Human: A Book for Free Spirits*. 1878. Translated by R.J. Hollingdale, Cambridge, Cambridge University Press, 1986.

———. *Untimely Meditations*. Leipzig, Verlag von E.W. Fritzsch, 1876.

O'Donovan, Rocky. "Reclaiming Sodom." *Reclaiming Sodom*, edited by Jonathan Goldberg, New York, Routledge, 1994, pp. 247–48.

O'Healy, Áine. "Imagining Lampedusa." *Italian Mobilities*, edited by Ruth Ben-Ghiat, and Stephanie Malia Hom, New York, Routledge, 2016, pp. 152–74.

Orsito, Fulvio. "Percorsi Mediterranei." *Il cinema di Marco Tulio Giordana: interventi critici*, edited by Federica Colleoni, et al., Vecchiarelli Editore, 2015, pp. 203–22.

Orwell, George. *1984*. London, Martin Secker and Warburg, 1949.

Ottieri, Maria Pace. *Quando sei nato non puoi più nasconderti: Viaggio nel popolo sommerso*. Rome: Nottetempo, 2003.

Pallanch, Luca. "Terra di Mezzo, Ospiti, Estate Romana: Fotografando la Realtà." *Non solo Gomorra: Tutto il Cinema di Matteo Garrone*, edited by Pierpaolo de Sanctis, et al., Cantalupo in Sabina, Edizioni Sabinæ, 2008.

Parati, Graziella. *Migrant Writers and Urban Space in Italy: Proximities and Affect in Literature and Film*. New York, Palgrave Macmillan, 2017.

———, *Migration Italy: The Art of Talking Back in a Destination Culture*. Toronto, University of Toronto Press, 2005.

Pasolini, Pier Paolo. "Analisi linguistica di uno slogan." *Scritti corsari*, Milan, Garzanti, 1973.

———. *Divina mimesis*. Turin, Einaudi, 1975.

———. *Lettere luterane*. Turin, Einaudi, 1976.

———. "Limitatezza della storia e immensità del mondo contadino." *Scritti corsari*. Milan, Garzanti, 1974.

———. *Lutheran Letters*. Translated by Stuart Hood, Manchester, Carcanet Press, 1983.

Works Cited

———. *Passione e ideologia: 1948–1958*. Milan, Garzanti, 1960.

———. *Petrolio*. Turin, Einaudi, 1992.

———. "Pier Paolo Pasolini parla della lingua italiana." by RAI. *YouTube*, uploaded by Flavio Gipo, 22 Feb. 1968, www.youtube.com/watch?v=wkqoc8blFvI.

———. "Supplica a mia madre." In *Poesia in Forma di Rosa*. Milan, Garzanti, 1964.

———. "The Mature Auteur: La Dolce Vita and Beyond." *Perspectives on Federico Fellini*, edited by Peter Bondanella, and Cristina Degli-Esposti. New York, G.K. Hall & Co., 1993.

Pastorino, Gloria. "Voyeurism and Desire Keeping *The Right Distance*." *NeMLA Italian Studies,* vol. XXXIV, 2012, pp. 128–39.

Patierno, Francesco. "Intervista (Venezia 68) www.rbcasting.com." *YouTube*, 2011, www.youtube.com/watch?v=mBqlFxrTaMw.

Patruno, Nicholas. *Understanding Primo Levi*. Columbia, University of South Carolina Press, 2008.

Pickering-Iazzi, Robin. "Ways of Looking in Black and White: Female Spectatorship and the Miscege-National Body in *Sotto La Croce del Sud*." *Re-Viewing Fascism, Italian Cinema, 1922–1943*, edited by Jacqueline Reich, and Piero Garofalo, Bloomington, Indiana University Press, 2002, pp. 194–222.

Quandt, James. *Roberto Rossellini's War Trilogy, Myth and Manipulation*. New York, The Criterion Collection, 2009.

Re, Lucia. "Fascist Theories of 'Women' and the Construction of Gender." *Mothers of Invention: Women, Italian Fascism and Culture*, edited by Robin Pickering-Iazzi, Minnesota, University of Minnesota Press, 1995, pp. 76–99.

Ricciardi, Alessia. *After La Dolce Vita: A Cultural Prehistory of Berlusconi's Italy*. Stanford, CA, Stanford University Press, 2012.

Richardson, Robert. "Waste Lands: The Breakdown of Order." *Federico Fellini, Essays in Criticism*, edited by Peter Bondanella, Oxford, Oxford University Press, 1978, p. 111

Riviello, Tonia Caterina. *Woman in Italian Cinema*, edited by Tonia Caterina, Rome, Fabio Croce Editore, 2001.

Romeo, Caterina. "Italian Postcolonial Literature." *California Italian Studies*, vol. 7, no. 2, 2017, pp. 1–43.

Rossellini, Roberto. "Presentazione." *La città di Rossellini*, edited by Antonio Leto, Salerno, Plectica editrice, 2004.

Said, Edward. *Orientalism*. New York, Vintage Books, 1978.

Sartre, Jean-Paul. *Critique de la raison dialectique*. Paris, Gallimard, 1960.

———. *Critique of Dialectical Reason*. Translated by Alan Sheridan-Smith, London and New York, New Left Books, 1976.

———. *La nausée*. Paris, Gallimard, 1938.

———. *Nausea*. Translated by R. Howard, New York, New Directions, 2007.

Scalzo, Domenico, editor. *Gianni Amelio: Un posto al cinema*. Turin, Lindau, 2001.

Scego, Igiaba. *La mia casa è dove sono*. Milan, Rizzoli, 2010.

Schneider, Helga. *Lasciami andare, madre*. Milan, Adelphi, 2001.

———. *Mother, Let Me Go*. Translated by Shaun Whiteside, New York, Walker Publishing, 2004.

Segre, Andrea. "Director's Notes." *Io Sono Li: Press Kit*, 2011, www.iosonoli.com/press-kit/.

———. "Intervista al regista Andrea Segre." *YouTube*, uploaded by ImmigrazioneOggi, 2012, www.youtube.com/watch?v=xM004Spcc5I.

———. "Intervista esclusiva ad Andrea Segre per Io sono LI." *YouTube*, uploaded by Rete degli Spettatori, 2013, www.youtube.com/watch?v=G5iKrt1OJJ0.

Sinopoli, Franca. "Caratteri transnazionali e translinguismo nella letteratura italiana contemporanea." *La Modernità Letteraria*, no. 8, 2015, pp. 53–63.

Spackman, Barbara. "Fascist Women and the Rhetoric of Virility." *Mothers of Invention: Women, Italian Fascism and Culture*, edited by Robin Pickering-Iazzi, Minnesota, University of Minnesota Press, 1995, pp. 100–20.

Spanjolli, Artur. *I Nipoti di Scanderbeg*. Lecce, Besa, 2012.

Steimatsky, Noa. *Italian Locations: Reinhabiting the Past in Postwar Cinema*. Minneapolis, University of Minnesota Press, 2008.

Tamburri, Anthony Julian. *To Hyphenate or Not to Hyphenate*. Montreal, Guernica Editions, 1991.

Taylor, Charles. "The Politics of Recognition." *Multiculturalism: Examining the Politcs of Recognition*, edited by Amy Gutmann, Princeton, Princeton University Press, 1992, pp. 25–74.

Terdiman, Richard. *Discourse/Counter-Discourse: The Theory and Practice of Symbolic Resistance in Nineteenth-Century France*. New York, Cornell University Press, 1985.

"The Odd, Award-Winning Migration Movie *Fire at Sea*." *The Economist*, 9 June 2016, www.economist.com/prospero/2016/06/09/the-odd-award-winning-migration-movie-fire-at-sea.

Tomlinson, John. *Globalization and Culture*. Chicago, University of Chicago Press, 1999.

Trento, Giovanna. "Pier Paolo Pasolini in Eritrea. Subalternity, Grace, Nostalgia and the 'Rediscovery' of Italian Colonialism in the Horn of Africa." *Postcolonial Italy: Challenging National Homogeneity*, edited by Cristina Lombardi-Diop, and Caterina Romeo, New York, Palgrave Macmillan, 2012, pp. 139–53.

Triulzi, Alessandro. "Hidden Faces, Hidden Histories." *Postcolonial Italy: Challenging National Homogeneity*, edited by Cristina Lombardi-Diop, and Caterina Romeo, New York, Palgrave Macmillan, 2012, pp. 103–13.

Troiano, Francesco. "Cose dell'altro mondo." *Italica*, www.italica.rai.it/scheda.php?scheda=patierno_cosedellaltromondo&cat=cinema.

Urban, Maria Bonaria. "Cities and Landscapes: Physical Spaces and Topos of Identity in Films by Giuseppe Tornatore, and Carlo Mazzacurati." *Italy on Screen: National Identity and Italian Imaginary*, edited by Lucy Bolton, and Christina Siggers Manson, Oxford, Peter Lang, 2010, pp. 173–86.

Valli, Bernardo. "Lalbania contro Lamerica." *La Repubblica*, 11 Jan. 1995.

Vattimo, Gianni. "Dialettica, differenza, pensiero debole." *Il pensiero debole*, edited by Gianni Vattimo, and Pier Aldo Rovatti, Milan, Feltrinelli, 2010, pp. 12–28.

Verga, Giovanni. *I Malavoglia*. Milan, Fratelli Treves, 1881.

———. *The House by the Medlar Tree*. Translated by Mary A. Craig, New York, Harper and Brothers, 1890.

Virilio, Paul. *Ville Panique*. Paris, Editions Galilée, 2004.

Voltaire. 2015. *Candide*. Translated and introduced by Philip Littell, Fairhope, AL, Mockingbird Classics.

Vorpsi, Ornela. "In una lingua svestita d'infanzia." *Il paese dove non si muore mai*, Rome, Minimum Fax, 2018, pp. 113–15.

———. *Tu convoiteras*. Paris, Gallimard, 2015.

Waller, Marguerite. "Whose Dolce Vita Is This, Anyway? The Language of Fellini's Cinema." *Federico Fellini: Contemporary Perspectives*, edited by Marguerite Waller, and Frank Burke, Toronto, University of Toronto Press, 2003, pp. 107–20.

Welle, John. "Fellini's use of Dante in *La dolce vita*." *Perspectives on Federico Fellini*, edited by Peter Bondanella, and Cristina Degli-Esposti, New York, Maxwell Macmillan International, 1993, pp. 110–18.

Works Cited

Filmography

A Day without a Mexican. Directed by Sergio Arau. Altavista Films, Televisa Cine, 2004.

A Sud di Lampedusa (South of Lampedusa). Directed by Andrea Segre, et al. ZALab, 2006. *Accatone*. Directed by Pier Paolo Pasolini. Arco Film, 1961.

Alfredo, Alfredo. Directed by Pietro Germi. Cineriz, 1972.

Anija: La Nave (The Ship). Directed by Roland Sejko. Istituto Luce Cinecittà, 2012.

Appunti per un'Orestiade Africana (Notes for an African Orestes). Directed by Pier Paolo Pasolini. Gian Vittorio Baldi, 1970.

Cetrangolo, Mirko, and Anita Rivaroli, creators. *Summertime*. Netflix, 2020.

Come un Uomo sulla Terra (Like a Man on Earth). Directed by Andrea Segre, et al. Asinitas Onlus, ZALab, 2008.

Cose dell'Altro Mondo (Things of Another World). Directed by Francesco Patierno. Rodeo Drive. Medusa Film, 2011.

Darabont, Frank, creator. *The Walking Dead*. AMC Networks, Entertainment One, 2010.

Divorzio all'Italiana (Divorce Italian Style). Directed by Pietro Germi. Lux Film, 1961.

Ettore Fieramosca. Directed by Alessandro Blasetti. Nembo Film. E.N.I.C.,1938.

Europa '51. Directed by Roberto Rossellini. Carlo Ponti, Dino De Laurentiis. Lux Film, 1951.

Eyes Wide Shut. Directed by Stanley Kubrick. Warner Bros., 1999.

Fuocoammare (Fire at sea). Directed by Gianfranco Rosi. 01 Distribution, 2016.

Germania anno zero (Germany Year Zero). Directed by Roberto Rossellini. Salvo D'Angelo Produzione, Tevere Film. G.D.B. Film, 1948.

Gjenerali i Ushtrisë së Vdekur (The General of the Dead Army). Directed by Vladimir Prifti. RTSH, 1975.

Gomorra (Gomorrah). Directed by Matteo Garrone. Fandango, RAI Cinema, 2008.

I 100 passi (One Hundred Steps). Directed by Marco Tullio Giordana. Istituto Luce, Medusa video, 2000.

Il generale dell'armata morta (The General of the Dead Army). Directed by Luciano Tovoli. Antea Cinematografica, 1983.

Il grande appello (The Great Appeal). Directed by Mario Camerini. Artisti Associati, 1936.

Works Cited

Il Ladro dei Bambini (The Thief of Children). Directed by Gianni Amelio, Erre Produzioni, Alia Film, Rai Due, Arena Film, Vega Film, 1992.

Il pilota ritorna (The Pilot Returns). Directed by Roberto Rossellini. ACI, 1942.

Il Toro (The Bull). Directed by Carlo Mazzacurati. Mario & Vittorio Cecchi Gori, 1994.

Io Sono Li (Shun Li and the Poet). Directed by Andrea Segre. Kodak. RAI Cinema, 01 Distribution, 2012.

Kthimi I Ushtrisë së Vdekur (The Return of the Dead Army). Directed by Dhimiter Anagnosti, Shqipëria e Re, 1989.

L'armata ritorna (The Army Returns). Directed by Luciano Tovoli. Antea Cinematografica, 1983.

L'innocente (The Innocent). Directed by Luchino Visconti. Cineriz, 1976.

L'Orchestra di Piazza Vittorio (The orchestra of Piazza Vittorio). Directed by Agostino Ferrente. Lucky Red, Eurozoom, 2006

La dolce vita. Directed by Federico Fellini, Riama Film, Pathé Consortium Cinéma. Cineriz, 1959.

La Giusta Distanza (The Right Distance). Directed by Carlo Mazzacurati. Fandango, RAI Cinema, 2007.

La Malombra (The Bad Shadow). Directed by Andrea Segre, and Francesco Cressati. Jolefilm, 2007.

La meglio gioventù (The Best of Youth). Directed by Marco Tullio Giordana. BiBi Film, 2003.

La mia Classe (My Class). Directed by Daniele Gaglianone. Axelotil Film, Kimerafilm, Relief, RAI Cinema. 2014.

La nave bianca (The White Ship). Directed by Roberto Rossellini. Scalera Film, 1941.

La Nave Dolce (The Sweet Ship). Directed by Daniele Vicari. Indigo Film, Apulia Film Commission, RAI Cinema, 2012.

La Promesse. Directed by Jean-Pierre Dardenne, and Luc Dardenne. Lucky Red, 1996.

La terra trema (The Earth Trembles). Directed by Luchino Visconti. Salvo D'Angelo Produzione, Universalia, 1948.

La Tregua (The Truce). Directed by Francesco Rosi. Guido De Laurentiis, Leo Pescarolo Film. Mikado Film, 1997.

Ladri di biciclette (The Bicycle Thieves). Directed by Vittorio De Sica. P.D.S., 1948.

Lamerica. Directed by Gianni Amelio. Mario & Vittorio Cecchi Gori, 1994.

Works Cited

Le Conseguenze dell'Amore (The Consequences of Love). Directed by Paolo Sorrentino. Medusa Film, Fandango, Indigo Film, 2004.

Le Fate Ignoranti (The Ignorant Fairies). Directed by Ferzan Özpetek. Medusa, 2001.

Le notti di Cabiria (Nights of Cabiria). Directed by Federico Fellini. Dino De Laurentiis, Paramount Pictures, 1957.

Lo squadrone bianco (White Squadron). Directed by Augusto Genina. Roma film, 1936.

Mare Chiuso (Closed Sea). Directed by Andrea Segre, and Stefano Liberti. ZALab, 2012.

Marghera Canale Nord (Marghera North Channel). Directed by Andrea Segre. StudioImmmagine, 2003.

Marrakech Express. Directed by Gabriele Salvatores. Mario & Vittorio Cecchi Gori, 1989.

Mediterraneo. Directed by Gabriele Salvatores. Pentafilm Distribuzione, 1991.

Modern Times. Directed by Charlie Chaplin. Charles Chaplin Productions. United Artists, 1936.

Otto e mezzo (8 ½). Directed by Federico Fellini. Cineriz, 1963.

Pasolini, un delitto italiano (Pasolini, an Italian Crime). Directed by Marco Tullio Giordana. Cecchi Gori Group, 1995.

Passar la vita a Diol Kadd (Spending Life in Diol Kadd). Directed by Gianni Celati. Pierrot e la Rosa, Vitagraph, 2011.

Pater Familias. Directed by Francesco Patierno. Istituto Luce, 2002.

Pescatori a Chioggia (Fishermen in Chioggia). Directed by Andrea Segre. RAI3, 2001.

Po Dezju: Before the Rain. Directed by Milcho Manchevski. Gramercy Pictures, Electric Film, 1994.

Prove d'orchestra (Orchestra Rehearsals). Directed by Federico Fellini. Gaumont/Sacis, 1978.

Quando sei nato non puoi più nasconderti (Once You're Born You Can No Longer hide). Directed by Marco Tullio Giordana. Cattleya, 2005.

Roma. Directed by Federico Fellini. Ultra Film, Les Productions Artistes Associés. Ital Noleggio Cinematografico, 1972.

Roma Città Aperta (Rome Open City). Directed by Roberto Rossellini. Minerva Film, 1945.

Salò o le 120 giornate di Sodoma (Salò, or the 120 Days of Sodom). Directed by Pier Paolo Pasolini. P.E.A/P.A.A. 1975.

Works Cited

Scipione l'africano (Scipione the African). Directed by Carmine Gallone. Consorzio Scipione, 1937.

Sentinelle di bronzo (Sentinels of Bronze). Directed by Romolo Marcellini. Fono Roma, 1937.

Sotto la croce del sud (Under the Southern Cross). Directed by Guido Brignone. Mediterranea Film. CINF, 1938.

Star, Darren, creator. *Sex and the City*. Darren Star Productions, HBO Entertainment, 1998.

Swept Away. Directed by Guy Ritchie. Screen Gems. Medusa Film, 2002.

Taken. Directed by Pierre Morel. 20th Century Fox, 2008.

Taken 2. Directed by Pierre Morel. 20th Century Fox, 2012.

Terra di Mezzo (In-Between Land). Directed by Matteo Garrone, Archimede, 1997.

Travolti da un insolito destino nell'azzurro mare d'agosto. Directed by Lina Wertmüller. Medusa Film. 1974.

Umberto D. Directed by Vittorio De Sica. Dear Film, 1952. Italy.

Un'altra vita (Another Life). Directed by Carlo Mazzacurati. Erre Produzioni, RAI, 1992.

Uomo della croce (Man of the Cross). Directed by Roberto Rossellini. Cines, 1943.

Index

abortion, 9, 62, 77, 79, 158, 159
Accattone (Pasolini), 80, 94
Africa, 9, 11, 36, 38, 39, 89, 95, 154, 187–89, 191–93, 197, 223, 228, 295n72; immense peasant's world", 8. *See also* colonialism; migration
Agamben, Giorgio, 4–5, 10, 16, 45–47, 51–52, 282n7, 286n27, 300n27; being "simply men", 5, 73, 282n8; interpretation of Levi's "nonhuman", 5, 46, 47, 52, 75, 163, 271. *See also* Arendt, Hannah
Agro Pontino, 21, 23–25, 74
Albania / Albanian, 3, 9, 11, 13, 39–40, 171–85, 192, 199, 203–05, 207–09, 221, 223–24, 234, 237–38, 252–53, 257, 263–64, 275, 278, 281n2, 292–94, 296n73, 297n75, 300, 302n104. *See also* Amelio, Gianni; migration
Alvaro, Corrado, 1–10, 21–25, 49–50, 56–57, 64, 71, 74, 156, 253–54, 281n3, 282. *See also* new man; Soviet Union
Amelio, Gianni, 2, 9, 11, 171–73, 175, 177, 180, 192, 208, 263, 266, 274, 292, 294–95; perspective on "extra modern people", 11, 263. *See also* Albania / Albanian; extra modern
Amendola, Giovanni; first use of "totalitarian" (adjective), 5. *See also* totalitarianism
anthropological shift (Pasolini), 6, 9, 80, 153; anthropological mutation, 83, 87, 93. *See also* consumerism; Pasolini, Pier Paolo
anthropological perspective, 134, 142–43
"anthropological telescope", 8, 130–32. *See also* Celati, Gianni
Appiah, Kwame Anthony, 255, 301
Apulia, 9, 11, 180, 208, 263
Arendt, Hannah, 4–5, 13,

325

Index

15–17, 45, 47, 52–53, 57, 60, 64, 73–74, 171, 249, 271. *See also* Agamben, Giorgio; stateless persons
A sud di Lampedusa, (Segre), 194–96, 205, 217
Attali, Jacques, 4
Auschwitz, 1, 5, 16, 45–47, 74–75, 280

Balkans, 11, 39, 175, 184. *See also* Albania / Albanian; migration
Banti, Anna, 27–28
Bauman, Zygmunt, 8, 12, 122, 137, 145, 158, 168, 199, 227, 232–33, 241, 246, 267, 271, 297n82, 301n100. *See also* closed communities; consumerism; *homo eligens*
belonging, 13–14, 42, 46, 68, 74, 86, 115, 137, 148–49, 157, 161, 163, 196, 249–58, 261, 263–64, 271–72, 274–75, 278, 295n70, 300n95, 301n100; all possible, 68; citizen, 74; cultural, 196, 258; in earlier cultures, 86; transition between forms of, 13, 250; mono, 137, 250; multi-belonging, 13–14, 128, 137, 148, 157, 163, 249, 253, 255–58, 261–62, 272, 275, 301n100; national, 161, 278; non–belonging, 6, 13, 137, 148, 163, 249, 252–53, 258, 263–64, 271, 300n95, 301n100;
Ben–Ghiat, Ruth, 36, 38–39
Berardinelli, Alfonso, 8–9, 121, 286
Berlin, 1, 4–5, 21, 24, 58, 61–62, 65–66, 68, 73, 165, 169, 171, 178, 219, 259, 278, 282n4; as totalitarian capital, 1, 5, 61, 73, 282n4; *Germania anno zero* setting, 1, 58, 61–62, 65–66,68,; Wall ,165, 178, 259, 278. *See also* Rossellini, Roberto
biopolitical. *See* biopolitics
biopolitics, 5, 16–18, 45–47, 51, 53, 76; in Agamben, Giorgio,5, 16, 45, 47, 51; in Esposito, Roberto, 16; in Foucault, Michel, 5, 16, 45, 51, 53. *See also Agamben; Giorgio, Esposito, Roberto; Foucault, Michel*
"biracial", 38–39, 76, 277
border crossing, 11, 167, 217–18, 266
Bossi–Fini Law, 10, 165, 182, 225, 245, 264, 270; impact on citizenship, 10, 264. *See also* migration; Salvini Decree
Bourdieu, Pierre, 14, 256, 302n103
Bolshevism. *See* Soviet Union
bourgeois, 3, 6, 43, 84–85, 135, 143, 153, 161, 213, 270, 297n76.

Index

Calabria, 5, 21, 23, 151, 223, 281n3
Calvino, Italo, 2,7–9, 12, 14, 80–81, 83–92, 97, 111–28, 134, 136–38, 140, 146–48, 150–51, 154–59, 163, 166, 191–92, 206, 211, 243, 270, 284, 285n21, 286–87, 288n35, 289n36, 291n52. *See also* incomplete human being, open encyclopedia, cultural map
Castle of Crossed Destinies, The (Calvino), 115, 119, 125, 288n35
Celati, Gianni, 8, 9, 11, 95, 112, 130–32, 160, 187–92, 266, 295n72; perspective on "extra modern people", 11
CIE (Centre for Identification and Expulsion), 200–01, 208, 296n73
citizenship, 10, 37, 49, 166–67, 183–84, 199, 201, 249, 256, 264, 269, 279n2, 298n97, 300n108; economic means, 9, 182, 264; European, 166, 184, 199, 201, ; dual, 183, 281n2; Italian, 38, 300n97; Ius culturae, 9, 256; Ius scholae, 9, 256, 299n102. *See also* migration; "national man"
city, 7, 14, 21, 27, 45, 50, 56, 66–70, 72–73, 75–76, 80–81, 83, 92, 112–15, 118, 121, 124–26, 129, 132, 134–37, 140–41, 144–45, 147–50, 152, 154, 157, 169, 182, 188, 195, 203–04, 221–22, 224,227, 228–30, 240, 245, 267, 282n4, 287n29, 296n74; center of, 70, 92, 154; countryside dichotomy, 21, history of, 149–50; outskirts of, 70, 136, project, 69, 75
Città invisibili. *See Invisible Cities*
closed communities, 12, 168, 228, 231, 233, 246, 267. *See also* gated communities; Lakhous, Amara
Cold War, 9–10, 77, 153, 159, 165, 167, 180, 184, 200, 265, 268, 278, 293n65
colonial cinema, 4, 36–37; extension of Fascist ideology, 4; propaganda tool, 4, 35, 75
colonialism, 37, 171, 184–85, 192–93; Italian, 37, 192–93, 197; *See also* Africa
collective imaginary, 3, 185, 204, 211, 265
concentration camps, 10, 16, 93
consumerism, 6–7, 85, 100–02, 107–08, 153–54, 162, 235; *in Pasolini, Pier Paolo*, 6–7, 85, 100–02, 107–08, 153–54
Corpo presente (Hajdari). *See Present body*

327

Index

Cose dell'altro mondo (Patierno), 228, 236, 241, 269, 270, 296n86; protagonist: Mariso Golfetto, 137–38
cultural capital, 14, 255–58, 264, 302n103
cultural discourse, 3–4, 9–10, 31, 75, 182–83, 245
cultural map, 8, 127, 147, 163

de–individualization, 23, 55–57, 291n50
Del Grande, Gabriele, 13, 195, 296n74, 297n74
demography, 12, 161
"desire for community", 12, 227, 267
deterritorialization, 201, 240–41.
divorce, 9, 32, 77, 79, 145, 158–59, 162, 243, 244
documentary cinema, 35–36, 65, 109, 179, 182–83, 188–91, 196, 198–99, 214–23, 225, 242, 244, 265, 283n11, 293n66, 295n78; migration narratives, 182–83, 188–90, 194–98, 215–20, 244–45, 265, 297n78; Like a documentary, 220–25, 297n78; contrast with mainstream cinema, 11–13, 167–68, 214, 216–17, 265
Drowned and the Saved, The (Levi), 47, 55–56, 58, 62–63
dystopian, 27, 101

eastern borders, 3, 10, 185
economic boom, 6–7, 79–80, 141, 162
economic development, 18, 158, 239, 297n80
economic profile, 9, 182, 264
emancipation, 27, 34, 53, 71, 160–61, 254
encyclopedic knowledge, 111, 112
encyclopedic novel, 111, 118, 123, 124, 126
Esposito, Roberto, 16
Europe, 2, 4, 7, 17, 46, 51, 63, 69, 70, 73, 75, 77, 86, 132, 144, 154, 161, 165, 169, 172, 175, 178, 182–83, 192, 194–95, 198–201, 205, 209, 213, 218–219, 237, 240, 245, 255, 259–60, 264, 269, 271, 275, 278, 293n65, 294n70, 296n74, 301n98
European borders, 198, 200, 219
European citizenship, 10, 166, 184, 199, 201
extension of youth, 8, 12, 143, 269
extra modern, 9, 11–12, 190–91, 263

Fascism, 3, 5–6, 21, 24–25, 27–28, 31, 35, 37, 42, 76, 85, 101–02, 104–05, 132, 150, 153–54, 165–66, 171–74, 176–77, 181, 184, 193, 265, 268–69, 292n61,

293n64, 300n97; masculinity, 4, 33–36, 39, 161; women, 2, 27–29, 32–38. See also Gentile, Giovanni; Marinetti, Tommaso; Mussolini, Benito
Fellini, Federico, 8, 12, 72, 79–80, 87, 130, 132–34, 137–43, 146, 148, 150–51, 156–58, 161–62, 242, 246, 290–91
Ferrente, Agostino, 14, 246, 267, 270
Forti, Simona, 4, 6
Foucault, Michel, 16, 45, 51, 53, 99, 201, 282n9, 283n9
frontier, 116, 200–01, 210, 259
Fuocoammare (Rosi), 218–20

Garrone, Matteo, 11, 221–23, 265–66, 297
gated communities, 12, 168. See also closed communities
gender, 2–3, 27, 29, 33–36, 39, 76–77, 104, 158–59, 161, 163, 266–68, 288n34, 302n108; ideology, 35–36, policies, 3, 39, 76, 77; politics, 35, 76, 104, 302n108
Gente in Aspromonte (Alvaro), 21–22, 281
Gentile, Giovanni, 3–4, 28–32, 35, 76. See also Fascism
geographic human being, 9, 165, 166
geography, 2, 6–8, 10–11, 100, 151, 154, 156, 157, 159–61, 166, 168–69, 181, 197, 230, 265; capitals and change, 4; global, 7–8, 119; ideological, 154; polarized, 157, 160; political, 6
Germania anno zero (Rossellini), 1, 5, 58, 60–61, 65–66, 69–70, 172, 283n13; protagonist: Edmund, 1, 61, 67–69, 220, 283n10
Giordana, Marco Tullio, 9, 11, 14, 99, 207–13, 266, 297n75
Gjenerali i Ushtrisë së Vdekur, 172, 174, 178; as novel (Kadare), 172, 174; as film (Prifti), 172, 178
gulag, 49, 62, 74

Hajdari, Gëzim, 13, 249, 252–53, 257–58, 300n95, 302n104. See also bilingual; belonging–multibelonging
holocaust, 18, 27, 55. See also: Auschwitz, concentration camps, Levi, Primo
homo eligens, 133, 137, 158
human being, 2–3, 6–7, 9, 15, 17, 18–19, 22, 25, 31, 46, 51–52, 55–56, 59, 62, 69, 71, 73–77, 99, 103, 105, 109, 111, 114–16, 118, 127, 134, 137, 141, 147, 148, 152–53, 156–58, 162–63, 165–66, 169, 197, 199–201, 221, 223,

237, 246, 263–64, 266, 275, 278
Human Condition, The (Arendt), 15–16, 47
humanity, 5, 22, 51, 53, 55, 58–60, 73, 116, 190, 195, 232
hybrid, 137, 218, 220–21, 235, 267, 273, 288n33
hybridization, 222, 225, 233, 266, 289n37
hyphenated literatures, 271, 273

ideology of representation, 100, 124, 155, 167
If on a Winter's Night a Traveler (Calvino), 112, 118–20, 125–28, 137, 147, 243
If this is a man (Levi), 1, 5, 18–19, 45–48, 52, 59–60, 63
Il castello dei destini incrociati. See *Castle of Crossed Destinies, The*
Il Generale dell'armata morta (Tovoli), 172, 290n62
I maestri del diluvio: Viaggio in Russia (Alvaro), 1–2, 49–51, 56–57, 64, 253–54
Imaginary, 3, 13, 27, 43, 167–68, 185, 187–88, 204, 207, 210–11, 213, 220, 222, 241–44, 265, 267–68, 278, 296n74; collective imaginary, 3, 185, 204, 210, 265; Italian imaginary, 167, 185, 187, 210

imagination, 131, 182, 193, 200, 206–07, 210, 228, 256, 267, 297; unpredictable development of subjectivity, 206, 267
immigration, 9–11, 167, 171, 173, 177, 179, 181–83, 185, 187, 197–99, 206, 212, 215, 217–18, 228, 236, 239–40, 242, 246, 263, 266, 272, 275, 281n2, 295n73, 299n88
incomplete human being, 7, 114, 116, 134, 137, 141, 156, 158, 162
internal border, 201, 214, 220, 224, 265
interruption of tradition, 55, 58, 74
Invisible Cities (Calvino), 8, 119, 122, 126–27, 129, 134–35, 137–38, 147, 150, 287n29, 288n35
Io sono Li (Segre), 12, 239; protagonist: Bepi, 230–32, 235 297n81 protagonist: Shun Li, 228–32, 235; setting: Chioggia, 229–32
I sommersi e i salvati. See *Drowned and Saved, The*
Italian Fascism's Empire Cinema, 36, 38–39
Italy, 3–14, 24–25, 35, 62–63, 65–66, 73, 75–77, 80, 85–89, 91–93, 95, 97, 99–100, 103–06, 111, 121, 131–32, 138, 153, 158–59, 161, 165–68, 171,

173–74, 176–85, 189–90, 193, 197–99, 204, 207–09, 212, 215–19, 223, 229–31, 239, 244–46, 250, 252, 256–58, 263, 266–69, 272–73, 275, 278, 281n3, 282, 290n41, 292n61, 293, 294n66, 295n73, 296, 298n85, 299n88, 302n108, 303n110; Fascist, 10, 25, 165, 173; *Postcolonial,* 184–85, 193; post-war, 75, 100, 153, 158–59; today's, 244, 269; towards, 8, 179, 181, 190, 193, 278

Kadare, Ismail, 172–76, 274, 292n59, 293n62

La dolce vita (Fellini), 6, 8, 14, 79–81, 129–30, 132–34, 138–41, 143–45, 151, 158, 162, 269, 284n14, 290–91; protagonist: Emma, 133, 136, 141–42, 162; protagonist: Maddalena, 133, 135–36, 142, 145, 162, 290n46; protagonist: Marcello, 8, 43, 130–36, 139–43, 145, 147–48, 157–58, 162, 176, 237, 242, 290

lager, 16, 19, 48–49, 51, 56, 59–61, 63, 93, 154

La giusta distanza, (Mazzacurati), 11, 233; protagonist: Hasan, 233–35, 270, 289n37; protagonist: Mara, 12, 234–35, 267, 270

Lakhous, Amara, 12, 168, 241–44, 258, 267

Lamerica (Amelio), 2, 9, 11, 171–73, 175, 177, 179, 181, 182–83, 207–09, 212, 214, 263, 294n67, 295n71

Lampedusa, 11, 194–96, 198, 205, 216–20

landscape, 1, 22, 40, 61, 66, 100, 107, 126, 137, 143, 145, 153, 188, 206, 264, 267, 282n5, 302n106

language, 6–7, 13, 47, 83, 88–91, 108, 122, 135, 140, 153, 155, 181, 223–24, 237–38, 249–54, 256–58, 260–61, 271–72, 274, 281n3, 285n22, 287n31, 288n33, 301n101, 302n104; foreign, 91, 155; Italian, 90, 155, 224, 250; modern, 90, 155, national, 6, 153, 155; write in more than one, 13, 249, 271

Lasciami andare, madre. See *Mother, Let Me Go*

Le lezioni americane: Sei proposte per il prossimo millennio. See *Six Memos for the Next Millennium*

Le Sens pratique (Bordieu), 256, 302n103

Lettere Luterane. See *Lutheran Letters.*

Levi, Primo, 4–6, 13, 18, 45–48, 52, 55–57, 59–60, 62–63, 73–75, 163, 215,

249, 271, 282n9, 283n9
Liquid Life (Bauman), 122, 137, 158
L'Orchestra of Piazza Vittorio, (Ferrente), 14, 244–46, 271
L'uomo è forte (Alvaro), 21, 23–25, 281n3, 282n6
Lutheran Letters (Pasolini), 80, 84–86, 92–94, 159, 161, 284n15, 285n19

Magnani, Anna, 42, 62, 244
mainstream, 11, 12, 102, 166–68, 214, 216–17, 277; media, 167–68, 214, 216–17, 277; non-, 168, 265; productions, 11; representations 11, 12, 166, understanding of the movie, 102
Mamadou va a morire: La strage dei clandestini nel mediterraneo. (Del Grande), 13, 195
Marcovaldo ovvero: Le stagioni in città (Calvino), 114, 122, 152
Marinetti, Filippo Tommaso, 4, 28, 32–35. *See also* Fascism
material conditions, 60, 62, 75
Mazzacurati, Carlo, 12, 236, 239–40, 267, 298
Medea (Hajdari), 13, 252
Mediterranean, 13–14, 169, 193, 198, 200, 212, 218, 234, 295n72, 296n74
middle class, 7, 9–11, 84, 86–87, 92, 94, 128–29, 148, 153–54, 157, 161–62, 253, 286n25
migrant women, 208, 211, 213–14
migrant boat, 193–94, 198, 208–211, 214, 216, 218, 225, 264
migration, 9, 18, 77, 158, 165–67, 180, 183, 196, 198, 201, 203, 218–19, 224, 240, 264, 268, 270, 274, 276, 294n74, 300n100; dynamics, 165, 167, 183, 205–06, 263, 268, 272
mobile border, 199, 201
mobility, 9–10, 38, 73, 76–77, 83, 157–58, 162, 165–66, 168, 201, 205, 255, 264, 272, 277; control on, 10, 73, 83, 165–66, 201, 264; international mobility, 9, 77, 165
modernity, 2, 6–7, 9, 11, 14, 16–17, 23, 25, 33, 52, 57, 59, 67, 74, 83, 86, 90, 92, 95, 100, 102, 112, 122, 124, 143, 154, 155, 160, 180, 182, 187–91, 195, 206, 240, 243, 268, 279, 286n26, 289n39; impact on tradition and culture, 59, 83; interpretations of, 86, 90, 92, 95, 100, 102, 122, 124, 154, 155, 180, 286n26, 289n39; the advent of, 52, 57

Moscow, 2, 4–5, 73
Mother, Let Me Go (Schneider), 13, 249–50, 299n91, 300n92
mothers in cinema, 40, 42–43, 69–71, 142, 160, 166, 174–75, 229, 235, 237, 277, 290n43
mothers of the race, 3, 9, 27, 31–32, 35, 76
mother tongue, 13, 249, 250, 261, 299n91
multi–belonger. *See* multi–belonging
multicultural. *See* multiculturalism
multiculturalism, 13, 14, 156, 213, 232, 237, 245–46, 255, 266–67, 270–72, 274–75, 301n99; missing model, 13, 267, 275
multiethnic, 14, 169, 221, 233, 301n98
Mussolini, Benito, 4, 24–25, 32, 65, 132, 172, 174
myths, 28, 59, 67, 98–99, 102, 107–08; building, 28, 59, 67, 98, 102; of Sodom, 99, 107–08

national border, 184, 229, 264
national human being, 75, 77, 169, 264
"national man", 10, 13, 87, 252, 264
nationalism, 10, 18, 77, 201, 213
Nazism, 2–3, 5, 16, 18, 21, 24, 28, 57, 61–62, 67–69, 93, 105, 165, 300n97
neorealism, 14, 41–42, 62, 65–66, 69, 75, 80, 87, 138, 221, 223, 243, 267. *See also Germania anno zero*, neorealist novel / film, *Roma città aperta*; Rossellini, Roberto
neorealist novel / film, 41, 66–67, 87, 180–81, 218, 220. *See also* neorealism
network novel, 112–14, 118, 120, 125, 127, 147–48, 156, 163, 242
network human, 7, 127, 147–48, 156–57
new geographies, 7, 9–10, 146
new man, 1–3, 7, 9–10, 13, 15, 17–19, 23, 25, 31, 51, 57, 61, 64, 71, 73–75, 88, 95, 155–56, 163, 252, 254, 279, 284n16, 300n98, 301n98. *See also* anthropology; Soviet Union; Fascism; incomplete human being; nationalism; Nazism; transitional human being
"new poor", 9, 263
New York, 4, 8, 14, 112, 144, 151, 162, 251, 258, 279
nightmares, 179, 181, 185, 194, 200, 211, 213, 260, 278–79
non–belongers. *See* non–belonging
non–choice, 135, 137, 145, 162

333

nonhuman, 5, 14, 46–47, 52, 75, 148, 163, 249, 271–72. See *also* stateless persons, subhuman

On Revolution (Arend), 52–53, 64
open encyclopedia, 14, 113, 140, 163.
open form, 137, 140, 144, 157, 291n52
Orientalism (Said), 207
Origins of Totalitarianism, The (Arendt), 16, 17, 47, 53, 57
outlook on modernity, 9, 11, 187

Pasolini, Pier Paolo, 6, 8, 11, 80, 83–87, 89–90, 92–95, 97–103, 106–09, 140, 153–55, 157, 159–61, 166, 180, 187, 191–93, 211, 244, 263, 284n15, 285n19, 291, 294n70, 295. See *also Accattone*, Africa; anthropological shift; consumerism; extra modern
Passare la vita a Diol Khad (Celati), 11, 188
Patierno, Francesco, 12, 236, 239, 267, 298n86, 298n87
piazza Vittorio, 12, 14, 168–69, 241–45, 270. See *also* Lakhous, Amara; Ferrente, Agostino
postmodernity, 87, 118, 121–26, 146–47, 149, 155, 285n22, 287n30, 288n34, 289; postmodern (as adjective), 118, 121–26, 146–47, 285n22, 285n30, 288n34, 287n30, 289; postmodernism (movement), 87, 122–24, 126, 146, 149, 155, 287n30, 289n37
Preliminari allo studio del fanciullo (Gentile), 3, 29–31
Present body (Hajdari), 13, 249, 252, 300n96

Quel che resta di Auschwitz. See *Remnants of Auschwitz*

racial laws, 27, 38–39, 52, 277
representation, 9, 11, 37, 66, 80, 100, 109, 111, 113, 116–17, 119, 125–25, 127, 129, 138, 147, 150, 155–56, 167, 180, 188, 193, 203, 208, 211, 213–18, 222–26, 242, 265–67, 272, 288n34, 289n39, 292n61; colonial Italy, 37, 193; geography, 126, 156, 225; ideology of, 100, 155, 167, 265; immigration and borders, 9, 11, 180, 214–15, 225, 268; levels, 225–26; media, 188, 211, 216–17; politics, 216, 288n34, 289n38; testimony instead of, 223
re–representation, 111, 113, 119, 127, 140, 208, 285n20; literature as, 111;

of the world, 127, 140;
    technologies of, 285n20;
    topics like, 113
Remnants of Auschwitz
    (Agamben), 5, 16, 45–47,
    51–52, 282n7
Roma (Fellini), 81, 131,
    140–41, 149–50
Roma città aperta (Rossellini),
    41–42, 65, 67–68, 70, 76,
    171, 283; protagonist: Pina,
    42–44, 67, 76
Rosi, Gianfranco, 11, 218–20,
    265–66,
Rossellini, Roberto, 4–6, 41,
    43–44, 58, 60, 62, 65–66,
    68–70, 72, 74–76, 87,
    111, 138, 180, 216, 243,
    283n11, 285n23

*Salò o le 120 giornate di
    Sodoma* (Pasolini), 97–103,
    107–09, 191
Salvini Decree Law (2018),
    10, 291n2. *See also* Bossi–
    Fini Law; immigration
Schneider, Helga, 13, 249–50,
    299n91, 300n92. *See also*
    language; multibelonging
Segre, Andrea, 11–12, 194,
    196, 198–99, 205, 216–17,
    219, 223, 225, 228, 230,
    232, 236, 239, 265–66,
    297, 299n88. *See also* closed
    communities; immigration
Senegal, 11, 188–90, 192
*Se questo è un uomo. See If this
    is a man*

*Se una notte d'inverno un viag-
    giatore. See If on a Winter's
    Night a Traveler*
Sex and the City (Star), 144–
    45, 161
*Scontro di Civiltà per un
    Ascensore a Piazza Vittorio*
    (Lakhous), 12, 168, 241,
    243–44, 256, 299n89
per un Ascensore a Piazza
    Vittorio
"simply men". See "simply
    man"
"simply man", 5–6, 18, 73,
    282n8
*Six Memos for the Next
    Millennium* (Calvino), 91,
    111, 113, 121, 124–25,
    284n17, 285n17, 287
socialist realism, 2, 284n16
Soviet Union / USSR, 3, 10,
    14, 23, 29, 35, 73, 95, 105,
    154, 159, 165, 253, 265,
    301n98; appeared in, 253;
    atheist, 29; camp, 159; in-
    dustrialization of, 3; nature
    of, 154; situation in, 105
spatial categories, 126, 146
stateless persons,4, 5, 13,
    18, 53, 73, 77, 196, 249,
    263–64, 271; Arendt's
    analysis, 4, 13, 53, 73,
    249, 271; connection to
    nonhuman, 4, 13, 249;
    connection to non–belong-
    ing, 13, 263; connection to
    "simply man", 5–6, 18, 73.
    See also Arendt, Hannah;

Index

non–belonging; non–human; "simply man"
stepmother, 13, 252
Stigmate (Hajdari), 252, 253, 257, 300n96
stripped man, 45, 52, 93
sub–human, 5, 47, 93
subjectivity, 102, 121, 125, 135, 206, 267
sub–Saharan, 191, 215, 218
survivor, 56, 59, 172, 198, 215, 218–19, 231, 234, stories 56, 59; narratives, 172, 215, 218–19, 231, 234; migrants, 198, 215

Termini della politica (Esposito), 16
Terra di mezzo (Garrone), 220–21 223–24
Terra nuova (Alvaro), 22–24, 29, 282n5
territorial human being, 221, 266

totalitarian. *See* totalitarianism
totalitarianism, 2, 4–6, 10, 16–17, 21, 28–29, 31, 47, 49, 51, 53, 57, 61, 73–75, 77, 154, 165, 167, 171–72, 252, 281n3, 282n9. *See also* Arendt, Hannah, Fascism; nationalism; Nazism; Soviet Union
Tovoli, Luciano, 172, 176–79
transitional human being, 73, 99, 156, 162, 275. *See also* new man; incomplete human being
translingual, 256, 271–72, 274–75
transportation revolution, 8, 10, 14, 149, 151, 156, 166, 264

Una pietra sopra (Calvino), 86, 89–91, 116–17, 285n21,
universal man, 15, 17, 19, 74
urban, 4, 7, 12, 14, 21, 25–26, 62, 67, 69, 73, 79–80, 87, 134, 143–46, 148, 151–54, 156, 160, 162, 168–69, 187, 192, 222, 224, 228, 240–41, 265–68, 270; areas, 80, 154, 160, 162, 168, 265; anthropology, 14, 145; centers, 145, 168, 222, 224, 267; environments, 156, 187, 241, 266, 270; explorer, 79, 151; landscape, 145, 153; life, 67, 143; maps, 152, 169; realities, 12, 134, 168; space, 146, 169, 268
urbanization, 21–22, 26, 71, 80, 100, 126, 146, 165, 240; acceleration of, 22; against, 165; domains of, 126, 146; expansion of, 100; progress of, 26; result of, 21; themes of, 71. *See also* economic development; economic boom

Venice, 4, 27, 69, 177, 230, 298n83

About the book

This book analyzes the crisis of the idea of human being based on timeless notions, in the Euroamerican context, as seen primarily through literature and cinema. It focuses on Italy, which has been and remains a crossroads for diverse cultural and political currents—open to Mediterranean cultural influences while remaining within a typically Western cultural context. The "new man," defined by Corrado Alvaro during his trip in Russia in 1934 as "transitional," implies a human being with a fundamental need for change. Instead of the "new man," Italo Calvino in the 1960 preface to his *I nostri antenati* wrote about the incomplete human being who is always changing, always being completed without ever reaching completion, and thus always in transition.

In these pages, the author examines the twentieth- and twenty-first-centuries Italian metamorphosis of the concept of the human being, mirroring closely at every historical turn the contextual demands of the country. From Brignone's film *Sotto la croce del sud* (1938), and its faulted "biracial" protagonists to the Netflix series *Summertime* (2020), characterized by the intentional lack of problematization of a multicultural society; from the Fascist manhood represented by Roberto Rossellini's aviator "modern knight of our time"(1942), to Fellini's Marcello who chooses to not choose (1959); from Marinetti's idea of the woman who belonged "to the race's development" (1919) to Mazzacurati's Mara, who wishes "to live thirteen different lives" (2007); from Primo Levi's non-humans and stripped men, to not-belonging, to Arendt's stateless persons, to migrants crossing the desert and the Mediterranean sea in Segre's and Rosi's movies (2008, 2016): the journey chronicled in these pages is a surprising one, as today's Italy is very different than that imagined toward the second half of the nineteenth century.

About the author

Ron Kubati holds two PhDs: one in modern and contemporary philosophy from the Università degli Studi di Bari, and one in Italian studies from the University of Chicago. He is a lecturer at Pace University, New York campus, and his articles have been published in edited volumes and peer-reviewed journals. He has also published a collection of poems in Albanian (1992), as well as four successful novels in Italian: *Va e non torna* (2000, *Leaving with No Return*), *M* (2002), *Il buio del mare* (2007, *The Darkness of the Sea*), and *La vita dell'eroe* (2016, *The Hero's Life*).

www.ingramcontent.com/pod-product-compliance
Lightning Source LLC
Chambersburg PA
CBHW061425300426
44114CB00014B/1547